The Knowledge of Childhood
in the German Middle Ages, 1100–1350

University of Pennsylvania Press
MIDDLE AGES SERIES
Edited by
Ruth Mazo Karras,
Temple University
Edward Peters,
University of Pennsylvania

A listing of the available books
in the series appears at the
back of this volume

The Knowledge of
Childhood in the
German Middle Ages,

1100–1350

James A. Schultz

University of Pennsylvania Press

Philadelphia

Library of Congress Cataloging-in-Publication Data

Schultz, James A. (James Alfred), 1947–
    The knowledge of childhood in the German Middle Ages, 1100–1350
/ James A. Schultz.
        p.   cm. —(Middle Ages Series)
    Includes
    ISBN 0-8122-3297-6
        1. Children—Germany—History.   2. Social history—Medieval,
500–1500.   3. Children in literature.   I. Title.   II. Series.
HQ792.G3S376   1995
305.23'0943'0902—dc20   95-17057
                                                                CIP

for my parents
SHIRLEY AND WILBERT SCHULTZ

Contents

Contents   ix

Acknowledgments

More years ago than I care to calculate, it seemed like a good idea to turn a footnote I had written in an earlier book into an article on childhood. When I thought I had completed the article I showed it to Ingeborg Glier, then my senior colleague at Yale University, and she, noting that it was already too long to get published in a journal, suggested it really ought to be a book. Without her suggestion I never would have started, without her encouragement I never would have finished, and without her invaluable criticism at nearly every stage this book would be much less than it is.

From early on I have benefited from the friends and colleagues who read portions of the manuscript, made valuable suggestions, and directed me to useful sources: Efraín Barradas, John Boswell, Gloria Flaherty, Artin Göncü, Sibylle Jefferis, Bruce Murray, Norbert Ott, Ibrahim Sundiata. Sem Sutter came to my aid on numerous occasions at the Regenstein Library of the University of Chicago. I never would have completed this book if I had not been able to count on Efraín Barradas, John Boswell, George Chauncey, Peter Hawkins, Karma Lochrie, Peggy McCracken, and Nicolas Shumway for the support that only dear friends, all of them academics, can provide. Above all, I could not have gotten this far without Mitchell Matsey, who may be even more relieved than I that this project has finally come to an end.

For me the greatest pleasure in finishing is being able to dedicate this book to my parents, whose love has supported me and whose example has inspired me for so many years. Let the dedication stand as a small token of a much greater gratitude and admiration.

As my friends, especially the academics, have lost few opportunities to remind me, I have been very fortunate in the amount of fellowship support I have received to pursue my work on this project. That I am thus envied I owe to the generosity of the John Simon Guggenheim Memorial Foundation, the National Endowment for the Humanities, and the Institute for the Humanities at the University of Illinois at Chicago. The Campus Research Board at the University of Illinois at Chicago has generously provided a publication subsidy. Finally let me thank Theodore M. Andersson, Michael Curschmann, Ingeborg Glier, and Eckehard Simon, without whose support over the years I might never have had an academic career at all.

Abbreviations

In the notes I have referred to Middle High German and a few other texts by the following abbreviations. For full information about the editions used see the bibliography.

MIDDLE HIGH GERMAN TEXTS CITED

AdamEv	*Adam und Eva*
AdlSwb	Anna von Munzingen, *Adelhausener Schwesternbuch*
Alban	*Albanus*
AlxusA	*Alexius A*
AlxusB	*Alexius B*
AlxusC	*Alexius C*
AlxusF	*Alexius F*
Anegng	*Das Anegenge*
AplTyr	Heinrich von Neustadt, *Apollonius von Tyrland*
ArmHnr	Hartmann von Aue, *Der arme Heinrich*
ArmSch	Heinrich der Klausner, *Der arme Schüler*
ArPhlB	*Aristoteles und Phillis* [*B*]
ArPhlS	*Aristoteles und Phyllis* [*S*]
AvaJes	Frau Ava, *Leben Jesu*
AvaJnG	Frau Ava, *Das Jüngste Gericht*
AvaJoh	Frau Ava, *Johannes*
BertvR	Berthold von Regensburg, *Predigten*
BitDlb	*Biterolf und Dietleib*
Blnsdn	*Blanschandin*
BMärtr	*Buch der Märtyrer*
Brchta	*Berchta*
Bussrd	*Der Bussard*
Crone	Heinrich von dem Türlin, *Diu Crone*
DtCato	*Der deutsche Cato*
Dulcfl	*Dulciflorie*

EkrtPr	Meister Eckhart, *Predigten*
ELgAur	*Die Elsässische "Legenda aurea"*
Eneit	Heinrich von Veldeke, *Eneit*
Englhd	Konrad von Würzburg, *Engelhard*
EngSwb	Christine Ebner, *Engelthaler Schwesternbuch*
Eracl	Otte, *Eraclius*
Erec	Hartmann von Aue, *Erec*
ErnstB	*Herzog Ernst B*
ErnstD	*Herzog Ernst D*
ETrist	Eilhart von Oberg, *Tristrant*
Exdus	*Altdeutsche Exodus*
FlorBl	Konrad Fleck, *Flore und Blanscheflur*
Floyrs	Trierer *Floyris*
FrdSwb	*Friedrich von Schwaben*
Fridnk	Freidank, *Bescheidenheit*
Frndst	Ulrich von Liechtenstein, *Frauendienst*
Frnlst	*Frauenlist*
Gänsln	*Das Gänslein*
GbrEi	*Das gebratene Ei*
Gensis	*Altdeutsche Genesis*
GottNf	Gottfried von Neifen
Greg	Hartmann von Aue, *Gregorius*
GrMarl	*Grazer Marienleben*
GrshPr	*Grieshabersche Predigten I*
GRudlf	*Graf Rudolf*
GTrist	Gottfried von Straßburg, *Tristan und Isold*
GTrojk	*Göttweiger Trojanerkrieg*
GuFrau	*Die gute Frau*
GuGrhd	Rudolf von Ems, *Der gute Gerhard*
Häsln	*Das Häslein*
Helmbr	Wernher der Gartenære, *Helmbrecht*
HgMarg	Hartwig von dem Hage, *Margaretenlegende*
HlbDek	*Die halbe Decke A*
Hlgnlb	Hermann von Fritzlar, *Heiligenleben*
HnrKgd	Ebernand von Erfurt, *Heinrich und Kunegunde*
HoffPr	*Hoffmannsche Predigtsammlung*
HvKemp	Konrad von Würzburg, *Heinrich von Kempten*
Ioland	Bruder Hermann, *Leben der Gräfin Iolande von Vianden*
Irmgrd	Elisabeth von Kirchberg, *Irmegard-Vita*

Jakobr	Kunz Kistener, *Die Jakobsbrüder*
JnaMrt	*Jenaer Martyrologium*
JngTit	Albrecht, *Jüngerer Titurel*
JohBap	Priester Adelbrecht, *Johannes Baptista*
Jüdel	*Das Jüdel*
Judenk	*Der Judenknabe*
Jünglg	Konrad von Haslau, *Der Jüngling*
JWeltc	Jans Enikel, *Weltchronik*
KAlxus	Konrad von Würzburg, *Alexius*
Klage	*Die Klage*
KndJsu	Konrad von Fußesbrunnen, *Die Kindheit Jesu*
KPantl	Konrad von Würzburg, *Pantaleon*
KrbSwb	Elisabeth von Kirchberg, *Kirchberger Schwesternbuch*
KrlGal	*Karl und Galie*
KSilvr	Konrad von Würzburg, *Silvester*
Ksrchr	*Kaiserchronik*
KTirol	*König Tirol*
KTrojk	Konrad von Würzburg, *Trojanerkrieg*
Kudrn	*Kudrun*
LAdam	Lutwin, *Adam und Eva*
LAlexr	Lambrecht, *Alexanderlied*
S	*Straßburger Alexander*
V	*Vorauer Alexander*
Lanzlt	Ulrich von Zatzikhoven, *Lanzelet*
LBarlm	Otto II. von Freising, *Laubacher Barlaam*
LebChr	*Leben Christi*
Lohgrn	*Lohengrin*
LpzgPr	*Leipziger Predigten*
Magzog	*Der Magezoge*
MaiBfl	*Mai und Beaflor*
MarBrt	Ein Scholar, *Marias Bräutigam*
Marglg	*Margaretenlegende des XII. Jahrhunderts*
MarlKg	*Marienleben der Königsberger Hs. 905*
MEbner	Margareta Ebner, *Offenbarungen*
Melrnz	Der Pleier, *Meleranz*
MfRmbl	*Mittelfränkische Reimbibel*
MHMarg	*Die Marter der heiligen Margareta*
MönNot	Der Zwingäuer, *Des Mönches Not*
MOswld	*Münchner Oswald*

MtdtPr	*Mitteldeutsche Predigten*
Niblgn	*Nibelungenlied*
Nchtgl	*Die Nachtigall A*
ObalPr	*Oberaltaicher Predigtsammlung*
ObSrvt	*Oberdeutscher Servatius*
Orendl	*Orendel*
ORmchr	Ottokar von Steiermark, *Steirische Reimchronik*
PartMl	Konrad von Würzburg, *Partonopier und Meliur*
Parz	Wolfram von Eschenbach, *Parzival*
Passnl	*Passional*
H	Parts one and two: *Das alte Passional*, ed. K. A. Hahn
K	Part three: *Das Passional*, ed. Karl Köpke
PhMarl	Bruder Philipp, *Marienleben*
Pilat	*Pilatus*
PKonPr	Priester Konrad, *Predigtbuch*
M	*Predigtbuch des Priesters Konrad*, ed. Volker Mertens
S	*Altdeutsche Predigten*, 3, ed. Anton Schönbach
PrdsAI	*Paradisus anime intelligentis*
PrLanc	Prose *Lancelot*
PyrThs	*Pyramus und Thisbe*
Rabens	*Rabenschlacht*
RAlexr	Rudolf von Ems, *Alexander*
RBarlm	Rudolf von Ems, *Barlaam und Josaphat*
Rennew	Ulrich von Türheim, *Rennewart*
Rennr	Hugo von Trimberg, *Der Renner*
RnfrBr	*Reinfried von Braunschweig*
Rolndl	Pfaffe Konrad, *Rolandslied*
Rother	*König Rother*
RpParz	Claus Wisse and Philipp Colin, *Rappoltsteiner Parzifal*
RWeltc	Rudolf von Ems, *Weltchronik*
SaeldH	*Der Saelden Hort*
SAlexr	Seifrit, *Alexander*
Schnkd	*Das Schneekind A*
ScholM	*Der Scholar und das Marienbild*
Schwsp	*Schwabenspiegel*
La	Landrecht
Le	Lehnrecht
SfHelb	*Seifried Helbling*
SlPrsA	*Der Schüler zu Paris A*

SlPrsB	*Der Schüler zu Paris B*
SlPrsC	*Der Schüler zu Paris C*
SpecEc	*Speculum Ecclesiae*
Sperbr	*Der Sperber*
StAdal	Nikolaus von Jeroschin, *Sent Adalbrechtes leben*
StdabA	*Studentenabenteuer A*
StdabB	Rüdeger von Munre, *Studentenabenteuer B*
StDrth	*Von sent Dorothea*
StElis	*Das Leben der heiligen Elisabeth*
StEuph	*Sand Eufrosin leben*
StFran	Lamprecht von Regensburg, *Sanct Francisken Leben*
StGeor	Reinbot von Durne, *Der heilige Georg*
StGrPr	St. Georgener Prediger
StKatM	*Katharinen Marter*
StLudw	Friedrich Köditz, *Das Leben des heiligen Ludwig*
StMarM	*Sante Margareten Marter*
StPlPr	*St. Pauler Predigten*
StrKrl	Der Stricker, *Karl*
StUlrc	Albert von Augsburg, *Das Leben des Heiligen Ulrich*
StVeit	*S. Veit*
SwrzPr	Der Schwarzwälder Prediger
F	*Fest- und Heiligenpredigten*, ed. Peter Schmitt et al.
P	*Predigten*, ed. Gerhard Stamm
TandFl	Der Pleier, *Tandareis und Flordibel*
TKdlbg	*Thomas von Kandelberg*
TößSwb	Elsbet Stagel, *Tösser Schwesternbuch*
Treuep	Ruprecht von Würzburg, *Treueprobe*
UAlexr	Ulrich von Etzenbach, *Alexander*
UlmSwb	*Ulmer Schwesternbuch*
UWilhm	Ulrich von dem Türlin, *Willehalm*
A	*Arabel*, ed. Werner Schröder
W	*Willehalm*, ed. Samuel Singer
Väterb	*Väterbuch*
VBüMos	*Vorauer Bücher Mosis*
VChrGb	*Von Christi Geburt*
Virgnl	*Virginal*
VlSrvt	Heinrich von Veldeke, *Servatius*
VorNov	*Vorauer Novelle*
VrJngf	*Passienbüchlein von den vier Hauptjungfrauen*

Walthr	Walther von der Vogelweide
Warng	*Die Warnung*
WerMar	Priester Wernher, *Maria*
Wglois	Wirnt von Gravenberg, *Wigalois*
Wigmur	*Wigamur*
WilOrl	Rudolf von Ems, *Willehalm von Orlens*
WilÖst	Johann von Würzburg, *Wilhelm von Österreich*
WilWnd	Ulrich von Etzenbach, *Wilhelm von Wenden*
Winsbk	*Winsbecke*
Winsbn	*Winsbeckin*
WldAlx	Der Wilde Alexander
WlGast	Thomasin von Zerklaere, *Welscher Gast*
WlMarg	*Wallersteiner Margareta-Legende*
WlMarl	Walther von Rheinau, *Marienleben*
WolfdA	*Wolfdietrich A*
WolfdB	*Wolfdietrich B*
WolfdD	*Wolfdietrich D*
WTitrl	Wolfram von Eschenbach, *Titurel*
WTotnz	*Würzburger Totentanz*
WWilhm	Wolfram von Eschenbach, *Willehalm*
WzMarg	Wetzel von Bernau, *Margareta*
ZwöMön	*Die Legende vom zwölfjährigen Mönchlein*

OTHER ABBREVIATIONS

MHG	Middle High German
VL	*Die deutsche Literatur des Mittelalters: Verfasserlexikon*, 2nd edition, edited by Kurt Ruh
ıVL	*Die deutsche Literatur des Mittelalters: Verfasserlexikon*, 1st edition, edited by Wolfgang Stammler and Karl Langosch

On Notes, Translations, and Names

In order to reduce the number of interruptions that would occur if readers felt obliged to consult all the footnotes, I have adopted the following practice. A note attached to a passage *within* a paragraph will contain only specific documentation (the original for a passage quoted in translation, references to a source that is cited). A footnote placed *at the end* of a paragraph may contain this sort of material if it documents something in the last sentence of the paragraph. But it may also include additional evidence for the topic discussed in the paragraph, references to secondary sources, or comment on scholarly issues. The differentiation between these two sorts of notes means that, unless you want to know the specific source for a particular citation or claim, there is no reason to consult any of the footnotes to passages within the paragraph.

In order to simplify the notes somewhat I have employed a slightly unorthodox procedure when citing foreign languages *only*. First I indicate the source, most often an abbreviation for a MHG text followed by line numbers, but sometimes an abbreviated reference to a scholarly work followed by page numbers. This information ends with a colon and is followed by the quotation *without quotation marks*. This means that any foreign language in the notes that follows a reference and a colon is a quotation from the place indicated even though it is not surrounded by quotation marks. Any foreign words that are not quotations appear in italics.

Readers who compare the MHG cited in the notes with the translations that appear in the text will discover a number of discrepancies. First, I have not marked ellipses in the translations. Second, the MHG passages in the notes may occasionally include material that does not appear in the translations in the texts. Since I want to offer those who consult the original languages something that makes sense, I have tried to provide a minimally intelligible unit even if various parts of the original did not make it into the translation. Third, I have taken the usual translator's liberties of replacing pronouns with nouns and the like. Unless otherwise noted all the translations are my own.

Although my treatment of MHG names may seem inconsistent, it is not meant to be. I have used English names where they exist (King Mark) and modern German forms where they do not (Rüdiger). However, I have preferred the MHG names in cases where they can help differentiate between related texts: rather than Isolde (the most common form in English), I have kept Isalde (as the heroine is called in Eilhart's *Tristrant*) and Isold (as she is called in Gottfried's *Tristan*).

1. Zingerle's Rattle: History and the Knowledge of Childhood

All of us have some knowledge of childhood. We were children once. We encounter children daily, as parents or teachers, as shoppers or travelers, on television or in the newspaper. We learn about children from what we have been told, from what we read in magazines or books, and from what we ourselves observe. Some of this knowledge reflects the biological facts of childhood: we all know that infants must be fed. But most of it we have picked up without much thought from the world around us. Most North Americans, for instance, know that a child's early experiences determine her subsequent development. We could have learned this from Freud, who was convinced that "the events of the child's first years are of unequaled significance for her whole later life."[1] Or from Dr. Spock, who believes that "it's in the first 2 to 3 years of life that children's personalities are being most actively molded."[2] Most likely we acquired our knowledge simply from having grown up in an American culture that, throughout its entire history, has believed in "the doctrine of the primacy of early experience."[3] The fact that this doctrine is under "serious attack"[4] among psychologists because "there is insufficient scientific support"[5] for it has done little to undermine our belief. We *know* that the experiences of infancy determine the subsequent development of the individual, just as we know that infants must be fed.

German speakers of the Middle Ages also knew that infants must be fed, but they did not know that the experiences of infancy would set the course of a person's life, at least if one can judge from the surviving texts in Middle High German (MHG). Although these texts contain hundreds

1. Freud, *Abriss*, 113: die Erlebnisse seiner [des Kindes] ersten Jahre seien von unübertroffener Bedeutung für sein ganzes späteres Leben.
2. Spock, *Baby and Child Care*, 44.
3. Kessen, "American Child," 267.
4. Kessen, "Child and Other Inventions," 31.
5. Kagan, *Nature*, xv.

of stories about children, they betray little interest in the first years of life, often ignoring them completely. According to the MHG texts, the individual life is determined less by the experiences of early childhood than by the nature with which the individual is born. Thus, although Parzival is kept ignorant of knighthood until he has nearly grown up, as soon as he has a few words of instruction he is transformed into an expert, defeating the first five knights against whom he jousts. He succeeds not because of early childhood training, of which there was none, but because of "the nature that he had inherited from Gahmuret,"[6] his father, which guarantees that he will become an excellent knight. The writers of texts in MHG can ignore the first years of life because they know that the course of the individual life is determined not by early experience but by inherent nature. This knowledge affects the way they treat their children.

Obviously, what MHG writers know about childhood differs from what we know about it. Their knowledge of childhood, like ours, is specific to a particular time and place. In the chapters that follow I will attempt to describe the particular knowledge of childhood that one finds in German texts of the Middle Ages, but before beginning I want to use this introductory chapter to define my undertaking more precisely. I will situate it in relation to previous work done on the history of medieval childhood, explain what I mean by the "knowledge of childhood," describe the nature of the evidence on which the book is based, and offer an outline of the chapters that follow.

Historiography from Ariès to Zingerle

Ideas about childhood affect not only the way we treat children in the present, but also the way we treat children of the past: they affect the way we write the history of childhood. For the historiography of medieval childhood two paradigms have been particularly important. According to one, childhood is primarily an historical phenomenon, but a very recent one: thus there was nothing in the Middle Ages that deserves the name. According to the other, childhood is primarily a natural phenomenon, governed by immutable laws: therefore childhood in the Middle Ages must have been very much like childhood nowadays. The first, associated above all with the work of Philippe Ariès, has become the common knowledge

6. Parz 174,24: diu Gahmuretes art.

on the subject, at least among educated nonspecialists. Over and over in the course of my work, when I mentioned that I was investigating child-hood in the Middle Ages, I have been told there was no such thing. The second, which I will associate with Ignaz Zingerle, of whom more later, is the older paradigm. It still has a large number of adherents, however, people who, never mind Ariès, refuse to believe that childhood in the past was not essentially like childhood today.

Ariès's *Centuries of Childhood*, first published in French in 1960, in English in 1962, and in German in 1975, established the framework within which historians have discussed medieval childhood ever since. Among Ariès's most famous assertions are his claims that the Middle Ages lacked "an awareness of the particular nature of childhood," that "medieval civili-zation failed to perceive" the difference "between the world of children and that of adults," that, in short, "the idea of childhood did not exist" in medieval society.[7] The apparent clarity of these assertions is obscured somewhat by the fact that Ariès neglects to state what he actually means by the "idea of childhood" or the "particular nature of childhood." One can only assume, however, that these formulas refer to some idea or awareness that Ariès himself has and that, judging from his failure to offer any defi-nition, he believes his readers have and share with him. Thus Ariès's "idea of childhood" and his "awareness of the particular nature of childhood" can only be a modern "idea" or "awareness." What Ariès is actually say-ing is that medieval society lacked *our* idea of childhood and *our* awareness of the particular nature of childhood. If this idea of childhood is absent from the Middle Ages, then there was *no* idea of childhood. There simply is no other.[8]

Ariès discovered a second absence in the medieval attitude toward children, an absence of affection, and this too has become well known. He claims that medieval parents, and those of later periods as well, regarded their children with indifference, at least when the children were very young. "This indifference," he believes, "was a direct and inevitable consequence of the demography of the period,"[9] that is, of the fact that so many children died while still young: "People could not allow themselves to become too attached to something that was regarded as a probable loss."[10] Ariès feels that this indifference is an index of "the gulf which separates our concept of

7. Ariès, *Centuries*, 128, 411–12, 128.
8. On Ariès's discovery of absence: Wilson, "Infancy," 139, 142–43.
9. Ariès, *Centuries*, 39.
10. Ariès, *Centuries*, 38.

childhood from that which existed before the demographic revolution."[11]
Here Ariès does seem to admit the possibility of a "concept of childhood"
in times past. But he does so only to dismiss it at once as "strange"[12] because the gulf that separates it from our own is so vast. Once again, Ariès's
standard for judging past times is the present.

Ariès's claims have not gone unchallenged. His work has been called
"badly flawed in both its methodology and its conclusions,"[13] his method
"utterly unsound,"[14] his thesis that there was no concept of childhood
"a totally indefensible viewpoint."[15] Nevertheless his claims about pre-
modern childhood, especially the two points mentioned above, have at-
tracted considerable attention. They have done so partly because they were
so startling and partly because they were taken up by a number of other
historians in the decades following the publication of Ariès's book. John
Demos, writing about the Puritans of Plymouth Colony, finds that "childhood as such was barely recognized."[16] Lawrence Stone believes that one
of the reasons relations between upper-class parents and children were so
remote in sixteenth-century England "was the very high infant and child
mortality rates, which made it folly to invest too much emotional capital in
such ephemeral beings."[17] These and a number of other influential family
historians helped establish Ariès's two kinds of absence as the common
knowledge concerning childhood in preindustrial Europe.[18]

Of course there is an alternative, even within the binary system in
which Ariès operates: one can look at the past and find the present. Since
this practice has a long tradition I will take as the paradigmatic case a book

11. Ariès, *Centuries*, 39.
12. Ariès, *Centuries*, 38.
13. Stone, "Massacre," 28.
14. Wilson, "Infancy," 147.
15. Pollock, *Forgotten Children*, 263.
16. Demos, *Little Commonwealth*, 57.
17. Stone, *Family*, 82.
18. Others who assert that there was no idea of childhood in past times: Flitner and
Hornstein, "Kindheit," 312–15; Hausen, "Familie als Gegenstand," 185; Johansen, *Betrogene
Kinder*, 7; Klapisch, "Attitudes," 64; Le Goff, *Medieval Civilization*, 287–88; Shorter, *Modern
Family*, 169; Ta-Shma, "Medieval German Jewry," 278. —Others who assert that parents in
the past had little emotional involvement in the lives of their children: Johansen, *Betrogene
Kinder*, 118; Le Goff, *Medieval Civilization*, 287–88; Riché, "L'Enfant," 96; Shorter, *Modern
Family*, 168, 172; Turner, "Anglo-Norman Royalty," 43; Wiedemann, *Roman Empire*, 16. The
best critique of this position, along with a useful bibliography, is Wilson, "Motherhood."
—Not surprisingly, there is a substantial body of commentary on Ariès and the work he in-
spired. For recent surveys: Bellingham, "Some Issues"; Graff, "Beyond Infancy?"; Fishman,
"History of Childhood"; Stone, "Family History." The most sophisticated critique of Ariès is
Wilson, "Infancy."

published in 1868 by Ignaz Zingerle, *Das deutsche Kinderspiel im Mittelalter*, devoted, as the title indicates, to children's games of the German Middle Ages. Zingerle begins his study with the rattle, because, he claims, "the rattle was surely the child's first toy among our ancestors, as it still is among us today."[19] One's confidence in this claim is somewhat undermined when Zingerle admits that he was unable to find a single reference to the rattle in any of the medieval texts he consulted. Zingerle, however, is not to be deterred by the lack of evidence: "even though we do not find any references to this toy in MHG literary texts," he insists that "we can nevertheless be certain that it was used, since so little changes in the world of children."[20]

While Ariès looks at the past and finds nothing familiar, Zingerle looks at the past and finds familiar things that aren't even there. He is able to do so by relying on the very powerful premise that present and past are the same. Since Zingerle knows all about childhood in the present—for him, as for many of his contemporaries, it is "the golden age of innocent pleasure and happy play"[21]—and since he knows that "little changes in the world of children," Zingerle therefore knows all he needs about childhood in the Middle Ages: it is the same as childhood today. Relying on this principle Zingerle can draw on the present to fill in the gaps in the past: since rattles are a child's first toy in the present, he is sure they must have been a child's first toy in the past, even when he can find no evidence of them.

Zingerle is not by any means the only one to have discovered the present while investigating childhood in the past. Quite a few others have done so too, most of them writing after Ariès and usually in explicit opposition to him. In their eagerness to disprove his claims about the Middle Ages they seem not to have noticed that, in spite of the many very real flaws in his arguments, Ariès did succeed in discrediting the naive conflation of present and past. This is his invaluable contribution. "At a stroke," writes Adrian Wilson, Ariès "historicized the family."[22] The disciples of Zingerle write as if this had never happened.

The closest to Zingerle are the sentimentalists. Like him, they rely on a common-sense certainty about what children are really like, often

19. Zingerle, *Kinderspiel*, 3: wie es heutzutage noch der Fall ist, war wohl das erste Spielzeug des Kindes auch bei unsern Vorfahren die Klapper.
20. Zingerle, *Kinderspiel*, 3: Finden wir in den mittelhochdeutschen Dichtungen auch keine Belege für dieses Spielzeug, so ist dessen Gebrauch doch sicher anzunehmen, da sich in der Kinderwelt so wenig ändert.
21. Zingerle, *Kinderspiel*, 1: Die Kindheit ist die goldene Zeit der harmlosen Freude, des fröhlichen Spieles.
22. Wilson, "Infancy," 136.

tinged with a nostalgia for the lost paradise of childhood. Ilene Forsyth, discussing a ninth-century "representation of Truth as an innocent child," maintains that it "suggests a ready empathy with virtues peculiar to children such as their clear, unsullied, level vision of life, received by them directly from mother earth herself."[23] The sentimental historians know certain things to be true about childhood, and they judge medieval images or texts successful or not according to whether they find such truths represented. The truths on which their verdicts depend are the same sentimental beliefs about childhood that Zingerle invoked over a century ago: Forsyth's "innocent," "unsullied" child would be completely at home in Zingerle's "golden age of innocent pleasure."[24]

While the sentimental approach to the history of childhood relies on a knowledge of childhood that is assumed to be self-evident, the psychological approach is more demanding: it requires a familiarity with modern psychology, at least with the writings of Erik Erikson. In her recent book on medieval childhood Shulamith Shahar cites Erikson on the developmental tasks to be accomplished by a child about age two so that she can talk about toilet training, and she cites him on the oedipal stage so that she can treat the death of Giovanni Morelli's father as an oedipal disaster.[25] Yet toilet training, as Shahar freely admits, is not mentioned in any of her sources, and one can be pretty sure the oedipal stage isn't either. Shahar invokes Erikson not to "elucidate" the sources, as she claims,[26] but to fill in their gaps. Having filled in the gaps with modern elements, she can then write about medieval childhood as if it really were modern childhood. The psychological historians take modern categories for timeless truths, transport them into the past, and then act as if the imports were indigenous. All the while they, like the sentimentalists, are merely looking at what they have brought there from the present: for Zingerle it was a rattle, for Shahar it is a potty.[27]

---

23. Forsyth, "Early Medieval Art," 32.

24. Shahar's book on medieval children is awash in this sort of confident sentimentality. She praises one story because it shows an "understanding of . . . the workings of the childish imagination" (*Childhood*, 106), and she is always eager to identify which medieval "comments" are "unquestionably" (81) or "undoubtedly the fruit of observation of small children" (99; similarly: 84, 107, 118–20). Gray is equally confident of her ability to detect which MHG texts reveal their author's "knowledge" and which betray their author's "ignorance of the nature of children" (*Bild des Kindes*, 9, 25: Unkenntnis des kindlichen Wesens; 16: Kenntnis des kindlichen Wesens). See also Arnold, *Kind*, 66; Löffl-Haag, *Kinder*, 62–63; Swanson, "Sermons," 321, 326, 329.

25. Shahar, *Childhood*, 98, 159.

26. Shahar, *Childhood*, 30.

27. Shahar's claim that she follows "Erikson's model" (*Childhood*, 30) is not even true:

One can also bring the past and present closer together by trying to discredit the specific arguments of those who assert they are different. This has been the goal of many medievalists, who have been nearly unanimous in insisting against Ariès, first, that "medieval society knew the age of child-hood"[28] and, second, that medieval "children were loved."[29] The evidence I have found in MHG texts strongly supports these claims.

The revisionists, however, have not been content with challenging Ariès's representation of medieval attitudes; they have gone a step further, insisting that medieval attitudes are the same as modern ones. Emmanuel Le Roy Ladurie, while admitting some differences, insists that medieval parents "probably loved their children just as intensely as we do, and perhaps even spoiled them too."[30] Klaus Arnold believes that medieval children "were loved and were occasionally felt to be burdensome by their parents and others around them, just as they are in every age."[31] Focusing on a different issue, Barbara Hanawalt claims that the "motor skills [of medieval peasant children] and their relationship to their environment develop within the stages that are familiar to us." She believes this suggests "a strong biological basis for child development as opposed to decisive cultural influences."[32]

---

right after she has sketched his developmental scheme, which has four stages before puberty, she adopts another model, which has two (21, 22). Shahar is not interested in following Erikson's model, only in borrowing bits and pieces with which she can supplement her account of the past. She drops the names of other psychologists as well: Freud (6, 115); Piaget (6, 21, 31); others, sometimes anonymous (67, 115, 134–35, 157, 160, 162, 214, 218). —Erikson was particularly popular among historians of childhood in the 1970s: Demos, "Developmental Perspectives"; Demos, *Little Commonwealth*, 129, 138–39; Hanawalt, "Childrearing," 19; Hunt, *Parents and Children*, 11–31. Although Hanawalt claims to have abandoned Erikson in the 1980s (*Ties*, 305 n. 32), she still cannot refrain from introducing the modern notion of "infantile sexuality," even though, as she admits, her sources "contain no evidence that children suddenly took their fingers out of pots and put them on their genitals instead" (182; see also 171). Weinstein and Bell seem to rely on a watered-down version of Erikson's "identity crisis" when they define adolescence as "the onset of maturity and the quest for identity" and speak of it is as "the appointed time for . . . a contest of wills, a power struggle between parent and adolescent" (Weinstein and Bell, *Saints*, 244, 59). —For more general criticism of the use of modern psychological categories by historians of childhood see Mitterauer and Sieder, *European Family*, 60; Spiecker and Groenendijk, "Betrogene Kinder?"

28. Weinstein and Bell, *Saints*, 19.
29. Holmes, "Medieval Children," 172.
30. Le Roy Ladurie, *Montaillou*, 213.
31. Arnold, *Kind*, 86: Sie wurden geliebt und von ihren Eltern und der Umwelt zuweilen als lästig empfunden wie zu allen Zeiten.
32. Hanawalt, *Ties*, 171. —Medievalists who maintain there was a concept of childhood in the Middle Ages: Arnold, "Kindheit," 448; Borst, *Alltagsleben*, 310–19; Forsyth, "Early Medieval Art," 33, 60; Hanawalt, *Ties*, 187; Kroll, "Concept," 385, 391; Le Roy Ladurie, *Montaillou*, 263; Loffl-Haag, *Kinder*, 182; Nicholas, *Domestic Life*, 109, 208; Shahar, *Childhood*, 1–4, 95–97; Weinstein and Bell, *Saints*, 19, 58–59, 241–43. —Those who maintain that medieval

I suspect there are two impulses that generate these claims. The first is the temptation, to which medievalists often succumb, to make the Middle Ages more accessible to modern readers by showing that they are not so strange as is frequently thought: medieval men and women behaved "just as we do" or in ways "that are familiar to us"; even better, they acted "just as parents do in every age." For all their apparent innocence, such statements are merely weak versions of the second, much more clearly ideological claim articulated by Hanawalt, that children's development is determined primarily by their inevitable biological growth and only very slightly by the culture in which they grow up. The revisionists are not so blatant as Zingerle: they do not transport evidence from the present into the past. But then they don't need to. They look at the past and find that the present is already there. Indeed, when it comes to childhood they seem to have eyes only for that part of the historical record that is "familiar to us." One is tempted to agree with Hayden White when he writes that "history has become increasingly the refuge of all those 'sane' men [and women] who excel at finding . . . the familiar in the strange."[33]

The sentimentalists, the psychologists, and the revisionists all look at the records of the past and discover there the image of the present. And when they have done so, they cite their discoveries as evidence against the "negative stereotype"[34] of childhood in the Middle Ages first advanced by Ariès. Thus it is that the issues first raised by Ariès have continued to dominate the scholarship on childhood in the Middle Ages, even among those who disagree with him most strongly. Shahar makes her opposition to Ariès into the "central thesis" of her book and proclaims it boldly at the top of page one.[35] Although Shahar and the others present rich collections of data on medieval childhood, they feel constrained to devote a disproportionate part of their interpretive effort to disproving the claims

---

parents were attached to their children: Arnold, *Kind*, 82–86; Boswell, *Kindness*, 37–39; Hanawalt, *London*, 89; Hanawalt, *Ties*, 185; Herlihy, *Households*, 125–27; Le Roy Ladurie, *Montaillou*, 209–11, 212; Loffl-Haag, *Kinder*, 78; Martin and Nitschke, *Sozialgeschichte*, 12–27; Nicholas, *Domestic Life*, 149, 153, 171, 208; Orme, *Childhood to Chivalry*, 3–4; Shahar, *Childhood*, 74, 145–55; Weinstein and Bell, *Saints*, 47, 245–46. —For a detailed survey of, coupled with a vigorous attack on Ariès and his followers see Pollock, *Forgotten Children*, 1–67. Others who claim that past and present are the same: Hanawalt, *London*, 42; Holmes, "Medieval Children," 172; Nichols, *Domestic Life*, 208. Loffl-Haag suggests that in a number of ways medieval children might have been better off than those of today (*Kinder*, 174–82).

33. White, *Tropics*, 50.
34. Herlihy, *Households*, 112.
35. Shahar, *Childhood*, 1.

of Ariès. Thus it is that the "Father of Family History"[36] has stunted the growth of his child.[37]

The Knowledge of Childhood

But perhaps Ariès and Zingerle and their disciples have not exhausted all the possibilities. Perhaps, along with Doris Desclais Berkvam, we should ask "whether there might not have existed, in the Middle Ages, a consciousness of childhood so unlike our own that we do not recognize it."[38] If we are to have any hope of doing so we will need a history that is different from the ones that have dominated the study of medieval childhood so far. Such a history will respect the alterity of the past, allowing the possibility of an idea of childhood that is different from ours but that is nevertheless an idea of childhood. It will respect the complexity of the past, acknowledging the likelihood that there are more aspects to childhood than the pair of absences authorized by Ariès and the corresponding presences discovered by others. Finally, it will insist on the historicity of its object, regarding childhood as "a cultural and historical fact," as "an artifact of human making."[39] This different history of childhood will attempt a comprehensive and differentiated description of a culturally constructed, therefore inevitably different, knowledge of childhood.

Our knowledge of childhood is constituted in a variety of ways. We know a few rudimentary biological facts: that infants must be fed, for instance. We can know, if we care to, what the various sciences that study children have to say about them: psychoanalysis, represented by Dr. Freud, and pediatrics, represented by Dr. Spock, both tell us that the events of early childhood exercise a profound influence on later development. More important is the voice of cultural tradition: we know that early childhood is of paramount importance because everyone around us thinks so, and in

---

36. Demos, *Past, Present*, [v].

37. Even those who write on childhood in cultures that Ariès does not discuss feel obliged to answer his claims. Golden spends nineteen pages of his study of childhood in ancient Greece arguing, in explicit opposition to Ariès and Stone, that Athenian parents loved their children and were upset when they died (*Athens*, 82–100). Martin and Nitschke, in their introduction to a collection of essays on childhood in cultures throughout the world, fill sixteen pages with evidence from those essays showing that high child mortality does not prevent parents from loving their offspring (*Sozialgeschichte*, 12–27).

38. Berkvam, "*Nature*," 165.

39. Wartofsky, "Construction," 193.

fact most Americans have thought so for a very long while. Our knowledge of childhood is articulated not only in what we think or say about children but also in the way we treat them: American parents try to provide stimulating environments for their children, even in the crib, in order to get them off to a good start. Sometimes what we know about children takes institutional forms: we have established programs like Head Start in order to enrich the early years of those children whose early years seem to need enrichment.

Our knowledge of childhood is what we make of children—both how we make sense of children and how we make them into children. It is our way of giving shape to "the incoherence of the young"[40]—both conceptually and practically. The knowledge of childhood is the culturally constructed meaning of childhood, as articulated in discourses, practices, and institutions.

In such a knowledge, theory and practice are inextricable. Most everyone will recognize that what we think about children affects the way we treat them: because we believe that the early years are of paramount importance, we buy special toys for our children's cribs and establish special programs like Head Start. What we think about children affects not only the way we treat them but, as a consequence, what they actually become: because American parents believe that children should sleep through the night, five-month-old American babies have learned to sleep eight hours without interruption, while babies of the same age in cultures where uninterrupted sleep is not an issue sleep only four hours without waking.[41] Only a few months after birth, infants have already begun to become the children their culture expects them to become.

But it also works the other way around: practice determines theory. A great deal of research has been done on the development of children's memory, logical reasoning, and ability to classify unrelated objects. The knowledge of childhood generated by this research is dependent on the practice of compulsory schooling, for it is in schools that such abilities are cultivated, and it is only in a country with compulsory education that enough children would be learning these skills to attract the attention of science.[42] The lives of children, in this case the institutional lives of children, determine what we know about them.

40. Kessen, *The Child*, 129.
41. Rogoff and Morelli, "Perspectives," 345.
42. Rogoff and Morelli, "Perspectives," 344.

There are, of course, certain biological constants. Children are born, children must eat, children grow in size: these can safely be taken as biological facts. However, the biological facts are not the solid ground of childhood they are often assumed to be. Among social historians, at least, it is well known that the age of puberty is significantly lower now than it was 200 years ago: in most countries of northern Europe girls in the first decades of the nineteenth century did not begin to menstruate until they were on average about 16 or 17, whereas in the 1970s the average age of menarche was 12 or 13; in the same parts of Europe boys in the early nineteenth century were still growing in their mid-twenties, whereas now they reach their full height at about 18. These changes were caused, in part at least, by improved nutrition and the decrease in child labor.[43]

Not only do the biological facts change over time, but the understanding of these facts changes as well. In the Middle Ages nursing children were understood to imbibe the attributes of their nurse's character and lineage along with their milk. At the turn of the century Freud believed nursing children "already enjoy sexual satisfaction" from the activity.[44] Nowadays we are more likely to regard nursing as "analogous to adult trust."[45] The fact that children must be nursed acquires meaning in the context of a medieval belief that mothers' milk is a form of blood that transmits attributes, a turn-of-the-century theory of psycho-sexual development, and a contemporary American concern for the quality of personal attachments.

Although the biological facts are modified by history and mediated by culture, there are limits. Biological facts limit the effects of history: the age of menarche does not seem to be falling very much any more, probably because it is already as low as is biologically possible.[46] And biological facts limit interpretation: it is hard to imagine that any culture would regard feeding children as harmful, because the need is so obvious. Since biology limits the kinds of facts that can be known and the meanings that can be attached to them, biology helps constitute the knowledge of child-

43. Mitterauer, *Jugend*, 13–14. —Medievalists are not taken in by such data. Even in her most recent book Hanawalt insists that "children's biological development, including increases in both motor skills and psychological maturity, has not changed over the centuries" (*London*, 42). It is hard to imagine that "psychological maturity" (here understood as a kind of "biological development") could remain completely unaffected by a fluctuation in physical maturity of 25 percent or more.

44. Freud, *Drei Abhandlungen*, 133: Es schien uns vielmehr, daß das Kind . . . schon bei der Nahrungsaufnahme sexuelle Befriedigung mitgenießt.

45. Kagan, *Nature*, 84.

46. Steinberg, Belsky, and Meyer, *Infancy, Childhood*, 439.

hood in any culture. But it does not determine that knowledge. "It is culture," insists Jerome Bruner, "not biology, that shapes human life and the human mind."[47]

Anthropologists will hardly be surprised by a proposal to study childhood as a cultural construction. They have been doing so at least since Margaret Mead set out for Samoa to find out whether adolescence there was anything like adolescence back home in North America.[48] More recently, psychologists, inspired by the "six-culture study" of Beatrice Whiting and John Whiting, have been investigating the ways in which cultural forces shape childhood.[49] Nor will my argument seem surprising to those who are familiar with recent work in women's studies, African-American studies, or the history of sexuality. In these fields the categories of gender, race, and sexuality, which, like childhood, are often assumed to be biologically given, are understood to be culturally constructed.[50] Thus Joan Wallach Scott defines gender as the culturally specific "knowledge about sexual difference,"[51] much as I have defined a culturally specific "knowledge of childhood." Lest there be any confusion, let me note here that when I write of gender in the following pages I will always use it in that sense: not the biological difference between female and male but the cultural knowledge of what it means to be female or male, feminine or masculine.

Obviously my history of childhood is inspired by concerns of the moment. How could it be otherwise? But this is no cause for regret: such entanglement in time and place is not only inevitable but also useful. On the one hand, it puts us in a position to "learn things the past did not understand about itself."[52] The medieval indifference to early childhood would have seemed natural and would therefore have been invisible to thirteenth-century Germans, but it becomes obvious in comparison with a culture like ours that is fixated on the first years of life. I will not claim that the MHG indifference exists in any absolute sense, like Ariès's "idea of childhood," but only in relation to other possibilities for constructing childhood, in this case our own. On the other hand, acknowledging our own historicity enables us to learn something about ourselves. Comparison with other cultures reveals that our own anxiety about the experiences of a child's first years is actually rather unusual. By enabling such comparisons the history

47. Bruner, *Acts of Meaning*, 34.
48. Mead, *Samoa*, 1–13.
49. Whiting and Whiting, *Six Cultures*.
50. See Scott, *Gender*, 1–11, 28–50; Appiah, "Race," 274–87; Foucault, *Use of Pleasure*, 4.
51. Scott, *Gender*, 2.
52. Bynum, *Fragmentation*, 23.

of childhood defamiliarizes the present and makes the natural strange. In this way it helps us, in Foucault's eloquent formulation, "to learn to what extent the effort to think one's own history can free thought from what it silently thinks, and so enable it to think differently."[53]

The Nature of the Evidence

Nearly everything I have mentioned so far has concerned history, yet what follows is a book that relies almost entirely on literary sources. Can one write a history of childhood based on MHG literary texts? These texts are, after all, profoundly shaped by literary tradition, by the circumstances of their patronage and performance, and by a host of other factors that make it absurd to suppose they might somehow offer an accurate representation of extraliterary childhood. MHG texts seem particularly unrepresentative. They discriminate by class: almost all the children in these texts, whether religious or secular, are of noble birth. They discriminate by sex: males appear in greater number and in a greater variety of roles than females. And they are relentlessly idealizing: their young heroes and heroines are, with hardly an exception, flawless in every regard. These biases are not hard to explain. MHG literary texts, nearly all of them written by men, were commissioned by men and, less frequently, women of the nobility and the church, themselves usually of noble birth, who regarded literary patronage as a way of glorifying themselves and legitimating their power.[54] It is not surprising that the texts represent the interests of those who paid for them. But it would be foolish to think that they represent the real children of the German Middle Ages.

Unfortunately, however, the MHG texts are the best we have. The more usual kinds of historical sources waste hardly a word on children, even on those who, like Frederick Barbarossa and Elizabeth of Hungary, were born into the highest nobility and who grew up to capture the imagination of their contemporaries. For the most part, medieval chroniclers share the attitude of Ottokar von Steiermark, who greets the birth of a future king of Hungary by declaring: "I don't want to write any more about him now; he'll have to wait until he gets older."[55] Nor do we know much about

---

53. Foucault, *Use of Pleasure*, 9.
54. Bumke, *Mäzene*, 65; Schreiner, "Hof," 86; Wenzel, "Höfische Repräsentation," 107.
55. ORmchr 11652–55: von dem ich iezuo niht mê tihten wil noch schrîben: er muoz alsô belîben, unz daz er wirt elter.

the courts and other settings where medieval children grew up. Partly this is the fault of the documents, which contain "significant blind spots and blank spaces" where court culture is concerned.[56] Partly it is the fault of the historians, whose "investigation of [even] the royal court of the high Middle Ages has only just begun."[57] However, while records of medieval children and the institutions where they grew up are scarce, representations of children in medieval literary texts are not. Under such circumstances it is not surprising that historians like John Boswell or Josef Fleckenstein have drawn on literary texts to supplement the historical record—although, as historians, they clearly feel some uneasiness about using literary material and go out of their way to explain why they do so.[58]

If one wants to describe the medieval German knowledge of childhood, then literary texts are less an embarrassing necessity required by the lack of other material than essential, perhaps even privileged sources of information. They are privileged, first, because the knowledge of childhood is the culturally constructed *meaning* of childhood, and literary texts are rich sources of cultural meaning, richer perhaps than census records or school reports. Second, the representations of children in the literary texts are themselves part of the historical knowledge of childhood. They rely on that knowledge and incorporate elements of it—otherwise they would have been incomprehensible. At the same time the behaviors and ideals represented in the texts help constitute that knowledge—doubtless, in many cases, providing models for behavior. One can argue over the meaning of the MHG texts, just as one argues about the meaning of census figures, but it would be foolish to ignore so rich a source of information about the knowledge of childhood just because what one can learn from it does not have the clarity of an arithmetic sum. Whatever its limitations, the surviving corpus of MHG texts constitutes the entire linguistic remains of the most productive community of German speakers in the high Middle Ages. It provides our best, indeed our only access to the discursive practices that articulated their understanding of the world, including their knowledge of childhood.[59]

56. Schreiner, "Hof," 67: Wer wissen möchte, welche Kulturbedeutung dem 'Hof' um 1200 zukam, stößt in Urkunden und Chroniken des Mittelalters auf beträchtliche Blind- und Leerstellen.

57. Spieß, "Königshof," 204: Die Erforschung des hochmittelalterlichen Königshofes steht . . . noch ganz am Anfang.

58. Boswell, *Kindness*, 6–23; Fleckenstein, *Curialitas*, 463–64.

59. The fundamentally linguistic definition of the corpus is reflected in two solecisms I

It is true that the MHG texts are unrepresentative, focusing almost exclusively on nobles and preferentially on males. Yet noble males, both secular and ecclesiastical, constituted the hegemonic groups in the German Middle Ages and therefore played a disproportionate role in the production of cultural knowledge, including the knowledge of childhood. Because the interests that dominate the texts are the same as those that dominated the historical world, the MHG texts are more useful guides to the general knowledge of childhood in medieval Germany than they might at first seem. It is also true that the MHG texts idealize their heroes and heroines and the world in which they live. Yet heroes and idealizations are cultural products and are themselves part of the world in which they circulate. Even historians, in this case Josef Fleckenstein writing about the education of future knights, recognize that the idealized representations found in contemporary literary texts are themselves "definitely a part of reality."[60] As "part of reality," even the most implausible aspects of childhood in MHG texts will necessarily have affected the lives of real children to some degree.

This must have been particularly true in the noble culture of the high Middle Ages, which strove in many ways to give life the ideality of literature. Courtliness is one result: C. Stephen Jaeger maintains that "court life is literature operating in the medium of reality rather than the written word."[61] The courtly festival is another: Walter Haug writes of "the precariousness of the festival, its ideal dimension and utopian character hovering between performance and reality."[62] The class of knights is a third: relying on little more than a few rituals, a handful of words, and a vague ideological program, medieval rulers united in the single real but artificial category of "knight" those ranging from impoverished mercenaries to the emperor himself. In such a context, where life aspires to the artificiality of literature, one cannot dismiss the textual representation of childhood, no matter how artificial or idealized, as "merely literary." The real power of the class that cultivated these ideals means that the ideals themselves have real constitutive power.

---

will use repeatedly: "the MHG knowledge of childhood," which is the knowledge of childhood articulated in MHG texts, and "MHG children," the children represented within the discursive realm of Middle High German.

60. Fleckenstein, *Curialitas*, 464: Insofern sind sie [ideale Züge] durchaus ein Teil der über sich hinausstrebenden ritterlichen Wirklichkeit.

61. Jaeger, *Courtliness*, 258.

62. Haug, "Idealität zur Orgie," 163: das Prekäre des Festes . . . , seine ideale Dimension und seinen utopischen Schwebecharakter zwischen Spiel und Faktizität.

Since MHG texts offer our best access to the knowledge of childhood of German speakers in the Middle Ages, I have tried to consult
as many of these texts as possible. The largest body of evidence comes
from "childhood narratives," that is, stories about children. Some childhood narratives are independent texts, like the *Kindheit Jesu* of Konrad von
Fußesbrunnen, which is devoted entirely to the childhood of Jesus, but
most are part of longer texts, like the story of Obilot, which fills book seven
of Wolfram von Eschenbach's *Parzival*. Childhood narratives are found in
courtly romances, heroic epics, saints' lives, *Mären*, pious tales, sermons,
and chronicles. Although narrative accounts form the core of my study, I
have also consulted lyric, didactic, legal, and homiletic texts. Doubtless I
have failed to find all the children I was looking for, but I would be surprised if those I missed will seriously alter the conclusions I have reached.

Since I have defined the object of investigation primarily in linguistic
terms I have thereby determined the date at which I must begin. The first
MHG texts appear around 1050, after a gap of about a century and a half
in which hardly anything appears to have been written in German. Since
no children of any significance appear in MHG texts before about 1100,
that is when I start. The year at which I end can also be justified on linguistic grounds, since 1350 is often given as the (admittedly arbitrary) date at
which Middle High German becomes Early New High German.[63] History
and literature suggest other reasons for ending at 1350. By 1300 population growth, which had been substantial for several centuries, has ceased;
agricultural production has reached the limits of its technical capability;
and a period of economic crisis has commenced that will cause a fundamental restructuring of the noble class.[64] The great flourishing of medieval
German courtly culture, which began in the middle of the twelfth century,
comes to an end.[65] The literary landscape changes as well. After 1300 those
genres disappear that had dominated literary production since the twelfth
century: *Minnesang*, *Spruchdichtung*, and courtly romance. Younger forms
take their place: religious drama, prose, allegory, mystical writing, and the
various genres of short couplet texts.[66] In order to see whether the MHG
knowledge of childhood is affected by the dramatic changes already begin-

63. Bach, *Geschichte*, 224; Eggers, *Sprachgeschichte*, 1:282.
64. Sablonier, "Situation," 19, 22.
65. While many extend the period from 1100 to 1300 (Borst, *Barbaren*, 333; Bumke, *Höfische Kultur*, 31), Fleckenstein argues that courtly culture in Germany does not begin in the
full sense until the accession of the Hohenstaufen ("Miles und clericus," 311).
66. Glier, *Literatur im späten Mittelalter*, 8–10; Schirmer, *Motivuntersuchungen*, viii, 56;
Wehrli, *Geschichte*, 465.

ning by 1300 it is necessary to pursue the investigation beyond that date. I
have continued up to 1350.

The Shape of the Argument

I have approached the body of evidence just described in two ways. The
first puts me in the positivist lineage of Zingerle: I have tried to collect,
organize, and make accessible as much information about MHG childhood
as I could find. The second puts me in the historicizing lineage of Ariès: I
have tried to discover the culturally specific knowledge of childhood that
informs those sources. Of course the MHG discourse on childhood was affected by nondiscursive historical practices—oblation, fosterage, marriage,
inheritance: where something relevant is known about these I will try to
mention it. The MHG writing on childhood was also influenced by writing in Latin and French, on which a large proportion of the MHG texts
depend: where it seems appropriate I will refer to these traditions as well.
But I will do so only to place the German texts in a broader context since,
closely related as they may be, the Latin and French traditions are necessarily different from the German. More inclusive studies, surely desirable,
will require scholars with greater patience or greater learning.

   This project takes the MHG knowledge of childhood as a single
discursive formation and attempts to describe it without preconceptions
about the divisions it might contain. Therefore I do not begin with authors and their works, with literary genres, with literary history, or with
the familiar stages of childhood development. I do not presuppose that
Lambrecht will necessarily have different ideas about childhood from Jans
Enikel, that childhood in Arthurian romance will differ from that in didactic texts, or that MHG writers distinguish, as we do, between childhood
and adolescence. Instead I have assumed that all MHG texts are authen-
tic witnesses to the MHG discourse on childhood—the least of the many
lives of St. Margaret no less than the sophisticated and self-conscious pro-
ductions of Wolfram, texts that recount the ancient stories of Jesus no less
than those that tell of contemporary figures like Elizabeth of Hungary. All
indicate the kinds of things that could be said about children in medieval
Germany. I have not offered readings of individual texts but have attempted
rather to sketch the cultural knowledge of childhood in relation to which
the individual childhood narrative would have been meaningful.

   Let me give an example. As Gottfried begins to describe Tristan's education he pauses to lament that the study of books represents Tristan's "first turning away from freedom," the end of his "joys" and "the beginning of his worries."[67] Some take these lines as a commentary on "the high price"[68] of Tristan's own education, showing "how his childish freedom is curtailed by the educational plans of his devoted foster father."[69] Others understand them as a commentary on education in general, as lines in which, "remarkably, Gottfried distances himself from study and learning."[70] The first reading is hard to reconcile with the actual description of Tristan's education, in which the young hero is shown to master every discipline with ease: where is there even a hint of worry or of regret for lost freedoms and joys? And the second is hard to reconcile with the practice of a poet like Gottfried, who delights in nothing more than in parading his mastery of rhetoric, dialectics, and other school subjects: why would he distance himself from study and learning? The lines on freedom, joy, and worry make better sense if they are understood not in relation to Tristan or Gottfried but rather in relation to widespread MHG attitudes toward the nature of the child: children, by nature, pursue pleasure and joy, which distinguishes them from adults, who are burdened with worry. It also helps to know something about MHG attitudes concerning nurture: with the help of education the undisciplined "freedom" characteristic of children, which may be indulged when they are very young, is replaced by the discipline expected of adults. Gottfried takes the beginning of Tristan's education as his "first turning" towards adulthood, and, like other writers of the first half of the thirteenth century, he allows himself a bit of nostalgia for the undisciplined "freedom" and pursuit of "joy" that are natural to children but that must be sacrificed as one becomes an adult. The "worry" that Tristan begins to feel is best understood not as a commentary on education but as a commonplace on growing up.

The knowledge of MHG childhood necessary to situate this passage from *Tristan* in its cultural context can only be had by examining a large number of texts for what they show about nature, nurture, history, and other topics. In this book I try to provide that background. I have isolated

67. GTrist 2068–69: sin erstiu kere uz siner vriheite; 2079: vröuden; 2086: siner sorgen anevanc.

68. Werner, "Tristan," 171: den teueren Preis.

69. Bindschedler, "Bildungsgedanke," 33: wie seine kindliche Freiheit eingeschränkt wird von den Bildungsabsichten seines treuen Pflegevaters.

70. Huber, *Gottfried*, 23: An dieser Stelle kommt es zu einer bemerkenswerten Distanzierung zu Studium und Gelehrsamkeit.

seven topics, devoted a chapter to each, and then added two more general essays. This introductory chapter, concerned primarily with historiographical issues, is the first of the essays. The second concludes the volume. The seven studies that fall between are arranged so that the smallest units are treated first. Chapter two is devoted to the words that are used to refer to children and childhood. Chapter three treats the nature of childhood: those traits said to be natural to children by virtue of their status as children, by virtue of the lineage into which they were born, or because they are heroes and heroines. Chapter four treats the nurture of children: the care that is given to them by parents and others, as well as the training and education they receive. Chapters five and six describe the changing social relations of childhood. Five is devoted to the ties with which children are born (of lineage, for example, or religion), the ones that are broken (by abandonment or death of parents), and the new childhood ties that are contracted as they grow up (to tutors or foster parents). Six continues with the adult ties that can be formed either during childhood (love, religious commitment) or when a child comes of age (marriage, knighthood). Chapter seven investigates how the various elements already considered singly combine to form childhood narratives of different types—for virgin saints, brides, knights, and so forth. Chapter eight traces historical patterns, the changing fashions in the MHG childhood narrative over the course of 250 years, including the fates of the various genres, the changing attitudes towards sources, and other historical developments.

In the concluding essay, chapter nine, material from the previous chapters is drawn together in order to offer a comprehensive description of the knowledge of childhood in Middle High German. It contains evidence that may seem to support Ariès, evidence so contrary to our notions of childhood that it seems to deny childhood itself: while we regard childhood as a special time of life that deserves all the attention we can give it, MHG writers regard childhood as a time of deficiency that warrants little attention for its own sake. At the same time there is much evidence to support the revisionist critics of Ariès: those who challenge Ariès's charge of parental indifference will find vocal allies in MHG parents, who are extravagant in expressing love for their children. These data, however, represent more than discrete points of agreement or disagreement with Ariès or Zingerle: they represent elements of an historically specific knowledge of childhood that is more complex than either will acknowledge. In many ways the MHG knowledge of childhood is different from our own, and in many ways we might find it less attractive. Nevertheless, if we are interested in the history of childhood, we must note the differences as well as the similarities; we must acknowledge the unattractive as well as the attractive; above all we must respect the complex integrity of the knowledge of childhood in past times.

2. Words: Defining the Terms of Childhood

When the *Titanic* sank, it was women and children first. The men, presumed loyal to a code of behavior that C. S. Lewis and others would like to derive from medieval chivalry,[1] were expected to stand back, relinquishing their places in the lifeboats to those thought less able to fend for themselves in the cold waves of the north Atlantic. Many apparently did so. But what was expected of a young man of sixteen? Was he to stand back with the grown men and go down with the ship, or was he to take his place among the children and, perhaps, be saved? What if he was fourteen? or eighteen? And what of a young woman of sixteen? Was she in the lifeboat because she was a child or because she was a woman? And what if she was fourteen? or eighteen? We speak of men, women, and children and understand that we have included everybody, but the categories by which we do so are not equally precise. We can usually distinguish men from women without much difficulty but seem to be less sure when it comes to distinguishing children from adults. I have asked many people when they think childhood ends, and all of them agree with the dictionaries: childhood ends when adolescence begins, with the onset of puberty. But if adolescence comes between childhood and adulthood, then what of our formula for everybody? Surely when we say "men, women, and children" we don't mean to leave out adolescents.

Given these ambiguities, it seems important to clarify at the very outset what I mean by "childhood." I am concerned in this book with the stretch of life that begins at birth and lasts until adulthood, what we usually call "childhood and adolescence" or "infancy, childhood, and adolescence." Since, however, I do not want to assume that medieval Germans necessarily subdivided this stretch of life, as we do, into two or three stages, I need a single term for the years that fall between birth and majority. I have chosen to follow the example of the passengers on the *Titanic* (perhaps an

1. Lewis, *Allegory*, 3–4.

unwise choice), who knew that some English expressions—such as "men, women, and children"—do include in the category of "children" everyone who is not yet an adult. I have adopted such usage as my own and will refer to the object of this study as "childhood," the period of life from birth to adulthood, and to those who fall within this period as "children."[2]

While I can ask my friends what they understand by "childhood" and state what I mean by the term, it is no longer possible to ask MHG writers what they meant by the various words with which they refer to those who are not yet adults. Nevertheless, we will never discover what MHG texts can tell us about childhood in the German Middle Ages unless we have some idea of how we ought to understand the words we read—and words, as we well know, are tricky. This chapter is devoted, therefore, to an analysis of the MHG vocabulary of childhood.[3]

The MHG words for children fall into three categories, which can be illustrated with unusual clarity in the prose *Lancelot*. The story begins as the king and queen of Benewic set out for King Arthur's court in order to seek Arthur's help in defending themselves against a traitorous attack. They take with them their infant child Lancelot, who is regularly referred to as *daz kint*, "the child."[4] *Kint* is a word that designates Lancelot in a general way, without regard to sex, class, or vocation; it reveals only that he is young. Shortly after Lancelot's parents start their journey the infant Lancelot is stolen by the Lady of the Lake, who carries him off to her marvelous realm. Once there he continues to be called *kint*, but, especially when he is addressed by others, he is also called *juncherre*.[5] *Juncherre* means "young lord"; it places Lancelot in a category defined by relative youth, male sex, and noble birth. Somewhat later, when Lancelot is slightly over eighteen, the Lady of the Lake decides that he should be knighted. From the moment this decision is taken Lancelot is called almost exclusively *knappe*,

2. As will become clear in chapter five, I have followed the investigation of childhood only up to the earliest point at which adulthood might be thought to begin. Although a secular male is said to become a "man" when he is knighted, some might argue that he is not fully adult until later, when he has married and assumed his inheritance (see Duby, "Youth"). I assume childhood ends at the first threshold.

3. The following discussion does not attempt to satisfy the standards that might be set by a semanticist, standards that I am not in a position, either by training or by temperament, to meet. But it is not just a collection of random observations either. It is based on a systematic survey of nearly 100 childhood narratives and related texts, a survey in which I recorded all the terms for children and childhood that occur in each text, where in the course of the narrative each term occurs, and who uses it. The generalizations that follow are based on this substantial body of evidence.

4. PrLanc 1:6,13, 1:13,27, 1:14,10.

5. PrLanc 1:34,24, 1:37,28, 1:41,15.

"squire," until he receives his sword from Guenevere, from which point he is called *ritter*, "knight."[6] Used in this sense, *knappe* is a word that designates Lancelot according to his future vocation: he is a young male who hopes to become a knight.

Kint, juncherre, and *knappe* represent three classes of terms, each of which contains words that designate children from a different perspective. *Kint* is a *general* term, since it can apply to any child; *juncherre* is an *aristocratic* term, since it designates the child as noble; *knappe* is a *vocational* term, since it indicates the vocation towards which the child is headed. I will begin by describing each of these classes in its clearest form, and will then show some of the kinds of interference that occur among them.

General Terms

Until Lancelot is about to be knighted he is called *kint* more than anything else. And this is not unusual: *kint* is the single most frequently used term for MHG children. It is also the most inclusive, designating them without regard to sex, class, or future vocation, but only according to their relative youth. With hardly an exception MHG children are called *kint* as soon as they are born, and *kint* remains the preferred term throughout early childhood. It is practically the only designation for the young Jesus in Konrad von Fußesbrunnen's *Kindheit Jesu*, which follows its hero until he is twelve, and for Willehalm von Orlens until he is about the same age. In the *Grazer Marienleben* the Virgin is called *kint* until she is five, as is Sigune in *Jüngerer Titurel* until she falls in love.

The diminutive *kindelin* is also used for both males and females, although, contrary to what one might expect, it is neither limited to infants nor is it as frequent as *kint* as a designation for them. When the Virgin is born Bruder Philipp refers to her as *kint* and *kindelin*, and he continues to call her *kindelin* until she is seven.[7] Dietleib can still be called *kindelin* after he has left home and is just about to fight and wound the formidable Hagen.[8]

As children grow up *kint* begins to be used differently according to sex. Males can be called *kint* until they reach manhood and, occasionally, even later. For some—Gottfried's Tristan, Wolfdietrich A, and many saints—the

6. PrLanc 1:118,25, 1:131,28, 1:146,29.
7. PhMarl 372, 374, 376, 383, 389, 413, 425, 469, 472, 501.
8. BitDlb 2778; see also 3348.

term dominates until they come of age, when it is abandoned. For others—
Rudolf's Alexander, Wolfram's Parzival, and some of the saints in the *Väterbuch*—*kint* is soon supplemented and then replaced by other designations.
Although the use of *kint* for males decreases as they approach adulthood
and usually ceases when they come of age, it does occur occasionally as
a designation for young adults. Shortly after he has been knighted Wigalois fights Hojir, who, we are told, "was not able to hold out against the
kint."[9] In the *Nibelungenlied* the youngest of the Burgundian kings is often
called "Giselher the *kint*."[10] This is not just a literary usage. When Frederick II crossed the Alps in 1212, the seventeen-year-old was greeted as the
puer Apuliae, the "child from Apulia," even though he had come of age and
married several years earlier.[11] Chronicling the events of 1212 at the end of
the century, Jans Enikel respects the earlier usage and refers frequently to
"the *kint* Frederick" or simply "the *kint*."[12]

Passages like those just cited inspire the claim in the *Mittelhochdeutsches
Wörterbuch*, often repeated, that "the notion attached to [MHG] *kint* com-
prised a much longer part of life than we now attach to the word."[13] But
this is to take the exception for the rule. MHG infants and young male
children are always called *kint*. Only rarely does *kint* apply to males we
would regard as too old to be called children, and in these cases it is clearly
used to indicate relative youth. Wigalois is younger than Hojir, Giselher is
the youngest of the three Burgundian kings, and Frederick's successes are
rendered all the more remarkable by insisting on his youth. *Kint* can, after
all, also be used as an adjective meaning "young": sometime after Wigalois
defeats Hojir, another opponent tells him he is "too *kint*"[14] to undertake
the adventure he has in mind. Just as young children are regularly called
kint to indicate that they are young, so knights too are occasionally called
kint for the same reason. The key notion is relative youth.[15]

The use of *kint* for females differs in two ways from its use for males.
First, the term disappears at an earlier age and more completely: as soon as

9. Wglois 3021–22: dône mohter niht mêre gewern vor dem kinde.

10. Niblgn 267,2, 1098,2, 2191,2, among many others.

11. Kantorowicz, *Frederick*, 59–61.

12. JWeltc 27739: daz kint Fridrîch; 27714, 27721, 27727, among others. —Other knights
called *kint*: ErnstB 61; GTrojk 336, 337, 574; GuFrau 375, 539, 1265; Kudrn 1029,1, 1439,4;
MOswld 29; Parz 356,3, 357,11.

13. Benecke, *Wörterbuch*, 1:817: der begriff, den man mit *kint* verband, umfaßte eine viel
längere lebenszeit als der den wir jetzt damit verbinden.

14. Wglois 3384: ir sît ze kint.

15. *Kint* as a relative term: AplTyr 13005–6, 14810, 19201–12; Eneit 274,8; Frndst 151,1;
Orendl 388–90; Rabens 451,1; SfHelb 4,339; Virgnl 74,7, 161,7, 916,5–6, 861,13. —Old French
enfes exhibits a semantic range even greater than MHG *kint* (Berkvam, "Nature," 165–66).

a female has contact with strangers, especially with suitors, *kint* makes way for other terms, chiefly *maget*, "maiden." Walther von Rheinau calls the Virgin *kint* and *kindelin* until she is seven and joins the company of Temple maidens, when the terms disappear. Gottfried hardly ever calls Isold *kint*, even when she first appears in the story, although Tristan is frequently designated that way, even as he approaches the end of his childhood. Of course there are exceptions: the heroine of *Armer Heinrich* is called both *kint* and *maget* throughout.

Second, in the relatively few cases where *kint* is used for older females it does not mean "young," as it does for males, but "virgin." As a consequence, while a male can be called *kint* after he has been knighted, a female cannot be called *kint* after she has married. According to Priester Wernher, when Joachim wed Ann "he took a *kint* in marriage," but a few lines afterwards we learn that the *wip*, "woman," was very beautiful.[16] At marriage a female changes from *kint* to *wip*. Virgins, however, remain *kint* no matter how old they are. When Kudrun, who must be at least in her mid-twenties, is rescued from captivity along with Hildeburg, who is the same generation as Kudrun's *grand*mother, they can still be called *kint*.[17] The association of virginity with *kint* is so strong that the writer of the *Väterbuch* can refer to a monastery in which "there was a great assembly of God's servants, many pure *kint*, both old and young."[18] Even old men can be called *kint* if they are virgins.[19]

In the vast majority of cases *kint* does not distinguish between males and females: it designates infants and relatively young children of both sexes. However, as children grow up *kint* begins to differentiate according to gender. For males things are comparatively relaxed. *Kint* is used less and less as they grow older; it usually disappears when they come of age, although it can still refer to young adults. For females things are stricter. Early in life they must acknowledge the gender ideal of virginity, so *kint* makes way for the more explicit *maget*, "maiden." When *kint* occurs later in a maiden's childhood it submits again to the same ideal, functioning now as a synonym for *maget*. For older males *kint* is a relative term: male *kint* are relatively young. For older females *kint* is an absolute term: female *kint* are virgins.

16. WerMar D341: er nam ein kint ze siner e; D348.
17. Kudrn 1214,1, 1218,4.
18. Väterb 27691–94: Da was von Gotes gesinde An manigem reinen kinden, Beide alde und junge, Ein michel samenunge.
19. *Kint* used for older virgins: AplTyr 5940–44; BMärtr 25900, 25926; Erec 1318; HnrKgd 848; Kudrn 13,1, 1644,1; Lohgrn 477, 482, 497, 501; Niblgn 582,3, 616,3.

Of course there are times when writers want to differentiate clearly between males and females, and MHG has terms that enable them to do so. Males may be called *degen, kneht, knabe, knappe, jugent, junge,* and *jungelinc.* Females will be called *maget* and little else.

The MHG noun *degen* derives from an Indo-European root meaning "to beget" or "give birth," which developed on the one hand into words for "male child" (and "female child," *dierne*) and on the other into words meaning "servant" or "military retainer"—as in English "thane."[20] MHG reflects this development, using *degen* in two senses that, with uncharacteristic rigor, are kept quite distinct. First, *degen* can designate an infant as male: Paris is called "the newborn *degen*"; the Christchild is "a *degenkint.*"[21] Second, *degen* serves as a praiseworthy designation for adult warriors, especially but not exclusively in texts in the heroic tradition: Siegfried, Hagen, and the other heroes of the *Nibelungenlied* are often called *degen.* Between infancy and adulthood, however, males are usually not referred to in this way: Engelhard, Tschinotulander, and Tristrant, of whose childhoods we learn a good deal, are not called *degen* until after they have been knighted.[22] There are exceptions, however: the young hero of *Biterolf und Dietleib* is called *degen* on many occasions throughout his childhood, perhaps under the influence of the heroic tradition with which this text stands in a close and self-conscious relation.[23]

Although *kneht* was originally a general designation for a male child, in MHG it is much more common as a term for "servant," "attendant," or "squire." Nevertheless, it does appear occasionally in its original sense: Wilhelm von Wenden looks forward to the birth of his child "whether it is a *kneht* or a maiden."[24] And it does occur occasionally in reference to older children: Paris is said to have been well taken care of by his foster mother until "the *junge* became a well-grown *kneht.*"[25] The vast majority of childhood narratives, however, get by without *kneht* as a general term for young males. Like *degen, kneht* can also refer to adult fighters. Charle-

---

20. Kluge, *Etymologisches Wörterbuch*, 125, 134.
21. KTrojk 520: der niuweborne degen; WerMar D4260: ein degenkint.
22. Englhd 2631; JngTit 1224,2; ETrist 740.
23. BitDlb 2109, 2144, 2182, 2220, among many others. —Others called *degen* at birth only: Exdus 151, 175, 191; HlbDek 53; JngTit 1107,4; JWeltc 1275, 6179; SAlexr 579. Others not called *degen* until they leave home or are knighted: KrlGal 63,31; Lanzlt 434; TandFl 1985; WilÖst 2937. —On the relation of *Biterolf und Dietleib* to the heroic tradition: Curschmann, "Dichtung über Heldendichtung."
24. WilWnd 1275: wirt ez kneht oder maget.
25. KTrojk 578–79: biz der junge wart ein wol gewahsen kneht.

magne, Alexander, Erec, and Morold are all called *kneht* in situations where their knightly prowess is at issue.[26]

Probably the most common general term for male children is *knabe*. Its variant, *knappe*, is less frequent in general usage. Of the two, only *knabe* is used to refer to infants: Parzival is called *knabe* at birth, Paris the diminutive *knebelin*.[27] And, of the two, *knabe* is by far the more popular as a general designation: Dietleib, Engelhard, Meleranz, Tandareis, Rudolf's Alexander, Malefer, Helmbrecht, Pyramus, Eraclius, the Göttweiger Paris, the Zwölfjähriges Mönchlein, and the heroes of *Nachtigall* and *Studentenabenteuer A* are all called *knabe*, many of them frequently, but never *knappe*. Comparatively few texts, among them Wolfram's *Parzival* and *Willehalm* and Ulrich's *Alexander*, prefer *knappe* as a general term for boys. *Knabe*, but not *knappe*, can be also refer to adult knights: years after he has come of age Parzival can still be called "a strong *knabe*."[28]

The MHG distribution shows clearly how *knabe* and *knappe*, the second originally a synonymous variant of the first, are moving towards the modern distinction between *Knabe*, "boy," and *Knappe*, "squire" or "knight-in-training." The use of *knabe* but not *knappe* for male children of all ages, as well as the much greater frequency of *knabe* in all kinds of texts, indicates a distinct preference for *knabe* as the general term for young males. The rarity of *knappe* as a general term, as well as its absence as a term for infants and adult knights, reveals the tendency to restrict it to those, no longer infants and not yet adults, who hope to become knights. Yet the restriction of *knappe* to vocational usage is not absolute: young saints like Bernhard and Pantaleon can be called *knappe*, even though they have nothing to do with knighthood.[29] And Parzival is called *knappe* before he even knows that knights exist, before, that is, he could possibly be considered a knight-in-training.[30]

---

26. Rolndl 706; LAlexr S1809; Erec 834–35; ETrist 600. —Cases where *kneht* distinguishes male from female: KTrojk 14968–72; SlPrsC 53; StrKrl 135–37. Cases where *kneht* seems to mean "male child" in general rather than "attendant" or "squire": Englhd 501, 598, 936, 1024, 1258, 2402; Eracl 1373, 1706, 1811; Helmbr 22; Lanzlt 472; PKonPr M249,109–110. —On the medieval history of *kneht*: Schmidt-Wiegand, "Knecht," 895–96. On the relation of *kneht* to fighters: Bumke, *Höfische Kultur*, 88–89; Grimm, *Deutsches Wörterbuch*, 5:1382–84.

27. Parz 113,29; KTrojk 381.

28. Parz 290,6: ein strenger knabe.

29. Passnl K397,52; KPantl 964.

30. Parz 117,30, 119,9, 119,16. —To claim, like Dennis Green ("Naming," 110), that Wolfram takes *knabe* and *knappe* to be "synonymous references to the hero's young boyhood" or, like David Yeandle (*Commentary*, 281), that Wolfram uses the terms "without obvious distinction in meaning" is to underestimate Wolfram's art. Wolfram calls Parzival *knabe* only three

Jugent, junge, and *jungelinc* derive from the adjective *junc,* "young."
Jugent, a feminine abstract noun that ordinarily means "youth," is used,
very rarely, to designate young males: Gottfried's Tristan is addressed as
"dear fellow, sweet *jugent*" by Mark's hunters.[31] *Junge* and *jungelinc,* on the
other hand, are very common. *Junge* does not ordinarily occur until near
the end of childhood: Alexander is first called *junge* when he falls in love,
the hero of *Bussard* after he is already a student at Paris, Malefer when his
grandfather arms him and makes him his heir.[32] Others, like Engelhard or
Charlemagne, are not called *junge* until after they are knighted.[33] *Junge* is,
in fact, not at all uncommon as a term for adult heroes: Dietleib and Siegfried are both called *junge* in their climactic battle near the end of *Biterolf
und Dietleib.*[34]

  Jungelinc is as common as *junge* and seems to designate those of the
same age: Lanzelet is first called *jungelinc* when he sets out on his own,
Eilhart's Tristrant just before he is knighted, Abraham when he gets married.[35] It can also refer to adult fighters: Tristrant is called *jungelinc* just
before he fights the Irish dragon.[36] *Jungelinc* is unusual, however, for two
reasons. First, more than any other designation, it is explicitly placed in
sequence: Silvester, Ambrose, and the hero of *Mönches Not* are all said to be
kint who become *jungelinge.*[37] In such passages, at least, *jungelinc* must refer
to a relatively older child. Second, *jungelinc* seems to have been particularly associated with an ideal of young male beauty: Lancelot is regularly
referred to by those around him as "the beautiful *jungelinc*";[38] after describing the beauty of an angel Jans Enikel concludes that "the angel had the
appearance of a *jungelinc.*"[39]

---

times: when he is born, helpless, or foolish (Parz 113,29, 129,3, 138,9). Otherwise, against the
usage of nearly every other MHG writer, he prefers *knappe.* By insisting on a term that usually
means "future knight" and using it for Parzival before he has heard of knights, Wolfram
suggests Parzival's future vocation, even when the hero himself is still completely ignorant
of it.
  31. GTrist 3128: trut geselle, süeziu jugent.
  32. ArPhlS 147; Bussrd 101; Rennew 13285.
  33. Englhd 2880; KrlGal 75,51.
  34. BitDlb 11054, 11062, 11184. —*Jugent* designates a young male: GTrist 2277; JngTit
161,1, 806,1, 1168,1; RBarlm 332,2.
  35. Lanzlt 404; ETrist 346; Väterb 30709.
  36. ETrist 1644.
  37. KSilvr 130–31; ELgAur 283,20; MönNot 18–21.
  38. PrLanc 1:21,2: der schön júngling.
  39. JWeltc 3675–76: der engel was in der gebaer, sam er ein jüngelinc waer. —Very occasionally male and female are grouped together as *jungelinge*: FlorBl 599, 742, 6666, 7304;
Passnl H247,71. And very occasionally infants can be called *jungelinc*: FlorBl 599, 742; KTrojk
448, 502. —Males who *become jungelinge*: GTrist 3912–21; LAlexr V365–67; Passnl H348,56–
57, K397,29; Väterb 33517; WlMarl 6154–55, 6770–71. —*Jungelinc* is associated with beauty:

Two things should be noted about the words with which MHG designates male children. First, with the exception of the infrequent *knappe*, none of the general terms for young males rigorously distinguishes children from adults. *Junge* and *jungelinc* refer to those who are *relatively* young, but these can be children or young adults. *Degen*, *knabe*, and *kneht* can refer to children and adult warriors, even where youth does not seem to be an issue. Second, all of the terms imply some gender ideal: knightly vocation (*knappe*), warrior prowess (*degen*, *knabe*, *kneht*, *junge*, *jungelinc*), or male beauty (*jungelinc*). The terms for male children indicate sex absolutely, referring only to males. They imply gender ordinarily, since all are associated with knighthood or male beauty. But they signify age only relatively, since they can refer to males in the prime of life as well as to children.

While MHG offers a large selection of words that can designate male children, there is essentially only one term for females, *maget*, or "virgin." In Konrad Fleck's *Flore und Blanscheflur* it is the most common designation for the heroine between the ages of five and fifteen. The heroine of Hartmann von Aue's *Armer Heinrich* is introduced as "a *maget*, a *kint* of eight years,"[40] and *maget* remains by far the most common designation for her throughout the work. Kudrun is often called *maget*, and this is the most frequent term for the heroine of Pleier's *Tandareis und Flordibel*. Some females, like Dulciflorie or Wernher's Mary, are called *maget* or the diminutive *magedin* from birth; others, like the Wallerstein Margaret or Sigune, are called *kint* first and *maget* only later.[41] There is no female child who is never called *maget*.[42]

While it is not at all clear when, if ever, a male stops being a *knabe* or a *degen*, it is quite clear that a female ceases to be a *maget* when she first has sexual relations, at which point she becomes a *wip*. After Gahmuret and Belacane make love, "she who used to be called *maget* was now a *wip*."[43] A woman who never has sex will remain a *maget* until she dies. Thus Priester Wernher refers to the Virgin Mary as *maget* throughout the story of her life since, as he says, she "never became a *wip*."[44] *Maget*, then, is not primarily

---

Englhd 1370; ErnstB 79, 582; ETrist 822; GTrist 2123–35; Helmbr 519; KPantl 123; KTrojk 603, 688–89, 763, 1672–95; LAlexr V141–54, V365–67; Passnl K397,26–29; PrLanc 1:34,27; PyrThs 149.

40. ArmHnr 302–3: eine maget, ein kint von ahte jâren.

41. Dulcfl 75; WerMar D1025; WlMarg 151; JngTit 692,2.

42. Very occasionally a female child may be called *dierne* (Ioland 194, 307), *jugent* (JngTit 680,2, 730,1), or *diu junge* (Dulcfl 96, 174, 181, 448; GTrist 8027, 10222, 10535; WilÖst 2005).

43. Parz 45,24: diu ê hiez maget, diu was nû wîp.

44. WerMar D1340: div nie wart ze wibe; A4109, D4714, D4825, D5014.

a designation of age but of sexual status. When we are told that Tydomie "was a *maget* and not a *wip*"[45] we learn something about her sexual experience but nothing about her age. The association of *maget* with virginity is so strong that it can even refer to males who have not had sex, not only saints, like John the Baptist, but also secular figures like Mai or Bohort.[46] According to Berthold von Regensburg, "All of those who have kept themselves pure from the time that they were born, whether they are ladies or manservants, young or old, females or males, all of them are *megede*."[47.] Again, one should not take the exception for the rule: *maget* regularly refers to female virgins and thus regularly designates sex. At the same time one must recognize that the core meaning of *maget* does not concern age or even sex but rather the lack of sexual experience.[48]

The MHG words that designate children without regard to class or future vocation divide them into three classes. First, a group of children, who are called *kint*. Second, a group of males, who are called *degen, kneht, knabe, knappe, junge*, and *jungelinc*. Third, a group of virgins, who are called *maget*. Obviously, the criteria according to which these classes are defined are not commensurate. The first defines according to age, the second according to sex, the third according to sexual experience. The terms that distinguish male and female imply powerful gender ideals, but here too they are not really commensurate. Male children are defined as relatively young males using terms that can *also* be used for adult knights or squires; female children, however, are *defined* as virgins. Since the criteria for establishing these classes are not commensurate, the classes are not mutually exclusive. Thus, while a boy cannot also be a girl, it is possible for Mai to be a *junge* and a *degen*, and, at the same time, a *maget*.[49]

As these last examples indicate, the MHG categories do not correspond to modern ones. We divide children, an age class, into two commensurate classes according to sex, boys and girls. MHG does have a similar age class, those called *kint*. However, if it wants to indicate that a child is

---

45. Melrnz 2550: ein magt si was und niht ein wîp.

46. PKonPr S192,22–23; MaiBfl 93,3; PrLanc 2:79,25–26.

47. BertvR 1:310,4–7: Und alle die sich reineclîche behalten habent von der zît daz sie geborn wurden, ez sîn frouwen oder knehte, junc oder alt, frouwengeslehte oder mannesgeslehte, die sint alle samt megede.

48. Passages in which it is clear that the transition from *maget* to *wip* occurs with the beginning of sexual relations rather than with marriage: Häsln 153–56, 253–58; MfRmbl 217; Niblgn 631,3–4, 652,4; PartMl 1720–22; Parz 60,15, 84,6, 192,9–12, 202,22–23; PrLanc 2:297,14–17; RnfrBr 6194–97; RpParz 38,29–30, 544,39–44; RWeltc 6125; Sperbr 237; WTitrl 27,1–2; WerMar D3370–71. —*Maget* refers to males: Rennew 32297. *Maget* refers to old as well as young: WlMarl 2056.

49. MaiBfl 56,24, 65,3, 93,3.

male, MHG places him in the class of (relatively young) males. And if it wants to indicate that a child is female it places her in the class of virgins. A *knabe* or a *jungelinc* is not a kind of child but a kind of male, usually young but not necessarily a child. A child who thinks of himself as a *knabe* or a *jungelinc* thinks of himself not as one kind of child, the other being girls, but as a kind of male, the others being older. A *maget* is not a kind of child either but a kind of human, a virgin, ordinarily understood to be female. A child who thinks of herself as a *maget* thinks of herself not as one kind of child, the other being boys, but as a kind of female, the other being *wip*, women who have had sexual experience. When we distinguish children by sex we subordinate sex to age: a boy or a girl is a kind of child. When MHG distinguishes children by sex it subordinates age to gender: a *knabe* or a *maget* is a kind of male or female. We accord relatively more importance to age, MHG accords relatively more importance to gender. In order not to efface the differences between modern and MHG conceptualizations of sex difference in children, I will refer to MHG children not as "boys" and "girls" but as "youths" and "maidens." These seem to me the closest English approximations to the categories implied by the MHG terms.[50]

Aristocratic Terms

After Lancelot has been called *kint* for some time, this designation is augmented by *juncherre*, an aristocratic term. One day, for example, when

50. I do this not because I am a "purist" or because I believe "modern terms . . . are taboo" (Hanawalt, *London*, ix) but because I am trying to understand the categories in which medieval Germans understood childhood. If you refer to the heroine of *Armer Heinrich* as a "girl" or an "adolescent" living with her "family" then certain things inevitably come to mind. English is my native language, I hear these ideologically laden words constantly, and I cannot forget what I know even if you tell me that MHG speakers had quite different notions of "girl," "adolescent," and "family," words for which there were no equivalents in their language. My unwillingness to use certain familiar words is not a matter of purity: I cannot get by without "childhood," for instance; and I cannot purge my mind of modern notions of "family" no matter how I refer to medieval domestic units. It is a matter of strategy. By resisting the temptation to translate everything into familiar terms at the very first opportunity it becomes easier to perceive the differences between the MHG knowledge of childhood and our own. First, calling the heroine of *Armer Heinrich* a "maiden" living in a "household" more accurately registers those differences, since the terms come closer to attested medieval categories than "girl" or "family." Second, by their relative unexpectedness the less familiar terms remind us that such differences exist, discourage us from conflating past and present, and encourage us to see what unexpected connections might obtain among the unfamiliar terms. As a consequence, avoiding words like "girl," "boy," and "family" helps bring us closer to the unattainable but still heuristicly useful goal of trying to understand medieval childhood in its own terms.

Lancelot is already over ten, he rides away from his companions in pursuit of a deer; he comes upon a squire hurrying along on foot, leading his exhausted horse, and crying. When Lancelot asks him who he is and where he is going, "the squire saw that the *kint* [Lancelot] was a nobleman and answered him: 'Dear *juncherre*.'"[51] The squire, recognizing Lancelot's class, chooses the appropriate form of address and calls him *juncherre*, "young lord." The narrator still refers to Lancelot as *kint* and will continue to do so occasionally until Lancelot is knighted; *juncherre* does not replace *kint* but is used to acknowledge the noble class affiliation of an individual who according to age or sex might otherwise be called *kint*, *knabe*, or *jungelinc*. *Juncherre* means "young lord" not only in a general way, by virtue of a youth's noble birth, but also in specific feudal terms, in relation to his vassals. When telling of Rual and Floraete, who are the young Tristan's vassals as well as his foster parents, Gottfried will sometimes refer to Tristan as their *juncherre*, thus reminding us of the specific *feudal* ties that subordinate Tristan's foster parents to their "young lord."[52]

The equivalent term for females is *juncvrouwe*, "young noblewoman." Galie, the daughter of King Galaffers, is called "the beautiful, exalted *juncvrouwe*," and is thereby designated as a young woman of the highest nobility.[53] Galie's attendants use the term relatively, calling her "our *juncvrouwe* Galie."[54] They express thereby the relation between the (subordinate) attendants and their (superior) "young lady."

Although both male and female saints are born into wealthy, usually noble, families, male saints are seldom called *juncherre*; a larger number of young female saints, however, are called *juncvrouwe*.[55] Although employed originally in this context as an honorific, the term gradually became so infused with the aura of saintly virginity that, during the period under consideration here, it sometimes means "virgin," as it does in modern German *Jungfrau*. Already in the first half of the thirteenth century the heroine of the *Sperber* can be taken to task for her first sexual adventure with the words: "Now you have become a *wip*! And for that reason you will never again be called *juncvrouwe*!"[56] Writing close to 1350, Hermann von Fritzlar

51. PrLanc 1:36,34–35: Der knapp sah wol das das kint ein edelman was, und antwurt im alsus: 'Lieber juncker. . . .'
52. GTrist 1903, 2159, 3764, 3806.
53. KrlGal 26,41: De schone junffrawe gehere.
54. KrlGal 35,32: Unsse junffrawe Galya.
55. *Juncherre*: Passnl K303,19; Väterb 39140. —*Juncvrouwe*: GrMarl 388; Passnl K111,1, K111,49, K111,65, K113,3; Väterb 27788, 27796, 27874, 27889, 27961, 27976, 28044, 28083, 35787, 35798; WlMarg 233, 311, 317, 550, 590; WlMarl 1185, 1223, 2413.
56. Sperbr 237–41: Nu bistu worden ein wîp! . . . Des gewinstu niemer mêre Wider juncvrouwen namen!

can consider various opinions as to whether Mary Magdalen "was a *junc-vrouwe.*"[57] Having come to mean "virgin," the term can now be applied to males: Hermann states that St. Andrew "himself was a pure *juncvrouwe,*" as were John the Evangelist and Dominic.[58] Although these citations are harbingers of the future development of *juncvrouwe*, in the period under investigation it means "virgin" only rarely. Gregorius's mother is called *juncvrouwe* even after she is pregnant.[59] In the 1330s Aclervis "is called *junc-vrouwe,*" even after she has "lost the name of maiden."[60]

When *juncherren* or *juncvrouwen* grow up, they become *herren*, "lords," and *vrouwen*, "ladies." Just before Charlemagne fights his first combat as a knight he is called *juncherre*, immediately afterward *herre*.[61] Until St. Elizabeth is married she is usually called *maget* and *juncvrouwe*; afterward she is called *wip* and *vrouwe*.[62] Yet *herre* and *vrouwe* can also be used before children come of age. One moment a messenger refers to the young Meleranz as "my illustrious *juncherre*," the next as "my *herre*."[63] Tristan addresses Isold as "sweet *juncvrouwe*" and then three lines later he calls her "a *vrouwe*."[64] This kind of vacillation indicates that *juncherre* and *juncvrouwe* are not opposed to *herre* and *vrouwe* but subordinate to them; they designate varieties of *herre* and *vrouwe*, young ones, not something different from *herre* and *vrouwe*. In this context at least, social rank and sex are clearly more important than age. Whether the messenger calls Meleranz *juncherre* or *herre* he acknowledges him as his lord; whether Tristan calls Isold *juncvrouwe* or *vrouwe* he defines her as a woman of noble birth. That is the main thing. If it seems useful to indicate their youth, they can also be called *juncherre* or *juncvrouwe*—just as an older *herre* or *vrouwe* might be called *altherre* or *altvrouwe*[65]—but this is optional information.

57. Hlgnlb 164,12–13: Von dirre vrowen haben etelîche einen wân, daz si ein juncvrowe wêre.

58. Hlgnlb 9,30–31: her selber ein reine jungvrowe was; 38,10, 173,3.

59. Greg 658.

60. RpParz 37,29–30: ir megede nam verlor sü sam: juncfrowe und liep heisset nu ir nam. —On the history of *Jungfrau*: Kotzenberg, *man, frouwe, juncfrouwe*, 124–57. Although Kotzenberg continues to be cited on the subject, his claim that *juncvrouwe* was established in its modern sense at the end of the thirteenth century primarily through its use in connection with the Virgin Mary (146) is not supported by the texts I have investigated. *Juncvrouwe* occurs more frequently in the lives of the female saints than in the lives of the Virgin. And it is very rare in any of these texts that it has its modern meaning. —For others who are called *juncvrouwe* after they are no longer virgins: Parz 526,1–5, 528,22; WolfdB 93,1, 179,4.

61. KrlGal 67,29, 69,4, 69,62, 69,3.

62. StElis 675, 773, 1000, 1003, 1400, 1470, 1482, 1512, 1513, 1542, 1609.

63. Melrnz 2276: mîn juncherre klâr; 2297: der herre mîn.

64. GTrist 10154: süeziu juncvrouwe; 10157: ein vrouwe.

65. *Altherre*: Crone 21009, 29613; *altvrouwe*: MaiBfl 61,1, 130,23; Wglois 3751.

Vocational Terms

Just after his foster mother, the Lady of the Lake, has decided that it is time for Lancelot to be knighted he is called *knappe* for the first time.[66] And from then on the word is very common: between his arrival at King Arthur's and the moment, eighteen pages later, when he receives his sword from Guenevere, Lancelot is called *knappe* 131 times. The word refers to a youth who hopes to become a knight, a distinction for which Lancelot is extremely eager: "For my part I no longer wish to remain a *knappe*," he says to Ywan, "therefore tell my lord [Arthur] that he should make me a knight tomorrow."[67] *Kneht* is at least as common for a young man en route to knighthood. When the hero of *Mai und Beaflor* is just about to marry he decides that he must be knighted first: "I wish to be knighted before the marriage takes place. My lady shall never be warmed by the embrace of a *kneht*."[68] Even Mai, who has been ruling his country for some time already and is often called *vürste*, "prince," remains a *kneht* until he has been knighted. His sense of propriety is so fine that, en route to his knighting, "the prince rode behind out of good breeding. That was because he was still a *kneht*. It was right and proper that he avoided the knights and rode with his *knappen*."[69]

Some passages seem to imply that the path to knighthood begins not with the status of the *knappe* or *kneht* but with that of *kint*. In *Jüngerer Titurel* when Gamuret sneaks out of Kingrival, he takes "twenty *kint* of high, courtly lineage and eighty worthy *knappen*."[70] His retinue seems to include both *kint* and *knappen*. Although it is nowhere stated explicitly, it seems not unlikely that the *kint*, who are said to be both noble and young, will eventually advance to *knappen* and hope ultimately to be knights.[71]

To judge by the MHG narrative texts, clerics are the only ones besides knights who have a term for those young men who aspire to a particular vocation but who have not yet become full-fledged members: the aspirants are called *schuolaere*, "those who attend school." At the end of *Thomas von*

---

66. PrLanc 1:118,25.
67. PrLanc 1:131,28–29: mit mym willen blib ich nit lenger knapp; darumb sagent mym herren das er mich morn ritter mach.
68. MaiBfl 81,7–10: ich wil ritter werden ê . . . danne daz ergê. ez sol an eines knehtes arm mîn vrouwe nimmer werden warm.
69. MaiBfl 82,33–38: den vürsten man dâ schône sach rîten zühteclîchen nâch. daz was dâ von, er was noch kneht, und was daz billîch unde reht daz er die rîterschaft vermeit und bî sînen knappen reit.
70. JngTit 752,3–4: zweinzik kint von hoher art kurteise und ahzic werder knappen.
71. Other *kint* who seem to be pages: Parz 8,4–5, 429,8–12; WilÖst 224–25.

Kandelberg we learn that "very shortly afterward" the hero, a *"schuolaere,* became a priest."[72] This is the usual expectation—even though a number of the amorous *schuolaere* who set out for the university at Paris are not of a particularly priestly temperament.[73] Given the considerable attention paid to education in MHG narrative and the importance of school in saints' lives, it is surprising how few children are actually called *schuolaere*—only the heroes of a few *Mären* and a few miracles of the Virgin.[74]

Service

When Lancelot's parents leave home to seek help at the court of King Arthur, taking their infant son with them, they are accompanied by a *kneht* "who could serve well. He transported the *kint* before him in a cradle."[75] Possibly this *kneht* is a young squire hoping someday to become a knight. But he need not be, for the vocabulary of childhood is used not only to designate children but also, quite frequently, to designate servants or attendants of any age. The vocabulary of childhood overlaps so extensively with the vocabulary of service that one cannot discuss the former without addressing the latter.

Although *kneht,* as noted above, is one of the less frequently used general terms for youths, it is the most common term for male servants or attendants. When Willehalm von Orlens is living at the court of the king of England, "he served the king well, as a *kneht* should serve his lord."[76] But other terms are used as well. Iwanet, who helps Parzival when he first comes to Arthur's court, is said to be "lady Guenevere's *knappe,*" which implies that he serves the queen.[77] When Dietleib leaves home he sends three *knaben* on ahead to be ready to wait on him, but a bit later they are called *man;* apparently they are adult retainers or servants.[78] When Flordibel arrives at Arthur's court Tandareis is assigned to her "so that he might be her *juncherre* and attend her with service."[79]

72. TKdlbg 306–7: dar nâch in kurzen zîten Der selbe schuoler priester wart.
73. Bussrd 69–70, 88–91; SlPrsC 58–67; StdabA 159–60, 188.
74. *Bussard, Schüler zu Paris A, Schüler zu Paris C, Studentenabenteuer A, Scholar, Marias Bräutigam, Scholar und das Marienbild,* Heinrich der Klausner's *Armer Schüler, Thomas von Kandelberg.* —On *schuolaere* as the heroes of *Mären*: Fischer, *Märendichtung,* 121–22.
75. PrLanc 1:6,12–13: ein knecht . . . der wol kunde dienen. Der furt das kint vor im in eyner wiegen.
76. WilOrl 3907–08: Doch diente er dem herren wol, Als ain kneht sinem herren sol.
77. Parz 156,3: vroun Ginôvêren knappe.
78. BitDlb 2236, 2248, 2289, 2294, 2415.
79. TandFl 679–80: daz er ir juncherre sî unt ir wone mit dienste bî.

The words for young females are used in analogous ways. When Jeschute's fortunes have hit bottom she says that now she could not even be Orilus's *dierne*.[80] She means "servant" or "attendant." *Dierne* is, in fact, much more common in this sense than as a general term for maidens. When Kriemhild needs to provide splendid outfits for her brothers, she directs "thirty *megede* from among her *juncvrouwen*" to get to work.[81] The *megede* and *juncvrouwen* are her attendants. When Walther von Rheinau renders the Magnificat into German he translates the Latin *ancilla*, "handmaiden," as *juncvrouwe*; Bruder Philipp chooses the less ambiguous *dienaerinne*, "servant."[82] Walther's *juncvrouwe* is synonymous with Philipp's *dienaerinne*, and both are translations for *ancilla*. Although both *juncherre* and *juncvrouwe* are used as words for attendant, *juncvrouwe* is far more common. Noble youths in service are likely to be called *knappe* or *kneht*, while noble maidens are called *juncvrouwe*.

In many other languages words for children are also used for servants or slaves. This may be because all were equally subject to the authority of the head of the household, or because adult servants and slaves occupied the legal position of children, or because they were all liable to physical punishment. The emperor Faustinian recalls his father saying that "sons and servants [*kneht*] are equally subject to a single law" because they are beaten and otherwise subject to hardship.[83] Jans Enikel links children and servants historically: before Noah cursed Ham no one had any servants "other than his children. The child was the father's *kneht*."[84] The lexical conflation of servants and children was facilitated, in the Middle Ages at least, by the fact that children frequently did serve—sometimes just because they were children, sometimes as part of their knightly or courtly education.[85]

Because the words for children and those who serve are the same, it is often impossible to tell which is meant. When Tandareis first arrives at Arthur's court he is repeatedly called *knabe* in what can only be its general sense.[86] When Flordibel turns up, however, Tandareis is selected as the

80. Parz 259,25.

81. Niblgn 361,2–3: dô hiez ir juncfrouwen drîzec meide gân ûz ir kemenâten Kriemhilt diu künegin.

82. WlMarl 3031; PhMarl 1780.

83. Krschr 1391–92: der sun und der chneht haben algelîche ain reht.

84. JWeltc 3093–96: er hêt nieman dann sîn kint. . . . daz kint was des vater kneht.

85. On the lexical identity of children and servants or slaves: Boswell, *Kindness*, 27–28; Fenske, "Knappe," 99–100; Flandrin, *Families*, 64; Flekenstein, *Curialitas*, 463; Golden, *Athens*, 145. On the service of MHG children see chapter four.

86. TandFl 203, 206, 214, 224, 230, etc.

person she "is supposed to take as her *knabe*, who would serve her at all times."[87] Subsequently, when Tandareis is called *knabe*—and it is by far the most common designation for him—one cannot be sure whether it means "youth" or "attendant" or both at once. What appears at first to be a confusion turns out to be, in some senses at least, an equivalence. The most interesting lexical equivalence is, in fact, a conceptual reversal. Noble children, *juncherren* and *juncvrouwen*, are sent to court to serve and become attendants, *juncherren* and *juncvrouwen*. Thus, when Tandareis is called *ir juncherre* it can mean "their young lord," as it does in relation to the knights of his father's court, or it can mean "her attendant," as it does in relation to Flordibel.[88] The term that originally designated superior status comes, also, to designate subordinate status.

Abstraction

In addition to the various words for people who are not yet adults, the MHG vocabulary of childhood also includes two terms for the stretch of life that precedes adulthood. The first is *kintheit*. In the *Passional* one can read that "*kintheit* had departed from God's handmaiden" St. Margaret by the time she was fifteen, at which point she was suddenly found eligible for marriage, and that Ambrose acquired great fame "when he had completed his entire *kintheit* and became a man."[89] Such citations suggest that *kintheit* lasts until a child comes of age, with marriage or manhood. Yet things are not so simple. According to Priester Wernher, Gabriel tells Mary that her cousin, now past childbearing age, had "borne no offspring in her *kintheit*."[90] Apparently *kintheit* can last well into the years when a woman might be expected to bear children. After Wigalois has been knighted, when the narrator does not hesitate to call him a "brave man," Wigalois's traveling companion fears he will not survive the adventure ahead of him "on account of his *kintheit*."[91] Here *kintheit* must refer to Wigalois's relative youth. It seems that *kintheit* can designate a clearly defined stretch of life that "is completed" when a child comes of age but that it can also refer

87. TandFl 668–69: den solt si zeinem knaben nemen der ir diente zaller stunt.
88. TandFl 1534, 679.
89. Passnl K327,66–67: nu was itzu die kintheit getreten von der gotes maget; K241,88–89: do er uz aller kintheit gewuchs und ein man wart.
90. WerMar 2738–39: do si in ir kintheite neheinen wuocher gebar.
91. Wglois 2464: der küene man; 2461: si vorhte sîner kintheit.

to the relative youth of an adult. In this it resembles *kint*, the word from which it is derived.[92]

The other abstract noun, *jugent*, often seems to refer to a stretch of life that comes somewhat later than *kintheit*. According to Bruder Philipp, Jesus "entered his *jugent*"[93] after he had returned from Egypt, when he was about eight. Here *jugent* seems to follow some unnamed period. According to Pfaffe Konrad, Charlemagne "grew constantly in excellence from *kintheit* to *jugent*, from *jugent* into *alter*."[94] Here *jugent* clearly follows *kintheit*. However, considering the way *jugent* is positioned between *kintheit* and *alter* it may not refer to preadulthood at all but to the prime of life—like *iuventus* which, in certain schemes of the ages of man, falls between *adolescentia* and *senectus*. According to Johannitius's *Isagoge*, *iuventus* lasts from twenty-five or thirty to thirty-five or forty and "preserves the body in perfection."[95] This understanding seems appropriate to other passages as well. Hartmann von Aue calls Armer Heinrich "a knight in his *jugent*"[96] even after he has been a lord for some time, and Hugo von Trimberg writes of someone who is "in his *jugent* at thirty."[97]

And yet, *jugent* does not always follow *kintheit*. While the *Passional* claims that Ambrose did not complete "his entire *kintheit*" until he "became a man,"[98] the *Buch der Märtyrer* considers Ambrose "in his *jugent*" when he is still in the cradle.[99] According to the latter, *jugent* must begin at birth. Wirnt von Gravenberg can say of the young Wigalois that "God gave him physical beauty and every other excellence in his *jugent*" and two lines later that "he lived without blame in his *kintheit*."[100] *Kintheit* and *jugent* seem to be the same thing. In both manuscripts of Walther von Rheinau's *Marienleben* one finds a heading that announces the subject of the following section: the miracles that have remained hidden that Jesus performed

92. Cases where *kintheit* refers to the relative youth of an adult: ErnstB 234–35; GTrojk 2540–43; VBüMos 16,2–4; Wglois 1816–18. —Sometimes *kintheit* refers not to a stage of life but to a quality associated with that stage, "childishness": GTrist 290–300, 12427–30, 12436–38; PrLanc 1:36,15–17; Rabens 390,5–6; RWeltc 9047–49; UWilhm 30,1, 30,17–18.

93. PhMarl 3914–15: er begund . . . ane heben sîne jugent.

94. Rolndl 24–27: ie baz unt baz steic der herre zetugende uon kintheit ce iugente, uon der iugent in daz alter.

95. Johannitius, *Isagoge ad Tegni Galieni* as cited in Burrow, *Ages*, 22–23.

96. ArmHnr 34: ein ritter in sîner jugent.

97. Rennr 21778: in sîner jugent bî drîzic jârn. —See also Duby, "Youth," 112–13; Schultz, "Adolescence," 530–33.

98. Passnl K241,88–89: do er uz aller kintheit gewuchs und ein man wart.

99. BMärtr 4795–97: got lie sehen in seiner jugent.

100. Wglois 1244–48: Nu gap im got in sîner jugent schoenen lîp und ganze tugent. . . . âne missewende lebt er in sîner kintheit.

"in his *kintheit*"; the lines that follow immediately take up this same topic, the miracles that Jesus performed "within the term of his *jugent*."[101] It is difficult to imagine from such formulations what the difference between the two stages of life could possibly be. Thus, although those who compiled the *Deutsches Wörterbuch* clearly would like to believe that, "in the most exact sense, *kintheit* is *infantia* and is distinguished from *jugent*," they are obliged to continue by admitting that "already in Middle High German *kintheit* and *jugent* are also used as equivalents, both for early and for late childhood."[102]

Mention of *infantia* raises the question of the Latin terms for the stages of life and of the learned schemes for the ages of man. Although historians of medieval childhood are devoted to them,[103] such schemes can offer little help in understanding the MHG knowledge of childhood. As anyone who has studied them will discover, they differ greatly, both in the number of ages into which they divide life and in the number of years they accord each age, and these differences clearly reflect particular exegetical or expository needs rather than any shared medieval understanding about the stages of human development. Physicians, for instance, tend to prefer four ages, since four is the number of the seasons, the humors, and the temperaments. According to the tetradic schemes of Avicenna and Johannitius the beginning of life falls within *adolescentia*, which lasts from birth to twenty-five or thirty.[104] Theologians tend to prefer six ages, linked, since Augustine, with the days of creation and the ages of world history. Following Augustine, Isidore, Bede, Hrabanus Maurus, and others divide the beginning of life into *infantia*, from birth to seven, *pueritia*, from seven to fourteen, and *adolescentia*, from fourteen to twenty-eight.[105] A tradition of five ages goes back to Gregory the Great and his interpretation of the parable of the workers in the vineyard.[106] Elizabeth Sears and J. A. Burrows, the two recent authorities on these matters, insist that "the theme of the ages of man was a bookish one"[107] and that one can by no means

101. WlMarl following 6689: in sîner kintheit; 6690: in sîner jugende zil.
102. Grimm, *Deutsches Wörterbuch*, 5:763–64: im genauesten sinne ist *kintheit* infantia . . . und wird von *jugend* unterschieden. doch werden *kintheit* und *jugend* auch gleich gebraucht . . . beide vom frühen wie vom späten kindesalter, schon mhd. —Passages in which *kintheit* and *jugent* seem to be synonyms: Jakobr 265–67; JWeltc p. 544,30; SaeldH 6382–415.
103. Ariès, *Centuries*, 15–32; Arnold, *Kind*, 17–20; Hanawalt, *London*, 5–13; Shahar, *Childhood*, 21–31.
104. Burrow, *Ages*, 22–24; Sears, *Ages*, 14–20, 25–31.
105. Burrow, *Ages*, 80–92; Hoffmeister, "Puer, iuvenis," 289–91; Sears, *Ages*, 54–79.
106. Burrow, *Ages*, 60–66; Sears, *Ages*, 80–90.
107. Sears, *Ages*, 6.

assume that the numbers encountered in such schemes "bear any relation to the social or biological realities of the time."[108] It makes no sense then to expect such schemes to provide the key to any vernacular knowledge of childhood: they differ too much among themselves and they are too deeply rooted in their particular learned traditions.

The Power of Words

If the passengers on the *Titanic* were really strict about enforcing the principle of "women and children first" then it was a matter of some importance how one got classified. For a teenage male it was a matter of life and death. If he was considered a child he had a chance of getting into a lifeboat and being saved; if a man, he went down with the ship. Words indicate status, producing—or reproducing—hierarchical relations, both on the *Titanic* and in the German Middle Ages. "The forms of classification," writes Pierre Bourdieu, "are forms of domination."[109] To conclude this discussion of the MHG vocabulary of childhood I want to note three different hierarchies—service, gender, and age—in which children are placed because of the way they are classified.

Most of the words that designate children also designate servants. This is not so surprising for the vocational terms associated with particular forms of service. A *knappe* or a *kneht* ordinarily does perform service as part of his knightly training, and a *juncherre* or *juncvrouwe* is often expected to serve at court as part of his or her courtly education. But even those general terms, like *maget* or *knabe*, that are not associated with a particular form of child service, are also used to designate servants. Apparently their youth alone places children in the same subordinate position as those who serve. Thus, although a *vrouwe* might attend a more powerful noblewoman, *vrouwe* itself never means "attendant," while *juncvrouwe* does. It is because of *junc* that *juncvrouwe* means attendant. Youth subordinates.

Among those who are young, it is impossible to designate sex without invoking gender. Merely to call a maiden *maget*, virtually the only way to indicate she is female, invokes the gender ideal of virginity. It also defines her, inescapably, in relation to male sexuality. Physically, a *maget* is untouched by men, but conceptually she is defined in relation to and is

108. Burrows, *Ages*, 34.
109. Bourdieu, "Fieldwork," 24.

therefore dependent on them. The sex-specific terms for youths also invoke gender ideals, but in a much different way. Since the terms by which they are distinguished from maidens also designate adult warriors, merely calling them *degen* or *kneht* places them in a category that also includes adult males. While designating a child as female inevitably subordinates her to the hegemonic class of adult males, designating a child as male assimilates him to that class.

The most common term for children, *kint*, clearly indicates age: *kint* are young, at least relatively. Otherwise, however, the MHG vocabulary of childhood places somewhat less emphasis on age than we might expect. To acknowledge the noble class status of a child she may be called either *vrouwe* or *juncvrouwe*: the indication of age is optional. To indicate the sex of a child one must use terms that, like *maget* or *degen*, are not restricted to children. This does not mean that age is irrelevant to MHG writers: its importance is attested by the frequent use of *kint* and the optional use of *juncvrouwe* and *juncherre*. It does, however, mean that age is relatively less important in MHG than it is to us. When we want to indicate the sex of a child we say "boy" or "girl," thereby inevitably indicating age at the same time. When MHG writers want to indicate the sex of a child they say *maget* or *degen*, thereby indicating sex and gender but not age. This is the first of many contexts in which the mere fact of youth, childhood itself, will be found to be somewhat less interesting to MHG writers than it is to us.

Those who write on childhood in past times have often lamented that the "language of age," whether in ancient Greek or Latin, or in Hebrew, German, or English of later periods, is "hopelessly vague."[110] They are disappointed because these languages "lacked words for dividing childhood into separate parts."[111] To a certain extent this is true of MHG. *Kintheit* cannot be neatly distinguished from *jugent*, and *maget* does not distinguish children from adults. But this should not be a cause for disappointment. The expectation that the "language of age" should divide "childhood into separate parts" is a consequence of the modern obsession with dividing childhood into stages and giving each one a precise label. There is no reason, however, to expect that past cultures will have shared our obsession. They will have had other things to say about childhood. If we can over-

---

110. Gillis, *Youth and History*, 1. —Greek: Golden, *Athens*, 12–16. Latin: Arnold, *Kind*, 20; Metz, "Droit canonique," 11–15; Riché, "L'enfant," 95. Hebrew: Ta-Shma, "Medieval German Jewry," 272. German: Flitner and Hornstein, "Kindheit," 315–16. English: Orme, *Childhood to Chivalry*, 5–7; Kett, "Adolescence," 98.
111. Orme, *Childhood to Chivalry*, 7.

come our disappointment that the Middle Ages had not read Piaget, then we can discover what some of these other things are. The confusion of *kintheit* and *jugent* suggests that MHG speakers did not distinguish clearly, if at all, between different stages of childhood. The chronological inclusiveness of *maget* suggests that they considered gender as independent of age. Words have power, now as in the Middle Ages. But, rooted in a different language and culture, the MHG vocabulary of childhood articulates a knowledge of childhood that is inevitably different from our own.

3. Nature: The Determinations of Birth

What are little boys made of?
What are little boys made of?
    Frogs and snails
    And puppy-dogs' tails,
That's what little boys are made of.

What are little girls made of?
What are little girls made of?
    Sugar and spice
    And all that's nice,
That's what little girls are made of.[1]

Or at least that's what little boys and girls are made of according to this familiar English nursery rhyme. We find it strange to have children reduced to animal parts and baking supplies, but such a reduction is not without its utility. It enables a very precise definition, and this precision in turn enables a very clear distinction between boys and girls. Boys are slimy and active; girls are sweet and accommodating. Boys belong outdoors, girls in the kitchen. By reducing children to a few concrete elements the nursery rhyme is able to articulate a very clear conception of childhood gender.

If nursery-rhyme children are made of snails and spice, then what are MHG children made of and what does this tell us about MHG conceptions of childhood? Unfortunately the question cannot be answered with anything like the clarity permitted by the nursery rhyme, since the MHG evidence is distributed over hundreds of texts, is of many different kinds, and does not always agree. To bring some order into this mass of data, I have grouped it in three categories. This chapter describes the nature of the child, those things that constitute the child because they are inherent. Chapter four is devoted to nurture, the ways a child is constituted by those

1. Opie, *Nursery Rhymes*, 100–101.

who care for and educate her. Chapters five and six consider those things that constitute the child as a member of society: five treats the personal and social bonds, made and broken, that are characteristic of childhood; six treats those, made during childhood or on coming of age, that are typical of adulthood.[2]

MHG writers believe that one's inherent nature is the single most important factor in determining the course of one's life. It is composed of a number of elements, some of them shared with others of one's age, some inherited from one's lineage, and others peculiar to each individual. Sigune, the heroine of Wolfram von Eschenbach's *Titurel*, is a child and cannot help behaving according to the nature of children. Thus, when Schionatulander tells her he loves her, she doesn't know what he is talking about and asks foolish questions. That is because she is a child and children, by nature, lack wisdom and experience. No sooner does she realize that she too is in love than the two are separated. The separation casts Schionatulander into such despondency that he loses the "perfect appearance that was his inherited nature."[3] Wolfram understands Schionatulander's beauty as something he has inherited because it belongs to the nature of his lineage. The fact that Sigune and Schionatulander fall in love at such an early age is, of course, unusual and distinguishes them from most other children. Their precocious love sets them apart, even within the world of MHG narrative, and makes them worth writing about. It is part of their particular nature as hero or heroine. The inexperience that is Sigune's nature as a child, the beauty that is the nature of Schionatulander's lineage, and the precocious love that is their nature as hero and heroine represent the three kinds of nature that combine to constitute the nature of the individual. In what follows I will

2. Although the categories of nature and nurture will seem familiar, especially to medievalists, I did not adopt them out of piety. Instead, having assembled a huge collection of things that are said about children in MHG texts and looking for a way of organizing them, I adapted an idea of Juri Lotman's according to which a narrative event is generated by the crossing of a boundary. I considered two sorts of boundaries. The first (an elaboration of Lotman) is the boundary of the individual. Certain narrative events occur when something within the individual is expressed and becomes visible to the outside world. Such events disclose something about the individual nature. Other events occur when those around the individual try to get him or her to internalize ideas or behaviors. They constitute the category of nurture. The second sort of boundary is crossed as the individual moves through the world. A child is born, is sent to school, leaves home to seek adventure, turns to God— in such cases thresholds of various kinds are crossed, usually in a ways that mark significant articulations in the child's life. I have considered such events as a series of attachments that are made and broken. —On narrative boundaries: Lotman, *Artistic Text*, 231–39; Schultz, *Round Table*, 49–57.

3. WTitrl 89,1: von angeborner arte sô wunschlîch geschicke.

consider each in turn: the nature of the child, the nature of the lineage, and the nature of the individual hero or heroine.

The Nature of the Child

In writing about Sigune and Schionatulander, Wolfram mentions a number of traits that he believes are characteristic of children in general. When Schionatulander's despondency causes him to withdraw from knightly combat, Wolfram interprets this as a stage the novice lover must go through before realizing that love requires him to seek renown as a knight. In this Schionatulander is like a child, who must crawl before he can stand: "When children use chairs to help them learn to stand up, they must crawl over to them first."[4] Earlier, when Wolfram first mentions the love between his protagonists, he laments that "they are still too *tump* for such troubles."[5] *Tump* means "young," "inexperienced," and "foolish." Because Sigune and Schionatulander are children, they are necessarily too *tump*, that is, too young and inexperienced for love. Earlier still, when the narrator first mentions Schionatulander he refers to "his true child's sweetness," thereby drawing attention to another quality Wolfram considers "true" for children.[6] Wolfram's comments represent the three principal aspects of the nature of the child, each of them related to a deficiency. Children lack strength and coordination: therefore they must crawl. They lack the wisdom and experience that come with years: therefore they are too young for love. Their lack of experience also has positive consequences, however: they retain a sweetness and purity that adults have lost.

Although MHG writers clearly regard childhood as a time of "weakness, deficiencies, and helplessness,"[7] they have little to say about the weakness of the body. Nor do MHG writers have much to say about childhood illness, which we, at least, might understand as a consequence of physical weakness. A few secular figures become sick from unrequited love, and occasionally God uses illness as a tool: in order to keep Adalbert's parents from making him their heir, God afflicts the young saint with "a great and

4. WTitrl 86,4: swâ kint lernent ûf stên an stüelen, diu müezen dar zem êrsten kriechen.
5. WTitrl 48,1: si sint noch ze tump ze solher angest.
6. WTitrl 39,3: sîn wâriu kindes süeze.
7. PhMarl 3934–36: [Jesus] enphie die krankeit, gebresten unde bloedikeit die man mac ân sünde getragen.

powerful sickness so that his body cried out and his stomach grew large."[8]
Childhood illness is widespread only among the anonymous sufferers who
provide opportunities for saints to display their miraculous healing powers.
Of the 121 miracles attributed to Ludwig of Thuringia, between 26 and
40 percent involve children.[9] So many children are healed by the protagonists of medieval saints' lives that one modern study calls them "the true
pediatricians of times past."[10]

The efforts of the saints notwithstanding, it was common in the historical Middle Ages for "children, who are much loved," to be "carried off
by the wind of death."[11] Some estimate that 15 to 20 percent, others that
50 percent of medieval children died during their first year.[12] Some think
that 30 percent, others that over 50 percent died by age twenty.[13] Jans Enikel reports that Leopold III of Austria and his wife Agnes had eighteen
children, "seven of whom died in their *jugent*."[14] Whatever the incidence
of child mortality, it was certainly much higher in the historical Middle
Ages than it is in the MHG narratives, where very few children die. Significantly, those MHG children who do die do so not from weakness but from
strength. This is certainly true of the largest group, the martyrs. Margaret,
who resists torture and the devil, is killed and taken to her heavenly reward
because her "faith was so excellent" and "so steadfast."[15] The same is true
of secular figures. The sons of Etzel and the brother of Dietrich von Bern
are killed fighting the fierce Witege.[16] But before they die they display their
heroic mettle by provoking a fight with so formidable an opponent. Like
religious martyrs, their death demonstrates not so much their weakness as
children as their strength as heroes.[17]

8. StAdal 270–73: Daz kint er angesante ein sûch michel unde grôz, damit im der lîb
erdôz, daz im grôzer wart der bûch.
9. StLudw 70–97. The ambiguity reflects the impossibility of knowing how to count
the *juncvrouwen*. One is called *kint* (96), another is 20 (79), and the rest could be any age.
10. Alexandre-Bidon and Closson, *L'enfant*, 223: véritables pédiatres du temps passé.
—On weakness: WlMarl 4876–83. Others who become sick: ELgAur 536,11–14; Passnl
K395,72–396,8, K505,77–78. Other children cured or restored to life by saints: RWeltc 34390–
418, 36177–278; StFran 4622–27. —On childhood illness in the Middle Ages: Alexandre-Bidon
and Closson, *L'enfant*, 216–27.
11. Warng 1647–48: diu kint diu vil liep sint diu füeret hin des todes wint.
12. Russell, "Population," 45–47; Flandrin, "L'attitude," 174.
13. Russell, "Population," 45–47; Flandrin, *Families*, 53; Konner, *Childhood*, 197.
14. JWeltc p. 544,29–30a: der selben kint sturben sibneu in der jugent.
15. StMarM 23–25: si gewan einen stæten muot, ir geloube was sô guot: die wurden
alsô veste.
16. Rabens 376–459.
17. On child mortality in the fifteenth century: Wenzel, "kindes zuht," 145–48. For other
martyred saints see chapter six, note 112. Other deaths: EngSwb 3,11–13; WTotnz 203–06.

Whereas MHG texts show only modest interest in the physical deficiencies of children, they have considerably more to say about their intellectual deficiencies. The key term is *tump*. In some contexts it simply means "young," as when Ulrich von Liechtenstein's heart gives him good advice, "even though it is *tump* in years."[18] In other contexts it means "dumb" or "foolish": in the course of an argument Josaphat calls his opponent "a *tump* ass" and refers to the "*tump* people" whom the devil tricks into believing in pagan gods.[19] In still other contexts *tump* means "inexperienced": the victims of Witege mentioned above are said to be "too *tump* for fighting."[20] In most cases, however, it is impossible to distinguish the senses so clearly. When Josaphat's father tells him a "child should behave in a *tump* manner"[21] he means that those who are by definition *tump*—that is, young— should behave like those who are *tump*—that is, foolish and inexperienced. The connection between foolishness and children is so strong that foolish behavior turns one into a child: "No matter how old or young he is in years, if someone behaves in a *tump* manner, then," says Konrad von Haslau, "he's a child as far as I'm concerned."[22] The foolishness and inexperience of children manifest themselves in a lack of insight, a lack of speech, and a lack of seriousness.[23]

Because children lack wisdom and experience, they lack insight, which causes them to act without realizing the consequences. One child wants a fried egg, closes her eyes so that no one will see what she is doing, then reaches for the egg and sticks her hand into the fire: she "displayed the cleverness of a child, which is often not very clever."[24] Because they cannot recognize the truth behind appearances "children are easily deceived."[25] Diocletian tries to explain away Pancras's conversion to Christianity with the argument: "You are a child, and for that reason you are easily drawn onto the wrong path and deceived."[26] In a number of short narratives the sexual ignorance of children is treated as a manifestation of the foolish

18. Frndst Lied 3 2,1: swie tump ez von den jaren si.

19. RBarlm 326,16: ein tumber esel; 329,25: tumbiu diet.

20. Rabens 431,6: si wârn ze strîte ze tumbe.

21. RBarlm 207,4: kint tumplîche gebâren sol.

22. Jünglg 819–21: wie alt, wie junck er ist an jaren, wil er wan tumplich gebaren, zwar er muz mir sin ein kint.

23. On the foolishness and inexperience of children: Frndst 10,1–4; JWeltc 6504–06; WilWnd 5062–63; WWilhm 194,20.

24. GbrEi 11–12: und erzeigte eines kindes list, der dicke âne liste ist.

25. Erec 3876–77: kint lîhte ze triegenne sint.

26. Passnl K294,24–26: du bist din kint. . . . des bistu lichtlich gezogen in valschen wec und betrogen.

inexperience natural to those of their age. When a knight appears at a convent wall in the *Sperber* and seeks the love of a young nun, she responds: "Unfortunately, I do not know what you want. What you have told me about, calling it love, is unknown to me I'm afraid. In my chest I have only two pictures, three needles and a scissors, two new hair bands, my everyday clothes, and my psalter."[27] The knight is certain that he can find love nevertheless, and she agrees to let him try. He finds it twice, after which she tells him he can take as much as he wants.[28]

Some children are so young and inexperienced that they do not recognize situations of mortal danger. When the infant Paris sees his reflection in a sword raised over him, he "began to smile so very sweetly at the two murderous men" who had been commissioned to end his life "that they didn't want to slay him."[29] This scene, which occurs in a number of texts, is one of the very few in which MHG adults respond sympathetically to childish ignorance.[30]

Children's lack of insight keeps them from exercising the restraint that comes with greater experience. Lacking this restraint they reveal things that an adult might keep hidden. In *Berchta* a child confuses the monster of the title, a threat conjured up by his father, with the priest who has been visiting his mother—thereby revealing the liaison between the priest and the mother. Children, the narrator observes, "are quick to speak: they say what they hear and keep very little of it secret."[31] Because they do not always consider the consequences, "children speak the truth."[32] Children's lack of restraint affects not only their speech but also their behavior. A fourteenth-

27. Sperbr 129–39: Nu enweiz ich leider, waz ir welt. Daz ir mir hât vür gezelt Und ez minne hât genant, Daz ist mir leider unbekant. . . . Ich hân niht in mînem schrîn Wan zwêne bildære, Drî nâdeln und ein schære Und zwei niuwe hârbant Und mîn tegelîch gewant Und den mînen salter.

28. Other cases where acting childishly means acting foolishly: ArPhlS 353; Dulcfl 366–72; ETrist 1473–75; FlorBl 4064–78; GTrist 11299–300; JWeltc 6771–74; KrbSwb 113,22–23; Ksrchr 3344–48; KTirol 34,1–4; LAlexr S1856–60; LBarlm 1489, 11678–83; Niblgn 1468,3–4; Passnl H51,70–76; WlMarg 4–8; WolfdB 153,4. —On children's gullibility: PartMl 19344–45; RWeltc 9008–70; VBüMos 33,8–34,13; WolfdA 91,1–2. —Other narratives in which the sexual ignorance of children plays an important role: *Berchta, Dulciflorie, Gänslein, Häslein, Mönches Not.*

29. KTrojk 478–81: dô began daz kindelîn die zwêne mortgîtigen man sô rehte suoze lachen an, daz si'z ungerne sluogen.

30. Children who smile unknowingly in the face of danger: GTrojk 1357–58; Jakobr 947–48; RpParz 219,9–220,15; WolfdA 83,3–85,4. —Parallels in French texts: Schneider, *Wolfdietrich,* 277. This is a commonplace, not a consequence of "the fact that contemporaries were acquainted with five-year-old children," as Shahar seems to think (*Childhood,* 119).

31. Brchta 70–72: si sint mit rede gerne snel, Waz si hœren, daz si daz sagen, und sîn lüzzel iht verdagen.

32. Frnlst 303: diu kint diu redet die warheit.

century nun's life refers to the "wildness that is part of children's nature."[33] Armer Heinrich claims that children have "impulsive spirits: they are in a hurry to accomplish whatever comes into their heads, whether good or bad, but they regret it afterwards."[34]

Children lack not only foresight but also speech, and, since they cannot express their wishes in words, they must express them by crying. Different ages attach different meanings to the crying of children. Augustine considered it a sign of human sinfulness, of the child's unbridled desire and jealous greed.[35] In the nineteenth century, according to Jerome Kagan, "the protesting cry of the one-year-old following maternal departure was classified as similar to the willful disobedience of the adult. Today the same act is linked with the anxiety and sadness that follow loss of sweetheart, spouse, or parent."[36] MHG writers seem to regard crying primarily as a way of communicating discomfort: according to Hugo von Trimberg "a child makes known its pain by crying when it is inflamed by hunger or illness."[37] Thus, when the infant Paris has been abandoned in the forest, he "began to carry on very sadly on account of his hunger, since he had no other way of lamenting his distress."[38] Crying is so closely associated with children that they provide the standard in this regard: when Rual recounts the death of Tristan's mother, "he cried as if he were a child."[39]

Children's communicative skills progress beyond crying when they learn to talk, but at first they do so only imperfectly: they "stammer for a long time so that at most one hears half-words from them. Their tongues and lips are disobedient until practice brings them to where they can encompass whole words."[40] An example is provided by a young child who,

33. TößSwb 87,9–10: so ir darnach etwas wildikait begegnet, als sôlichen kinden von natur an ist.
34. ArmHnr 949–54: dû tuost als diu kint diu dâ gæhes muotes sint: swaz den kumet in den muot, ez sî übel oder guot, dar zuo ist in allen gâch und geriuwet si dar nâch. —On children's heedlessness: GTrist 301–2; PartMl 12078–85; UlmSwb 141.
35. Augustine, *Confessions*, 1.7.
36. Kagan, *Nature*, 84.
37. Rennr 20709–10: Ein kint sîn leit mit weinen kündet, Swenne ez hunger oder siuche enzündet.
38. GTrojk 1368–71: Daz kind von hunger sich gehaben Gar trurenklichen begunde, Won es nitt enkunde Anders clagen sine nott.
39. GTrist 4216–17: er . . . weinete, als er ein kint wære. —Other cases where a child cries from hunger or need: ELgAur 34,13; Frndst 2nd Büchlein 213–17; GuFrau 1731–34; KTrojk 522–29; SaeldH 10816–24, 10852–55. Other references to crying: GTrist 2485–86; JWeltc 20058–59; Parz 118,7–22; Rennr 23357–59, 23360–62; RWeltc 36180; WolfdB 164,4. —On medieval attitudes towards children's crying: Demaitre, "Idea," 470; Shahar, *Childhood*, 90–92.
40. WlMarl 4896–903: an der rede anevange Stôzent diu kint vil lange, Sô daz kûme hälbiu wort Von in werdent gehôrt. Diu zunge in ist ungehôrsam Und ir lespelîn alsam, E daz si diu gewonheit Uf ganzer worte mâze treit.

when asked the name of the saint who has just cured him, responds: " 'Ciku Ciku.' He wanted to say Franciscus but because he was so young he was unable to say the name completely and had to break it in two."[41] Once children have learned to speak clearly they often fail to speak appropriately. When the daughter of Rudolf of Habsburg married the son of Wenzel of Bohemia they "were both children in years."[42] It is not surprising therefore that, according to Ottokar, they talked to each other "in a childish fashion,"[43] she of her dolls, he of his hunting birds. Where Shulamith Shahar would find this charming, Ottokar finds it ludicrous: "Anyone who heard them would have been overcome with laughter."[44]

Young people also lack seriousness: they "always seek pleasure," writes Freidank, "while those who are old and wise live with worry."[45] This is as it should be, at least according to Hugo von Trimberg: "I shudder when very small children speak wise words or are serious."[46] Sometimes the pursuit of pleasure leads to catastrophe. When Paris gave the apple to Venus, showing thereby that he cared nothing for wisdom or wealth, he "did as the young do, who are by nature of such a disposition that nothing is so dear to them as pleasure and delight."[47]

Children's pursuit of pleasure often takes the form of play. Nowadays we attach great importance to play, regarding it as "a form of learning" that "serves a critical function during development."[48] Dr. Spock holds that "play is serious business," in which children are "learning about the world" and "sorting out their feelings."[49] For MHG writers, however, "childish games" are nothing more than a particularly characteristic form of "childish behavior."[50] They are just the opposite of "serious business." Thus *kindes*

---

41. StFran 4603–9: Ciku Ciku. . . . Franciscus wold ez hân geseit: done moht ez vor kintheit des namen niht gar gesprechen, des muost iz in enzwei brechen.

42. ORmchr 17981–82: an jâren beidiu kint wâren.

43. ORmchr 17984: si reten kintlich.

44. ORmchr 17979–80: swer daz solde hân vernomen, der wære lachens wol bekomen. —Other references to childish speech: AplTyr 4725–28; GottNf 50,1,7–9; GrMarl 330–33; GTrojk 1412–13; LAdam 1886–91; Parz 170,10; PhMarl 412–14, 425–26, 3700–3701; Rennr 12290–92; SlPrsC 58–60; WilOrl 2713–14, 3832–33.

45. Fridnk 51,25–52,1: diu jugent ie nach fröden strebt, mit sorgen witze und alter lebt.

46. Rennr 14953–54: mir gruwet, swenne gar kleiniu kint hant wisiu wort und ernsthaft sint.

47. KTrojk 2718–21: er tet alsam die jungen tuont, die von natûre sint der art, daz in sô liebes nie niht wart, sô vröude ist unde wunnespil. —Lack of seriousness: Magzog 378–79; Rennr 6219–22, 14945–54, 14983–86, 18329–32; Winsbn 4,5. Indifference to wealth: ELgAur 805,23–24; GTrist 4508–21.

48. Konner, *Childhood*, 305.

49. Spock, *Baby and Child Care*, 376, 460.

50. PhMarl 3975: kintlîchiu spil; 3972: kintlîch site.

spil, "child's play," comes to mean, as in modern English and German, any activity that is easy or trivial. Although MHG writers attach little value to play itself, they cite it frequently on account of its emblematic clarity. When Christ appears to the nuns at Engelthal, he "played like a tiny child,"[51] thereby giving an unmistakable indication of the form in which he has chosen to reveal himself. When Darius sends a golden ball to Alexander, he wants to insult him: "by the ball he meant that it would be much more suitable for him to go play ball with other children."[52] Dolls are also closely associated with children: Morhold drags "armed knights into his saddle in front of him, just as children play with dolls."[53] Other pastimes and games mentioned as typical of children include: hearing stories, playing in the flowers, digging in the streets, playing on swings, playing marbles, playing with rings, drawing straws, playing peek-a-boo, and tormenting birds that leave their nests too soon.[54]

Children "seek pleasure" not only in children's games but also in fostering that collective joy, *vreude*, which, for courtly society, is one of the most desirable conditions. The pious young Iolande is urged to enter into the life of the court, since "youth wants to have its pleasure [*vreude*] and the world wants the same."[55] What this entails is clear from Freidank's admonition that "youth should sing and dance"[56] and from Hartmann's

51. EngSwb 24,7–8: vor irm tod spilt unser herre in einez cleinen kindelins weise. Also EngSwb 29,6–7, 36,4–6.
52. LAlexr S1464–67: Mit dem balle meinter daz, daz ime gezême michilis baz, daz er mit anderen kinden des balles spilen gienge.
53. JngTit 1403,3–4: da sach man in verwapent ritter zocken fur sich in den satel sin, als da diu kinder spilent mit den tocken.
54. On *kindes spil*: Zingerle, *Kinderspiel*, 1 n. 2, 2 n. 1. —The following games are said to be characteristic of children in general. Dolls: WWilhm 222,18; Virgnl 203–5. Hearing stories: WGast 1079–86. Playing in the flowers: WilÖst 1843–61; WldAlx 5.1,1–2,3. Digging in the streets: Rennr 11426–27. Hobby horse: Rennr 2693–94. Playing on swings: Parz 181,7–9. Playing marbles: Rennr 14904–5. Playing with rings: WWilhm 327,7–8. Drawing straws: Rennr 2695; Walthr 66,7–8. Peek-a-boo: KTirol 34,1–3. Tormenting birds: Frnlst 295–97; Winsbk 32,1–4; Winsbn 9,5. —The following games are mentioned in connection with particular children. Ball: Crone 692; WilÖst 1874–2136; ZwöMön 134–53. Dancing: StElis 881–85. Dolls: Dulcfl 366–71; JngTit 492,4, 689,1–3; 731,1–3; MaiBfl 175,40–176,2; ORmchr 17985–87; Parz 372,15–18; Rennr 12530; WilOrl 3820–24; WTitrl 30,1–3, 64,1–3; WWilhm 33,24–26, 318,12. Hide and seek: WerMar D2350–56. Tag: StElis 710–14. Running, jumping, throwing, wrestling: Passnl H82,32–36; PhMarl 4338–39. Throwing things into water: ELgAur 435,19; SaeldH 11170–76; StLudw 92,9–11. Spinning a top: Parz 150,16–18. Playing with rings: ELgAur 809,12–13; Parz 368,12; StElis 3608–19. Shooting birds: Parz 118,4–6; JngTit 4443,4–4444,1. Keeping a pet bird: WilOrl 3820–24. —On children's games: Alexandre-Bidon and Closson, *L'enfant*, 174–86; Arnold, *Kind*, 67–76; Loffl-Haag, *Kinder*, 89–125; Shahar, *Childhood*, 103–05; Zingerle, *Kinderspiel*.
55. Ioland 314–16: dy jungent wil hir vrôide han. . . . sô wilt dy werelt ôich alsô.
56. Fridnk 52,6: singen, springen sol diu jugent.

description of Brandigan, a city "in which there were many pleasures [*vreuden*], dancing and every sort of entertainment that was suitable for young people."[57] The social pleasures of singing and dancing are characteristically attributed to "youth" and "young people" rather than to "children." Although this can include those who are still called children—like Iolande at the time she was urged to participate in court life—it doubtless also includes young adults.

Of all the attributes of children, the most admirable, surely, is their freedom from sin. Needless to say, MHG writers were not about to challenge the doctrine regarding the "sin [that] is called original,"[58] which holds that "a newborn infant cannot be without sin."[59] And yet there is a clear tendency to downplay the sinfulness of children without denying it completely: an abbot tells Rennewart that "children are *very nearly* free of sin."[60] Such ambivalence has a long tradition in the West. The Greeks and Romans, who, like medieval Germans, viewed children as basically deficient, nevertheless accorded them a special role in religious rites because, not having been polluted by the world, they were considered purer than adults.[61] Jans Enikel reports a Roman rite performed by "pure children under seven years of age."[62] The Christian church, although it insisted that even infants are burdened with original sin, also taught that those who would be saved must, in Jesus' words, "become like children."[63] The MHG tendency to downplay children's sinfulness runs parallel to theological developments in the twelfth and thirteenth centuries: questions were raised concerning the damnation of unbaptized infants that led Aquinas to define the *limbus puerorum*, an antechamber to purgatory where they could escape the punishments meted out to more active sinners.[64]

Sometimes children's lack of sin is taken quite broadly, as when the

---

57. Erec 8062–64: dâ was inne vreuden vil, tanz und aller slahte spil daz jungen liuten wol gezam.

58. PhMarl 357–58: diu selbe sünde ist geheizen originale.

59. RBarlm 81,13–14: ein niubornez kindelîn mac âne sünde niht gesîn.

60. Rennew 11282: die kint vil nah bar sünden sint.

61. Golden, *Athens*, 10, 49; Eyben, "Sozialgeschichte," 331–32.

62. JWeltc 20275–76: diu ungemeilten kint, diu under siben jâren sint.

63. Matthew 18.3.

64. Herlihy, "Medieval Children," 126. —Other references to original sin: ELgAur 72,11–13; PhMarl 350–64; StGrPr 63,2; VorBüM 48,19–23; Winsbk 70,1–3. Other children nearly free of sin: ArmSch 861; BertvR 1:337,13–17; SpecEc 31,9; StElis 1093–97; VorNor 33–34; Winsbk 70,1–3. —For children's innocence in antiquity and Christianity see, above all, Herter, "Das unschuldige Kind." See also, in addition to the studies cited in note 61, Burrow, *Ages*, 106; Flitner and Hornstein, "Kindheit," 320–23; Martin and Nitschke, *Sozialgeschichte*, 13; Néraudau, *Rome*, 135–37.

Schwarzwälder Prediger holds up children as a model of that which is "pure and simple." "You should be just like a child," he admonishes his auditors, "that is, you should overcome pride and be without envy and without hatred and without ill-gotten gain, and without unchastity and all sin, just as children are without sin."[65] In some cases "the purity of a child" is understood in more narrowly sexual terms, as when Elizabeth of Hungary regrets that, as a wife and mother, "she would not [be able to] preserve a noble chastity with the purity of a child."[66] It is important to recognize that when MHG writers hold that children are pure they do not mean that children are innocent in the essentialist way children are often called innocent today. According to one twelfth-century sermon, those who died in the Slaughter of the Innocents were pure only "because they had not yet come to the age in which they would have acquired any guilt on account of their human weakness."[67] Like Augustine, who believes that children are innocent only because they lack the ability to sin,[68] MHG writers believe children are pure only because they lack the opportunity to sin.[69]

The purity of children is doubtless the reason why the blood of those younger than two—or of maidens—can cure leprosy.[70] It must also be related to the "childish modesty"[71] regarded as natural to children, especially maidens. When Irmengard is married "she wept profusely. Thereby she showed her modesty and also her feminine breeding."[72] The most profound form of this modesty is displayed by those, youths no less than maidens, who are unaware of what is expected of them on their wedding night. When Malefer and Penthesilea go to bed, "the children acted like children," and the narrator must call on Love to help get things started.[73] MHG writers are not the least bit sentimental about the sexual ignorance of children: either they regard it as an instance of the foolish inexperience

65. SwrzPr P59,40–41: die als lûter vnd als ainualtich sint als diu kint; P60,63–66: so soltu reht sin als ain kint. dc ist dc du an hochuart sigest. vnd ân nît vnd ane has vnd an vnreht gût. vnd an vnkûsche vnd alle sûnde. reht als diu kint ane sûnde sint.
66. Passnl K619,19–23: daz si die edelen kuscheit nicht mit kindes reinekeit . . . solde . . . behalden.
67. PKonPr M216,8–9: wan div seligen chint dannoch zû dem alter niht chomen waren, das si von ir menslicher blode dehein schulde iht heten.
68. Augustine, *Confessions*, 1.7.
69. On the purity of children: ArmHnr 690–92; BertvR 2:172,27–33; EkrtPr 2:424,2; ELgAur 248,14–17; LBarlm 7461–66; SaeldH 1323; WlMarg 125–31.
70. ArmHnr 224–32; Englhd 5456–77; JWeltc 25275–349; Jakobr 769–75, 897–906; Ksrchr 7818–27.
71. StGrPr 224,1–2: kintlichû scham.
72. Treuep 164–66: diu maget sere weinte. damite si bescheinte ir kiusch und ouch ir wiplich zuht.
73. Rennew 32287: diu kint nach kinden taten.

natural to children, as discussed above, or they treat it as a sign of modesty, a virtue to which we should all aspire.[74]

The disparate attributes that are said to exemplify "the nature of the child"[75] are united only by their opposition to various characteristics of adults. Children lack strength, insight, self-control, articulate speech, discretion, gravity, and sin—all of which adults, with the experience of years, are thought to possess. Of course, not all the deficiencies are to be lamented: to be free of sin is surely admirable, while to lack gravity is hardly a great failing; and in any case it is proper to young people and therefore right. Even the foolishness of children will occasionally elicit a sympathetic response, as when the infant Paris smiles at the sword raised to kill him. Still, that even the most admirable aspect of the child's nature, purity, is conceived as a lack (of the opportunity to sin) indicates the extent to which the nature of the child is understood to be deficient. The child is the deficient other of the adult.

One should keep in mind that the opinions on the nature of the child are scattered very sparingly throughout the corpus and never figure in anything approaching a general description of "the child." On those rare occasions where they occur, they serve either to explain a particular narrative event (Paris cried because that's how children express hunger) or to enforce particular behavior among adults (you should remain pure like a child). These opinions are explanatory and prescriptive in very particular situations. They are not fragments of a general theory. That MHG writers limit their statements on the general nature of the child to very occasional remarks in very specific contexts suggests that the general nature of the child is not a subject in which they have a great deal of interest.

The Nature of the Noble Lineage

MHG writers believe that the nature of the individual child results not only from the nature that child shares with other children but also from the nature of the lineage into which he was born. The very first thing Wolfram says about Schionatulander is that he was "born of a race of princes and of such a lineage that he refrained from everything that undermines

74. On the modesty of children: MaiBfl 93,3–10; Niblgn 1684,4; StGrPr 224,1–11; WilOrl 8177–78, 9019–20, 12450, 13457–60, 13816–17, 13916–20. On children's ignorance of love: BitDlb 2250–60; JngTit 456,1–458,2; Parz 201,21–203,11; PrLanc 2:79,27–30; WilÖst 1515–1770.
75. WilÖst 1062: kindes art.

renown."[76] Apparently Schionatulander has inherited from his princely ancestors a devotion to worldly renown. Later, when Schionatulander declares his love, he asks Sigune to let him profit from the fact that, as he has heard tell, she is "born of a lineage that never tired of helping with their reward those who suffered any distress on their account."[77] Schionatulander expects that Sigune will have inherited from her forebears this same predisposition to repay services rendered. Just as Schionatulander has inherited fame and Sigune has inherited a sense of obligation, so it is assumed throughout the world of MHG narrative that the individual nature will be determined in very specific ways by the nature of the lineage into which one is born—at least if the lineage is a noble one.

The MHG word that encompasses both individual nature and lineage is *art*. In some cases it seems to refer only to the nature of the individual. The narrator of the prose *Lancelot* says of his hero: "Never before had a child been seen of his *art*."[78] Since there had certainly been other children of Lancelot's lineage, *art* here must refer to his individual nature. In other cases *art* refers to ancestry. Hoping to discover who it is that he has been fighting, "Rennewart attempted to see if he could find out from him what lineage this brave person was descended from," and said: "'I would like to hear you tell me your *art*.'"[79] In most cases, however, it is impossible to distinguish the two aspects. When the young Charlemagne fought his very first opponent, he was already "so proud spirited, so brave and of such high deeds" because, we are told, he acted "at the urging of his noble *art*."[80] He performed such lofty deeds because of the noble nature he had inherited from his noble lineage. *Art*, which can refer either to lineage or to individual nature, usually implies both: that "nature" possessed by an individual because he or she is descended from a lineage distinguished by certain qualities.[81]

76. WTitrl 38,1–3: ein kint . . . erborn von vürsten künne und von der art, daz muoste sich mâzen aller dinge, dâ von prîs verdirbet.

77. WTitrl 58,2–4: dû sîs erborn von der art, die nie kunde verdriezen, si enwæren helfec mit ir lône, swer durch si kummerlîche nôt emphienc.

78. PrLanc 1:36,11–12: Noch nye wart kint gesehen von syner art.

79. Rennew 17666–72: Rennewart daz versühte ob er ervinden daz mæhte an im, von welhem geslæhte sin kûner lip wære komen. 'ich hete gerne daz vernomen . . . daz du mir sagtest dinen art.'

80. KrlGal 64,16–18: Dat Karlle do was so stoltz gemoet, So kone ind van so hoer daet, Dat rede eme allet syn edel art.

81. There are few passages in which it is clear that *art* refers *only* to the individual nature of a person, although there are some referring to objects that, since they are unique, can only have an individual nature: the grail (Parz 441,1); the sun (WrMarl 548); the magnet mountain (ErnstB 3944–47). —Passages where *art* means lineage alone: AplTyr 1972; GTrojk 37,

The favorite metaphors for the relation of lineage and individual nature are arboreal. At the beginning of *Iolande* we are told that "one is sure to see sweet fruit on sweet trees in due season."[82] This botanical fact is then elaborated into a metaphor of human generation: Iolande's parents "were the trunk of a sweet tree that brought into the world sweet fruit," that is, "excellent, pure children"; one can find these children occupying exalted positions in the world—they are bishops, counts, royalty—and doing so "without blemish according to their inherited nature [*art*]."[83] Although *Iolande* offers an unusually elaborate example, the arboreal topos is widespread. It invokes a law of nature, that trees bear fruit according to their kind; it appropriates the authority of Scripture, "a good tree always yields good fruit";[84] and it exploits the dual meaning of MHG *vruht*, both "fruit" and "offspring," to assert a necessary and natural resemblance between parents and children, the same conflation of lineage and individual nature one finds in the word *art*.[85]

Notions concerning what can be inherited vary widely. Freud believes there is an "*archaic* legacy which the child, influenced by the experience of his ancestors, brings with him into the world before any experience of his own" and that parts of this inherited experience appear in dreams.[86] Nowadays most of us assume that children inherit little besides physical traits (eye color) or, at most, general aptitudes (coordination). Recently, however, psychologists have been making stronger claims—that particular cognitive abilities, personality factors, even attitudes and beliefs are all heritable.[87] MHG writers go even further: they believe children inherit very specific physical traits as well as very particular skills and virtues.

1830; HgMarg 368; Ioland 57, 62, 78; JngTit 704,1; Rennew 17705, 17745, 17788, 17833, 17834, 17852, 32651; RWeltc 19416–19; WilWnd 113, 5256; WTitrl 41,1. —The classic discussion of *art* is Schwietering, "Natur und *art*." See also Heinzle, *Stellenkommentar*, 9; Yeandle, *Commentary*, 63–64. —MHG *geslehte* can also combine the notion of lineage with that of inherited nature, although it is more likely than *art* to be restricted to the former.

82. Ioland 75–76: an sûzen bôime man gesît wol sûze vruht ze rehter zît.

83. Ioland 82–91: sy wâren sûzen bôimes stam, der reinen lîves sûze vruht zûr werlde brahte sûze vruht an gûden reinen kinden, dy sich wol lyzen vinden nâch hiren arde sunder meil. . . . bischove, grêve, kuniges kint.

84. Matthew 7.17; see also Luke 6.43–44.

85. Other instances of the botanical metaphor: AlxusF 45–82; RBarlm 268,21–24; Englhd 774–75; HnrKgd 732–44; Ioland 5027–33, 5058–61; JngTit 105,1–108,3, 480,1, 482,1–3, 708,1–2, 781,2; Lohgrn 3814–16; Parz 128,26–28; Passnl H4,60–62, K6,30–31; KTrojk 632; Väterb 1596–98, 1609–14; WTitrl 103,2; WilÖst 12358–60. —*Vruht* in the sense of "offspring" or "child": Dulcfl 47, 148; GTrojk 1329, 1882, 11211; KTrojk 17793–95; RnfrBr 24590–95; UAlexr 1163–64, 1193–97; Väterb 30636; WilOrl 3740; WTitrl 33,3.

86. Freud, *Abriss*, 89: . . . Teil der *archaischen* Erbschaft . . . die das Kind, durch das Erleben der Ahnen beeinflusst, vor jeder eigenen Erfahrung mit sich auf die Welt bringt.

87. Plomin, "Environment and Genes," 105–8.

MHG writers share our assumption that children will take after their parents. The St. Georgener Prediger, for example, asserts that "every person is the child of two persons: his mouth resembles his mother's and his eyes his father's." [88] MHG writers differ from us, however, in believing that the physical resemblance is so close that one can determine the parents by looking at the child. Terramer takes one look at an unknown infant and declares: "Looking at the youth I see that he is of my lineage [art]"; "he is the image of my son Rennewart," whom Terramer has not seen since he was abducted as a child but who is, in fact, the father of the infant.[89] Without hesitation Terramer correctly identifies the unknown child solely on the evidence of his appearance.[90]

MHG children do not only inherit the "image" of their lineage, they also inherit very specific skills, attitudes, and virtues. Malefer possesses "brave prowess from his lineage" for "he is born of manly bravery."[91] Sigune and Schionatulander are predisposed to love by "the nature [art] of their lineage—they were born of pure love."[92] Rennewart's actions are governed by "a sense of propriety that was part of his inherited nature [art]."[93] Young knights can inherit specific skills, like jousting. In *Winsbecke* the father tells his son to "sit tight [in the saddle] and use up the woods [by splintering lances] according to the nature [art] you have inherited from your lineage."[94]

The attributes the MHG children inherit—beauty, bravery, susceptibility to noble love, loyalty, skill at jousting, renown, and a sense of proper behavior—are all attributes celebrated in noble adults and claimed by the nobility for itself. The inheritance of these distinctions is guaranteed by

88. StGrPr 243,27–29: ain ieglich mentsch ist zwaier menschen kint, und ist an dem munde siner mûter glich und an den ogen dem vatter.

89. Rennew 10026–27: ich sehe wol an dem knaben daz er ist von miner art; 10060–61: sin bilde daz ist gar getan als min sun Rennewart.

90. Appearance reveals lineage: LpzgPr 324,4–7; MaiBfl 196,8–17; Melrnz 1974–77, 2140, 2213–17, 2285–87; PrLanc 1:38,22–39,20, 2:624,25–625,10, 2:656,2–8, 3:4,10–16; Rennew 13618–38, 14483–93, 14936–39; RpParz 283,40–43; WWilhm 272,26–30, 291,27–30.

91. Rennew 12559–61: manlich ellen nach dem geslehte. . . . sin lip uz manheit ist erborn.

92. WTitrl 53,1–2: diu art ir geslehtes, (si wâren ûz lûterlîcher minne erborn).

93. WWilhm 213,5: von arte ein zuht.

94. Winsbk 20,5–6: sitz ebene und swende sô den walt, als dir von arte sî geslaht. —Inherited skills and virtues: BitDlb 196–97; Englhd 259–60; JngTit 716,1–2, 811,1–2, 1147,2–4, 1354,3–4; Klage 1894–1903; Lanzlt 258–60; RBarlm 258,9–12; Rennew 17666–81; Parz 55,30–56,24, 174,24–25, 717,22–23; UWilhm W24,13–15, W29,26–28; Väterb 37690–95; WilWnd 5064–69, 5192–94; WTitrl 128,1–2. —The notion of inherited traits seems to have been of particular importance to Wolfram—which is not surprising considering his obsession with consanguinity—and to his followers, who seem to have regarded it as one the requisites of Wolfram's manner. This may account for the very high percentage of citations in the last few paragraphs from these works (JngTit, Parz, Rennew, UWilhm, WTitrl, WWilhm).

what might be called the "rule of noble genetics": just as MHG children inevitably inherit the class status of their noble parents, so they inevitably inherit the attributes that distinguish their noble lineage. Thus the Lady of the Lake can say to Lancelot: "If you knew your father's lineage and your mother's you could hardly doubt that you will become an excellent man. A lineage as lofty as yours could never produce a worthless man."[95] Of course there are also non-noble children in MHG narratives, although not very many, and, while some of these are of questionable character (Helmbrecht, the clever students in *Studentenabenteuer A* and *B*) most are quite admirable. Nevertheless, none of the non-noble children is said to have inherited his distinguishing attributes, good or bad, from his lineage. It seems that admirable qualities are accidental among non-nobles while they are an essential part of the noble genetic code, necessarily passed on from one generation to the next.[96]

The full impact of the rule of noble genetics can be understood only if it is seen in connection with a second rule, that of exalted lineage: in MHG narrative it is assumed that almost any child whose story is worth telling will be of noble or otherwise exalted lineage. The exceptions to this rule are quickly enumerated. First, there are seventy tales, primarily devoted to saints or biblical figures, in which the status of the parents is not indicated in any way.[97] Second, there are a number of short narratives in which children are born of parents who are said to be other than noble: a few merchants, two farmers, several bourgeois, two Jews, and, in the same story, two knights.[98] The heroes of three miracles of the Virgin, said to be poor, are almost certainly not highborn.[99] Third are a number of

95. PrLanc 1:124,22–24: Bekentet ir auch uwers vatters geslecht und uwer mutter, ir dörfftent wenig daran zwyveln, ir wurdent ein gut man. Von so hohem geslecht als ir sint enmag nymer böse man werden.

96. Very occasionally base characteristics are transmitted from one generation to the next, but usually this occurs in *noble* lineages: Gregorius and Albanus, born of incestuous relations, grow up and marry their mothers. Only Pilate acts ignobly because one of his parents is baseborn (Passnl H82,46–53).

97. BMärtr Agnes, Ambrose, Boniface, Jerome, John the Baptist, Silvester; Brchta; ELgAur Agnes, Dominic, John the Baptist, Judas, Peter Martyr, Remi, Vitus; Exdus Moses; Gänsln; GbrEi; GrshPr John the Baptist; Hlgnlb Aquinas; HoffPr Nicholas; JnaMrt Agapitus, Eulalia, Felicula, Margaret, Thecla; Irmgrd; KSilvr; MarBrt; MHMarg; MönNot; Passnl Augustine, Francis, Jerome, Judas, Remi; PKonPr Mary of Egypt, Silvester; RWeltc Moses; SealdH John the Baptist; SlPrsA; SpecEc John the Baptist, Martin; Sperbr; StFran; StdabA; StdabB; StPlPr Lawrence; Väterb Helenus; VBüMos Moses; VorNov; WzMarg.

98. Merchants: Schnkd 1; Treuep 29–31. Farmers: ArmHnr 267–75; Helmbr 10, 21. Bourgeois: HlbDek 1; SlPrsA 8–15; SlPrsB 53–56; SlPrsC 131. Jews: Jüdel 124,30; Jüdenk 6. Knights: Nachtgl 11, 26.

99. ArmSch 68; ScholM 28–31; TKdlbg 109.

biblical figures as well as early Christian saints who are born of illustrious stock, even though they are not said to be noble. Their fathers may be patriarchs, priests, senators, or imperial Roman officials.[100] Others are said to be wealthy.[101] All other children in MHG narrative fall into the fourth category, those who are clearly of noble (or divine) birth. This includes the child heroes of a number of *Mären*[102] as well as a considerable number of saints[103] and, above all, the child protagonists of secular romance and epic, *all* of whom are of noble, often royal, birth.

I have identified about 375 children in the MHG texts under consideration, of whom approximately 300 can be identified by class. Of these, about 6 percent are clearly not of noble birth, 16 percent are saints of exalted, but not explicitly noble, ancestry, and all the rest, about 78 percent, are children of noble lineage. Combining the last two categories, one finds that 94 percent of the children in MHG narratives are of noble or otherwise exalted birth. This fact, which I will call the "rule of exalted lineage," doubtless reflects the dominance by the nobility—secular and ecclesiastical—in the production and reception of vernacular texts.[104]

100. AvaJoh 19–20; BMärtr Mary of Egypt 5209–10, Margaret 11804–5, Pantaleon 13393, Alexis 18290, Martin 22979, Nicholas 25857; ELgAur Eustace 698,14, Gregory 220,13–18, Ambrose 283,11–12, Servatius 348,6–13, Margaret 423,16, Martin 724,10–11, Pantaleon 787,4; Hlgnlb Vitus 134,24–25; JnaMrt Barbara 89; KPantl 100; Marglg 8–10; Passnl Gregory K192,10, Justina K492,6–9, Margaret K327,20; StDrth 47–57; StPlPr John 116,9; VlSrvt 199–239; WlMarg 115–19.

101. ELgAur Nicholas 20,25, Bernhard 536,2–3, 536,30–32; Eracl 66; GrMarl 11–41; Hlgnlb Alexis 161,1; JnaMrt Hilarion 72–73; Passnl Nicholas K6,7, Agnes K111,30, Benedict K217,5, Ambrose K241,15, Vitus K301,4, Martin K492,6, Dominic K353,34; PhMarl 27, 55–68; StVeit 56; Väterb Anthony 253, 308, Euphrosyne 27634–35, Abraham 30636, Abraham's niece 32273, Margaret 35793, Alexis 39035; WerMar D291–336; WrMarl 132–50.

102. ArPhlS 93–94; Bussrd 49, 79–80, 110–16; Dulcfl 104, 195–97; Häsln 61–62; HvKemp 50–59; PyrThs 25–28; SlPrsB 33; SlPrsC 37–43.

103. AlxusA 17; AlxusB 2; AlxusC 19–20; AlxusF 25; BMärtr Gregory 3198, Eustace 7219–24, Martin 22973, Katherine 24651; ELgAur Anastasia 47,2–3, Pancras 346,22–23, Margaret 423,24–25, Alexis 426,4, Christine 442,9, Nazarius 462,15–17, Eugenia 596,4, Jerome 656,12, Ursula 688,24, Cecilia 738,2, Clement 744,2, Katherine 755,15, Ulrich 779,4, Maximilian 805,10, Elizabeth 809,7, Ottilia 817,16; GrshPr Martin 450a,8–9; HgMarg 385; Hlgnlb Agnes 67,10–11, Elizabeth 242,13–14, Katherine 253,20; HoffPr Margaret 120,7; Ioland 29; JnaMrt Gertrude 19, Cunibert 80; KAlxus 75–59; LpzgPr Agnes 280,6–7; MarlKg 1.12–13; ObSrvt 248–49; Passnl Mary H5,48–55, John the Baptist H345,52–57, Pilate H81,76–77, Agatha K176,16–17, Pancras K293,3, Bernard K395,9, Eugenia K471,18–22, Elizabeth K618,6, Katherine K669,7; PKonPr Martin S239,25; SaeldH Mary Magdalen 5868–73; StAdal 201–08; StElis 71–127, 325–33; StKatM 466–71; StMarM 61–63; StUlrc 57; Väterb Mary of Egypt 34411–17, Eustace 36711; VrJnfg Margaret 135–36; WlMarg 181–85, 209–12; ZwöMön 45.

104. The numbers can only be approximate. Including every child whose birth or marriage is noted would have raised the number to well over 400. Reducing the list to the more substantial narratives (a necessarily subjective standard) leaves about 300 but does not affect the percentages given in this paragraph.

It also reflects well-established literary traditions, both secular and hagiographic. Perhaps most striking is the latter, in which exalted birth was
long a requirement for sainthood. Medieval writers assumed that, just as
Christ was born to the royal lineage of David, so saintliness would manifest
itself in certain royal, or at least noble, families; thus, if little was known
about the lineage of a particular saint, hagiographers did not hesitate to
claim that she was of exalted birth.[105] Four unrelated medieval versions of
the legend of Mary the Egyptian independently added the information that
she was born into a noble lineage.[106] The Christian valorization of poverty
and humility seems to have applied only if they are voluntary, and for that
one must be rich and noble to start with.[107] A treatise written around 1300
and attributed to Albertus Magnus explains how the Virgin Mary had to
have been of the highest lineage, because, among other reasons, only then
would her profound humility be meaningful.[108] The rule of exalted lineage
is so powerful that it even affects the one group that is clearly excluded: of
the families explicitly said to be of other than noble station, nearly all are
at least said to be rich.[109] For centuries then, and not only in MHG, virtually the only children considered worth writing about were those born of
noble or otherwise exalted lineage.

MHG texts offer a very clear argument with regard to the nature of the
noble lineage. They assume that class-specific, noble attributes will necessarily be passed on from one generation to the next and that this transmis-
sion is an inevitable consequence of biological reproduction. According to
the narrator of *Wilhelm von Österreich* this is a fact of nature: "Whoever is
born of the nobility," he claims, "is chosen by Nature for noble affairs."[110]
Lesser groups are virtually excluded from MHG narrative, and where they
do appear, nothing is said about the class-specific traits they might have
inherited. The entire MHG corpus thus presents a powerful argument that
noble virtues are inevitably, naturally, preserved from one generation to
the next and, further, that the distinguishing attributes of other groups—
which, in any case, seem barely to exist—are hardly worth mentioning, let
alone inheriting. It is an argument that cannot but have appealed to the

---

105. Vauchez, "Beata stirps," 398, 404.
106. Kunze, *Maria Aegyptiaca*, 141–42; Kunze, "Märterbuch," 444.
107. Weinstein and Bell, *Saints*, 199–200, 216.
108. Schreiner, "Hof," 133–35.
109. ArmHnr 281–82; HlbDek 1; Jüdel 129,30; Jüdenk 6–9; Nchtgl 17, 27; Schnkd 14;
SlPrsA 11; SlPrsC 131; Treuep 41–43.
110. WilÖst 12331–33: Swaz von adel ist geborn, daz hat diu Natur erkorn zu adellichen
sachen.

noble men and women who were the patrons and the first audiences for these texts.

The Nature of the Hero/ine

After Wolfram has told us something about the early childhood of Sigune and Schionatulander, he introduces his principal subject: the love that "arose early between the two children."[111] Although the narrator laments this development, since "they are still too young and inexperienced for such anguish,"[112] their love nevertheless represents an ideal: "it developed so purely that no one could find any of the world's dullness" in it.[113] Clearly the lovers are special. They share a perfect love even though they are too young to love. And that is why they are heroine and hero: they behave like exemplary adults even though they are only children.[114]

The MHG childhood narratives are full of passages like these that contain signs of their protagonists' special nature. I have grouped them into three categories. The first comprises the general signs: they show the child to be exceptional in a general way because of something she is—beautiful, well mannered, clever. The second comprises the vocational signs: they promise future distinction in a particular calling, usually because of something the child does—displays a precocious love, or valor, or piety. The third group consists of the prophetic signs: these show that the child will be remarkable by means of an external agency or circumstance—portents, or prophecies, or dreams.

The most common of the *general signs*, indeed, the one distinction shared by all MHG child heroes from the moment they are born, is physical beauty. At birth the Gute Frau was "the most beautiful little daughter ever seen by the eye of man."[115] Of St. Silvester at a slightly later age we are told "that he was so completely beautiful that he had the countenance of an angel."[116] At the threshold of adulthood these children are still with-

---

111. WTitrl 46,3: minne huop sich vruo dâ von zwein kinden.
112. WTitrl 48,1: si sint noch ze tump ze solher angest.
113. WTitrl 46,4: diu ergienc sô lûterlîche, al diu werlt möhte ir truopheit niht bevinden.
114. Ruh ("Liebessprache," 505–6) finds it remarkable that scholars have made little of the fact that these children actually manage their love affair quite well. But that is precisely the point: they are hero and heroine, and therefore able to manage parts of their lives, at least, every bit as well as adults. —On their love: Curschmann, *Oswald*, 157–59.
115. GuFrau 38–39: daz schœneste töhterlîn daz mannes ouge ie gesach.
116. BMärtr 27988–89: daz er wêr so schöne gar, daz er engels antlicz hiet.

out peer. When Lancelot arrives at King Arthur's court just before he is knighted "the king took him by the chin and thought him so beautiful that nothing about him could be improved in this world."[117] The examples could be increased almost without limit, since beauty is felt to be an essential attribute of all MHG child protagonists: male and female, secular and saintly, infant and near adult.

Three things should be noted about beauty. First, the beauty of MHG children, even very young children, is described in adult terms. Just after Beaflor is baptized we are told that "her cheeks were white and red, her eyebrows small and brown, arched just the right amount; her bright eyes were perfectly sized. Her brow, her nose, her chin blossomed from true love. Her mouth, which invited kisses, burned from heat redder than a fire. Her throat, her arms, her hands were without the least flaw. Her beauty vanquished all beauty. She bore the emblem of love."[118] The infant Beaflor is described just like an adult romance heroine. There is no beauty peculiar to children.

Second, beauty is not merely a personal distinction; it is has dramatic effects on those who witness it. When Moses, whose "beauty could overpower a great many people, was carried into the street, they abandoned whatever they were doing and paid attention to nothing else."[119] When servants are ordered to kill the infant Paris, they find him "such a beautiful child" that they decide to abandon him instead; a shepherd comes upon the abandoned infant, "delighted in his very beautiful appearance," and takes him home.[120] Beauty can also elicit unwelcome reactions. Olybrius sees St. Margaret tending sheep and "she pleased him more and more, since that vessel of God's grace was young and beautiful";[121] he is seized by desire and wants to marry her, she refuses, and, in the end, is martyred. The beauty of MHG maidens often attracts suitors, not all of them as unwelcome as Olybrius.[122]

117. PrLanc 1:131,7–9; Der konig nam yn mit dem kyne, und ducht yn so schön das in der welt nicht an im zu beßern ware.
118. MaiBfl 9,38–10,12: ir wängel wîz unde rôt, dâ bî kleine brûne brâ gewelbet ze mâze hie unt dâ, ir ougen lieht ze rehte grôz. nieman ze sehene sî verdrôz. ir stirne, ir nase, ir kinne erbluote ûz rehter minne. ir kuslîch munt vor hitze bran noch rœter danne des viwers gan. ir kel, ir arme, ir hende ân alle missewende. . . . ir schœne al schœne nider sluoc. der minne wâfen si truoc.
119. RWeltc 9179–83: sin schöne konde twingen der lúte mere danne gnûg. swa man ez an die straze trûg, da liezens ir ummûze gar und namen da niht andirs war.
120. KTrojk 492: ein sô klârez kint; 558–59: der hirte vröute sich dur sîn vil clârez bilde.
121. Passnl K327,83–85: si geviel im baz und baz, wand daz gotes genadenvaz was beide schone unde iunc.
122. Moses' beauty as an infant is equal to Beaflor's: JWeltc 6351–55, 6432–33. Beauty

Third, beauty carries meaning. It can signify nobility. When the emir of Babylon first sees the captive Blanscheflur "her appearance told him that she might be of noble birth because his eyes had never seen a more beautiful woman."[123] More commonly beauty is said to reveal the favor of God. Vitus "was so well formed that his beauty was without equal, since God in heaven had poured his grace on him."[124] In the Christian tradition physical beauty was not only "a sign of supernatural endowment, it was also a worldly temptation."[125] But there is very little concern in MHG texts for the danger that this temptation represents. The beauty of Euphrosyne, who disguised herself as a man and entered a monastery, "troubled the brothers' hearts greatly"; as a result the abbot asks the new monk to keep to his cell because his "beauty causes the weak brothers to fall."[126] But the abbot is just about the only one to articulate such reservations. The function of beauty as a sign of the hero's special nature, of noble lineage, or of God's favor is too important to do without.[127]

MHG child heroes and heroines do not only have the beauty of adults, they also possess an adult wisdom. They are *wis*—old, wise, experienced—like adults, rather than *tump*—young, foolish, inexperienced—like children. The maiden in *Armer Heinrich* "spoke in such a *wis* manner" that she "violated human nature"; no child "could ever display such wisdom and sense."[128] Often the combination of youth and wisdom is reduced to a formula: Iolande is "a child in years, a woman in sense, young in body, old in spirit."[129] Such precocious wisdom can bring eloquence: when the Virgin "was three years old [she] spoke as well and as perfectly as if she were thirty."[130] More commonly child heroes reveal their extraordinary mental

---

saves a child's life: FlorBl 6790–978; KTrojk 5652–56; PartMl 9002–15. Beauty dispels sorrow or sickness: GuGrhd 2953–57; JngTit 1158,4; ORmchr 17780–82; RnfrBr 23346–61; WWilhm 155,4–6.

123. FlorBl 1682–89: ir angesiht tet im kunt, daz sî edel wesen mehte an gebürte . . . durch daz sîniu ougen nie schœner frouwen erkurn.

124. BMärtr 8998–9001: nün was er also wol getann, das seiner schön nicht was geleich; wann in Got vonn himelreich mit seinen gnaden begossen het.

125. Weinstein and Bell, *Saints*, 27.

126. Väterb 28466–67: betrubete Der brudere herze genuc; 28512–13: die selbe schonheit Den cranken brudern ist ein val.

127. Beauty in courtly culture: Bumke, *Höfische Kultur*, 419–25; Krüger, "Verhöflichter Krieger," 339–40. On Parzival's beauty see Yeandle, *Commentary*, 167 and the literature cited there.

128. ArmHnr 855–62: Dô . . . daz kint . . . sô wîslîchen sprach unde menschlich reht zebrach, si begunden ahten under in daz die wîsheit und den sin niemer erzeigen kunde dehein zunge in kindes munde.

129. Ioland 144–45: der jâre ein kint, der witze ein wîf, des lîves junc, des mûdes alt.

130. GrMarl 330–33: dô si was drîer jâre alt, dô rette diu reine tugentrîch als wol und alsô vollectîch als ob si hiete drîzec jâr.

gifts by their success at book learning: Eraclius is taught to read at age
seven and shortly thereafter all who see him agree that "there was no one
alive at that time who was so learned." [131]

The topos of the wise child, the *puer senex*, known since Pindar, became very popular in late antiquity, especially among Christian writers.[132]
The story of the twelve-year-old Jesus in the Temple, when "everyone who
heard [him] was stunned by his wisdom," [133] provided a scriptural model.
Such a topos is only meaningful in cultural contexts where children are
ordinarily expected to be foolish, for it is only where children are thought
to be *tump* by nature that a child can give evidence of her special nature
by being *wis*. Some MHG texts attribute this wisdom directly to the individual nature: Wilhelm von Österreich "grew wise by nature" rather than
instruction, excelling on his own even in school subjects, "in the liberal arts
and in knowledge of philosophy." [134] More frequently precocious wisdom
is understood as a sign of God's favor: the Armer Schüler "was smart on
account of the instruction of the Lord, who gave the scholar such ability
that he was very learned." [135]

The beauty and wisdom of the MHG child heroes and heroines are so
striking that they become famous while still young. When Willehalm von
Orlens first arrives in London the king greets him with the observation: "I
have heard more about your many excellences than I ever did of any other
child." [136] Willehalm is only thirteen but already his fame has spread to for-

131. Eracl A439–43: alle die jahen Die in ie gesahen . . . Ez enlebte niemen bi siner zit
Der so wol gelerte wære. —Others who are young but wise: AplTyr 14971–80, 17292; ArPhlS
76–81; Crone 357; ELgAur 135,19–23, 347,13–14; FlorBl 706–07; Greg 1179–80; HgMarg 159–
69; Hlgnlb 67,10; JngTit 680,1, 1523,1; Kudrn 81,4, 162,4; LAlexr S2504–6; Lohgrn 932; Passnl
K111,18–23, K294,37–43, K301,24–27; PrLanc 1:36,15–17, 1:93,24–25; RnfrBr 18020–29; StAdal
246–48; StElis 699–702; StLudw 16,16–17; WerMar 1134–38; WilOrl 3941–43; WilWnd 146;
WlMarl 1060–68, 1585, 5156–62; WWilhm 23,10. —Others who are eloquent when young:
BMärtr 10383–85; GTrist 3094–95; GTrojk 374–75; LAdam 1883–91; PrLanc 1:93,24–25; WilÖst
3254–55. —Others whose wisdom brings them success in school: AlxusF 146–55; ArPhlS 76–
81; BMärtr 3205–10, 4831–40, 13411–17, 24670–78; Bussrd 71–81; FlorBl 678–83; Greg 1159–97;
GTrist 2088–92; Hlgnlb 99,13–15; LAlexr S5318–20; Passnl K192,26–37, K241,78–81, K354,76–
89, K396,36–43, K415,24–56, K505,13–45, K669,12–32; RBarlm 25,9–27; RAlexr 1851–61; SAlexr
597–604; SlPrsC 75–78; Väterb 30692–97, 39119–26.
132. Eyben, "Sozialgeschichte," 335; Herter, "Das unschuldige Kind," 148.
133. MtdtPr 305: alle die daz horton erscraken. von siner wishait.
134. WilÖst 632: er wart von natur wis; 646–47: in artibus . . . und in phylosophie kunst.
135. ArmSch 76–79: Daz kint hatte sinne Von unses hêrin meisterschaft. Der gap dem
schüler sulche craft Daz her gar gelernit was. —Others who are wise by nature: KTrojk 6442–
47; RBarlm 25,4–27. Others who are wise by God's grace: AlxusF 146–52; BMärtr 4831–41;
FlorBl 836–41; Kudrn 105,2; Jüdel 130,33–39; Passnl K192,30–31, K241,78–81, K301,24–27; Väterb 39114–26. —On the *puer senex*: Burrow, *Ages*, 95–134; Curtius, *Latin Middle Ages*, 98–101,
381; Goodich, *Vita Perfecta*, 87–89; Shahar, *Childhood*, 15–16; Weinrich and Bell, *Saints*, 29.
136. WilOrl 3530–33: Ich han mer von dir vernomen Tugentlicher râte Danne ich ie
getâte Von dekaime kinde.

eign countries. The virtues of MHG children make them not only famous but also beloved of all with whom they come into contact. After the Virgin joins the Temple maidens, "everyone who saw her became fond of her."[137] The fame and devotion that the MHG children enjoy are not superficial responses to their many virtues but important distinctions in a world that "accorded worldly glory a central value"[138] and in which "it was a token of success . . . to make oneself beloved of all."[139]

In addition to the general signs like beauty and wisdom, which are distributed very broadly throughout the population of MHG child protagonists and reveal a sort of general excellence, there are also a number of *vocational signs*, those that reveal a more particular excellence and predict a more specific future. Exceptional size and rapid growth indicate that a youth is destined to become a great fighter. Malefer grows so fast—he is the size of a five-year-old by the time he is baptized—that he requires the services of ten nurses.[140] His uncle interprets this as a predictive sign: "If you're going to keep growing like this you will be able to conquer the whole world."[141] The future fighter's vocation is often indicated more actively by feats of precocious strength: when Wolfdietrich is three-and-a-half he throws against the wall any dog that tries to take food out of his hand.[142] Often those youths destined to excel as knights show a strong attraction to knighthood as children. "Even though Fivianz was only a few years old, he began to pursue knighthood with bold deeds. Wherever he found tournaments, there he wanted to be, until he became familiar with knightly games and deeds."[143]

137. WerMar 1153–54: daz ir alle holt wâren die si an gesâhen.

138. Bumke, *Höfische Kultur*, 428: Die höfischen Dichter . . . haben dem weltlichen Ruhm . . . einen zentralen Wert zuerkannt.

139. Jaeger, *Courtliness*, 43. —Others who are famous: ErnstB 76–79; KTrojk 6360–61; MaiBfl 13,22–25; Väterb 27797–801; WerMar 1343–54. —Others beloved of all: Alban 47–48; ETrist 1036–50; Greg 1460–61; GTrist 2144–48, 3744–49; Ioland 341–59; Ksrchr 1365–74; LBarlm 1200; MaiBfl 195,23–196,5; Parz 148,30–149,1; RBarlm 29,40–30,7; Väterb 39134–38; Wglois 1262–64, 1407–10; WilOrl 2693–2703; WilWnd 5096, 5458–64, 5539–44, 5659–64; WlMarl 1589–1656.

140. Rennew 9273–75, 10212–27.

141. Rennew 10184–85: wiltu sus wahsen für sich, du maht betwingen gar die welt.

142. WolfdA 38,2–4.

143. UWilhm A358–63: nv begvnde nach ritterschefte iagen Fivianz mit frecher tat. swie klein er doch der iare hat, swa er ie tvrnyre vant, da wolt er sin, biz er bekant ritterlicher tete spil. —Other young heroes who are extraordinarily large: JngTit 4444,2–4; LAdam 1883–85; LAlexr S142–44; Parz 112,6–8; Passnl H82,11–14; PrLanc I:34,6–7; Rennew 9062–67, 11738–42, 32622–24, 32649–55, 32662–77; RpParz 215,34–35; RWeltc 20494–506; Wglois 1226–27; WilWnd 2317–19; WolfdA 233,3–234,4. —Discussions of the Slaughter of the Innocents, which consider the size of child heroes in the past: ELgAur 74,21–23; SwrzPr F57,178–58,200. —Other examples of precocious strength: ELgAur 702,12–13; GTrojk 1469–78, 1512–35, 1588–1615, 1678–83; KrlGal 22,34–35; Pilat 536–37; UAlexr 1299–1306; WolfdA 234–37. —On Parzi-

Others manifest as children the virtues appropriate to leaders and rulers. Paris, who is selected to adjudicate disputes by the young shepherds among whom he grows up, is named Paris from *par* "on account of his evenhanded justice";[144] he becomes famous for his decisions and settles many disputes. Lancelot is a model of liberality: "He distributed among his companions all that he could win."[145] Even before his education begins "Alexander bore himself as if he were prince of the whole world."[146]

While Alexander reveals his secular vocation as a young child, saints reveal their holy calling as soon as they are born. "In their earliest childhood," according to the *Passional*, "many of them grafted their chaste lives onto the tree of life with complete purity and immaculateness."[147] The consequences of this graft—contrary to the rule in botany—are evident in the nature of the fruit they bear. Some are precocious ascetics. The infant Nicholas nurses only twice on Wednesdays and Fridays, an abstinence that is read as a predictive sign: "God indicated in his exalted youth what a strict life he should lead later on."[148] Others mortify their flesh, like Vitus, who wears a hair shirt at age twelve, or Iolande, who has another child flagellate her when she is a bit over nine.[149] Some perform good works, like Elizabeth, who distributes food and alms to the poor.[150] Those destined to be doctors of the church display an extraordinary aptitude for learning, like Aquinas, who "was smart from youth on. Even as a child he had no equal among those of his age."[151] One of the nuns memorialized in the *Engelthaler Schwesternbuch* "had a prophetic spirit from the days of her childhood."[152] The most dramatic demonstrations of election are offered

val's strength: Yeandle, *Commentary*, 106–7. On Wolfdietrich's size and strength along with parallels from Old French: Schneider, *Wolfdietrich*, 277. —Others eager to become knights: BitDlb 2028–31, 2191–98; JngTit 184,4; Kudrn 24,1–25,3; Parz 66,15–22; RAlexr 1406–8; SAlexr 608–10. —Others who know they must become knights even though they have been kept from knowledge of knighthood include Parzival, Gregorius, Lanzelet, Wigamur. —Some future knights fight before they are knighted: BitDlb 2767–3092; PartMl 3260–82, 3547–6137; Rabens 447–48, 451; Wglois 1610–21; Wigmur 576–650.
144. KTrojk 663: dur sîn gelîchez reht.
145. PrLanc 1:36,10: Alles das er gewinnen mocht das deilt er under syn gesellen.
146. LAlexr V161–62: ime was ouch sîn gebâre, alser ein furste von allen landen wâre. —Others who display liberality: LAlexr S181–89; Wglois 1249–53; WilOrl 3069.
147. Passnl K5,54–57: so heten sumeliche ir leben kusche von kindes beine, luter unde gar reine gepfropfet uf des lebens stam.
148. Passnl K7,13–15: got . . . wisete an siner edelen iugent, wie strenge er dar nach solde leben.
149. BMärtr 8760–64; Ioland 76, 199–218.
150. Hlgnlb 242,18–29; StElis 747–63, 874–80.
151. Hlgnlb 99,13–15: daz kint . . . was klug von jugent ûf. Nôch den tagen sînes alders sô enwas ime nimant glîch under anderen kinderen.
152. EngSwb 10,17–18: die het von irn kintlichen tagen einen wissagenden geist gehabt.

by those children who perform miracles: while still a Temple maiden the Virgin cures the sick with her touch.[153] Just as saints reveal their future vocation as children, so do great sinners: Pilate kills his half brother, Judas his foster brother.[154]

Whereas vocational signs can appear any time during childhood, the third sort of heroic sign, the *prophetic sign*, occurs most often in connection with birth. The future glory of many MHG children is indicated by the fact that they are born to barren parents: "When a child is born contrary to the course of nature," an angel tells Joachim, "that is a gift of God, and therefore the child will become all the more perfect."[155] As the angel asserts in a religious context, so one must assume in a secular one as well: children born contrary to the course of nature are destined to become especially remarkable.[156]

Sometimes the illustrious destiny of a child is revealed at birth through natural signs. "The knowledge of astronomy,"[157] which "was popular at the time,"[158] enables Clinsor to prophecy the birth of St. Elizabeth.[159] The

153. WerMar 1522–28.

154. Pilat 358–99; Passnl Pilate H82,46–53, Judas H315,14–32. —Other instances of the grafting metaphor: AlxusF 61–77; Passnl K667,6–21. The details of the graft are different in each case, as they are in Romans 1.17–42, which is doubtless the inspiration for them. —General statements of precocious piety: ArmHnr 863–69; ArmSch 118–26; BMärtr 23014–26; Passnl H261,44–49, H348,38–55, K217,6–19, K293,1–3, K396,44–397,15, K618,16–33; StElis 665–83; StVeit 16–19; Väterb 248–51; WzMarg 130–37. —Others moderate in nursing or eating: ELgAur 21,5–9, 348,13–15; ObSrvt 254–60; PhMarl 389–92; UlmSwb 141; StUlrc 67–104. Moses refuses to nurse from a heathen woman: VBüMos 32,18–33,8. See also Weinstein and Bell, *Saints*, 24–25. —Those who shun games and social pleasures: LBarlm 11939–53; Passnl K7,44–47; StElis 710–14, 881–97; TößSwb 87,5–7; UlmSwb 141; Väterb 272–73. See also Opitz, *Frauenalltag*, 55–56. —Youths who resist temptation by beautiful women: BMärtr 8835–52; ELgAur 371,24–28; Passnl K302,15–29, K397,26–398–15; LBarlm 12244–963; RBarlm 290,17–309,24. —Others who display great learning: BMärtr 3205–10, 4831–40, 24670–78; Greg 1159–97; Passnl K192,26–37, K241,78–81, K354,76–89, K396,36–43, K505,13–45, K669,12–32; UlmSwb 141. —Other children who perform miracles: BMärtr 8978–9016; ELgAur 799,10–20; PKonPr M246,15–249,117; WlMarl 4218–821, 4951–97. —On the miracles of the child Jesus: Masser, *Bibel, Apokryphen*, 286–88.

155. ELgAur 574,23–24: Wenne was wider der naturen löf wurt geborn, das ist us göttelicher goben; do von wirt es deste follekomenre.

156. Children born to long barren parents: Alban 1–2; AlxusA 94; AlxusB 32–45; AvaJoh 2,5, 4,1–3; BMärtr 18311–15; Dulcfl 41–48; ELgAur 115,23–24, 386,7–387,19, 574,7–10; Gensis 1652–74, 1686–87, 1768–73, 2113–20; GrMarl 65–67; Hlgnlb 161,10; Jakobr 86–91; JngTit 147,1–4; JWeltc 3597–730; Ksrchr 11348–69; MarlKg 1.36–71; MfRmbl 104–30; Passnl H7,44–67, H345,71–76, K93,40–41; PhMarl 98–106; PKonPr M225,24–29, S190,25–191,34; RAlexr 655; RBarlm 7,33–8,4; RnfrBr 12952–73; RWeltc 5409–14, 6281–87, 20411–14, 21757–59; SaeldH 2371–75; SlPrsC 44–47; SpecEc 80,8–81,12; StPlPr 116,2–117,16; SwrzPr F96,27; UAlexr 192–203, 1189–91; Väterb 27636–46, 39074–81; VBüMos 16,13, 26,11; WerMar D395–402; WilÖst 178–83, 420–37; WlMarl 267–70. —See also Weinstein and Bell, *Saints*, 20–23.

157. WilÖst 580: diu kunst von astronomie.

158. Pilat 231: sî was lieb bî der zît.

159. StElis 233–90; StLudw 10,31–11,10.

birth of Alexander is accompanied by earthquakes, storms, eclipses, and strange births;[160] in the account of Rudolf von Ems, Philip understands these as signs that Alexander's life will bring great suffering to the world, since his birth did the same.[161] A child's destiny can also be revealed through miracles. When Ambrose is still an infant in his cradle a swarm of bees lights on his face without harming him in the least; according to the *Passional*, "God wanted to make known" in the saint's "earliest childhood that his name would become well known later in the days of his maturity."[162] Sometimes dreams bring prophetic information. The accounts of the Trojan War report that Hecuba, while pregnant with Paris, dreams of a flaming torch that grows out of her heart and burns Troy to the ground.[163] Priam interprets this to mean that she is bearing "a dangerous offspring. My entire country could be completely destroyed by him"[164]—which, of course, it is. The clearest signs of the hero's special destiny are explicit prophecies. Aquinas's mother is visited by a hermit to whom it has been revealed that she will bear a child "who shall enlighten the entire world with his life and his teaching, who shall enter the order of preachers, and shall be called Thomas."[165]

The signs of the special nature of the hero or heroine are many and

160. LAlexr 129–38; RAlexr 1237–55; SAlexr 555–64; UAlexr 1172–86.

161. RAlexr 1269–72.

162. Passnl K241,16–19: got wolde an im kunt tun in siner kleinen kintheit daz sin name wurde breit hernach in sinen alden tagen.

163. GTrojk 1–11; JWeltc 13515–29; KTrojk 350–63.

164. KTrojk 391–93: Diz ist ein schedelîchiu fruht. mîn lant möht allez mit genuht von im zerstœret werden.

165. Hlgnlb 99,10–11: der sal irlûchten alle dise werlt mit lebene und mit lêre, und sal varen in den orden der predier, und sal Thomas heizen. —Other examples of astronomical divination: JWeltc 19871–77; Melrnz 1795–97; LBarlm 690–739; Pilat 224–42; WilÖst 572–91. —Other examples of dramatic natural signs: AvaJes 143–296; ELgAur 42,16–45,24; Passnl H19,81–22,72, H23,72–26,45; PhMarl 2236–429; SAlexr 565–77; SpecEc 11,22–13,13; VChrGb 124; WerMar D4192–436; WlMarl 867–84, 3536–929. —Other miracles: ArmSch 701–38, 840–82, 1131–32, 1909–92, 1209; BMärtr 697–731, 4798–830; ELgAur 283,13–20; Hlgnlb 242,18–29; JnaMrt 80; Jüdel 132,70–133,9; Judenk 556–67; Passnl K302,44–49; PhMarl 768–85; VChrGb 95–109; WerMar 1389–1406. —Secular miracles: FlorBl 2736–82; RAlexr 2173–240; UAlexr 1657–82; Wglois 1477–1544; WilÖst 4280–93, 4976–91; WolfdA 105,2, 106,3–4, 113,1–2. —Other prophetic dreams: ELgAur 115,17–27, 251,22–30, 499,5–11, 536,5–10; GTrojk 805–46; JnaMrt 7; Parz 103,25–104,30, 476,27–30; Passnl H312,87–313,35, K93,25–47, K354,6–46, K395,44–71; RAlexr 725–84, 928–94; RnfrBr 14915–86; SAlexr 343–84, 433–68; UAlexr 625–88; WolfdA 20,1–23,4. —Cases in which the child has a vision: BMärtr 21079–120; Judenk 170–93; Passnl K396,9–27, K505,66–506,36. —Other prophecies: AplTyr 4235–37; ELgAur 115,13–27, 386,10–24, 574,16–576,6, 799,13–20; GrMarl 420–25; JngTit 162,1–164,2, 169,4–170,3; JWeltc 6657–850; Ksrchr 2012–53; KTrojk 4570–616; Lanzlt 94–95; PhMarl 181–264; PrLanc 2:350,21–351,10, 2:539,23–540,8, 2:626,14–17; Rennew 5171–213; RpParz 591,20–592,24; SaeldH 1885–919; SAlexr 405, 515, 567; SpecEc 13,13–14; StUlrc 191–206; WlMarl 365–452, 581–622, 2815–907; WolfdA 31,1–32,4.

various, yet nearly all of them show the child to be like an adult. There is no heroism of children except in adult terms. Thus it is that, in the areas of their particular heroism, heroic children overcome the deficiencies of their childish nature and display the perfection of an adult. Partonopier is not weak but strong: when he is "still a child in years," his "youth is enriched with the great strength of a man."[166] Agnes is not *tump* but *wis*: when she "was considered a child in years, she was nevertheless old in wisdom."[167] Margaret receives the most general praise: when she "was in the years of her youth, many who saw her claimed that she did not seem to be a child."[168] Although the heroic children in MHG narrative are children and in certain ways act like children, they are exemplary in adult terms: Albinus attained such excellence "in his childhood [that] he was a model to adults."[169]

The Nature of Change

The English nursery rhyme quoted at the beginning of the chapter defines children in static terms: boys are made of frogs and snails, girls of sugar and spice, and that's all there is to it. The various kinds of nature discussed in this chapter also seem to define things in static terms: children cry and play games, noble children inherit beauty and bravery, heroes and heroines are wise and renowned, and it will always be thus. Yet change is one of the most obvious features of childhood. Although the MHG texts seem to regard the nature of the child, the lineage, and the hero/ine as static, these categories actually imply notions of change. Two deserve special mention: the inevitable change from childhood to adulthood; and the apparent change caused by the gradual revelation of the individual nature.

By nature the child is deficient. As a child ages, however, the weakness, heedlessness, crying, games, and relative freedom from sin characteristic of a child are replaced by the strength, discretion, articulate speech, gravity, and sinfulness characteristic of an adult. The deficiency of childhood is re-

166. PartMl 4872–77: sô bistu noch der jâre ein kint. . . . dîn jugent ist gerîchet mit hôher mannes krefte.
167. ELgAur 135,21–22: Die waz ein kint gescheczet an den ioren vnd waz doch alt an den sinnen.
168. HgMarg 166–69: in ir iungen iâren Vil maeng, die si gesâhen . . . iâhen, das si nit als ain kint erschin.
169. JnaMrt 15: he was den aldin ein bilde an siner kintheit. —Others who receive similar praise: Crone 356–57; ELgAur 348,18–19; GTrist 3641–45; Passnl K6,54–57, K397,10–15; Rennew 17828–31. —On the projection of adulthood back into the heroic childhood: Masser, *Bibel, Apokryphen*, 288; Opitz, *Frauenalltag*, 43–44.

placed by the plentitude of adulthood. Education has some role to play in these changes, as will be seen in the next chapter, but to a large extent they are regarded as inevitable. One cannot change from *tump*, "young," to *wis*, "old," without also changing from *tump*, "inexperienced" and "foolish," to *wis*, "experienced" and "wise." As childhood passes, so, naturally, does the nature of the child. This inevitable change, however, is limited to those attributes one has by virtue of being a child.

The nature that one has inherited from one's lineage, on the other hand, and the nature that one has as a hero or heroine, remain static. Nicholas does not become an ascetic as he grows up; his moderate nursing shows he is already an ascetic as an infant. Beaflor does not become beautiful as she matures; she already possesses an adult beauty as a very young maiden. The attributes of the noble nature and of the heroic nature are, after all, attributes admired in adults. There is no reason for them to change as the child grows up. Some children do experience change in the form of a dramatic conversion, but this is rare, even for saints. And others seem to change, but this change is only apparent. When Sigune and Schionatulander fall in love for the first time even they think something new has taken place. But in fact they are merely realizing "the nature of their lineage" which has been theirs from birth: "they were born of pure love."[170] While Sigune and Schionatulander seem to change, they, no less than the ascetic infant Nicholas, are merely revealing their unchanging nature. To a large extent the events of a MHG childhood do not represent gradual development but gradual revelation.[171]

There may be a certain tension between the deficient but dynamic nature of the child and the excellent but static nature of the hero. St. Ulrich, for example, when he was still too young to go to school, "revealed clearly in his outward behavior what filled his heart within, to the extent that his childhood enabled him to do so."[172] Ulrich's inherent nature, "the heart within," is already "full"—of the fear of God, disdain for lasciviousness, and the like.[173] And even when very young, Ulrich "revealed" this nature "clearly." But only up to a point, since the revelation is lim-

---

170. WTitrl 53,1–2: diu art ir geslehtes, (si wâren ûz lûterlîcher minne erborn).

171. MHG narrative is not alone in believing the individual to be basically immutable. The "idea that personality can change was almost completely alien to Greek and Latin biography. . . . a *vita* is an account of what sort of person [an individual] was, throughout his life" (Wiedemann, *Roman Empire*, 50).

172. StUlrc 150–52: als vil er mohte uor siner kintheit v̊zen zeiget er an den geberden wol wes sin herze was innen vol.

173. StUlrc 145–52.

ited by Ulrich's "childhood." What fills Ulrich's heart will be revealed fully only when "childhood" ceases to restrict the realization of the individual nature, in other words, when the child becomes an adult. MHG writers agree with Aquinas, who considers childhood "a defect [that] is not of the essence." Since "childhood is not of the essence of being human," Aquinas writes, "the same person who was a child becomes an adult."[174] The essential nature of the individual is static and adult: the adult is "*the same person* who was a child." Ulrich's heart does not change. It is fully realized, however, only when the deficiency of childhood, the "defect that is not of the essence," has passed.

174. Thomas Aquinas, *Summa Theologiae*, 2a2ae.4,4: Sed quando imperfectio non est de ratione rei imperfectæ. . . . sicut pueritia non est de ratione hominis, et ideo idem numero qui erat puer fit vir [translation, 31:129].

4. Nurture: The Limits of Intervention

In the United States, children of my generation were raised according to "Dr. Spock." And apparently we were not the only ones. Benjamin Spock's *Baby and Child Care* is still in print after more than 50 years, having sold well over thirty million copies. The book contains a wealth of information on how parents can foster the physical and emotional health of their children, all of it predicated on the assumption that the kind of care children receive is the primary factor in determining what sort of adults they will turn out to be. If they are loved they will be loving and disciplined; if they are respected they will trust themselves; if they are raised in an intelligent family, they will grow up to be intelligent.[1] Schools are equally important. If they are good they will foster cooperative, enterprising, and creative children who will grow up to be happy and useful adults.[2] Over and over Spock stresses the crucial importance of nurture, both at home and at school, in determining the way children grow up and the kind of adults they become. And we believe him: as a society we invest huge amounts of time and money in the care and education of our young. Presumably we expect it to make some difference.

Children in MHG narrative are also nurtured by their parents and instructed by their teachers. Isold's mother first engages a clerical tutor and then the accomplished Tristan to ensure that her daughter learns all that would be most impressive in a courtly lady. The efforts are successful: after instruction by Tristan, Isold can enchant a courtly audience with her musical skills. But the relation between teaching and accomplishment is not always so clear. Gregorius is sent to a monastery school, where he receives a thorough education in grammar, theology, and law. He does not become a monk, however, or a theologian, or even a lawyer. Instead he sets forth to pursue knighthood and, although he has received no training, he is successful in his very first knightly contests. How is it that Gregorius turns his

1. Spock, *Baby and Child Care*, 45, 406, 46, 293.
2. Spock, *Baby and Child Care*, 460, 479, 484–85.

back on the career he has been trained for and succeeds in one for which he has had no training whatsoever? To answer this question it will be necessary to learn something about the MHG attitude towards nurture and about the way MHG writers understand its relation to nature.

Nurture is of two kinds. Just after Mary has been born, Walther von Rheinau explains that her parents "raised her with care,"[3] and, as an example of this care, that Mary nursed at her mother's breast. After three years have passed we are told again that her parents "raised her well with great care" but, in addition, that they "taught her proper behavior, as one should":[4] virtue, modesty, patience, humility, and, above all, chastity. The first kind of nurture that Mary's parents provide, *care*, includes those activities, like nursing, that are directed primarily toward the child's physical well-being and of which the child is the more or less passive recipient. The second kind of nurture, *education*, includes all the various ways in which one might train, instruct, and discipline a child in order to shape her intellect or her behavior; such activities are fruitless unless the child is aware of what is going on. In what follows I will first discuss care, then education, then a number of general pedagogical topics, and finally the relation of nature and nurture.

Care

As soon as Mary is born she must be nursed, a task that is performed by her mother: "The pure, noble child did not suck the milk of a wet nurse, since her mother drew her to her own breast; she did not want to neglect to feed her herself."[5] Other kinds of care are mentioned a few lines later when Walther praises the purity and cleanliness of the infant: "The child was so clean that you couldn't find any spots on her swaddling bands when she was lifted up or swaddled, or when she was put in her cradle or taken out of it."[6] The care the Mary receives includes not only nursing but also swaddling, being laid in a cradle, picked up and put down.

3. WlMarl 899–901: Die friunt . . . zugen ez mit flîze.
4. WlMarl 1017–20: Diz edel kindelîn . . . Von vater und von muoter wart Mit allem flîze erzogen wol Und zuht gelêret, als man sol.
5. WlMarl 902–8: Daz edel reine kunne Souc keiner ammen spunne, Wan daz ez diu muoter sîn Wante an ir selber brüstelîn Noch wolde des nit vergezzen, Sin gaebe im selbe ze ezzen.
6. WlMarl 919–24: Ouch was daz kint sô reine, Daz man grôz noch kleine Flecken an sînen tuochen vant, Sô man ez ûfhuop ald bewant Noch swenne ez in die wiegen kam Ald sô manz ûf von dannan nam.

According to Berthold von Regensburg, parents must begin to care for their child from the very moment of conception. They must make sure that no children are conceived while the mother is menstruating, since such children are invariably blind, lame, or deaf, or suffer from leprosy, mean-spiritedness, or demonic possession.[7] Twelfth-century theologians regarded deformities and sickliness in children as punishment for their parents' violation of the Levitical prohibition against sex during menstruation, while those of the thirteenth century invoked natural laws according to which children conceived during menstruation are formed of corrupt menstrual blood and therefore deformed.[8] Care must also be taken during pregnancy, Berthold claims, since, "as soon as the child is alive in the mother's body and has received a soul, the devil is always there at once with his traps trying to prevent it from ever being born alive."[9] To this end the devil incites the husband of a pregnant mother to strike her and urges the mother to run and jump and lift things.[10] The devil hopes, of course, that the child will die before it is baptized and that it will therefore be condemned to perdition. The desire to forestall such a calamity motivates the *Schwabenspiegel* to specify that, no matter how grave an offense a pregnant woman has committed, she should not be punished in such a way as to endanger the child, "since then a beautiful soul would be lost, and a life."[11]

Very occasionally there is some indication of the attention a child receives immediately after birth. Wolfdietrich B was bathed, inspected for any marks on his body—a good thing, since he was later identified by the cross between his shoulder blades—and swaddled in rich clothes.[12] Swaddling, although widely practiced in the Middle Ages, is mentioned only rarely in MHG texts.[13]

7. BertvR 1:322,31–324,8.

8. Flandrin, "L'attitude," 155–57, 187–88.

9. BertvR 1:30,38–31,2: Und als daz kint in der muoter lîbe lebende wirt unde die sêle enphæhet, sô ist der tiuvel sâ zehant iemer dâ mit sîner lâge, wie er daz erwende, daz ez an die werlt iemer kume lebende.

10. BertvR 1:31,6–7, 14–16.

11. Schwsp La256: wan da wurde ein schoenv sele verlorn . vnd ein lip. —On the power of herbs to affect the growth of a fetus, a knowledge originating with Adam and transmitted after the Flood by women: RnfrBr 19716–853. On monstrous births: RnfrBr 19683–932.

12. WolfdB 139,3–141,4.

13. On bathing at birth: Alexandre-Bidon and Closson, *L'enfant*, 72–73; Hanawalt, *Ties*, 172. —Other MHG references to swaddling: Passnl H19,47–57; PhMarl 2072–93; PrLanc 2:624,22; SaeldH 1265–67, 1317–39, 1541, 1570; StDrth 740; WilWnd 2247–57; WlMarl 919–21. —On swaddling in the Middle Ages: Arnold, "Kindheit," 456; Le Roy Ladurie, *Montaillou*, 213; Shahar, *Childhood*, 84–88. Discussions of why swaddling is not the inhumane practice many take it to be: Chisholm and Richards, "Swaddling"; Kagan, *Nature*, 251–52; Konner, *Childhood*, 67–69; Wilson, "Motherhood," 194–95.

No aspect of child care receives as much attention from MHG writers as nursing. Many infants, like Parzival, are nursed by their mothers: "she was his nurse who had carried him in her womb."[14] Frequently, however, infants are entrusted to a wet nurse: after Beaflor was born "the child was given to its nurse."[15] Here, as in most cases where the mother is alive, the nursing seems to take place at the parents' home under the mother's supervision. In some cases the child is given to a wet nurse not by choice but by necessity: Tristrant's mother has died, Paris was abandoned, Lancelot has been abducted, and the wife of Wilhelm von Wenden does not produce a sufficient supply of milk.[16] The evidence from the MHG narratives corresponds roughly to what historians believe was the situation among the medieval aristocracy: maternal nursing was the ideal and was advocated by doctors, but wet-nursing was common.[17]

At the beginning of the twentieth century nursing was thought to resemble adult sexual intercourse. Freud believed that children "already enjoy sexual satisfaction at the same time they take nourishment"[18] and that the "expression of blissful satisfaction" on a child's face after nursing "will be repeated later after the experience of a sexual orgasm."[19] Nowadays, according to Jerome Kagan, nursing has become "analogous to adult trust rather than to sexual passion."[20] In MHG narrative nursing is related to two quite different responsibilities, one religious and one familial. When Herzeloide nurses Parzival she recalls the Virgin, "the highest queen, [who] offered her breasts to Jesus."[21] Herzeloide here invokes the feminine gen-

14. Parz 113,9–10: selbe was sîn amme diu in truoc in ir wamme.
15. MaiBfl 9,15: daz kint man sîner amme gap.
16. ETrist 122–25; KTrokj 566–71; PrLanc 1:20,34–35; WilWnd 2260–66, 2355–58.
17. Maternal nursing: GTrojk 133–39; JngTit 1109,4; Lanzlt 88–90; Passnl K6,70–7,12, K395,22–29; Pilat 300–302; RWeltc 8983–86; SaeldH 2156–58; StLudw 11,21–25; WlMarl 903–1008. —Wet nursing: BitDlb 2030–31; ELgAur 423,17–18; FlorBl 347–51; GottNf 50.2,1–6; HgMarg 115–22; KTrojk 28668–69; Marglg 19–22; Rother 4779–81; SaeldH 2097; StMarM 71–72; StUlrc 103–4; VrJngf Margaret 35–40; WlMarg 133–35; WzMarg 138–396. Others wet-nursed by necessity: AplTyr 2609–14; Hlgnlb 242,15–17; JWeltc 6439–40, 6651–52; Rennew 10212–47, 32637–41; StElis 510–11; WolfdB 177,1. —Nursing by animals: JWeltc 13653–62; KTrojk 530–41, 6026–51; GTrojk 1386–1402. Pepin is said to have been so short because his ill mother had to nurse him out of a horn: GuFrau 3029–30. —Attitudes and practices concerning nursing: Alexandre-Bidon and Closson, L'enfant, 112–31; Berkvam, Enfance, 50–54; Demaitre, "Idea," 474; Goodich, "Bartholomaeus," 80; McLaughlin, "Survivors," 115–17; Loffl-Haag, Kinder, 54–55; Shahar, Childhood, 53–76.
18. Freud, Drei Abhandlungen, 133: Es schien uns vielmehr, daß das Kind . . . schon bei der Nahrungsaufnahme sexuelle Befriedigung mitgenießt.
19. Freud, Vorlesungen 324: wenn [der Säugling] an der Brust gesättigt einschläft, zeigt er den Ausdruck einer seligen Befriedigung, der sich später nach dem Erleben des sexuellen Orgasmus wiederholen wird.
20. Kagan, Nature, 84.
21. Parz 113,18–19: diu hoeste küneginne Jêsus ir brüste bôt.

der ideal of the *Virgo lactans*. A different sort of obligation is cited in the *Passional* to explain why the mother of Bernard "nursed her children herself with her own milk, without a nurse. She wanted to give her children the vital nourishment directly from her pure lineage and to prevent them from acquiring additionally the attributes of another lineage [another *art*] from their nurse."[22] Here one finds expressed the widespread notion that a nurse's milk transmits to the child not only nourishment but also the qualities of the nurse. This should not surprise us. Since medieval writers believed that the attributes of the lineage were passed on through blood, and since they also believed, in the words of Konrad von Megenberg, that milk was nothing "other than a woman's blood that is transformed in the organs that nature has provided for this purpose,"[23] it makes perfect sense to assume that a child will acquire the qualities of the woman who nurses him. The narrator of *Jüngerer Titurel* cites this as a general law—"a child always turns to virtue [or not] according to the milk" it gets as an infant— and goes on to blame the decline in worthiness among the nobility on the fact that noble mothers no longer nurse their children themselves.[24]

The subject of feeding older children receives little attention, none of it in narrative texts. Berthold von Regensburg urges his listeners not to give their children too much to eat: if children acquire the habit of eating moderately when young they will preserve it as adults and remain healthy.[25] Konrad von Haslau condemns the opposite extreme, feeding children too little: children who are always hungry will act ignobly, will never share, and will always be looking for handouts.[26] Note that Berthold is only partly and Konrad not at all interested in the short-term physical consequences for the child of over- or underfeeding; they are much more concerned with the effect of childhood feeding on the development of adult habits. As with nursing, so with feeding: nurturing activities that might seem to us primarily physical are of concern to MHG writers for their role in shaping less tangible qualities of the individual.[27]

The kinds of care discussed above—to which one might add baths,

---

22. Passnl K395,22–29: die muter mit ir selbes spune ir kint zoch sunder amme. von irme reinen stamme wolde si vil ebene die libnar zu dem lebene iren kinden selbe geben und nicht lan schepfen sie beneben von der amme ein ander art.

23. Konrad von Megenberg, *Yconomica*, 1.2.8 [p. 79,18–19]: Nam quid aliud est lac quam sanguis femine iterato digestus in organis a natura deputatis?

24. JngTit 1110,1: Ein kint ie nach dem spunne sich an di tugende wendet.

25. BertvR 1:35,24–28.

26. Jünglg 1131–60.

27. On children's eating: BertvR 1:433,26–434,1, 2:205,19–206,3; Rennr 9541–45.

cradles, and soothing music[28]—are considered appropriate to young children and are ordinarily provided by women. Care for young children is, according to Pharaoh's mother, "the privilege, duty, and custom of women."[29] Those mothers are most admirable who perform this duty themselves: Wigalois's "faultless mother did not want to leave him for a single day; out of love she cared for him herself, along with many other noblewomen."[30] But many delegate responsibility to other women: Margaret's "father and mother gave the child to a good nurse, who raised her very tenderly."[31]

Education

Mary's education begins at home, where, from the time she is three, "her father and mother taught her proper behavior, as one should."[32] Mary's parents expect a lot. She is supposed to be virtuous and modest, to seek the friendship of good people, to be patient and humble, just in her works and straightforward in speech, to honor old people and be merciful to the poor, "to preserve chastity above all," and to "lead her entire life according to the teachings of the Prophets."[33] Then, when she is seven, Mary is sent to Jerusalem to become one of twelve maidens who serve in the Temple. She "learned from them whatever could be considered excellent in a woman."[34] Although Mary "had soon learned how to weave, sew, spin, and ornament

28. Bathing: ELgAur 21,5–6; KndJsu 1798–1809; Passnl H35,63–69, K6,52–64; PhMarl 3010–21; StElis 497–504; StLudw 14,14–18; WlMarl 4355–57; WolfdB 139,3–4, 172,1. —Cradles: JWeltc 12322–23; KndJsu 1196–99; Kudrn 1501,4; PrLanc 1:6,12–13; SaeldH 1265–67; StElis 505–9; StLudw 14,7–9; SwrzPr P62,125–29; WolfdB 141,1; WTotnz 216. —Music: EngSwb 1,17–19; GottNf 50.1,7–9; SaeldH 1605.
29. JWeltc 6437–38: ich wil nach frouwen reht heizen ziehen disen kneht.
30. Wglois 1222–25: sîn reiniu muoter woldez nie von ir gelâzen einen tac; vor liebe si sîn selbe pflac und ander manic vrouwe hêr.
31. WlMarg 133–35: dô gab ez vater und muoter einer ammen guoter, diu ez vil zartlîche zôch. —Child care: BitDlb 2030–31; ETrist 120–25; GrMarl 312; GTrist 2045–55; GTrojk 1419–37; Jakobr 2569; JngTit 782,2–4, 807,1, 1109,3–4, 1111,2; KTrojk 572–79; Kudrn 23,1–3, 198,1–4; MaiBfl 15,24–26; Melrnz 170–71; Passnl H82,8–14, H314,41–44, K7,20–23, K93,64–65, K327,50–56; PrLanc 1:20,34–35; RAlexr 1282–95; RnfrBr 23342–419; RpParz 143,34–38; Väterb 34422–28; Wglois 3373–74; Wigmur 131–43; WlMarl 1017–52; WolfdA 34,1–2; ZwöMön 24–25. —In a few cases care is provided by a man: AplTyr 7151–53; GuFrau 125–33; JngTit 673,1–2, 677,1–2; KTrojk 597–601; MaiBfl 194,31–40; UAlexr 1247–49.
32. WlMarl 1017–20: Diz edel kindelîn . . . Von vater und von muoter wart . . . zuht gelêret, als man sol.
33. WlMarl 1031–32: Vor allen dingen die meit Lêrte man behalten kiuschecheit; 1051–52: nâch der lêre der wîsagen Solde si al ir leben tragen.
34. WlMarl 1165–66: [Marîâ] lernete von in, Swaz wîbes frome mahte sîn.

silk with gold,"[35] we are never told who actually taught her. She seems to learn these skills on her own.

These passages illustrate three important characteristics of MHG education. First, as Mary's mother and father are clearly aware, education is primarily the responsibility of parents. Second, MHG parents, like Mary's, often delegate immediate responsibility for the education of their children to others. Third, the special nature of MHG heroes and heroines, like Mary, often enables them to know things without having received the instruction one would expect. In what follows I will consider each of these in turn.

The belief that parents have primary responsibility for raising their children rests on powerful authority. Paul exhorted fathers to give their children "the instruction, and the correction, which belong to a Christian upbringing."[36] Augustine taught that of the three "goods" of marriage, the second, offspring, "means that children are to be lovingly received, brought up with tender care, and given a religious education."[37] In general, the thirteenth century saw an increase in the importance theologians attached to parents' responsibility for child rearing.[38] Not surprisingly, MHG preachers and social critics share these views. Berthold von Regensburg admonishes his listeners: "for just as you and your children desire heaven, so should you raise your children yourselves, since no one owes it to them as much as you."[39] Hugo von Trimberg, typically, appeals not to the hope of heaven but to the certainty of hell: anyone, he writes, who "does not put a stop to his children's bad ways in their youth will earn God's anger along with them and his soul will perish on account of his negligence; thus it is written in the Book of Kings."[40]

Threats and promises notwithstanding, only a few MHG parents are actually shown instructing their children. In religious texts parents encourage virtue and piety: Adam "taught Cain valuable lessons, as a father does

35. WlMarl 1179–82: Weben, naejen, spinnen, Sîden mit golde zinnen Diu edel maget drâte Wol gelernet hâte.
36. Ephesians 6.4.
37. Augustine, *Genesis*, 9.7 [p. 78].
38. Brundage, *Law, Sex*, 430.
39. BertvR 1:35,2–4: wan iu und iuwern kinden des himelrîches als nôt ist, sô sult ir iuwer kinder selber ziehen, wan sîn in nieman sô wol schuldic ist als ir.
40. Rennr 16893–97: Swer sînen kinden in der jugent Mit flîze niht wert ir untugent, Der verdienet mit in gotes zorn Und wirt üm sîn lazheit verlorn; in der künige buoche ist daz geschriben. —On parents' educational obligations: BertvR 1:35,12–16, 2:58,22–37; Crone 314–16; DtCato 88; JngTit 504,4–505,2; KTrojk 597–99; StFran 418–45; SwrzPr F67,522–68,531; Warng 1495–98; WilOrl 2532–39; WilWnd 1248–55. —See also Flandrin, *Families*, 174–80; Shahar, *Childhood*, 112–17.

for his child,"[41] admonishing him to love and serve God, to do good, not to swear, curse, or bear hatred and envy in his heart. In secular texts one finds three kinds of parental instruction. Some mothers teach their daughters about love: when Lavinia poses the impatient question, "For God's sake, who is this Love?"[42] her mother offers an introductory lesson. One bourgeois mother teaches her daughter to read the Psalter—the Psalter being the text on which reading was taught in the Middle Ages and one particularly associated with women's reading.[43] Other parents make speeches when their sons leave home. As Willehalm von Orlens sets out for the English court his foster father urges him to love God, to be loyal, virtuous, chaste, well behaved, generous, and moderate; not to lie or brag or promise more than he can perform; to seek the company of those who are loyal, to honor women, and to follow good advice.[44] A number of didactic texts—*Winsbecke*, *Winsbeckin*, the *Magezoge*—are structured as dialogues of instruction between a parent and a child. They, like the parents in the narratives, are primarily concerned not to train children in particular skills but to impart general precepts of virtuous and admirable behavior.[45]

Most MHG parents do not educate their children themselves but delegate at least part of the responsibility for their children's education to some other person or institution. There are four arrangements by which this can be done: the tutored court education, in which the child grows up under the direct supervision of a personal tutor, usually at the court of her parents or guardians; the fostered court education, in which the child serves at a foreign court under the general supervision of the head of the court; the school education, in which the child is sent to a nonmonastic school; and the monastic education, in which the child is educated at a religious house.

41. LAdam 1842–43: Er begunde yme gute lere dun, Als vatter sinem kinde dut.
42. Eneit 261,27: dorch got, wer is diu Minne?
43. StdabA 182–204; Bumke, *Höfische Kultur*, 474; Grundmann, "Frauen und Literatur," 133–34; Rösener, "Höfische Frau," 217–18.
44. WilOrl 3386–450.
45. Parental instruction: JWeltc 1287–304; Magzog 115–28; PartMl 268–71; PhMarl 471–92; Schnkd 35–42; UWilhm W17,1–5; Väterb 252–60, 27763–75, 34439–43; Winsbk 1,1–10. —Mothers who teach their daughters about love: Niblgn 14,1–17,4; Winsbn 21,1–45,10. Rennewart tells his son Malefer about love: Rennew 19259–99. —Parental speeches of valedictory instruction: Englhd 336–75; FrdSwb 33–52; Greg 243–65; Jakobr 341–58; Parz 127,13–128,10; PrLanc 1:120,3–123,31, 1:128,12–13; RnfrBr 11618–784; UWilhm W21,14–28,19. Such speeches may be related to the folk-tale pattern in which a young man is given advice on setting out into the world (Green, "Parzival's Departure," 364, 381). —Similar speeches after the children are adults: JngTit 500,1–600,4; Wglois 11518–52. Ulrich von Etzenbach appends to his *Alexander* a completely independent speech of parental instruction: UAlexr 27780–993. Meliur speaks to Partonopier in a similar vein when he leaves her to defend France: PartMl 2840–930. —Fathers' instruction as opposed to tutors': Kästner, *Lehrgespräche*, 231–32.

The most luxurious education available to MHG children is the *tutored court education*, in which children remain at home and are taught by one or more private tutors. Tutors, as Berthold von Regensburg explains, are assigned by sex: "the [male] children of high lords are given [male] tutors, who are always with them and teach them proper behavior at all times; and young noble women are given female tutors, who teach them proper behavior and virtue at all times."[46] For youths this represents a change in the sex of their caregivers, since they, like maidens, spend their earliest years in the care of women. An aspiring macho like Dietleib welcomes the change: "he was delighted to be parted from the nurses who had cared for him previously" and to be "placed in the company of warriors."[47] Although the status of the tutors varies considerably, their social rank is always less than that of their charges: Aristotle, "wise and quite gray with age," is Alexander's "master";[48] "a monk disciplined Lancelot and taught him courtliness,"[49] while "the worthiest knights took charge of Wigalois."[50]

The paramount goal of a tutored court education is to "teach courtliness,"[51] a project in which the "proper behavior" mentioned by Berthold plays a large role. Dulciflorie is taught "to behave well, to stand and to bow, to speak and to be silent, as well as self-control and how to acquire a good name."[52] Wigalois is taught "to speak and to stand as good manners require."[53] Often the requirements of courtly speech receive special mention. The Schneekind learns "to speak and to remain silent as is fitting."[54] Males are also taught courtly behavior toward women. Graf Rudolf be-

---

46. BertvR 1:34,31–34: dar umbe gît man der hôhen herren kinden zuhtmeister, die alle zît bî in sint unde sie ze allen zîten zuht lêrent; unde den juncfrouwen eine zuhtmeisterin, diu sie alle zît zuht unde tugent lêret.

47. BitDlb 2030–31: vil gerne er sich scheiden liez von ammen die sîn phlâgen ê; 2028–29: den jungen recken . . . bî helden dô man wesen hiez.

48. ArPhlS 40–42: der künec im gewinnen bat einen meister, der was wise und gar von alter grise.

49. PrLanc 1:20,36: ein mönch . . . yn zuchtiget und yn wyßte hubscheit.

50. Wglois 1236–38: die tiursten . . . rîter dâ . . . underwunden sich sîn sâ. —A few maidens are tutored by males: GTrist 7708–27, 7962–8141; JWeltc 14636. —Hagen is also eager to escape the care of women: Kudrn 24,1–25,4. —Academic tutors: AlxusF 144–45; RAlexr 1352–89; UAlexr 1259–92. Clerical tutors: BMärtr 27975–83; Bussrd 59–65; FlorBl 662–63; GTrist 7696–727; KSilvr 116–21. Knightly tutors: BitDlb 2028–29; GTrist 10770–74; HvKemp 94; Kudrn 574,2–4; PrLanc 1:131,15–17, 33–34; WilOrl 3313–21. —Requirements for a good tutor: KTirol 44,1–7; SfHelb 7.1147–54. Bad tutors: Fridnk 49,17–18.

51. GRudlf γb 28: wisen zu der hovischeit; PrLanc 1:34,10: húbscheit leren.

52. Dulcfl 160–63: wol gebâren, Stân unde nîgen, Sprechen unde swîgen, Dar zuo zuht und êre.

53. Wglois 1239–40: si lêrtenz . . . mit zühten sprechen unde stên.

54. Schnkd 39: mit zühte sprechen unde swîgen.

lieves a youth should be taught to "go willingly to the ladies; he should stand before them and sit beside them with propriety."[55]

In addition to manners, those who receive a court education may be taught "an abundance of courtly pastimes."[56] Lanzelet is taught "to sing bravely."[57] Isold is instructed to "play the fiddle admirably in the French manner, to touch the lire expertly, and to draw tones from the harp with mastery."[58] Lancelot is taught "chess and backgammon and all those games that one can play with one's hands."[59] Some of the youths are also taught hunting and falconry: Tristan learns "to track and to hunt,"[60] and Alexander is taught how "to handle hunting birds in a courtly manner."[61]

Those who receive a court education frequently receive some instruction in foreign languages. Schoifloris is taught Greek, Italian, and Latin.[62] Isold knows Irish, French, and Latin; Tristan knows a half a dozen other languages as well.[63] Mastery of French, a sign of courtliness, enables one to participate in the international discourses of courtly culture. When Beaflor, who is Roman, lands on an unknown coast and encounters Mai, who is Greek, she facilitates their acquaintance by saying: "You strike me as so courtly, sir, do you know any French?"[64] As it turns out, he does, so they fall in love. A passage like this recalls the historical situation in the twelfth and thirteenth centuries, when French had acquired the status of an international language, a secular equivalent to the church's Latin.[65]

55. GRudlf γb 36–38: zu den vrouwen sal er gerne gan, gezogentliche vor in stan unde ouch bi in sizzen. —General instruction in courtly manners: MaiBfl 195,30–31; RAlexr 1387–89; Wigmur 342–43; WlGast 402–4, 577–80. —Instruction in proper speech: ETrist 152–58; Ksrchr 1648–51; Lanzlt 261; Magzog 243–44, 281; WilOrl 3413–22; Winsbk 23,5; WlGast 389–90, 405–10, 465–66, 581–90, 711–60. —Gurnemanz's fateful advice to Parzival (Parz 141,17–21), often reduced to an injunction against asking too many questions, is little more than an elaboration of the standard teaching just cited from the *Schneekind*. See Hennig, "Gurnemanzlehren."—Courtesy toward women: ETrist 163–65; Lanzlt 256–60; Parz 172,7–173,6; WilOrl 3433–37; Winsbk 8,1–16,10; WolfdD 3.2,1; Virgnl 361,5.
56. KTrojk 6168–69: von allen hovewunnen . . . den überfluz.
57. Lanzlt 266–67: die vrouwen lêrten in . . . baltlîche singen.
58. GTrist 7986–93: si kunde . . . videlen wol ze prise in welhischer wise. ir vingere die kunden . . . die liren wol gerüeren und uf der harpfen vüeren die dœne mit gewalte.
59. PrLanc 1:34,25: schachzabel und wurffzabel und allerhand spiel das man spielen mocht mit den handen.
60. GTrist 2118: birsen unde jagen.
61. RAlexr 1868–69: mit vederspil gebâren hovelîche. —Instruction in courtly pastimes: AplTyr 1893–930; ETrist 132–35; GTrist 7981–97; KTrojk 6164–67; Lanzlt 262–67, 290–91; RAlexr 1867; Schnkd 35–42; Wigmur 344–45; WilOrl 2776–80.
62. MaiBfl 195,8.
63. GTrist 7984–86, 11946–49, 3690–3703.
64. MaiBfl 57,11–12: ir dunket mich sô kurtois: herre, kunnet ir iht franzois?
65. Bischoff, "Foreign Languages," 210. —Others who learn languages: ErnstB 70–71 [French or Italian, Latin]; FlorBl 825–43 [Latin]; LAlexr S202 [Greek, Latin]; RpParz 47,37–

Mastery of Latin enables one to participate in the world of school learning. Aristotle introduces the young Alexander to "the letters A B C D E,"[66] and Willehalm von Orlens is "taught to read in books."[67] In the medieval context this means elementary instruction in Latin. Greater knowledge brings more interesting lessons: Flore and Blanscheflur first learn about love from books, Titurel from reading Ovid.[68] In a few cases young heroes are offered a relatively elaborate educational program. According to Rudolf von Ems, Alexander was instructed in "the seven liberal arts"—although the only ones mentioned are music, geometry, and rhetoric.[69] Although didactic writers like Thomasin von Zerclaere and Hugo von Trimberg insist on the importance of learning for noble children and especially for future princes,[70] reading and other school subjects figure in the stories of only a few of the MHG children who receive a tutored court education— Lambrecht's Alexander, Tristan, Isold, Flore, Blanscheflur, Willehalm von Orlens, Rudolf's Alexander, Titurel, Meliur, Seifrit's Alexander.[71]

While literacy was rare among the medieval German nobility in general, learning was more strongly associated with kingship.[72] Historically it was not uncommon for the first member of a dynasty who became king to be unlettered, but to make sure his heir received a careful education.[73] While this pattern is not always honored in the literary texts—Tristrant, Siegfried, and Charlemagne, all kings' sons, are taught nothing of books— in the case of Meliur it is applied to an emperor's daughter. Since her father had no sons, she reports, he has her taught by "the greatest masters who could be found," so that "when he left the empire in my hands after his death I would be better able to guide the country and its people and preserve their glory."[74] Others, like Alexander, are given more specific

---

40 [Latin]; WilOrl 2754–65 [Latin and others]; WWilhm 283,21–22 [French]. —Foreign words as an ornament to courtly speech: GTrist 2282–92. —Foreign languages in Gottfried's *Tristan*: Werner, "Tristan." Historical evidence of the value placed on knowledge of foreign languages: Bumke, *Höfische Kultur*, 436–37.

66. ArPhlS 70–71: die buochstaben a b c d e.

67. WilOrl 2764–65: lerten . . . an bûchen lesen.

68. FlorBl 712–47; JngTit 190,1–2.

69. RAlexr 2158: liberâles septem artes; 2161: der siben liste meisterschaft.

70. WlGast 9197–298; Rennr 1245–52.

71. Reading: FlorBl 712–17; GTrist 2065–86; JngTit 184,3; SAlexr 600; UAlexr 1277–80; WlGast 9197–200. —For the seven liberal arts see note 118. —A few texts indicate the age at which their heroes and heroines began the study of books and languages. Five: WilOrl 2744– 71. Six: FlorBl 627; SAlexr 597–600. Seven: GTrist 2056–67; RAlexr 1352–53. Schoifloris seems to have mastered his languages by the age of eight: MaiBfl 196,24–26.

72. Jaeger, *Courtliness*, 226.

73. Bumke, *Höfische Kultur*, 603–6.

74. PartMl 8080: die besten meister, die man vant; 8074–77: swenn er daz rîche lieze nâch sîme tôde in mîner hant, daz ich liute, êr unde lant berihten künde deste baz.

instruction in kingship: Aristotle delivers a long lecture about choosing counselors, administering justice, waging war, displaying mercy and liberality, and avoiding loose women and drunkenness.[75]

Of the disciplines that can constitute a tutored court education, MHG writers devote the most attention to knighthood—which, as Tristan himself explains, "must always take its beginning in childhood or it will never grow strong."[76] There seem to be two not always clearly differentiated aspects to this training. The first is the more general training of the body. Lanzelet, for example, is not taught knighthood until he leaves his childhood home, but while still there he does receive instruction in fencing, running, jumping, wrestling, throwing stones, and hurling the spear.[77] The second is knightly training proper. Wigalois was taught "a great deal about every kind of knightly skill: riding the bohort and jousting, breaking strong spears, fencing and throwing the lance."[78] Future knights are also instructed in the ideology of "the order of knighthood,"[79] often at the time of their knightly investiture by the person who performs the rite: Mark tells Tristan that he should be humble, upright, truthful, and well-mannered, kind to the poor and proud to the rich; that he should honor women and, above all, display liberality and loyalty.[80]

While the subjects taught in a tutored court education vary widely in number and content, MHG writers clearly feel they all belong together. Sometimes the subjects are collected into a single list. According to Lambrecht, Alexander's education—in Greek, Latin, music, astronomy, fighting, and statecraft—is provided by a group of tutors numbered one through six. In the description of Schoifloris's education, reading, sing-

75. RAlexr 1401–830; UAlexr 1383–642. —Education in kingship: GTrist 2131–43; LAlexr S245–51; Parz 170,21–171,12; RBarlm 25,1; UAlexr 27783–993; WilOrl 2801–21.

76. GTrist 4417–20: wan ritterschaft . . . diu muoz ie von der kintheit nemen ir anegenge oder si wirt selten strenge.

77. Lanzlt 278–99.

78. Wglois 1254–58: aller hande rîter spil lêrten in die rîter vil: buhurdieren unde stechen, diu starken sper zebrechen, schirmen unde schiezen.

79. PrLanc 1:119,8–9: dem orden der ritterschafft.

80. GTrist 5023–24, 5018–40. —Physical training: Erec 9281–85; ETrist 140–44; GTrojk 1454–62; JWeltc 13667–76, 14555–58; KTrojk 4730–48, 6052–161, 6174–273, 6308–30; Wigmur 342–48; WolfdB 264,1–265,4. —Knightly training: AlxusA 175–79; BitDlb 2116–43; ETrist 145–52; GRudlf 7b 17–18, 30–32, 41–44; KTrojk 6238–57; Kudrn 3,2–4; LAlexr S227–44; MaiBfl 196,21–23; Parz 156,4–158,12, 173,11–174,9; PrLanc 1:34,15–20; RAlexr 1862–66; SAlexr 608–15; Wglois 1237–39; WilOrl 2769–75; Winsbk 17,1–21,10; WolfdD 3.3,1–4,4. —Ideology of knighthood: JngTit 1143,1–1147,4; MaiBfl 83,29–38; PrLanc 1:119,39–123,31; Virgnl 210,7–211,13. —Of those texts that indicate when their heroes begin to receive instruction in knighthood, most give the age of twelve: AlxusA 175–79; RAlexr 1862–69; SAlexr 608–10; Wglois 1234. Tristan is said to learn knighthood between seven and fourteen (GTrist 2056–67, 2131–37) and Willehalm von Orlens sometime after he is eight (WilOrl 2769–71). Paris begins physical education at ten (JWeltc 13663–64).

ing, wrestling, and fencing all figure in the same sentence.[81] In other cases the entire curriculum is entrusted to a single tutor: Kurneval, Curvenal, Chiron, Tristan, and Dulciflorie's "loyal tutor"[82] are teachers of all subjects. In these ways MHG writers indicate that the seemingly heterogeneous "disciplines" that appear in a tutored court education actually constitute a single "knowledge."

In an important sense this is knowledge for its own sake. While the children who receive a tutored court education will have many opportunities to display as adults some of the things they learned—primarily courtly manners and knighthood—other subjects that they are taught play no subsequent role in the plot. Lambrecht's Alexander never makes use of his Latin, nor does he display his accomplishments in singing or astronomy. Lanzelet never plays the harp or the fiddle, nor is Dulciflorie ever seen embroidering. Conversely, adults sometimes reveal skills absent from the accounts of their education. Dulciflorie cites information that "one reads in books,"[83] Wolfdietrich A is "learned"[84] enough to comprehend a crucial document, and Beaflor is "so courtly" that she can "read you any story you want in French."[85] Yet none of these is said to have received instruction in reading or languages as a child. There seems to be no necessary relation between the skills children are taught and the skills they display as adults. They are taught things that they do not use, and they know things that they were not taught.

Nor is there any simple relation between the educational programs represented in MHG texts and the education offered at German courts in the twelfth and thirteenth centuries. Surely noble youths were taught knightly skills (the sons of Frederick Barbarossa by two of the most distinguished imperial ministerials),[86] and there is evidence that maidens were taught needlework.[87] However, there is not much evidence that the elaborate educational programs depicted in the Alexander romances of Lambrecht or Rudolf were common at medieval German courts. "One searches in vain," according to C. Stephen Jaeger, "for indications in Germany that it was customary for the sons of nobles to receive an education in letters."[88] Until well into the fourteenth century most German nobles, including fig-

---

81. MaiBfl 195,3–6.
82. Dulcfl 128: Eine getriuwe meisterin.
83. Dulcfl 360: Man liset an den buochen.
84. WolfdA 304,1: ir sît gelêret.
85. MaiBfl 230,30–32: ich lâze iu mîne tohter lesen swelch mære ir welt in franzois. mîn tohter ist sô kurtois.
86. Fleckenstein, "Mainzer Hoftage," 401.
87. Opitz, *Frauenalltag*, 63.
88. Jaeger, *Courtliness*, 224.

ures like Frederick Barbarossa and Henry the Lion, were illiterate.[89] The educational program that is detailed in the case of Alexander and the others receives attention not because it is required by the plot nor because it represents historical practice but because it itself is of interest. It seems to represent an ideal of courtly education that is considered worthy of elaboration in its own right.

This ideal has a pedigree. It appears in two classes of MHG texts, of which the first, those in which Aristotle teaches Alexander, tend to stress school learning and kingship: Lambrecht's *Alexanderlied*, Rudolf's *Alexander*, and to a lesser extent both versions of *Aristoteles und Phyllis*. Texts in the second group, those based directly on French romances, tend to place more emphasis on courtliness and knighthood: *Tristrant*, *Graf Rudolf*, *Lanzelet*, *Parzival*, *Wigalois*, *Lancelot*; *Tristan*, *Flore und Blanscheflur*, and *Willehalm von Orlens* also stress book learning. Before 1200 tutored court education appears in all secular texts that narrate that part of childhood that might include education. After about 1200, however, although the tutored court education is represented in a substantial number of texts, other narratives are written from which it is absent. In romances that are not based directly on French sources (*Titurel*, *Tandareis und Flordibel*, *Meleranz*) the protagonist receives a fostered court education (discussed below), and in other texts (*Nibelungenlied*, Stricker's *Karl*, *Karl und Galie*, *Crone* [Arthur], *Wolfdietrich A*, *Rennewart* [Malefer], Ulrich's *Willehalm*) educational details are completely missing. After 1250 the tutored court education is rare. Schoifloris, in the only text of this group possibly based on a French source,[90] is the only one held to the traditional curriculum.[91] In Ulrich's *Alexander*, despite a long speech by Aristotle, the educational program is less comprehensive and coherent than in earlier accounts.[92] Wigamur and Konrad's Achilles receive relatively detailed educations—not at court, however, but in the wilderness.[93] The education of other children is fragmentary (Dietleib, Wolfdietrich B, Titurel)[94] or missing (Paris in Konrad's and in the Göttweiger *Trojanerkrieg*, Achilles in the latter, Wilhelm von Wenden and his sons), or fostered (Alyze and Fivianz, in Ulrich's *Willehalm*),[95] or takes place at the university (prince in *Bussard*).[96]

89. Bumke, "Bestandsaufnahme," 453–55; Bumke, *Höfische Kultur*, 601–6; Grundmann, "Frauen und Literatur," 142; Jordan, *Heinrich*, 26; Wendehorst, "Wer konnte lesen," 18.

90. Fechter, VL, 5:1165.

91. MaiBfl 195,1–196,26.

92. UAlexr 1260–1642.

93. Wigmur 342–50; KTrojk 6052–469.

94. BitDlb 2121–43; WolfdB 264,1–266,4; JngTit 184,1–197,4.

95. UWilhm 316,2–333,17.

96. Bussrd 49–103. —Careful education also appears in *Dulciflorie* and *Wigamur*. I have

Throughout the Middle Ages education was the province of the church. Thus it is not surprising that young saints, especially those destined for a clerical career, routinely go to school, as will be seen below. And yet clerical education, while mentioned frequently, is treated perfunctorily: it is so well known that it is of little interest. The writers of secular texts, however, drawing on the authority of Aristotle, tutor of princes, and the cultural cachet of France, capital of courtliness, turn education into part of a cultural argument. They represent an ideal of courtly education that is to a certain extent independent of the needs of the narratives in which it appears and to a greater extent an idealization of the historical practice of the medieval German nobility. We have our own liberal arts, they seem to be saying—manners, languages, chivalry, music, and so forth—and these must be acquired by systematic instruction in the same way grammar, rhetoric, logic, and the rest must be learned. We also have our own great teachers, Aristotle, for example, just as the church has Gregory or Augustine. This claim, fully justified neither by narrative need nor historical practice, seems to have been part of the larger effort of the secular aristocracy to establish a cultural position of its own, an effort in which the development of a vernacular literature itself had a large role to play.[97]

The ideal of courtly education and the claim it implies are advanced most vigorously in the second half of the twelfth century but decrease in importance in the course of the thirteenth. The thirteenth century is the same period in which the debate over the nature of true nobility, whether it was the result of birth or of individual virtue, is gradually settled, for nobles at least, in favor of the former.[98] And it is the same period in which the class of knights becomes restricted to those who are of knightly birth.[99] The three phenomena cannot be unrelated. Education makes sense in a world where distinction can be attained through discipline and effort, but

included Gottfried's Tristan among those who receive a tutored court education because the source and the program of his education are similar to the others. Tristan's education does not take place at court, however, but while traveling about in foreign countries (GTrist 2060–63). —Support for the assumptions concerning sources and chronology can be found in chapter 8. —During just those years when German writers had a particularly high opinion of education, Wolfram, in adapting his source, modified it so that Parzival is more profoundly affected by those who teach him than was Perceval (Huby, "Entwicklung," 261–63). That Parzival should thus serve to illustrate the efficacy of education is all the more remarkable in that, among MHG children, he is one of those most completely determined by his inherited nature—as Huby also recognizes (266).

97. On courtly liberal arts: Bumke, "Bestandsaufnahme," 453; Kuhn, "Determinanten," 84–85.

98. Borck, "Adel, Tugend," 453.

99. Fleckenstein, "Abschließung," 375–76.

it is hardly worth the trouble in a world where distinction is determined by birth alone. The claim that we are special because we can shape ourselves is gradually overpowered by the claim, which in any case had always been quite strong, that we are special because we were born that way.

Many MHG children are educated not at the courts of their parents but at other courts to which they have been sent for the purpose, where they receive a *fostered court education*. While those who stay home are taught by specialists who are their social inferiors, those who are sent away learn by serving members of the court who are their equals or superiors. Although they are sometimes assigned a particular mentor—Arthur "entrusted Wigalois to Sir Gawein," who "took charge of the youth with his teaching"[100]—for the most part they learn not from precept but from imitation and practice. Fosterage means service.[101] Children serve in the bedchamber: whenever Guenevere "went to bed Lady Flordibel never failed to be with her in her chamber, early and late, to serve her as was appropriate."[102] They serve at meals: whenever the king of England "sat at table, Willehalm did not neglect to serve him well, as was his custom."[103] And they serve knights: whenever they travelled to tournaments Wigalois "was more than ready [to serve] all the knights of the Round Table."[104]

The purpose of such service is to learn courtliness and knighthood. Kudrun's father "sent her to her closest relatives in Denmark to learn courtly behavior."[105] A heathen king leaves his nephew "in Partonopier's service so that he might master the language of the country and become familiar with the ways of the courtly French."[106] Some children are first tutored at home and then sent elsewhere to complete their education. The mother of Herzog Ernst B "had him taught both French and Latin" at home before "she sent him to Constantinople to learn good conduct and manners."[107] There is considerable evidence that fosterage was not just a literary but also an historical practice. In 1162 Landgraf Ludwig II of Thu-

100. Wglois 1594–96: [er] bevalch in . . . dem herren Gâwein; 1601–2: her Gâwein underwant sich sâ des knaben mit sîner lêre.

101. Bumke, "Bestandsaufnahme," 455 n. 151.

102. TandFl 995–99: swanne diu künegîn slâfen gie, vrow Flordibel daz niht enlie si waere vruo unt spâte bî ir zer kemenâte unt diente ir, als ir wol gezam.

103. WilOrl 5245–46: Der künic do ze tische sas, Wilhelm des niht vergas Er diente im wol nach sinen sitten.

104. Wglois 1610–11: den von der tavelrunde was er allen vil bereit.

105. Kudrn 575,3: die sant er ze Tenemarke durch zuht ir næhsten mâgen.

106. PartMl 6524: in sîme dienste; 9905–9: durch das er . . . die sprâche von dem lande gelernet unde erkande der hübeschen Kärlingære site.

107. ErnstB 70–73: daz kint bat sie dô lêren beide welhisch und latîn. ouch sande sie daz kindelîn durch zuht ze Kriechen.

ringia wrote to the king of France asking him to accept two of his sons at the French court.[108] In 1211 the four-year-old Elizabeth of Hungary arrived at the Thuringian court, to be raised there in anticipation of her marriage to Ludwig IV. At the end of the century the Bavarian *Hofordnung* of 1294 prescribes that eight *juncherren*, noble children from the country, should always be at court to serve.[109] Except for Ulrich von Liechtenstein, who learns to write love letters,[110] none of the MHG children receive instruction in letters while serving at court, which seems to correspond to historical practice, at least in Germany.[111]

When MHG writers represent their child protagonists serving at court they are not so much interested in the educational arrangements, which are mentioned only in passing, as they are in the narrative developments that may occur. Fosterage brings Wigalois and Meleranz to King Arthur's, where they acquire renown and meet adventure. It brings Tandareis and Flordibel together so they can fall in love. Writers are drawn not to the educational but to the narrative opportunities that fosterage provides.

Many MHG parents arrange for their children to receive a *school education*. When Alexis "entered his eighth year," writes Hermann von Fritzlar, "he was placed in school, according to the custom of the noble Romans."[112] Hermann is right, many Romans did send their children to school,[113] and the parents of many early Christian saints do the same. In school, as Eugenia reminds her schoolmates, they "plumbed the recondite logic of Aristotle, the wisdom of Plato, and the opinions of Socrates."[114] She and others become learned "in the seven liberal arts."[115] Those who are brought up as Christians follow a different curriculum: Alexis learned "the New Testa-

108. Brandt, "Hermann I. in Paris?"
109. Bumke, *Höfische Kultur*, 434.
110. Frndst 33,2–5.
111. Fenske, "Knappe," 76–89. —Fostered court education: AlxusA 185–86; BitDlb 3209–401; Erec 1273–77, 2867–68, 9281–85; Frndst 16,2–3, 22,1–6, 26,3–5, 29,2–8, 44,6–8; Klage 2076–83, 2182–93; Ksrchr 14296–307; Lohgrn 7261–86; Niblgn 1194,4–1195,3, 1916,1–1917,1; RpParz 47,41–44; Parz 94,24–26, 145,11–12, 344,19–348,22, 528,17–21, 667,19–21; ORmchr 22945–65; Passnl H83,21; PartMl 256–61; StElis 646–55; TandFl 198–201; UWilhm 29,16–31, 316,2–13; WilOrl 3509–23, 3577–79; WWilhm 23,1; WolfdB 3,3–4,4. —According to Hugo von Trimberg, fosterage used to make sense, but nowadays courts have declined so drastically one might as well send one's children to a tavern (Rennr 535–54). —On historical fosterage: Boswell, *Kindness*, 356–60; Bumke, *Höfische Kultur*, 433–34; especially Fenske, "Knappe."
112. Hlgnlb 161,15–17: Dô daz kint in sîn achte jâr trat, dô saste man iz zu schule nôch den siten der edelen Rômêre.
113. Eyben, "Sozialgeschichte," 343–44; Néraudau, *Rome*, 311.
114. ELgAur 596,23–25: Wir hant die heimeliche beschliessunge Aristotilis, die kunst Platonis, die meinunge Socratis durch gründet.
115. ELgAur 596,9: in den suben künsten.

ment and the Old and how one should obey the Commandments, as they are written."[116]

In general MHG writers are not so eager to detail school curricula as they are to demonstrate the precocious wisdom and piety that their protagonists display at school: Alexis "grasped entirely whatever they could teach him, no matter how much it was, and learned even more"; because "he understood Scripture extremely well, he realized that God loved virginal purity and chastity; his heart became so inflamed by God that he put on at once the pure garment that virgins wear in eternity."[117] Medieval writers seem to have found it odd that so many maidens were sent to school in antiquity and go out of their way to explain this exotic custom: "in their pride," notes the narrator of the *Passional*, "the Greeks and [the inhabitants of] many neighboring lands, whether they were poor or freeborn, used to want their daughters, along with their sons, to have wise insight into Scripture."[118]

The inhabitants of stories set in the Middle Ages also send their children to school, at least their sons. These are urban schools, a cathedral school in the single case where one can make a more specific determination.[119] All we are told about the curriculum in such schools is that they taught "singing and reading," or, in one unusually detailed account, "declension, singing, and reading."[120] In the Middle Ages elementary instruction did, in fact, consist of singing, so that the pupils could assist at church services, and reading, that is, Latin, the mastery of which was the para-

116. AlxusA 171–73: die niuwen ê unt die alten unt wie man solte behalten diu gebot, als sî geschriben sint.

117. AlxusF 146–48: swie vil siez lêren kunden, des was ez gar begriffenlich und lernde mê; 154–58: [dô] er die schrift vil wol verstuont, dô . . . wart im kunt, daz megetlîche reinekheit got minnete unde kiuscheit; 197–200: Sîn herze wart sô enzunt von gote, daz er an der stunt an sich nam daz reine kleit, daz meide tragent in êwikheit.

118. Passnl K669,22–27: die Criechen pflagen do durch guft und ouch der lande vil da bi, si waren arm oder vri, daz si die tochtere mit den knaben wolden in den schriften haben durch wisliche inschowe. —Others who attend schools in late antiquity: AlxusB 55–57; AplTyr 14967–80; BMärtr 581, 4831–32, 3205–10, 21065–73, 25860; ELgAur 47,5, 303,3–4, 426,12–14, 656,13–21, 744,31–745,1, 746,26; Hlgnlb 161,15–17, 253,20; JnaMrt 3; KndJsu 2940–61; LpzgPr 280,9; Passnl K7,26–31, K111,32–40, K192,26–37, K217,10–17, K241,78–81; StKatM 476–508; Väterb 27791–94, 39119–21. —The schooling of two medieval saints, Dominic and Bernard, is noted very briefly: ELgAur 499,13–16; Passnl K354,76–355,5, K396,38–43. —References to the seven liberal (and other) arts: BMärtr 3205–10; ELgAur 426,13, 550,8–11, 551,1–2, 596,7–9, 744,31–745,1, 779,7–10, 782,6–7, 805,14–15; Hlgnlb 253,20–21; Rennr 1245–52; SlPrsB 40–41; WlGast 8899–9150. —Comments on the education of maidens in Alexandria and Rome: Passnl K471,34–38; Väterb 27605–7, 27791–94; Hlgnlb 67,12–14.

119. ArmSch 73–75, 202–6, 1118–24.

120. StdabA 18: singen unde lesen; Jüdel 129,54: decleinen singen vnt lesen.

mount goal of a medieval school education.[121] Some of the pupils in these texts are clearly preparing for a clerical career—like Walther in *Partonopier*, who then changed his mind and became a knight. But others are not—like the heroes of *Studentenabenteuer A*, whose fathers, trying to dissuade them from university study, insist: "you have [already] learned as much as a layman needs to know."[122]

As usual, the wealthy are much in evidence, but medieval schools were also obligated to accept "the child of poor people."[123] The heroes of the *Armer Schüler*, *Thomas von Kandelberg*, and *Der Scholar und das Marienbild* are, in fact, the only representatives of the poor to make their way into the MHG childhood narratives.[124] Being poor and young, these anonymous pupils (none of them has a proper name of his own) seem particularly vulnerable. This quality, along with their devotion to the Virgin, elicits her miraculous intervention, the principal event in many of these stories. MHG writers do not send poor children to school for educational reasons—they have little to say about the "singing and reading" that are taught there—but because poor, pious schoolboys attract miracles of the Virgin.[125]

Some MHG youths, setting their sights on higher learning, depart for what we would call the university but which the texts designate as a "school" or, at best, that "school of great learning which is called Paris."[126] We never find out what the youths learn in Paris, however, because the stories are not really about education at all but about love: the heroes' status as students gives them a freedom that is useful for carrying out a love affair but that does not require them to attend any lectures. Some of the would-be scholars do not even get to Paris before an erotic adventure takes over the plot.[127] This unstudious bunch seems fully to warrant the bitter

---

121. Köhn, "Schulbildung," 226–27.

122. StdabA 64–65: ir sît des wol gelêret swaz ein leie kunnen sol. —Singing and reading: ArmSch 80–82; BertvR 1:48,1–2; PhMarl 3995–99; StKatM 498. —Post-classical children sent to school: ErnstD 61–62; Hlgnlb 100,6–20; Jüdel 30–38; Judenk 6–45; MarBrt 1–3; Passnl K396,36–43; ScholM 4–7. —Recommendations to send children to school: WlGast 6505–20; SaeldH 6219–21. —Bad teachers: BMärtr 9734–74; Kunze, "Märterbuch," 446–47. Bad scholars: Rennr 13515–28, 16087–94, 16555–74, 16765–68, 17461–584, 21511–12. —The following ages are given for the beginning of schooling. Five: AplTyr 14967–70; Eracl B395–411; RpParz 47,34–35. Enters sixth year: AlxusB 55–57. Seven: AlxusA 168–76; Eracl A395–411; RAlexr 1352–53; SaeldH 6219–21. Enters eighth year: Judenk 12–13.

123. ArmSch 69: armir lûte kint; Feilzer, *Ständegesellschaft*, 233; Limmer, *Bildungszustände*, 140.

124. ArmSch 69; TKdlbg 109; ScholM 28–31.

125. Hugo von Trimberg has sympathetic words for students who must endure poverty (Rennr 17507–25).

126. StdabA 27–29: ein schuole von grôzer meisterschaft . . . diu wære Pâris genant.

127. The heroes of the *Studentenabenteuer A* set out for Paris but only get as far as Arras

words of Hugo von Trimberg, himself a teacher at Bamberg and deeply suspicious of travel in the first place: "Many a one goes off to Paris who learns little and spends a lot. At any rate, he has seen Paris, something fools like us can't claim!"[128]

Quite a bit more serious is the *monastic education* provided in religious houses. Some of those who receive this sort of education are oblates, those who "were given in the years of their childhood to a monastery into a spiritual life."[129] In the convent where the *Sperber* takes place, "a school-mistress taught" the future nuns "how to sing and read, how to behave properly, both in speaking and walking, to bow and to stand in the choir according to the rule of the order";[130] apparently they also learn how to write and embroider.[131] Others who are not oblates, like Hartmann's Gregorius or St. Ulrich, also receive a monastic education, the latter at St. Gall, although it is not clear under what circumstances they do so.[132] In the historical Middle Ages some children lived for a time as temporary members of monastic communities and attended the *scholae interiores* along with the oblates; others attended the *scholae exteriores*, which some houses established for those outsiders who wanted an education.[133] While monastic education can inspire diligent study on the part of the pupils (Ulrich, Gregorius) and detailed description on the part of the writers (*Gregorius*, *Sperber*), it often serves less scholarly narrative ends: by cutting children off from the world from an early age oblation can preserve a touching purity (*Zwölfjähriges Mönchlein*) or an astounding sexual naiveté (*Sperber*, *Mönches Not*), each useful for a different sort of plot.[134]

(StdabA 27–29, 114–15). In spite of the title, the hero of the *Schüler zu Paris C* says nothing about school or Paris when he leaves home and gets only about 100 miles before he enters an unnamed city, falls in love, and dies (SlPrsC 119–23).

128. Rennr 13435–38: Maniger hin ze Pârîs vert, Der wênic lernet und vil verzert: Sô hât er doch Pârîs gesehen: Des müge wir tôren niht gejehen! —Heroes who find love in Paris: Bussrd 59–76; SlPrsA 26–32; SlPrsB 37. On academic authority in Paris: Bussrd 88–103. —Herzog Ernst D is sent *ze schuole* in France and Greece, although nothing is said of what he learns there (ErnstD 110–14). —On Hugo's attitude to travel: Huber, "Bemerkungen."

129. VorNov 29–33: diu wurden . . . in ir kintlîchen jâren zeinem klôster gegeben in ein geistlîchez leben.

130. Sperbr 38–43: Ez lêrte diu schuolemeisterîn Die jungen singen unde lesen, Wie si mit zühten solden wesen, Beidiu sprechen unde gân, Ze kôre nîgen unde stân, Als in der orden gebôt.

131. Sperbr 18–24.

132. Greg 1155–97; ELgAur 779,7–12; StUlrc 153–58.

133. Boehm, "Bildungswesen," 169; Johanek, "Klosterstudien," 65.

134. Others educated in religious houses: ELgAur 819,11–15; Ksrchr 1470–81; MönNot 9–18; Sperbr 50–74; Väterb 33586–89; ZwöMön 28–41. —The education that the Virgin receives at the Temple in Jerusalem resembles that provided for oblates in a convent—even though the Temple maidens are expected to marry when they reach the appropriate age

Pedagogy

Mary's parents have an easy time of it. They need only provide their daughter with a list of virtues—modesty, humility, patience, chastity, and so forth—and their work is done, for Mary accepts what they teach her without any resistance whatsoever: "This noble vessel of glory received the teaching of her father and mother obediently and retained it unfailingly."[135] Parents and teachers who have to deal with less noble vessels, however, will need to give some thought to how they are going to get children to accept the teachings they are supposed to retain: they will have to give some thought to the techniques of education. MHG pedagogical theory, found primarily in didactic and homiletic texts, focuses on three themes: discipline, fear, and habit. To these I will add two other pedagogical topics, drawn primarily from narrative representations: generational relations and educational goals.

The necessity of discipline is the most frequently stated general idea on education in MHG texts. Faustinian invokes Proverbs 13.24: "A father who spares the rod hates his son."[136] The threat to discipline is *zart*, tender, indulgent love. Zosimus believes "that it will surely go ill for the person who loves his child so tenderly [*zart*] that he spares the rod."[137] According to the narrator of Rudolf's *Barlaam*, true parental love *requires* parents to discipline their children: "he who often spares the rod and does not put an end to bad behavior shows no love [*zart*] for his child."[138] Although such beliefs were widespread in the Middle Ages,[139] the young heroes in the narratives are seldom disciplined, since, with few exceptions, they are such exemplary children. Wolfdietrich A is one of the exceptions. When he arrives at Berhtung's court he causes so much mayhem that Berhtung "beat him for his own good: as a result of which he had to stop his nonsense all the more quickly. He hit him very often, and the blows were painful."[140]

(ELgAur 576,10–17; GrMarl 387–93; KndJsu 113–19; PhMarl 499–514, 588–97; WerMar 1343–54; WlMarl 1069–211). —Needlework is emphasized in stories of the Virgin in the Temple: Passnl H9,32–49; PhMarl 570–71, 578–87; WlMarl 1167–82.

135. WlMarl 1053–56: Diz edel vaz der êre Vater und muoter lêre Enpfienc si zühteclîche Und hielt si vesteclîche.

136. Ksrchr 1377–78: Swer dem besem entlîbet den sun hazzet.

137. Väterb 33581–83: Zwem sin kint ist also zart Daz er die rute im vurspart, Daz ez im wol mac missegan.

138. RBarlm 380,1–3: wan im ist sîn kint niht zart, swer im die ruoten dicke spart und sîne unzuht niht stillet.

139. Alexandre-Bidon and Closson, *L'enfant*, 207–8; Arnold, *Kind*, 79–82; Hanawalt, *London*, 159.

140. WolfdA 254,1–3: sô sluoc er in ze fromen: des muoste er der unfuoge deste schierer abe komen. er sluoc in harte dicke, die slege im tâten wê.

Corporal punishment is particularly at home in the schoolroom, so much so that even Jesus cannot escape untouched.[141] This does not keep "many a foolish little child" from praying "to our Lady that she might deign to watch over him during the day in school and protect him from being beaten."[142]

It is of some comfort to discover that there are limits to the discipline that is meted out to children. First, there are limits of age. According to Konrad von Haslau, "immoderate discipline is a waste of time before a child can tell the difference between yes and no, good and bad, here and there."[143] Second, there are limits to the violence. Berthold von Regensburg, who recommends having a little switch on hand to punish children the first time they say wicked words, adds the following restriction: "You should not strike [your child] on her bare head with your hand because you could very well turn her into an idiot."[144] Finally, there are limits imposed by the danger that the children will rebel. After the young Otto III has been punished by his guardian, the archbishop of Cologne, Otto has a child's corpse put in his bed to make it appear that he has died. Later he tells the archbishop why: "You had me beaten too harshly with a switch when I was in the bath, and it made no difference how much I cried. Therefore I was angry at you and wanted to scare you."[145]

In light of these attitudes towards discipline one can understand an opposition that is assumed in several contexts between education and freedom or indulgence. In the *Kaiserchronik* a distinction is made more than once between the child who studies books and the one who "wants shamefully to go free."[146] This recalls the famous passage in which Gottfried's

141. KndJsu 2975–76; Passnl H55,76–79; PhMarl 3995–97.
142. Jüdel 129,69–130,3: manic tumbez chindelîn. [bat] vnser frowen daz si rvchte sein. Des tages inder schule phlegen. vnt ez behute vor den slegen. —Dangers of tender indulgence and the importance of discipline: Jünglg 101–4, 1107–26; Ksrchr 1380–82; KTrojk 13716–19; MaiBfl 195,11–14; Rennr 6984–90, 14821–24; RWeltc 21980–89, 22074–96; StFran 418–59; Walthr 23,26–31; WilOrl 2864–76, 2927–28. —Others raised tenderly: ELgAur 216,20; JngTit 162,1, 1109,3; RAlexr 1283–86. —Discipline or the threat of discipline: ArPhlS 150–56; ArmHnr 586–88; ArmSch 930–1010; FlorBl 650–53; Häsln 198–204; Judenk 60–67, 90–95; JWeltc 22961–23024; Lohgrn 7425–39; Magzog 115; Parz 174,7–9; SfHelb 7.1147–54; Sperbr 234, 244–45; StdabA 190–99; WlMarg 592–98.
143. Jünglg 1196–98: unmezige zuht ist gar einwiht, e daz kint erkenne nein und ja, ubel und gut, hie und da.
144. BertvR 1:35,8–9: ir sult ez aber an blôzez houbet niht slahen mit der hant, wan ir möhtet ez wol ze einem tôren machen.
145. Lohgrn 7434–37: dâ hiez dû mich slâhen in dem bade ze vaste mit der gerten . . . und half mich niht waz ich dar umb geweinet. Dâ von was mir zorn ûf dich und wolt dich drumb erschrecken. —Limits on discipline: BertvR 2:58,26–33; Jakobr 264; RpParz 143,18–25; Schwsp La185, La247; Walthr 87,1–8; VorNov 66–69. —Rennewart runs away from home from fear that he will be beaten (Rennew 17816–19).
146. Ksrchr 3355: wil iz aver bôslîchen frî gân; 1465–69; 1672–43.

Tristan begins his education and the narrator tells us: "that was his first turning from his freedom."[147] In other texts it is not freedom but indulgent love that comes to an end: Seifrit's Alexander "was raised very tenderly [*zart*] until he was six years old," when his schooling began.[148] The thirteen-year-old Willehalm von Orlens realizes that one "can never become a truly perfect man through indulgent love [*zart*],"[149] so he sets off for a more rigorous environment. In every case freedom and indulgence are opposed to education and the discipline of growing up. Children may be indulged when they are quite young and allowed their freedom, but ultimately the freedom natural to childhood must be replaced by the discipline (*zuht*) appropriate to adults, and this is accomplished through education. Although Gottfried's narrator laments the end of freedom in the case of Tristan, it is nostalgia for a loss that cannot be avoided.[150]

The threat of discipline is related to another cardinal element in the MHG theory of education, fear. According to Thomasin, "fear is good for putting the child in the mood to hear and to understand. A child cannot quickly forget what he has learned in fear."[151] It is a good sign, then, that even Alexander "began to fear his master" when he started school.[152] Thomasin believes fear is so important to learning that "noble children who are away from their teachers should figure out how to make themselves afraid."[153] Model pupil that he is, St. Erhard does just that: "the child feared his master when he was not present just as much as if he were always right there beating him."[154]

One of the principal purposes of MHG education is to instill good habits since, according to Berthold, " 'Whatever the child gets used to sticks

147. GTrist 2068–69: daz was sin erstiu kere uz siner vriheite.

148. SAlexr 597–98: das chind zach man gar zart, unczt das es sechs jar alt wart.

149. WilOrl 2927–28: Mit zarte ich niemer werden kan Ain rehter vollekomenr man.

150. The passage from Gottfried is discussed in chapter one. The commonplace about the loss of freedom also appears at the beginning of Alexander's education in *Aristoteles und Phyllis [S]* (72–81), once again in connection with a pupil who masters his lessons with no difficulty whatsoever. —On freedom and its dangers: AlxusF 121–36; HnrKgd 3653–56; StFran 408–09; Väterb 34493–95; Winsbn 4,5, 11,6–10. —Others raised tenderly, but only up to a point: JWeltc 13663–64; RpParz 47,34–35; HgMarg 131–35, 225–29.

151. WlGast 593–97: diu vorhte diu ist dâ vür guot daz si dem kinde bereit den muot ze hœren unde ze verstên. ez mag ein kint niht schiere vergên swaz ez mit vorhten glêret ist.

152. UAlexr 1281: den meister er vorhten began.

153. WlGast 601–4: dâ von suln diu edelen kint diu âne meisterschefte sint dar ûf gedenken . . . daz si in selben vorhte machen.

154. ELgAur 105,2–4: Öch forhte dis kint sinen meyster so sere so er nút gegenwirtig waz also er allezit mit schlegen gegenwirtig were gewesen. —Fear in didactic texts: Jünglg 817–18, 970–71; Rennr 261–68, 14825–28, 17381–93; Warng 1499–1506. Fear in narrative texts: JWeltc 22963–65; Ksrchr 1379–82; MaiBfl 195,15–17; WolfdA 291,1–2.

with him.' That is an old saying and a true one."[155] Freidank cites Horace: "The first flavor to get into new barrels cannot be gotten out; it is not easy for a man to give up a habit to which he has been accustomed from youth."[156] From assumptions such as these Berthold draws the obvious conclusion: "For this reason you should always direct your child to good things, since habit is often stronger than nature."[157] "Habit," says Konrad von Haslau, "is second nature."[158] The mother of Alexis articulates the relation between discipline and habit: "One should force children to good things through discipline since a person is not likely to abandon what he has acquired, whether good or bad: whoever learns well in youth will strive to do well in adulthood."[159]

Turning from the grim elements of MHG pedagogical theory to the more attractive representation of pedagogical practice, one notices a striking difference from what we expect today in the relation of the various age groups. Nowadays we regard the ability to make friends and work with peers as one of the crucial skills to be learned in childhood: Dr. Spock tells us that people's happiness as adults "depends a great deal on how they got along with other children when they were young," and he devotes a special section of his book to "helping children to be sociable and popular."[160] We regard schools as one of the most important environments in which children learn "to get along with other children." In MHG narrative, education does not serve this function. With hardly an exception, MHG children do not form important relations with the other children with whom they are educated.

Those who receive a tutored court education are taught alone, so such relations are out of the question. Those who receive a fostered court education presumably live and serve with other children at that court, but

155. BertvR 1:34,37–38: "swes daz kint gewont, daz selbe im nâch dont." Daz ist ein alt gesprochen wort und ist ouch wâr.
156. Fridnk 108,15–18: Den niuwen vazzen niemen mac benemen wol ir êrsten smac: den site ein man unsanfte lât, des er von jugent gewonet hât.
157. BertvR 1:35,30–31: Dâ von sult ir iuwer kint ûf guotiu dinc wîsen, wan gewonheit ist etewenne rîcher danne diu natûre.
158. Jünglg 1165: gewonheit ist die ander natur.
159. AlxusF 129–34: man sol die kintheit twingen mit zühte ze guoten dingen, wan waz der mensche gwunnen hât guot oder bœse, kûme erz lât: wer in der jugende lernet guot, in dem alder er ez gerne tuot. —On new barrels and education: BertvR 1:35,28–30, 2:58,3–6. On habit: Helmbr 244–46; Jünglg 270–78; KndJsu 73–77; RAlexr 1411–17; StElis 1059–92; UAlexr 1396–98; Winsbk 37,1–10; WlGast 157–84, 656–58. —For medieval authorities who stress the importance of establishing good habits in childhood: Shahar, *Childhood*, 170, 312 nn. 44–45.
160. Spock, *Baby and Child Care*, 469.

the narratives show no interest in these other children. Those who attend schools, urban or monastic, are inevitably in contact with other pupils, but there is only one text, *Thomas von Kandelberg*, where the protagonist's relation to his schoolmates is of any real importance. In most cases the other students seem to have been introduced merely as a foil against which the hero can appear all the more remarkable: Eraclius is so far superior to his classmates that he has to listen to their lessons and correct their verses; the young Dominican nun, Elsbetlein, who understands Scripture as well as an adult, teaches other children when she is not studying herself.[161] Schoolmates are of so little interest that there are many stories in which they are not even mentioned, even though it is clear that the young protagonist has been sent to school.[162] Because relations among children are suppressed, the only school ties that matter are those between children and their teachers—between Alexander and Aristotle, Dulciflorie and her "faithful tutor," the Armer Schüler and his "schoolmaster."[163] As will be seen in the next chapter, education is only one of a number of situations in which MHG narrative ignores the relations among children in favor of those between children and adults.[164]

Just as the learning child must focus on the adult teacher, so learning itself is focused on adulthood: "children," according to one of Faustinian's sons, "are taught good skills so that they can make their way when they are older."[165] Aristotle believes Alexander should "learn in [his] childish youth all the excellent qualities of manhood."[166] Flore's father does "as wise people still do, who teach their dear children *zuht, ere*, and *tugent*— for those lessons are most advantageous to children in their youth that will be useful to them later on."[167] *Zuht, ere*, and *tugent* are often advanced as the goals of education, but they are only meaningful in terms of the larger,

161. Eracl 430–37; UlmSwb 142,14–18.
162. AlxusA 168–74; AlxusB 55–63; AlxusF 144–52; BMärtr 3205–10, 4831–40, 21068–76, 24658–59; KndJsu 2941–3004; MarBrt 1–11; Passnl K7,26–32, K111,32–40, K192,26–37, K217,10–11, K241,78–81; ScholM 4–39; Väterb 39119–26.
163. Dulcfl 128: Eine getriuwe meisterin; ArmSch 930: Der schûle meister.
164. A few children are attached to a lover or close friend: Flore and Blanscheflur, the heroes of the *Studentenabenteuer A* and *B*, and the novices in the *Vorauer Novelle*. However, these pairs function in many ways like a single hero and are no more likely than Tristan or Parzival to form ties with lesser children of their own age.
165. Ksrchr 3357–58: man lêret diu kint durch daz guote liste, daz si sih in dem alter der mit fristen.
166. RAlexr 1411–12: lerne in kintlîcher jugent vollekomene mannes tugent.
167. FlorBl 630–36: er tet als noch die wîsen tuont, die liebiu kint . . . lêrent . . . zuht, êre unde tugent; wan den kinden in der jugent die lêre aller meiste frument die dâ nâch ze nutze kument.

adult society; they designate those forms of behavior (*zuht*) and those attributes (*tugent*) that are considered excellent in adult society and that enable one to amount to something and enjoy a good name (*ere*) among adults.[168]

The MHG didactic texts seem to have been written with these goals in mind. Although *Winsbecke*, *Winsbeckin*, and the *Magezoge* are structured as dialogues in which a parent instructs a child, the parents are concerned above all to teach their children to be good adults, not good children. In the *Magezoge*, for instance, the father gives advice on how his son should raise his own son: it is advice on how to be a father, not a child.[169] Thomasin directs the first book of the *Welscher Gast* to young people. Yet while some of his admonitions are particularly appropriate for children, most are not: "a young lady," for example, "should seldom say anything unless she is asked," while "a lady should also not speak much, and when she is eating she should definitely not speak at all." [170] Where is the difference? Thomasin does recommend stories that he thinks are appropriate for children. But they are the stories of Enite and Blanscheflur, Gawein, Iwein, and Arthur, the same stories told to adults.[171] It is clear not only from the contents but also from explicit statements that the authors of didactic texts have adults in mind as much as children. Although the very title of the *Jüngling* invokes the young, when the question is explicitly raised about the age of those to whom the text is addressed it turns out to be "anyone who, on account of age or youth, cannot recognize what disgraces a man," anyone who "behaves foolishly, no matter how old or young he is in years." [172] Although the first book of the *Welscher Gast* is directed to the young, the work as a whole, which comprises ten books, is addressed to "both women and men" so that they may benefit "both in youth and in old age." [173] It seems that even the didactic tradition has no clear sense that children need to learn anything other than what adults need to know.[174]

168. On the object of education: Judenk 25–29; KTrojk 5812–37; SaeldH 6214–21; WolfdB 29,1–4. —*Zuht, ere*, and *tugent* as the goals of education: ArPhlS 38–39; Dulcfl 157–63; ETrist 173; HnrKgd 3583–87; KSilvr 116–20; Kudrn 575,3; SaeldH 6219–21; SlPrsC 66; StElis 128–31; UAlexr 1276; Väterb 27771–73; VorNov 44–46; WilOrl 2871–74, 2922–24, 2985–89, 3314–21; WilWnd 5527–34.

169. Magzog 113–28.

170. WlGast 465–70: ein juncvrouwe sol selten iht sprechen, ob mans vrâget niht. ein vrowe sol ouch niht sprechen vil, . . . und benamen swenn si izzet, sô sol si sprâchen niht.

171. WlGast 1026–78.

172. Jünglg 813–14: wer vor alter oder vor jugent enkan erkennen, waz swachet einen man; 819–20: wie alt, wie junck er ist an jaren, wil er wan tumplich gebaren.

173. WlGast 27: beidiu wîp unde man; 32: bêdiu an alter unde an jugent.

174. According to Orme, "most medieval writers on education failed to distinguish be-

Of course, children in most cultures, including our own, are educated for adulthood: we too expect families and schools to prepare children for the roles that they will fill when they grow up. But we also teach our children how to be children. MHG texts consider play a natural activity of children but quite unrelated to education. Many of us regard play as a crucial aspect of a child's development and make a point of teaching children those games we think will be most beneficial to them according to their age. We teach them to play like children. Thomasin recommends that children be told adult stories. We too tell stories to children, but they are stories written especially for children and are often about children. Parents in MHG texts are concerned that their sons and daughters acquire the social skills that will enable them to make their way as adults. So do we. But we are also concerned that they be able to succeed in the society of their peers. Where MHG education teaches how to be an adult, modern education teaches how to be a child as well.

Nature and Nurture

Once Mary joins the maidens in the Temple her knowledge increases rapidly. She "learned to work whatever was placed before her, fine linen, brocade, or silk, according to her own abundant sense."[175] "In a few short days, she knew the meaning of all the Holy Scriptures, both the teachings of the Prophets and the law of Moses."[176] As far as one can tell, nobody teaches Mary how to work with linen, brocade or silk or how to "read and understand Scripture as one should."[177] She is able learn these things, it seems, relying on nothing besides "her own abundant sense." Clearly there is something special about Mary that allows her to learn without instruction. Although the issue is not raised explicitly, the passage assumes ideas about the relation of nature and nurture that are widespread in MHG texts.

These ideas are presented at some length in Konrad von Würzburg's *Trojanerkrieg*, in order to explain how it is that Achilles surpasses the other young nobles in the care of Chiron. Konrad claims that the young hero

---

tween adults and children. They directed their writings to people in general" (*Childhood to Chivalry*, 109). Similar statements: Arnold, "Mentalität," 259, 276; Elias, *Manners*, 141; Hofmeister, "Jüngling," 11.

175. WlMarl 1168–71: Swaz ir wart werkes für geleit, Ez waer bys, pfellel, sîde, Des lernete diu plîde Nâch ir sinne die vollen.

176. WlMarl 1186–89: Aller der heiligen schrifte [sin] Kunde si bî kurzen tagen, Ez waere diu lêre der wîsagen Alder Moysenes ê.

177. WlMarl 1191–92: Daz si die schrift, als man si sol, Kunde entstân und lesen wol.

was predisposed by nature to profit from instruction: whereas "that which is going to turn into a bramble becomes crooked very soon, whatever is predisposed to nobility by inherited nature doesn't need much teaching to attain it."[178] Achilles's natural predisposition is so strong that he can make quite exceptional progress: "His pure and malleable nature created in him the marvel that he surpassed his master's teaching; for the noble young man turned out [even] better than he was taught."[179] Achilles's extraordinary nature enables him to derive more from nurture than is actually there.[180]

This does not mean that nurture is superfluous. Just as wax or stone requires the intervention of seal or sculptor to take shape, so Achilles's extraordinary nature requires the intervention of a teacher to be realized.[181] Nurture is necessary. While Achilles is likened to a noble stone, lesser natures are compared to flint, and, as Konrad asserts, "it is a tedious business to fashion a pure image out of hard flint."[182] Such low-quality material will necessarily limit the quality of the results: "No matter how much a master fills a baseborn child with instruction, he will never be able to bring forth anything praiseworthy in this life."[183] This does not mean one should abandon the effort, for with diligent nurture such a child "may well become better than he was before."[184] These are the children that the writers have in mind who recommend the pedagogy of discipline and fear. For them education is indeed "a tedious business," in which the harshest weapons must be engaged to overcome the unreceptive natures of the students. And yet these writers too apparently believe it is worth the effort, in the hope that nurture might make the child even slightly "better than he was before."

Konrad understands the relation of nature and nurture as one of unequal symbiosis. Nature is the more powerful since it provides the raw material. It determines what sort of development is possible as well as how fast and how far it will proceed. Without nurture, however, nature remains only potential. Nurture awakens and shapes nature, helping it to a more perfect realization.[185]

---

178. KTrojk 6400–6401: swaz z'eime haggen werden sol, daz krümbet sich vil vrüeje; 6405–7: Swaz adellichen arten wil, zuo dem bedarf man niht ze vil rîlicher meisterschefte.

179. KTrojk 6442–47: sîn art senft unde reine geschuof an im daz wunder, daz er sich ûz besunder vür sînes meisters lêre schiet; wan der juncherre baz geriet, dann er gelêret würde.

180. Aquinas also surpasses his master: Hlgnlb 100,15–17.

181. KTrojk 6386–91, 6418–28.

182. KTrojk 6421–23: und ist ein lanc geverte, ê man ûz flinsen herte geschepfe ein bilde reine.

183. KTrojk 6428–31: swie vil ein meister villet unedel kint mit lêre, doch kan ûz im kein êre gewahsen ûf der erden.

184. KTrojk 6732–33: ez mac wol bezzer werden, denne ez vor gewesen ist.

185. On the priority of nature over nurture: GTrist 11634–35; Passnl H82,15–55, H314,53–

Nature determines not only the general susceptibility of children to nurture but also the particular kind of nurture to which they respond. Although Parzival has grown up without any knowledge of knighthood, a few words of instruction from Gurnemanz are all that is needed to transform him from an incompetent into a paragon, able to unhorse the first five knights who ride against him. He achieves this success, Wolfram explains, because "he was urged on by inborn manliness and the nature of the lineage [art] of Gahmuret," his father.[186] In other words, it is Parzival's nature to become a knight. Although Josaphat has been kept from any knowledge of Christianity, the moment Barlaam arrives he believes at once, assimilating thousands of lines of doctrine without the slightest difficulty.[187] This is because it is his nature to become a Christian, as was revealed in the stars at the time of his birth.[188] Although the young nun in the *Sperber* is raised in a convent in ignorance of sex, she responds with enthusiasm when a knight comes along and demonstrates the rudiments. Sexual desire is part of her nature. The response of the young nun seems natural to us in a way the responses of Parzival and Josaphat do not, since we believe sexual desire is part of everyone's nature. In MHG texts, however, knighthood or Christianity can be part of the individual nature no less than sexual desire. Thus just as the young nun responds at once to a stimulus that corresponds to her sexual nature, so does Parzival to stimuli that correspond to his knightly nature and Josaphat to stimuli that correspond to his Christian nature.

The specificity and responsiveness of the individual nature enables a very efficient sort of instruction. Aristotle lectures Alexander for four hundred lines on how a prince should govern, and when he is done Rudolf tells us simply: "the child welcomed the sweet teaching in his mind."[189] Mary's parents teach her piety, modesty, humility, and a host of other virtues, and after giving the whole list Philipp tells us: "the dear child locked [these teachings] in the shrine of her heart."[190] The education of Gregorius—in reading, grammar, divinity, and law—lasts from age six to age fifteen, but even at the outset he is "such a smart youth" that "he quickly surpassed

315,3; RBarlm 164,21–165,21, 292,3–294,25; WilWnd 5096–116; WlGast 353–62. —See also Berkvam, *Enfance*, 90–94; Berkvam, *"Nature,"* 168–77; Jaeger, "Magister," 126; Kästner, *Lehrgespräche*, 276–79; Shahar, *Childhood*, 163–66.

186. Parz 174,24–25: den twanc diu Gahmuretes art und angeborniu manheit.

187. RBarlm 40,17–161,16.

188. RBarlm 21,26–22,38.

189. RAlexr 1401–1830: 1831–32: Lieplîche in sînem muote enphie diz kint die süezen lêre.

190. PhMarl 493–96: daz liebe kint des niht enliez swaz ez diu muoter hiez, und swaz ez lêrt der vater sîn, daz slôz ez in sîns herzen schrîn.

in knowledge the children who had started school three years earlier."[191]
Whether they are given a few pointers, like Parzival, a long lecture, like
Alexander, a list of virtues, like Mary, or a list of disciplines, like Gregorius, MHG children never need to have things broken down or explained:
they assimilate speeches, lists, and entire disciplines at once. To a certain
extent this is a consequence of MHG narrative conventions: it is customary to present the hero's education as a speech or a list of subjects taught
and mastered. But there is truth in the convention. A MHG hero or heroine already possesses a nature predestined for a particular excellence. Thus
when she is presented with a particular knowledge that corresponds to her
particular nature she can comprehend it at once—just as Parzival masters
jousting.

In a few instances the heroic nature is so extraordinary that it needs no
instruction at all. The young Hagen, who has been dropped on a remote
island, comes upon the arms that he needs to defend himself and puts them
on: "When he considered the straits he was in, he learned what he thought
necessary; he raised himself himself."[192] And it is the same with Mary in the
Temple: she needs only to be presented with something—whether it is embroidery or the word of God—and she comprehends it at once. These are
cases where the individual nature is so perfect that nurture is not needed.
All that is necessary is an occasion for nature to manifest itself.

At the opposite extreme is Judas. Abandoned as an infant, he is raised
by the queen of Scariot, who treats him just like her own son, encourages
him to behave virtuously, and corrects him when he does wrong. Nevertheless, "it simply didn't make any difference. He was but a shadow of
nobility and had not been properly born to it."[193] In the end he kills his
foster brother and flees the country. The narrator comments: "Anyone who
takes a leopard skin and sews it over a donkey, expecting it to jump like a
leopard, is no smarter than a very young child."[194] Just as Mary's supremely
good nature requires no instruction to understand Scripture, so Judas's
supremely wicked nature cannot be improved by even the most conscientious instruction. Mary and Judas represent the extreme, where nature,

191. Greg 1178: sô sinnerîche jugent; 1173–75: Diu kint diu vor drin jâren zuo gesetzet
wâren, mit kunst ez diu . . . schiere ervuor.
192. Kudrn 97,4: er lernte swes er gerte, dô er nâch sîner nôt begunde sinnen; 98,4: jâ
zôch er sich selbe.
193. Passnl H314,85–88: swaz man in zv tugendē brach daz wolde vurbas nicht an ime er
was ot edelcheit ein schime vnde dran zv rechte nicht geborn.
194. Passnl H314,95–315,3: swer eines lepartē vel vber einē esel suwet vnde des an im
getruet er springe im lepartē sprunc der ist an wisheite harte iunc.

ordinarily understood by MHG writers to be more powerful than nurture, is in fact completely autonomous.

Mary is an exception in another regard as well, at least as her story is told by Walther von Rheinau. According to Walther, Mary is taught feminine virtues like chastity and humility. According to Bruder Philipp (author of the other life of the Virgin based on the *Vita rhythmica*) she is also taught needlework, as is Dulciflorie. Otherwise MHG maidens (even in other lives of the Virgin: Wernher's *Maria, Passional, Grazer Marienleben*) do not receive instruction in specifically feminine virtues, behaviors, and skills. Nowadays, in the real world, according to a life of St. Margaret, maidens "are raised in those virtues that will keep them from living in vain luxury when men take them in marriage."[195] And the MHG didactic texts, especially *Welscher Gast*, are full of instructions about how a woman is to act: she shouldn't look directly at a strange man, she shouldn't cross her legs when she sits, she shouldn't talk much, especially at meals, and so forth.[196] In the MHG narratives youths are coached in feminine behavior when they want to disguise themselves as maidens: Achilles is told that he must take small, gentle steps, not look around when he walks, eat and drink modestly, fold his hands in front of him, speak quietly and draw out his words.[197] Yet such instruction is almost entirely lacking in narratives about maidens. Gottfried devotes twenty-five lines to *moraliteit*, the art of proper behavior that Tristan teaches Isold and that the narrator particularly recommends to women—yet there is not a word that distinguishes proper behavior for women from proper behavior for men.[198] Of course gender functions negatively: maidens are excluded from training in knighthood or kingship, from attendance at medieval schools, and from study in Paris. But gender does not figure positively: maidens are not taught feminine virtues. The maidens in the medieval audience are taught how to behave like women, as is Achilles, but Isold is not. She, like the other exemplary maidens of MHG narrative, possesses this knowledge without instruction—by nature.[199]

195. Marglg 27–30: man di [junge megetîn] in der jugende zût zu solchen tugenden, daz si in ubbekeit iht leben, swanne si di man genemen.
196. WlGast 400–1, 411–12, 467–69.
197. KTrojk 14980–15068.
198. GTrist 8002–26.
199. Hugdietrich is also taught feminine skills, in his case sewing, spinning, and embroidery (WolfdB 22,2–26,4). —On the education of women in the Middle Ages: Arnold, "Mentalität"; Berkvam, "*Nature*," 170; Bumke, "Bestandsaufnahme," 455; Bumke, *Höfische Kultur*, 474–76; Bumke, *Mäzene*, 56, 416 n. 59; Ferrante, "Education"; Grundmann, "Frauen und Literatur," 133–39; Rösener, "Höfische Frau," 217–19.

Congruence and Contradiction

According to Dr. Spock there is very little about a child that is not determined by nurture. Even "intelligence," he believes, "has a lot more to do with environment than with inheritance"—an assertion for which he offers the following evidence: "Babies born to parents with low intelligence but adopted into average or bright families tend to develop an intelligence like that of their adoptive parents."[200] Konrad von Würzburg says very much the opposite: "Teaching and instruction are fine things; however, the person who from excellent inheritance has a mind rich in sense will know more than anything that can be learned from instruction."[201] Where Spock believes that nurture determines intelligence, Konrad believes intelligence results primarily from inherited nature. Neither is an absolutist, least of all Konrad: in spite of the priority he accords nature, he clearly believes that nurture is a fine thing. And so do all the MHG writers. But the relation of nature and nurture is a complicated one, exhibiting congruences and contradictions, and I would like to mention a few of these in conclusion.

The nature of the particular child determines the nurture of that child in a number of ways. Since heroic children are predisposed by nature to knightly prowess, courtly excellence, saintly piety, and the like, when they are schooled in these matters they offer no resistance. Heroic nature, which already incarnates adult virtues, and heroic nurture, which teaches adult skills and values, are congruent. For these children nurture serves as a catalyst, the mere presence of which enables their heroic nature to be realized. Ordinary children, however, lack adult virtues—strength, wisdom, discretion, and the rest—by definition. Since they too must be educated to become adults their nurture is a much more difficult affair. Parents and teachers must discipline their charges, instill fear in them, and force them to act like adults until it becomes a habit. The generally harsh characterization of the nature of the child (weak, foolish, headstrong) elicits a correspondingly harsh educational theory (discipline, fear, habit). On the one hand we find the happy coincidence of heroic nature and educational goals and on the other the bleaker correspondence between ordinary nature and educational technique.

However, the relation of nature and nurture is not always so harmo-

200. Spock, *Baby and Child Care*, 293.
201. KTrojk 6459–63: Lêr unde meisterschaft sint guot, swer aber sinnerîchen muot von angeborner tugent hât, des witze gêt vür allen rât, der von meisterschefte kumet.

nious. On the one hand, nature is immutable: it is inborn, unchanging, the inevitable consequence of lineage or divine determination. The Virgin is pure by nature and reveals her unchanging purity from the moment of her birth. Nurture, on the other hand, effects change: it shapes children, teaches them things they did not know, and changes them as a result. After Parzival has been instructed by Gurnemanz his behavior is transformed. Ideological issues are involved. The belief in unchanging nature sustains the hereditary nobility in its claims of legitimacy: the noble nature, like the heroic nature, must be inborn and immutable; nobility is a matter of birth. The belief in transformative nurture also buttresses claims of precedence: for centuries the clergy claimed a special status because it practiced a certain discipline and mastered a certain knowledge, and now the secular aristocracy can make a similar claim. Both the clergy and the aristocracy assert a collective agency: in educating, that is forming, their children, they fashion themselves.

The belief in immutable nature and the belief in transformative nurture are at odds: an essentialist paradigm of inborn nature that cannot be changed is difficult to reconcile with a constructionist paradigm of self-fashioning nurture that inevitably transforms. Since the texts do not acknowledge, much less resolve, these contradictions, the representation of nurture in MHG texts is inconsistent. Some children, for example, are taught more than they need. Tristan learns "more books than any other child before or after"[202] and Willehalm von Orlens learns five years' worth of Latin in one year.[203] Yet they never have any use for this learning. They are trained in books and Latin because the careful education of secular princes is part of the self-fashioning of courtly culture: transformative nurture is good. Other children are taught less than they need to know. Beaflor, like other MHG maidens, is taught nothing about proper feminine behavior, and Gregorius is taught nothing of knighthood. Yet Beaflor is a paragon of modesty and wifely devotion and Gregorius is an excellent knight. These things can be omitted from the education of Beaflor and Gregorius because they are feminine or knightly by nature: nature renders education unnecessary. MHG children are taught more than they need because education is important in its own right: it shows us—as a class of clerics or nobles—able to form ourselves. They are taught less than they know because inborn nature determines everything: we are saints or nobles, masculine or feminine, pious or courtly, by birth and the will of God.

202. GTrist 2090–92: daz er der buoche mere gelernete . . . dan ie kein kint e oder sit.
203. WilOrl 2754–61.

Nature and nurture both have their roles to play in MHG childhood and they are generally understood to stand in complementary relationship: nature provides the potential and establishes the limits; nurture provides the skills that enable this potential to be realized and, perhaps, even improved somewhat. Yet nature and nurture also represent two not entirely reconcilable paradigms. According to one, nature is fixed and childhood is a time in which that static nature is revealed. According to the other, nurture can shape the individual, and childhood is a time in which the individual is formed. The MHG knowledge of childhood embraces both the complementary and the contradictory relation of nature and nurture so that childhood is both a time in which the unchanging nature of the individual is revealed and a time in which the individual is transformed by nurture.

5. Relations: Attachment, Separation, and Strange Situations

Anyone who read the American press during the winter of 1987 learned a great deal about Baby M. More, doubtless, than most of us wanted to know. Baby M's mother, Mary Beth Whitehead, had contracted to bear a child for William and Elizabeth Stern, who were unable to have children of their own. She was paid $10,000, in return for which she agreed to be artificially inseminated with William Stern's sperm and to turn over the baby to the Sterns once it had been born. But, after the birth of her child, Mary Beth Whitehead discovered she couldn't part with her, and a long and highly publicized battle for custody ensued. During this period Baby M was shunted back and forth between her mother's and her father's families depending on the day of the week. Poor child, we thought, constantly on the move, never sure where she will be or who will be caring for her: what a dreadful way to spend the first year of one's life. We reacted in accordance with a principle that is dear to us and that played an important role in the judge's initial ruling on custody: children deserve a stable environment in which to grow up, one where they can count on a reliable source of affection and nurture. We assume that "exposing the infant to many caregivers [will] create permanent emotional insecurity."[1] We cannot imagine that an unsettled childhood is anything but a liability.

In MHG narrative, however, just the opposite seems true. Elizabeth of Hungary was betrothed when she was one, shipped by her parents to the court of her future husband at age four, married ritually on arrival, and married for real at fourteen. Although the treatment of Elizabeth strikes us as so cruel that her parents would probably be liable to criminal prosecution if they were alive today, the disruptions that Elizabeth endures are not felt to leave any debilitating scars: she grows up to be saint, a model for us all. If one considers the even more eventful childhoods of other MHG children—Parzival or Tristan, for example, who also grow up to

1. Kagan, *Nature*, 73.

become heroes—one sees that childhood dislocation in MHG narrative is both much more common and, ultimately, much less harmful than we would expect. Indeed, it is an essential part of a MHG childhood. The breaking of ties and the making of new ones generate a series of changing relations that define the child's place in the world—leading Elizabeth, for instance, to Thuringia and marriage to the Landgraf. The dislocations and disruptions, the making and breaking of ties, all the changing relations of childhood play an essential role in constituting childhood in the world of MHG narrative. It is to them that this chapter and the next are devoted.

The most important kinds of relations are illustrated in *Wolfdietrich A*. Wolfdietrich is the son of a king and queen of Greece. As a young child he grows so strong that the king's courtiers fear he will destroy the country when he comes of age, so they convince the king to have his son killed. The loyal vassal Berhtung is ordered to carry out the murder, but he cannot bring himself to perform the deed and leaves the child with a hunter and his wife. Some years later the winds change at court and Berhtung, accused of having murdered Wolfdietrich, is able to save his own life by fetching the child from his guardians and returning him to his parents. The king and queen entrust their son to Berhtung again, this time to be educated. Eventually Wolfdietrich's father dies and his brothers seize power, depriving Wolfdietrich of his share of the inheritance and sending the queen, their mother, into exile. When Wolfdietrich learns what has happened he resolves to take vengeance on his usurper brothers, and soon he sets out on his adult adventures.

From the moment of his birth Wolfdietrich already sustains certain relations to the world, relations that I will refer to as kinds of *filiation*. I use the term somewhat broadly to refer not only to bonds of parentage, but to any ties, such as class or religion, that are established at birth or immediately thereafter. In Wolfdietrich's case the bonds of filiation turn out not to be very durable, since his father attempts to have him killed. The rupture of the bonds between parent and child, indeed, the rupture of any important ties, I will call *exfiliation*. Ties, however, are not only broken but also made. Wolfdietrich's parents entrust their child to Berhtung to be raised, and Wolfdietrich, rather improbably, thinks Berhtung actually is his father. Ties like these that are forged after birth I will refer to as varieties of *affiliation*. The affiliations limited to childhood will be considered in this chapter, those that are carried into adulthood will be the subject of the next.

Filiation: Natal Relations

Immediately after Wolfdietrich's birth his mother, following instructions she had received in a dream, carries him to a nearby hermit to be baptized. "'Give me the little child,'" the hermit demands, "'your son shall become a Christian.' She resisted for a long time but in the end she did relinquish the child" to the hermit, who baptizes him and makes a prophecy about his future.[2] Two kinds of filiation are emphasized in this account of Wolfdietrich's birth, the natal attachment to his mother (she gives him life, she resists surrendering him) and the neonatal attachment to Christianity (he is baptized and becomes a Christian). These, like the other filiations of birth, are of fundamental importance, since they determine the child's essential place in the world. They may be obscured or violated, but they are never completely forgotten.

The bonds between child and parent begin to be formed long before the child is born, when parents first desire offspring. Of the reasons to want children, MHG parents most frequently mention the need for heirs. The parents of Alexis desire "a little child who might yet be heir to the rich and various revenues of which they controlled a marvelous quantity."[3] Princes may also be concerned, as they should be, for the future peace of their realms. The father of Wilhelm von Österreich wants a child "who would inherit my fiefs, over which [otherwise] much hostility would arise after my death."[4] Religious texts frequently mention the desire to avoid the shame that attaches to barrenness. Thus Zechariah prays for "offspring that might relieve him of the disgrace of which he was quite properly ashamed."[5] Barrenness is a sign of "God's curse."[6] In order to gain God's favor, childless couples make pilgrimages, as people did in the Middle Ages: Titurel's parents go to Jerusalem, Wilhelm von Österreich's father to Ephesus.[7] Reinfried von Braunschweig goes off to fight the heathen.[8] Although about 20 percent of couples in pre-modern societies remained childless,[9] all the bar-

---

2. WolfdA 26,2–3: "dîn sun sol cristen werden: gip mir daz kindelîn." si werte sich des lange: daz kint si im doch liez.

3. KAlxus III–14: ein kindelîn, daz noch ein erbe solte sîn der hôhen gülte manicvalt der wunder was in ir gewalt.

4. WilÖst 213–15: daz erbe miniu lehen, dar umme sich mihel vehen hûb nach dem ende min.

5. Passnl H346,6–8: vrucht . . . die im die schande neme der er billiche sich muste schamen.

6. PhMarl 104: gotes vluoch.

7. JngTit 146,1–159,1; WilÖst 198–522.

8. RnfrBr 13270–315.

9. Goody, *Family and Marriage*, 44; Shahar, *Childhood*, 36.

ren couples in MHG narrative eventually do have children. The offspring so fervently desired by the parents are, after all, required by the story.[10]

Just as parents' relation to their children begins before birth, so does God's. According to the *Elsässische "Legenda aurea"* a male receives his soul on the fortieth day after conception and "the soul receives the stain of original sin from its infusion into the body."[11] Females receive their souls after eighty days, because "the body of a female is not formed until after eighty days."[12] Among the reasons given for the divine sex discrimination are that God, who took human form as a man, "wanted therefore to honor male nature" and that since "the first woman sinned more grievously than the man, she thus deserves worse fortune both on earth and in her mother's body."[13] Once the soul has entered the body its eternal life has begun. As Berthold von Regensburg explains: "Even if the child only lives as long as it takes to turn your hand over, she must live for ever and ever, for as long as God lives, and her soul can never perish."[14]

In most cases the birth of the child is noted only briefly. More detailed accounts may mention the suffering the child's mother endures: before Cain is born "labor pains began to oppress Eve [from which] she had no respite. Anyone whose heart was not harder than stone would have felt pity for her."[15] Others mention the danger of childbirth: after the wife of Wilhelm von Wenden delivered her twin sons, Wilhelm "saw his only joy lying there completely weak and exhausted; she had almost lost her life."[16] Women do lose their lives in childbirth, like Alise, mother of Malefer— although the incidence of such deaths is very low in MHG narrative, probably much lower than it was in medieval Germany. Sometimes midwives

10. Desire for heirs: AlxusB 38–41; AplTyr 14147–86; ELgAur 426,10–11; Eracl 214–17; Jakobr 89–91, 115–19; ORmchr 67715–27; StLudw 21,28–29; Väterb 27640–41. —The curse of barrenness: ELgAur 387,17–19, 572,10–16; MarlKg 1.38–52, 1.125–51; PhMarl 91–108; Passnl H6,52–64, H6,87–7,7, H345,79–83; PKonPr M260,19–20; StGrPr 328,11; WerMar 402–4, 433–40; WlMarl 287–94. Pilgrimages to overcome barrenness: Arnold, "Kindheit," 458–59; Shahar, *Childhood*, 36–37.

11. ELgAur 185,11–12: die sele . . . von dem ingusse in dem lichomen wirt bemoset mit der erbesúnden.

12. ELgAur 185,19: von einem dohterlin der lip in ahzig dagen erst formieret wirt.

13. ELgAur 185,22: Do von wolte er menlich nature eren; 185,231–25: die erste frowe swerlicher súndete denne der man. Do von solte sú vnseliger sin uf ertrich vnd in irre múter libe.

14. BertvR 1:30,34–36: Und als ez niwan als lange gelebet als ein hant mac umbe gekêret werden, sô muoz ez iemer und iemer leben als lange als got lebt, unde mac niemer ersterben an der sêle. —On the beginning of life and the entry of the soul: EkrtPr 2:24,1–25,3; Parz 109,5–7; PhMarl 329–68; WlMarl 727–42.

15. AdamEv 290–93: diu wêhen begunden si twingen, Ruowe hete si deheine. sîn herze wær' herter dan ein steine, Den si niht wolde erbarmen.

16. WilWnd 2208–10: unmâzen kranc und kreftelôs sach er dâ al sîn fröude ligen: des lebens was sie nâch verzigen.

are on hand "who were proficient in those skills that are useful during childbirth."[17] Usually the child's father is not present, but a messenger may be sent to him to apprise him of the happy outcome. When Ludwig IV of Thuringia was told that Elizabeth had delivered their first child "he gave the messenger a lavish reward and was happier than he could say. All who were present there rejoiced and praised God."[18]

The filiation of parents and children brings with it reciprocal attachments of love and obligation. According to *Wolfdietrich A* "women particularly love their very young children."[19] According to the narrator of Rudolf's *Barlaam* "children are always loved" by their fathers.[20] According to Berthold von Regensburg, a mother's devotion to her children resembles God's devotion to humankind.[21] Not surprisingly, parents are disconsolate at the loss of the children they love so dearly. The emperor Faustinian recalls that when his sons seemed to have disappeared he "found their mother grieving, beating her breasts, weeping and lamenting, and suffering great distress. She cried out over and over: 'My dear son Faustinus! My dear son Faustus!'"[22] The empress does not remain helpless in her distress but sets off on a perilous, yet ultimately successful search for her children. These examples, which represent a vast number of similar ones, offer a massive challenge to Ariès's famous claim, echoed by other historians of the family, that until well after the Middle Ages parents regarded their children with indifference. In MHG narrative, at least, parents love their children almost without exception. This love is not said to serve any

17. Exdus 181–82: die chunden selbe den list, der zû chintpette gût ist.
18. StLudw 31,28–30: her gab dem botin ein richiz botinbrot unde wart unsprechlichin fro unde alle di da keinwertig waren frouwetin sich unde lobetin got. —Childbirth: AlxusA 140–43; AvaJes 113–36; Exdus 205–6; GrMarl 288–90; GTrojk 1318–21; GuFrau 34–39, 1636–48; Hlgnlb 99,13; Ioland 128–29; Jakobr 130–32; JngTit 1107,1; Judenk 10–13; KTrojk 380–81, 5777–83; LAlexr V105–6; Parz 112,5–8; Pilat 310–13; RAlexr 1205–35; RBarlm 20,20–23; SAlexr 553–54; StElis 325–33; UAlexr 1158–64; Väterb 27746–47; VBüMos 32,9; WolfdA 24,1; WolfdB 138,3–139,2; WTitrl 18,1; WzMarg 122–24. —Pain and danger of childbirth: FlorBl 580–81; Gensis 1141–50; GTrist 1741–50; LAdam 1647–50; Rennew 9023–61, 32587–617; Parz 112,7–8; StGrgP 63,2–5. Tristrant is born by caesarean section: ETrist 95–100. —Assistance at childbirth: AdamEv 352–80; GuFrau 1647–48; KndJsu 779–80; LAdam 1770–74; Passnl H347,37–56; SaeldH 952–62. Priester Wernher claims that holding his life of the Virgin will help a woman to an easy labor and protect her child from deformities (WerMar A2505–15, 3027–38). —Messengers sent to father: FrdSwb 2922–50; Jakobr 134–91; Ksrchr 13895–904; Rennew 9024–37; MaiBfl 5,27–30; RnfrBr 23422–42; UAlexr 1165–70; WolfdA 36,1–4.
19. WolfdA 34,3: vil gerne liep den frouwen ir jungiu kindel sint.
20. RBarlm 192,5–6: hât ein man ein liebez kint (als ie diu kint mit liebe sint).
21. BertvR 2:166,6–9.
22. Ksrchr 3831–36: unz ih di muoter vant riwege, an die brust bliwende, wainunde und clagende, michel nôt habende, si rief ze allen zîten sus: "lieber sun Faustînus! lieber sun Faustus!"

particular purpose, as it is often thought to today. It is not a prerequisite for future happiness. It is simply inevitable.[23]

The devotion of parents to their children is returned by a reciprocal devotion of children to their parents. Euphrosyne's "love for her father was great, and she bestowed it according to nature in virtuous goodness."[24] More frequently children's devotion is expressed not in terms of love but of obligation. The heroine's mother in *Armer Heinrich* reminds her "beloved daughter" what this means: "You should be a joy to both [mother and father], our happiness without sorrow, the radiant object of our regard, the delight of our life, a blossom to your lineage, and a staff in our old age."[25] Like many others, she buttresses her argument with the authority of Moses, reminding her daughter that God "commanded us to love and honor mother and father and promised as a reward salvation for the soul and long life on earth."[26] MHG children are often praised for their obedience and filial devotion. The Schüler zu Paris "never failed to do what his father told him to do nor what his mother wanted, as was only fitting and proper."[27] Jesus, too, was an obedient child, not however from any compulsion, according to a sermon in the *Oberaltaicher Predigtsammlung*,

23. Parents' devotion to their children: AplTyr 2598–608, 27356; AlxusF 83–84; AvaJnG 393–97; FlorBl 780–83; FrdSwb 7039–46; HgMarg III–12; Ioland 2018–23; Jakobr 271–73; Judenk 14, 46–47; JWeltc 3781–83, 19895; LBarlm 9853, 13898–903; PartMl 6642–43; Parz 367,7–12; RBarlm 28,23–24, 192,1–16, 211,5–6; Rennew II594–99, 18515–18; RnfrBr 5696–99; Rother 1528–29; SaeldH 6204–7, 10838–40; StAdal 237–42; StEuph 669–716; StKatM 471–73; StVeit 54–55; Wglois 1224; WilOrl 2508–10, 2630; WilWnd 6787–89; Winsbk I,I–2; Winsbn 34,I–4; WolfdA 4,I. —Parents' distress at the death or departure of their children: ArmSch II52–55; BitDlb 2088–89, 2330–55; FlorBl 2917–50; FrdSwb 3452–56, 3475–524, 6715–16; Greg 815–21; Jüdel 132,2–51; Judenk 408–15; JWeltc 6281–359, 23315–29; Ksrchr 1482–565, 2735–44; Melrnz 223–31; ORmchr II50–71; Passnl H44,13–18, K472,72–473,22; Rabens 1055,I–1070,6; Rennew 9310–99; RnfrBr II558–70; RpParz 252,5–30; RWeltc 32252–56; StdabA 109–II; StElis 586–90; Väterb 28573–683; Wglois 1384–1406; WilÖst 1401–48; WilWnd 7875. —Children are their parents' joy: ArmHnr 299–300, 651–57; BitDlb 2337; JngTit III6,4; Parz 743,21–22; RBarlm 21,2–3; Väterb 27774–75, 39099–109. —Parents fail to show the usual devotion if they themselves are wicked: some are adulterers (RpParz II3,19–II7,29), others remain heathen when their children convert to Christianity (HgMarg 179–92; JnaMrt 65). As part of her religious discipline Adleheid von Frauenberg struggles to control her love for her daughter (TößSwb 51,II–14). —For the historiography concerning the issue of parental love in the past see chapter one, pp. 4 n.18, 7–8 n.32.

24. Väterb 28959–61: So was ir liebe zu im groz, Die sie von nature goz in tugentlicher gute.

25. ArmHnr 653–57: jâ soltû, liebe tohter mîn, unser beider vreude sîn, unser liebe âne leide, unser liehtiu ougenweide, unsers lîbes wünne, ein bluome in dînem künne, unsers alters ein stap.

26. ArmHnr 641–46: jâ gebôt er unde bater daz man muoter unde vater minne und êre biete, und geheizet daz ze miete daz der sêle rât werde und lanclîp ûf der erde.

27. SlPrsC 69–72: Wan er nie daz geliez, Ern tete swazn sin vatir hiez, Ouch swaz sin mutir wolde, Als er van rechte scholde.

but "out of his goodness, to teach us thereby to honor our mother and our father."[28]

Filiation in the narrowest sense, the child's relation to his parents, entails filiation in its broader sense, the child's descent from a certain lineage. Speaking to her husband, Penthesilea refers to their child as "the lineage [*art*] of us both."[29] A child *is* its lineage. The role of lineage in determining the individual nature was discussed in chapter two. But lineage also determines class status. According to the *Schwabenspiegel*, "No one can acquire for himself a legal status [*reht*] other than the one he is born with. Every child retains the status of his father."[30] This principle lies at the heart of medieval social thought and is assumed throughout the world of MHG narrative as well. When Olybrius asks Margaret if she is free she answers: "God has granted me two sorts of freedom: the first is mine by birth. I have the advantage that I am not owned by any person."[31] Filiation also determines the particular station one inherits. When Kudrun and her brother are born "the news spread far and wide that the country and its castles were not without heirs."[32] Through their birth these children have inherited sovereignty over important territories.

Shortly after birth the child undergoes a "second birth, which is baptism,"[33] and "becomes the child of God."[34] Until a child has "received Christianity" through baptism he is "still a heathen."[35] Often a child is named at baptism, and, if he receives "a signifying name,"[36] its meaning

---

28. ObalPr 29,28–29: daz tet er durch sin gûte, daz er uns da mit lerte daz wir unser muter und unsern vater eren. —Filial devotion: AlxusB 74–76; AlxusF 325–414; BMärtr 7808–77; GrMarl 496–99; GTrist 1937–39; GTrojk 1647–62; Helmbr 330–37, 496–99, 1684–702, 1913–22; Hlgnlb 161,24–27; Ksrchr 2070–71; LBarlm 15660–63; KTrojk 15100–15101; MarlKg 2,91–93; MtdtPr 305; PartMl 7152–55; Passnl K187,34–35; PhMarl 3986–87; RBarlm 218,24–26; SaeldH 2319; Väterb 259–60, 39161–69; WlMarl 4948–51, 5232–37, 6088–93. —Fourth commandment: HlbDek 271–73; Ioland 4616–24; JngTit 533,1–3; Magzog 35–36; LBarlm 10303–10; RBarlm 291,7–12; Rennr 14921–24; RWeltc 11684–87; Winsbn 2,8–10. —Typically, Hugo von Trimberg takes a less rosy view of the relation of children to parents: Rennr 14895–924. —Citations from a wide range of medieval texts on children's obligations to their parents: Shahar, *Childhood*, 167–69.

29. Rennew 32651: unser zweier arte.

30. Schwsp La12: Nieman mac im selber ander reht erwerben danne als in an geborn ist. . . . Ein iegelich kint behaltet sines vater reht.

31. WlMarg 345–50: got hât an mich geleit zweier hande vrîheit. diu eine ist mich an geborn. . . . von einer hân ich den gewin deich keines menschen eigen bin.

32. Kudrn 573,3–4: daz niht ân erben wæren lant unde bürge, man sagete harte wîte disiu mære.

33. StGrgP 63,13: Dú ander geburt daz ist der tôf.

34. Passnl H56,51: [swer getouft wirt] wirt zv kinde got erkorn.

35. MönNot 490–92: mîn kint ist noch heide; Het' ez enpfangen die Kristenheit, so wær' zergangen mîn leit.

36. Exdus 417: ein bezeichenlîcher name.

is explained. "We will call him Tristan," the infant's foster father tells the priest, and the narrator continues: "*Triste* means sorrow; anyone who has ever read this tale realizes that his name corresponded to his life."[37] If godparents are present, which is not often, they contract certain obligations: Berthold says that they "should teach the child the Credo and the Lord's Prayer when she is seven years old; they owe it to her, since they are spiritually father and mother."[38] MHG texts accord other faiths analogous rites. "The baptism of the Jews," says Gyburg, "includes a peculiar custom: they perform it by cutting."[39] As soon as the pagan Aglye was born she "was carried into the temple into the presence of Apollo."[40]

There are two sorts of natal tie that we expect most children to have but that MHG children must largely do without: siblings and family. Almost without exception, the most famous child heroes—Tristan, Isold, Siegfried, Sigune—do not have brothers or sisters. And this is typical: in the entire corpus roughly two-thirds of all children are only children. Although there is evidence that the medieval German nobility followed a

37. GTrist 1998–99: "so nenne wir in Tristan." nu heizet triste triure; 2018–20: diz mære, der daz ie gelas, der erkennet sich wol, daz der nam dem lebene was gehellesam.

38. BertvR 1:44,4–7: Ez solten des kindes totten daz kint den gelouben und daz pater noster lêren, sô ez siben jâr alt würde, wan sie sint ez im schuldic, wan sie sint geistlîche vater unde muoter.

39. WWilhm 307,23–24: der juden touf hât sundersite: den begênt si mit einem snite. —Baptism without naming: ELgAur 464,12–13, 462,21–22; LBarlm 7393–98; RBarlm 169,27–177,36; StElis 334–39; VrJngf Dorothy 86–89. —Baptism and naming: AlxusA 157–65; AlxusB 53–54; FlorBl 591–97; GTrist 1968–73; Hlgnlb 161,14–15; Jakobr 193–247; JngTit 171,1–174,4, 676,1–3, 1109,1; JWeltc 25595–604; Kudrn 22,3–4; MaiBfl 190,10–191,20; Melrnz 161–64; MHMarg 115–18; PrLanc 2:350,17–351,10; Rennew 9246–69, 32711–19; RnfrBr 23320–41; Rother 4775–78; WTitrl 24,1; Väterb 27755–58, 36956–87; StVeit 62–65; WilOrl 2051–67; WilÖst 552–69; WolfdA 24,2–33,4; WolfdB 171,3–176,4. —Children the meaning of whose names is explained: Dulcfl 96–102; Exdus Moses 255–58, Gershom 414–18, Eliezer 426–32; FlorBl 592–97; GrshPr John the Baptist 445a,33–36; GTrojk Paris 1908–14; KTrojk Paris 658–77; LebChr 137–40; Passnl Mary H8,58, Jesus H14,42–45; RAlexr 1274–81; RWeltc Moses 8983–94, Silvius 26558–76; VBüMos Benjamin 31,11–16. Some children are named by combining their parents' names: JngTit 171,1–174,4, Secundille 2990,1; JWeltc Pilate 19896–905; Passnl Pilate H82,4–7; Pilat 319–32; VrJngf Dorothy 83–84. —Significance of baptism: BertvR 1:31,25–33,9; ELgAur 578,33–34; LBarlm 2877–929; RBarlm 81,7–82,4; StGrgPr 63,15–18; VBüMos 48,7–49,2. Baptism as second birth: Jüdel 133,2–4; LBarlm 2915–19; RBarlm 81,17–23, 81,34–82,4; Rennr 24085–90. Baptism makes a child Christian: ELgAur 578,33–34; Eracl 351–57, 387–88; JngTit 1108,1–1109,1; MaiBfl 6,25–9,12; VBüMos 48,19–22; WolfdA 26,2, 35,1. Gyburg's remark that a baptized woman bears a heathen child assumes that the child will only be made Christian when it is baptized: WWilhm 307,21–22. —Godparents: AlxusA 159–62; BertvR 1:32,14–30; ELgAur 499,9–11; ORmchr 70382–94; Rennew 2465–66, 9264–69, 32715–19; StElis 2360–69; WolfdB 113,1–3, 173,1–3, 176,1–4, 212,1–3. —Circumcision: AvaJoh 171–86; Exdus 871–84; JohBap 73–94; JWeltc 3585–96; KndJsu 1132–39; LebChr 248–58, 347–52; MfRmbl 135; Passnl H22,73–85, H347,65–348,9; PhMarl 2430–35; SaeldH 1641–49; SpecEc 14,29–15,5, 15,19–34; VChrGb 119–21; WerMar A3889–98; WlMarl 3964–69. Heathen equivalent of baptism: RBarlm 20,29–21,25.

"pattern of late marriages [for males] and few children" in an effort to preserve their patrimony,[41] it is unlikely that they had as few children as their
noble cousins in the literary texts. The birth rate in MHG narratives is well
below what would be necessary to maintain a preindustrial population.[42]

Those heroes or heroines who do have siblings often have good reason to regret the fact: Wolfdietrich A is disinherited by his brothers; Pilate
murders his half-brother.[43] The fate of those siblings who do become close
is often disastrous: Helmbrecht's sister eagerly pursues his ill-advised plan
to marry her into a band of robbers; Gregorius's father falls in love with
his own sister and rapes her.[44] There are a few siblings, like the sons of
Faustinian, who are clearly attached to one another. Yet the devotion of
the brothers to each other is tepid compared with their devotion to their
mother, at least if one can judge by their reactions on being reunited after
a long separation. When the brothers meet, "Hey, how they welcomed
one another! Then they rejoiced in God saying: 'Gloria tibi deo.'"[45] But
when they find their mother, "No human tongue could ever present to
you, either in words or in song, the great ecstasy they shared among themselves."[46] Siblings, it seems, are like the schoolmates discussed in chapter
four. Just as most MHG heroic children do not have fellow students, so
most of them do not have siblings. And just as those MHG child protagonists who do have schoolmates remain distant from them, so those who
have siblings remain, if not actually hostile, then only loosely attached. The

41. Freed, *Falkenstein*, 65.
42. If average female life expectancy is 70 years, then women who reach childbearing years must average 2.19 children for population to remain constant; if average life expectancy is 20, surely closer to the medieval situation, they must have 6.5 children (Coale,
"Population," 44). —The following are only children (line numbers refer to clear statements
that the child is without siblings; in the other cases their status is clear from the context):
AlxusA; AlxusF 86–88; FrdSwb Angelburg; Greg; GuFrau; JngTit Titurel, Sigune, Tschinotulander, Parzifal; Nchtgl heroine 17–19, hero 29–30; PyrThs 25–28; Jakobr; KrlGal Charlemagne, Galie 145,55–60; Kudrn Hagen 154,3, Hilde; LAlexr; Lanzlt; Lohgrn Elsam; MarBrt
14–15; Melrnz; MOswld; Niblgn Siegfried; Passnl Nicholas K6,24–29, Katherine K669,10–
11; RAlexr; RBarlm; Rother Constantine's daughter 1528; SAlexr; SlPrsB heroine 569; SlPrsC
40–54, 100–102; UAlexr; WTitrl Sigune, Schionatulander; Väterb Abraham's niece 32273–
77, Euphrosyne, Alexis 39144–45; Wglois; WilOrl; WilÖst Wilhelm, Aglye; WilWnd. —The
following appear to be only children: BMärtr Agnes, Gregory, Ambrose, Vitus, Boniface,
Margaret, Pantaleon, Jerome, Remi, Martin, Katherine, Nicholas, Silvester; Hlgnlb Anthony,
Agnes, Aquinas, Vitus, Alexis, Elizabeth, Katherine; Jüdel; Judenk; KPantl; Passnl Remi,
Agnes, Gregory, Pancras, Vitus; Schnkd; StUlrc; Treuep Bertram, Irmengart.
43. WolfdA 266,1–269,4, 308,1–4; Passnl Pilate H82,22–53; Pilat 357–99.
44. Helmbr 1293–1638; Greg 303–410.
45. Ksrchr 2958–60: hai wi si ainander enphiengen! in got frouten si sih dô, si sprâchen
"gloria tibi deo."
46. Ksrchr 3005–9: nehaines mennisken zunge nemahte iu die michel wunne niemer
vur bringen, gesagen noh gesingen, die si under in habeten.

important relationships are not those that might connect the young heroes and heroines to other children but those they sustain with adults—tutors, teachers, or parents.[47]

While most MHG children grow up without brothers and sisters, all of them grow up without families, at least in the most common modern sense of parents and children living together. There are logistical reasons why this is so: since MHG parents tend to have few children and since, as will be seen below, many parents die and many children leave home, it is uncommon for all the elements of a potential "family" to live together from a child's birth until that child comes of age. In this the literary representation resembles the historical situation, in which death frequently did carry off parents or children. But there are also conceptual reasons: Middle High German has no word to designate what we usually mean by "family." *Familie* does not appear in German until the sixteenth century, does not come into general use until the end of the seventeenth, and does not attain its modern meaning until the first half of the nineteenth.[48] There is no MHG term that approximates the modern concept. Nor does medieval Latin have such a term: *familia* refers to the property or dependents under the authority of a lord or head of household.[49] The Middle Ages did not seem to feel the need for a category that would designate the coresidential unit of parents and children that we consider so important to psychic health and social stability.[50]

To be sure, it is possible to find MHG children who grow up in what looks like a modern family. The two sons of Wilhelm von Wenden, for example, are raised by merchants and their wives, whom they take to be their parents, along with the merchants' own children. They do not think they are part of a "family," however, but of a "household": "Each of them

47. The following have one or more siblings: ArmHnr maiden 297–303; BMärtr sons of Eustace; BitDlb 4201–4; Englhd 228–29, 282–85; FrdSwb 16–23; Helmbr; Ioland; JngTit Frimutel 459,4, Anfortas 482,4–492,4; KTrojk Paris 1090–1101; Niblgn Kriemhild 4,1–4; Orendl 166–67; Passnl Pilate H82,22–25, Ambrose K241,58–74, Bernard K395,20–21, K395,36–41; Parz Obie, Obilot 345,19–25, 367,7–8; Pilat 357–65; PrLanc Parceval 2:787,1–2; RWeltc Moses 8885–86; SaeldH Mary Magdalene 6204–7; StDrth 89–94; StElis Ludwig 122–25, 132–35; StrKrl 136–60; UWilhm W16,6; Väterb Anthony 370–71, Abraham of Kidunaia 32273, Eustace's sons 36958–61; Virgnl Dietrich 74,4–11; VrJngf Dorothy 60–62; WilWnd Wilhelm's sons 2198–201; WolfdA 3,4–4,4; WolfdB 258,2–3; WolfdD 3.2,1, 3.6,1–2; ZwöMön 8–12.

48. Kluge, *Etymologisches Wörterbuch*, 183; Schwab, "Familie," 266, 271.

49. Herlihy, *Households*, 3; Bosl, "Familia," 409–19.

50. On the history of terms for "family": Herlihy, "Family"; Herlihy, *Households*, 2–4; Mitterauer and Sieder, *European Family*, 6; Schwab, "Familie." Only a few, however, have taken seriously the absence of "families" in the Middle Ages: Ariès, *Centuries*, 353–56; Turner, "Anglo-Norman Royalty," 17.

believed himself to be a son of the household [*hus*] and a beloved child there."[51] Later we learn that they cooked for the man we would call husband or father but who is here called the *wirt*, or "master of the house,"[52] and that "the members of the household [*gesinde*] were fond of them."[53] Siegfried too might seem to grow up in a "family," since he spends his entire childhood at his parents' home. In fact, however, he grows up in the company of the "wise and experienced adults" who "cared for him"[54] and "the people" at "court," who "were glad to see him."[55] Siegfried grows up at a court, which, in this context, is nothing more than a particularly grand household. While a modern family may comprise the same members as a household, it need not, and in any case the congruence would be coincidental, since the two are defined differently. A family is defined by biology: parents and their children. A household is defined by authority: those subject to the head, which includes his wife and their children as well as servants and other dependents.

While the household and the court represent, initially at least, the primary social institutions of childhood—and in this they parallel the modern family—MHG writers do not often stress children's ties to these institutions as such. Instead they emphasize the filiations discussed above. Bruder Philipp mentions parents and relatives: when Mary is born he reports that her "father and mother were filled with joyful gladness" and that "friends and relatives came there and rejoiced with them."[56] The author of *Mai und Beaflor* mentions political and religious ties: when Beaflor is born we learn that her father, a Roman king, "sent for the princes and told them the news [that] God had given him an heir" before announcing that his daughter would be baptized the following day "because she should receive Christianity."[57] If we want to describe the "consciousness of what belongs together articulated by [medieval speakers of German] themselves,"[58] then we will have to attend closely to the terms in which they themselves articulated that consciousness. And "family" is not one of them. According to

51. WilWnd 5060–61: ietweder doch wânde, er wære sun des hûses und dâ liebez kint.
52. WilWnd 5091.
53. WilWnd 5096: des het sie daz gesinde holde.
54. Niblgn 25,3: sîn pflâgen ouch die wîsen.
55. Niblgn 24,1–2: er ze hove reit. die liute in sâhen gerne.
56. WlMarl 773–74: Des vater unde muoter dô Geilhafter fröuden wurden frô; 858–60: Friunde und mâge kâmen dar . . . Unde fröuten sich mit in.
57. MaiBfl 5,34–37: nâch den vürsten sante er dô und sagte in daz mære, wie . . . im got het einen erben geben; 6,21–22: wan ez enpfâhen sol den kristentuom.
58. Schmid, "Problematik," 19: welchem Zusammengehörigkeitsbewußtsein die Adligen selbst Ausdruck gegeben haben.

MHG writers, a child "belongs together" with "father and mother," "relatives," "princes," the lands to which she is "heir," and the "Christianity" into which she is baptized. The most important filiations with which the MHG child is born do not serve to enclose her securely within the circle of the "family" but situate her instead at the intersection of genealogical, feudal, and confessional lines that extend, usually through her mother and father, well beyond the household out into the world.[59]

Exfiliation: Breaking Ties

The ties of filiation, although of fundamental importance, are not for that reason immune from assault—as is amply illustrated by the fate of Wolfdietrich, whose father tries to have him killed. Although the murder is thwarted, Wolfdietrich ends up in the care of a hunter and his wife, completely cut off from the lineage, the class, and the society into which he was born. The rupture of the bonds of filiation as well as of later attachments are instances of exfiliation, a category that includes all the ways that ties can be attenuated or broken. There are three types, natural, passive, and active, each of which will be explained in its turn.

After his birth and baptism, Wolfdietrich's life seems to get off to a comfortable and uneventful start. His mother "took good care of him with maternal devotion as a lady should care for her child."[60] Perhaps as a consequence of this maternal solicitude, "the dear little child grew splendidly."[61] As he became older he "was placed so that he stood by the table," and "when he could walk he was given pieces of bread."[62] By this time—Wolfdietrich is now three-and-a-half—he has grown so strong that he throws dogs against the wall when they try to snatch the food out of his hands. These events trace a number of stages in the natural growth of the child, each representing a decrease in his dependence on adults: first his mother must care for every need, then he is able to stand, later to walk, and finally he is strong enough to assert himself against challengers. Each of these is

59. On my use of "lineage" and "household" rather than "family" see also chapter two, note 50.
60. WolfdA 34,1–2: des phlac sîn muoter wol mit muoterlîcher triuwe, als ein frouwe ir kindes sol.
61. Wolfd 35,4: dô wuohs ouch vollichlîchen daz liebe kindelîn.
62. WolfdA 38,1–3: Dô sazte man den kleinen, daz er bî der tavele stuont. dô er geloufen mohte . . . dô gap man im . . . brôt.

an instance of *natural exfiliation*, the attenuation of filiative ties that results from natural development.

The developmental basis for natural exfiliation is the physical growth of the child. Occasionally, as in the line from *Wolfdietrich A* cited above, a MHG text will take note of this sort of gradual development for its own sake. More frequently, the physical growth of the child is linked to some other development: Priester Adelbrecht elaborates the connection merely implied in his source (Luke 1.80), telling us that John the Baptist "increased from year to year in size and in goodness."[63] Often the growth of the child is represented as a series of sudden breaks. Eilhart's Tristrant was cared for by his nurse "until the day when he was able to ride," when he is entrusted to his tutor, Kurneval; "Kurneval cared for the child until the very day when he had become strong and could endure both suffering and hardship"; then it is time for him to go abroad.[64] Here childhood is represented as a series of sudden transitions from one set of abilities to another rather than as a gradual development.[65]

Among the developmental milestones that may be noted are weaning, walking, and talking—although the ordinary development these skills is usually described only to emphasize the extraordinary autonomy of Jesus. Jesus weans himself on his own at age two—not like other children, "for whom," according to Walther von Rheinau, "the mother's breasts are made bitter so that they will be distasteful and the children will stop sucking when they discover the bitterness that has been applied to them."[66] Jesus also learns to walk on his own—not like other children, Bruder Philipp reports, who "must be guided and directed and led by the hand. They fall down frequently, and they must be helped back up again. They crawl on their hands and feet and hold on to the walls until they have learned to walk properly and are able to stand on their own."[67] When Jesus talks he also

63. JohBap 143–45: fon iare ze iare begund iz sich meren an der gewahste unde an der gûte.

64. ETrist H124–25: dú zoch eß biß an den tag, daß er möcht rÿten; D185–89: Kurneval deß kindeß pflag biß an den namelichen tag, daß ez czu den creftin tochte und vil wol geliden mochte beide leit und ungemach.

65. Natural growth linked to other kinds of development: AvaJoh 195–98; JngTit 811,1–3, 4443,4–4344,4; MtdtPr 305; Passnl K241,54–55, K303,32–34, K619,3–5; PrLanc 1:21,16–17, 1:34,14–19; RBarlm 27,9–10; SaeldH 2325–27; StAdal 237–38; StElis 707–9, 747, 780–82; StKatM 509; UAlexr 1259; Väterb 269; WerMar 1150–56, 1539–42; WilOrl 2710–14, 2744–68, 2769–821, 3941–64; WlMarl 6094–6105.

66. WlMarl 4917–23: Als andern kinden geschiht, Dien man ir muoter brüste Bittert dur ungelüste, Dâ von diu kint erwindent Sûgens, sô si bevindent Der bitterkeite, sô dar an Ist gestrichen.

67. PhMarl 3680–87: [diu andern kint] muoz man wîsen unde stiuren und ouch mit den

talks perfectly—not, Philipp continues, like ordinary children who, "when they first learn to talk, mangle half the words."[68]

Autonomy also increases when the child attains the age of reason. Rather than a single age of reason MHG texts mention a whole range of ages depending on the consequences that the attainment of reason is going to have. When Alexis "turned seven his mother realized that he possessed reason and great intelligence [*witze*]" and decided it was time for him to begin school.[69] When Berthold von Regensburg is asked a question about children and mortal sin he answers: "one child may be smarter or have more understanding [*witze*] when it is eight years old than another that is twelve. Therefore no one can be certain at what age a child commits a mortal sin except according to the degree of understanding [*witze*] it possesses."[70] When the mature Parzival explains his earlier assault on Jeschute he says that at that time "I was a fool and not a man, not having grown to reason [*witze*]."[71] Although the ages and the consequences differ, all three texts link understanding to an increase in the child's autonomy—through greater knowledge, responsibility, or awareness. The "age of reason" is not some particular age; it is, rather, *any* age at which a sudden increase in understanding entails greater autonomy.[72]

MHG texts also refer to the physical maturation of the body, in a few cases to a change in the color of the hair,[73] more frequently to the growth of

---

henden vüeren. ofte vallent sî dâ nider, ûf helfen muoz man in dan wider. sî gênt ûf vüezen und ûf henden unde habent sich ze den wenden unz daz sî wol gelernent gên und von in selben mugen stên.

68. PhMarl 3700–3701: von êrste, sô sî sprechen lernent, diu wort halbiu brechent. —Weaning: GTrojk 1437–39; GuFrau 1674–76; HnrKgd 3580–82; PrLanc 1:20,25–26; RWeltc 21872–92; WlMarl 931–33. On weaning: McLaughlin, "Survivors," 116; Shahar, *Childhood*, 79–80. —Mastery of movement: JngTit 765,4; Pilat 335–39; SaeldH 6881–87; WilOrl 2710–12; WTitrl 86,4. —Children's speech: see chapter three, n. 44.

69. AlxusF 92–95: dô er siben jâr alt wart, dô nam diu muoter an im war daz er vernunst unt witze gar hæte.

70. BertvR 2:58,18–22: ez ist einez ouch kündiger, und hât einez mêr witze, daz aht jâr alt ist, danne etelîchez, daz zwelf jâr alt ist. Dâ von mac nieman gewizzen, wanne ez tœtlîche sünde tuot, in welchem alter, wan ie darnâch, als ez witze hât.

71. Parz 269,24–25: ich was ein tôr und niht ein man, gewahsen niht bî witzen.

72. The argument made here can be reproduced with citations that use other terms for understanding (*sich versinnen, übel und guot verstan*): BertvR 1:36,4–9; Gensis 1151–54; Jünglg 1196–1206; Kudrn 105,2; MOswld 25–26; Niblgn 1054,1–2; Parz 112,16–20; Passnl K618,22–23; Rennew 12566–67; SlPrsC 58–67, 83–84; StKatM 476–81; WilÖst 625; WlGast 1079–86; WWilhm 283,2–4. —In saints' lives the sudden access of understanding often coincides with a sudden increase in piety: ELgAur 21,10–13, 348,25–27; Passnl H348,56–57, K7,20–25, K93,74–77, K354,60–63; StMarM 75–77; Väterb 32306–08, 33517–20. —On age and legal responsibility for one's deeds: Schwsp La117, La232. —See also Arnold, *Kind*, 20–23; Boswell, *Kindness*, 32–35; Demaitre, "Idea," 466.

73. PrLanc 1:35,16–18; JngTit 694,2–3; WTitrl 36,2–3.

breasts or beards. Of the former the narrator of *Rennewart* reports: "When a maiden is about to come of age and her breasts begin to form she is overcome by a nascent desire that slips into her heart and that, on account of the pain of the desire, upsets her spirits and teaches her the ways of her mother."[74] A passage like this, which links the first stirrings of sexual desire to the sexual maturation of the body, may seem to refer to the beginning of puberty. But it does not. The narrator is commenting on the situation of Alise, who is just about to marry and conceive a child. In this as in other cases the physical change does not mark the beginning of maturation but the arrival of adulthood—social majority being signaled by marriage and sexual maturity by the conception of a child.[75]

According to legal texts, it is the same with beards: to determine the maturity of a youth, according to the *Schwabenspiegel*, "you should grab above his mouth, under his nose, and if you find small hairs there that is one indication that he is fourteen or older."[76] Ottokar also links the first growth of beard with coming of age.[77] Literary texts, however, offer quite a different picture: there the first growth of a man's beard appears after, sometimes considerably after, he has already come of age. Long after Parzival has married and fathered children, "no one could detect even half of a beard hair" about his mouth "on account of his youth."[78] When the young knights in *Guter Gerhard* are "very nearly thirty years old, their beards bore their first hairs, which had never yet been cut."[79] Perhaps these beardless men are adults who have shaved rather than youths with no need to shave: the vocabulary of beards is ambiguous in MHG and close shaving had become the fashion in Germany beginning in the mid-eleventh century.[80] Yet the passages cited refer clearly to "first hairs" and give "youth" as the reason for their absence; they use the MHG word *gran*, which refers particularly to hairs on the upper lip, where the first ones are most likely to appear. Unless medieval German beards really did not begin to grow until men were

74. Rennew 4222–28: so die maget beginnet sharen und entwerfent sich diu brûstel, so bestat sie ein gelûstel, daz slichet ir in daz herze, und daz des gelustes smerze ir den mût gar verkeret und ir mûter site leret.

75. Growth of breasts: AplTyr 1629–34, 5762–66, 14217–18; FlorBl 6904–5; JngTit 694,2–3; MaiBfl 61,11–12; WTitrl 39,2–3.

76. Schwsp La27: man sol im grifen oben an den mvnt . vnder der nase . vindet man da cleines har . daz ist ein gezivc . . . daz er vierzehen iar alt ist . oder elter.

77. ORmchr 20971–74.

78. Parz 244,9–10: vor jugende niemen dran kôs gein einer halben gran.

79. GuGrhd 1540–45: vil bî gên drîzec jâren was ir ieglîches jugent. . . . die êrsten grane truog ir bart, die man nie dâ vor versneit.

80. Bumke, *Höfische Kultur*, 201–3; Constable, introduction to *Apologia de barbis*, 94–100.

thirty, one will have to conclude that MHG writers treated beards quite artificially. Perhaps they wanted to give their heroes by nature the smooth faces that men of fashion gave themselves by shaving.[81]

The ties of filiation are undermined not only by the growth of children but also by the death of parents, which is quite common. The fathers of Parzival and Willehalm von Orlens have died before their sons are born; the mothers of Malefer and Sigune die in childbirth.[82] King Arthur's father dies when he is six and the mother of Euphrosyne when she is twelve; the parents of Katherine of Alexandria and Nicholas die as their children come of age.[83] Not surprisingly, the death of one's parents can have negative consequences. Oswald "lived with worry morning and evening since his father and mother were dead."[84] Sigune laments: "I am an orphan, exiled from my relatives, my people, and my lands."[85] In some cases, however, the death of parents can free the child to pursue virtue more diligently than before. "It came to pass that Katherine of Alexandria was completely orphaned: her father and her mother died. Only then did this most excellent maiden devote herself entirely to attaining the kingdom of heaven."[86]

81. The first growth of beard: GuGrhd 3720–22; Parz 478,8–12; PrLanc 1:36,29–30; Wer-Mar A299–303; WWilhm 338,12–14. —Young men without beards: FlorBl 6337–43; Floyrs 232; Lohgrn 595, 872–73; MaiBfl 56,31–32, 84,25; Parz 174,23–27, 211,15–17, 227,28–30, 307,7–8, 446,30, 497,30; WWilhm 13,25–27, 67,14–16, Rennewart 191,29–192,2. —Beards that carry special meaning: Partonopier lets his beard grow as a sign of his despair (PartMl 9700–9701); Rennewart grows a beard as a result of Alize's kiss, a testimony to the power of love that only makes sense against the general assumption that he would ordinarily be too young to have a beard (WWilhm 270,28–271,5, 274,18–23, 286,8–287,19, 311,16, 423,16–19); when he is twenty Jans's Achilles applies an herb to his face to keep his beard from growing while he is dressed as a woman (JWeltc 14571–94). —For medieval beards in general see the references in the previous note and Schultz, "Adolescence," 529–30.

82. Parz 105,1–112,4; WilOrl 1632–1640, 1693–1717; Rennew 9057–62; WTitrl 19,1–2.

83. Crone 314–16; Väterb 27779–90; Passnl K669,36–41, K7,65–73.

84. MOswld 21–24: er lebt mit sargen abend und den margen; . . . wann im was vater und muoter tod.

85. JngTit 724,4: ich bin ein weise, miner mage, lûte und land ellende.

86. BMärtr 24679–84: Darnach cham es an die vart daz sy gar verwaisset wart; ir vater und ïr mütter starb. alrerst sy envollen warb, die magt tugentleich, um daz himelreich. —Fathers who die before their children's birth: GTrist 1676–711; JngTit 951,1–970,4; KSilvr 101–90. —Mothers who die in childbirth: Greg 203–4; JngTit 669,1–670,2; Parz 477,2–8; SaeldH 10798–815. —Children who lose their mothers after they are born: ELgAur 787,23–25; Englhd 1753–1812; FrdSwb 167, 7093–95; MaiBfl 13,26–31; Marglg 15–17; MHMarg 119; KPantl 204–5; RBarlm 20,20–23; StLudw 14,32–15,4; StMarM 73; VrJngf 41–43. Children who lose their fathers after they are born: ELgAur 220,22; ErnstB 60–61; Greg 823–52; Klage 3449–58; KrlGal 5,43–45; Lanzlt 97–175; PrLanc 1:13,17–22; StLudw 15,9–21; StrKrl 136–39; WilWnd 103–13; WolfdA 255,1–257,1; WolfdB 4,2–8,1. Those who lose both parents: ELgAur 346,23–24; Greg 185–272; GuFrau 92–93, 134–36; MarBrt 12–15; Passnl K293,6–7; SaeldH 6227–30; Väterb 302–7, 32273–89; WolfdB 258,4–263,2. —Parents' death frees children to pursue another affiliation: BMärtr 3221–26, 10401–19; ELgAur 220,22; Floyrs 343–69; Passnl K7,65–87, K192,79–90; StKatM 510–60; Väterb 302–7.

While natural exfiliation occurs more or less by itself, *passive exfiliation* is caused by the deliberate intervention of others in the life of the child. After Wolfdietrich's father has been convinced by members of his court to have his child killed, he forces the loyal Berhtung to agree to carry out the deed and, on the night they have set, Berhtung waits outside the royal bedchamber while the king and queen prepare to retire. As they do so they argue about their son, and in the course of the argument the king disinherits him: "I swear by my faith that he will never enjoy the least benefit from any of my lands nor gain any part of them, even if he lives forever." [87] Later the king goes to the bed of the child "that he intended to steal from his dear mother," [88] takes him, and hands him over to Berhtung. Within a few hours Wolfdietrich's father violates the bonds of filiation repeatedly and brutally: first he disinherits his son, then "steals" him from his mother, and finally sends him away to be killed. All the while the young hero remains sound asleep. These and other similar exfiliative acts that the hero must endure are instances of passive exfiliation.

While the behavior of Wolfdietrich's father represents a heinous violation of paternal obligations, many milder sorts of passive exfiliation occur in the ordinary course of growing up. Children may be entrusted to a nurse or tutor. They may be sent to a foreign court or to school, or given to a religious house. These practices attenuate filial ties but do not seriously threaten them, and they do not deliberately expose the children to danger. Since they are treated in detail elsewhere they need only be mentioned here. The forms of passive exfiliation discussed below are quite different. They represent major disruptions in the child's relations to parents and society and, although common in MHG narrative, can hardly be considered ordinary features of conscientious childrearing.

Some parents, rather than encouraging their children's gradual integration into society, try to prevent this by sequestering them, usually to prevent them from coming into contact with something the parents regard as a threat. Dulciflorie's father locked her up in a splendid palace "so that she would never take a man, no matter what his lineage, nor would any man have the good fortune to see her beauty, for as long as her father should live." [89] Josaphat's father had him locked up in a very comfortable

---

87. WolfdA 68,3–69,1: ich gibe dir des mîn triuwe . . . daz er aller mîner lande geniuzet nimmer umbe ein hâr, Noch nimmer teil gewinnet, und solte er immer leben.

88. WolfdA 73,2: daz er verstelen wolte der lieben muoter sîn.

89. Dulcfl 138–43: Daz bî sînen zîten Si nimmer man genæme, Von swelher arde er quæme, Noch ime solde sô wol geschehen, Daz er möhte gesehen Ir wunneclîchen lîp.

house "because he had been told a prophecy that his son would become a Christian. However, he hoped to forestall this."[90] In every case the parents hope to prevent their children from coming of age and assuming their adult roles. But they never succeed. By sequestering their children they thereby guarantee that the children will sooner or later succumb dramatically to precisely that from which they wanted to isolate them. Josaphat's father "could not deflect what God was going to send into his son's mind."[91]

A few young heroes are, like Wolfdietrich A, disinherited. Heinrich, the father of Wolfram von Eschenbach's Willehalm, "cast out all his sons, leaving them neither castles nor fields nor any of his wealth in this world."[92] When this event is retold by Ulrich von Etzenbach, Heinrich is criticized severely for having "turned his back on his obligations, on natural behavior, and on birth."[93] Disinheritance can also occur when children violate *their* natural obligations, at least according to the *Schwabenspiegel*, where the list of filial violations includes the following: if a son refuses to redeem his father from prison or to permit a priest to administer last rites; if he becomes a thief or a minstrel against his father's will; if he hits his father in the face or vilifies him "greatly and notoriously";[94] if he sleeps with his stepmother or another woman with whom his father has lain; "if a daughter lies with a man against her father's will before she is twenty-five; once she is twenty-five she may very well lose her honor, but she can never lose her inheritance."[95]

Children forfeit their rights as heirs not only if they are disinherited but also if they are illegitimate. Thus, in order to deprive him of his portion the brothers of Wolfdietrich B "claimed that he was a bastard and

90. LBarlm 793–95: wand im gewîssaget was, sîn sun würde ein kristen; dô wolt erz alsô fristen.

91. LBarlm 808–10: er enmoht ez niht erwenden swaz got wolde senden in sînes sunes gemuote. —Sequestered children: Blnsdn 1.1–4; JnaMrt 89; KrlGal 34,40–53; KTrojk 13922–25; MOswld 305–22, 787–804; Nchtgl 55–59; Parz 116,28–118,2; PyrThs 393–97; RBarlm 23,7–24,8; SaeldH 1951–85; WolfdB 18,1–19,4. Two princes, Rennewart and Charlemagne, are raised in kitchens (WWilhm; KrlGal). —Lanzelet, Wigalois, Lancelot, and Wigamur are raised away from society but, although they lack certain information (identity of parents, knightly skills), they are not sequestered in order to keep them ignorant. —Sequestered maidens in medieval literature: Rosenfeld, *Novellenstudien*, 491–92.

92. WWilhm 5,16–19: Von Narabôn cuns Heimrîch alle sîne süne verstiez, daz er in bürge noch huobe liez noch der erde dehein sîn rîcheit.

93. UWilhm W20,24–25: grâve Heimerich nû triuwe vlôch, natiurlîch gebaern unde geburt.

94. Schwsp La15.6: Daz sehst ist ob er in sere vnd merclichen bescholten hat.

95. Schwsp La15.14: ob ein tohter . . . man zů ir leit . ane ir vater willen . die wile si vnder fivnf vnd zweinzec iarn ist . kvmt si vber fvnf vnd zweinzec iar . so mac si ir ere wol verliesen . aber ir erbe kan (sie) niemer verliesen.

that he could not have any part of the inheritance."[96] Illegitimacy can have
even more serious consequences, as Tristan's mother explains after she has
conceived a child out of wedlock: "I am certain that if things should go
so well that my brother does not kill me, he will nevertheless disinherit
me and deprive me of wealth and honor. Furthermore, I will have to raise
my baby without the help of a father."[97] While illegitimacy, though not
uncommon, was a definite disability in the historical Middle Ages, in some
literary texts it is "not a flaw but a distinction"[98]: in three of the four MHG
accounts Alexander is illegitimate as are a considerable number of youths
in the prose *Lancelot*, including Galaad.[99]

Illegitimacy is among the reasons why a child's birth may be concealed, an act that necessarily obscures many of the ordinary natal ties. The
mother of Gregorius, whose brother is the father of her child, deliberately
arranged to get through "her labor in such a way that no one was aware
of it."[100] While the births of Gregorius and Wolfdietrich B are kept secret
to conceal an incestuous or illegitimate union, those of Moses and Tristan
are concealed to protect them from their enemies.[101] The secrecy of such
births is often compounded by abandonment, abduction, or the death of
the parents, which leaves the children ignorant of their true parentage for
much of their childhood.

Infanticide is the most extreme form of exfiliation, since it envisions
the child's death—and in MHG narrative the crime is especially heinous,
since it is always planned by one of the child's parents. Thus it violates the
natural love that parents are assumed to feel for their offspring: it is "contrary to nature."[102] But it is never successful. Either those entrusted with
the crime are moved by pity and cannot bring themselves to carry out the
deed (Paris and Wolfdietrich A), or the children are brought back to life,

96. WolfdB 267,4: si jâhn er wære ein kebeskint, ern möht niht erbes hân.
97. GTrist 1477–86: ich weiz wol, ob daz wol ergat, daz mich min bruoder . . . niht
ersterbet, daz er mich aber enterbet und nimet mir guot und ere. . . . dar zuo muoz ich min
kindelin . . . ziehen ane vater rat.
98. Ruh, "Gralsheld," 248: nicht Makel, sondern Auszeichnung.
99. Illegitimate children and those accused of illegitimacy: FrdSwb 7143–68; Greg
303–683; KTrojk 28688–93; Ksrchr 13905–14; PrLanc 1:174,25–27, 2:77,9–80,28, 2:294,3–299,8,
2:306,26–307,13, 2:601,9–10, 2:715,28–716,1; RAlexr 454–844; SAlexr 233–420; Schnkd 19–
34; UAlexr 293–756. —Illegitimacy and inheritance: Greg 2483–85; GTrist 5370–444; Ksrchr
13905–14, 14146–49; LpzgPr 324,4–7; RWeltc 19409–19; Schwsp La41; WolfdA 266,1–275,4.
—Illegitimacy in the Middle Ages: Buchda, "Kinder und Jugendliche"; Sprandel, "Unehe-
liche Kinder"; Wesener, "Rechtsstellung." Tristan's illegitimacy: Combridge, *Recht*, 29–42.
Illegitimacy in the prose *Lancelot*: Andersen, "Väter und Söhne," 216–20.
100. Greg 668–69: ir geburt sô ende nam daz der nieman wart gewar.
101. WolfdB 93,1–94,3; Exdus 187–210; RWeltc 8887–930; GTrist 2023–42.
102. LBarlm 13901: daz ist wider der natûre.

as a sign that the fathers who killed them were acting according to God's will (children of Engelhard and one of the Jakobsbrüder).[103] Many of these stories contain a moment like the one mentioned in chapter three, where the unknowing smile of the child undermines the resolve of those who are supposed to kill him.[104]

In the end Paris is not killed but abandoned, and thus he joins a larger number of MHG children who suffer the same fate. Some are abandoned from poverty (Romulus and Remus), some to save them from their enemies (Moses), some to forestall the disaster that they are prophesied to bring to pass (Judas), some to save their parents from having to acknowledge an illicit relationship (Albanus), one to punish her for having thwarted her father's incestuous desires (king of Russia's daughter). When parents abandon a child they usually try to arrange things so that the child will survive, be found, and raised to adulthood. Judas is put to sea in a casket that has been carefully prepared "so that the surge of the raging water would not take his life at once."[105] Albanus is discovered with "beautiful gifts," which have accomplished their purpose when the finder concludes "that the child came from a noble lineage."[106] The abandonment of children was not only a literary device, useful for its ability to generate surprising plot developments, but also an historical practice: Hugo von Trimberg criticizes women at the end of the thirteenth century who leave their children at the church door.[107]

A number of children are sold by their parents or guardians, although the reasons for doing so vary widely. Eraclius's mother sells him to the emperor to save him from hardship in accordance with "a custom the Romans had at that time. When it befell a man that misfortune robbed him of all his possessions and his wealth, if he had children he sold them at once. He did this so that they would fare better, earn something by their service, and not be destroyed by poverty."[108] A similar custom seems to have ob-

103. GTrojk 1–28, 805–53, 1318–67; KTrojk 346–519; WolfdA 40,1–104,4; Englhd 5957–6295; Jakobr 894–968.

104. See chapter three, note 30 for examples.

105. Passnl H313,65–66: daz im des tobendē wazzers vlut zvhant dē lib nicht an gewā.

106. Alban 2.6: die scone gaven; 2.5: dad dad kint wære cumen van edelem geslehte.

107. Rennr 18519–32. —Abandoned children: ELgAur 216,1–6; Exdus 211–22; Greg 699–788, 923–76; GTrojk 1334–67; JnaMrt 44; JWeltc 20031–43, 26817–885; KTrojk 470–521; PartMl 17930–35; Passnl H313,51–73; RWeltc 8931–45; VBüMos 32,10–15; WolfdA 78,1–104,4. —On abandoned children: Arnold, *Kind*, 43–58; Boswell, *Kindness*; Goodich, *Vita Perfecta*, 92.

108. Eracl C696–716: Es hetten romer Pey den czeiten einen sit . . . Wenn ein man also cham Daz im die unselde nam Sein hab gar und sein güt . . . Het er chind er verchaüft ez san Und tet daz umb daz Daz si sich begingen dester paz Und dürch armüt nicht verdurben Und mit dinst güt erwurben.

tained in thirteenth-century Germany—at least to judge by the *Schwaben-spiegel*, which states: "If a man sells his child on account of hardship that is legally compelling, he does rightly. However he shall not sell her into a whorehouse or so that she would be killed."[109] The sale of children by their parents occurred frequently throughout Europe until the end of the Middle Ages,[110] and medieval jurists cited Nehemiah 5.1–5 in support of the practice, at least in cases of poverty.[111] Thus it is possible that a medieval German audience might not have felt the same revulsion we feel at the idea. Most of the youths, at least, fare rather well: the sons of Faustinian are bought by a pious widow who "treated the little children as if they were her sons."[112] The maidens, on the other hand, are bought for sexual purposes: Tarsia is sold into a brothel, Blanscheflur to the emir of Babylon, who plans to marry her for a year and then have her killed.[113] Although the details of the stories vary considerably, one thing that they all have in common is the surprising absence of any substantial criticism directed at those who sell the children.[114]

Some of the children who are sold had been abducted first. Malefer "was stolen as he lay in his cradle. The nurse who had him in her care betrayed him to the merchants, with whom she departed."[115] This would never have happened, according to the narrator of *Reinfried von Braunschweig*, if Malefer had only been cared for with the proper attentiveness—as, he is happy to report, was the case for Reinfried's son.[116] Other children are carried off by animals: Hagen from his parents' court by a griffin; the sons of Eustace from their father by a wolf and a lion.[117] In cases of abduction the antecedent ties are broken quite violently and require much effort to be reestablished: it is many years before Malefer encounters his father and many years before Hagen finds a way to leave the desolate island where the griffin deposits him.[118]

109. Schwsp La357: Unde ist daz ein man sin kint verkovffet . durch ehafte not . daz tŷt er wol mit rehte . er sol ez aber niht verkouffen in daz hŷr hus noch daz man ez tœte.

110. Verlinden, "L'enfant esclave," 109.

111. Boswell, *Kindness*, 144.

112. Ksrchr 1454–55: Diu frouwe handelte diu kindelîn sam si ir sune solten sîn.

113. AplTyr 15526–83; FlorBl 1501–866.

114. Other children sold: JWeltc 20411–500; Passnl K194,49–56; Rennew 9719–949; Schnkd 51–60; WilWnd 2283–325, 5049–185, 6957–73, 7869–72; WWilhm 283,3–4.

115. Rennew 9298–302: man verstal daz kint daz in der wiegen lac. die amme die des kindes pflac wider die kauflŷte ez verreit, mit den sie von dannen shiet.

116. RnfrBr 23362–419.

117. Kudrn 50,1–72,4; Väterb 37242–84.

118. Abducted children: AplTyr 9639–74, 15397–428; BMärtr 698–701, 7675–93, 8978–9160; ELgAur 700,15–26; GTrist 2270–481; Hlgnlb 68,12–15, 99,17–18; JWeltc 13569–638;

Heroes that they are, many MHG children refuse to wait around until someone else picks them up or sends them off. Often they themselves will sever the ties that bind them to people and places, thereby accomplishing their own *active exfiliation*. As Wolfdietrich's childhood comes to an end he learns that he is not the son of Berhtung, who raised him, but of the Greek king and that he has been deprived by his brothers of his inheritance. At once Wolfdietrich vows to fight the usurpers until they return what he is owed. The loyal Berhtung promises to lend his aid but attempts to get Wolfdietrich to stay out of battle until he is older. He invokes "a custom that we have [here] in Greece: a man must be completely grown up before anyone will allow him to bear a sword."[119] But Wolfdietrich disdains custom: "'I fully intend to fight for my own kingdom,' he replied. 'I myself give myself leave.' 'To be sure,' the old man said, 'I cannot prevent you from doing so.'"[120] Although Wolfdietrich is devoted to Berhtung— and for good reason—he has just learned that by right he is king: at once he overrules his former master, suddenly transformed into his vassal. Actions like these, where a child severs ties of dependence on his or her own initiative, are instances of active exfiliation.

Some children sever ties for their own safety. Beaflor wants to escape the sexual advances of her father.[121] Judas flees to escape punishment after he has slain his foster brother.[122] Those who lack the training they will need as adults leave home in pursuit of education. Blanschandin has been deprived of all knowledge of chivalry, so he sets forth to make up this deficiency: "I will never turn back," he says, "until I reach a place where I can learn knighthood."[123] Others leave home to seek their fathers. Wigalois declares his intention "to seek him of whose excellence and prowess I have been told all my life; that is my father, lord Gawein."[124] Searches like Wigalois's are ostensibly attempts to recover one's origins and reestablish natal filiations, but in fact they, no less than the other kinds of active exfiliation,

---

Lanzlt 180–83; PrLanc 1:14,14–24; RpParz 251,14–25; Wigmur 110–66, 300–319; WolfdB 142,1–154,4; WWilhm 282,24–283,1. —On the commentary in *Reinfried* on the abduction of Malefer: Harms, "Epigonisches," 312–13.

119. WolfdA 315,3–4: des habe wir site ze Kriechen, er muoz volwahsen gar, daz im iemen swert erloube.

120. WolfdA 316,3–317,1: "ich wil entriuwen vehten umb mîn selbes künicrîch: ich erloube mir ez selbe" sprach Wolf Dietrîch. "Triuwen" sprach der alte, "ich tar ez dir niht wern."

121. MaiBfl 20,39–29,40.

122. Passnl H315,27–32.

123. Blnsdn 1,60–61: Ichn erwinde niemer ich envar Da ich ritterschaf gelerne.

124. Wglois 1302–5: ich wil den suochen von dem mir ie tugent unde manheit allez mîn leben ist geseit; daz ist mîn vater, her Gâwein.

always lead the hero not backwards but forwards: in seeking his origins he is led out into the world.[125]

When Wigalois sets out he is eager not only to find his father but also to acquire fame as a knight: "How shall my name become known," he asks his mother, "unless I ride off into other countries?"[126] Wilhelm von Österreich leaves home for love, determined to find the woman whose image he has seen in a dream, even "if the land of Austria," to which he is heir, "must remain foreign to me forever."[127] Wigalois and Wilhelm, like many other MHG knights, set out to become adult heroes—as fighters or as lovers—and break their ties to parents and home in order to do so. Some, like Wilhelm, attenuate these ties even further by concealing their true identity, thereby guaranteeing that they will receive neither assistance nor opposition from those who know their origins and that, as a consequence, whatever they accomplish will be the result of their own efforts alone.[128]

Religious heroes stand under an even stronger imperative to break filial ties. As a monk reminds Euphrosyne, "The son of God has prescribed for us the path that leads to eternal bliss. He says: 'Whoever does not leave all that he possesses for my sake cannot be a disciple of mine. And whoever loves his father and mother more than me, if he does not break away, he cannot be my disciple.'"[129] Young saints are quick to obey. Benedict "did not remain long with his relatives" but went to live in a remote ditch "because in the days of his youth his heart began to prod him to flee the world, withdraw from people, and live in poverty for God's sake."[130] Eu-

---

125. Others who flee home: BMärtr 8938–64; JnaMrt 89; Rennew 17809–44; StrKrl 168–78; VorNov 70–77. —Children who leave home to pursue their education: Parz 125,27–128,16; Passnl K505,20–24; ScholM 30–31; WilOrl 2975–90. —Others who want to seek their fathers: BitDlb 2032–36, 2077–80, 2114–15, 2356–62, 4529–31; FrdSwb 6630–734; Rennew 13106–27; WilWnd 5182–83, 5583–647; WolfdA 295,1–3. —On the search for the father: Cormeau, *Zwei Kapitel*, 26–27; van der Lee, *Vatersuche*, 145–55, 177–86.

126. Wglois 1350–52: wie sol mîn nam werden erkant ichn rîte ûz in andriu lant?

127. WilÖst 792–93: sôlt daz lant ze Osterrich mir ymmer wesen wilde.

128. Others who leave home to pursue fame and fortune: Englhd 270–325; Frndst 8,1–12,8; Greg 1492–503, 1558–624; Helmbr 361–88, 646–48, 419–21; Lanzlt 294–306, 349–51; SAlexr 823–50; SlPrsC 83–123; UAlexr 1721–62; Wigmur 1417–34. —Others who leave home for love: FlorBl 2567–950; TandFl 1436–589; WolfdB 9,1–38,4. —Others who conceal their identity: BitDlb 2296–313, 3407–8; ETrist 269–85; FlorBl 2102–6; GTrist 2689–721, 3081–131; Rennew 17834–38; StrKrl 200–201; WilÖst 1262–65; WolfdB 22,1–55,4; WWilhm 284,1–5. —On Tristrant's anonymity: Mohr, "Tristan," 61–62; Schindele, *Tristan*, 16–18.

129. Väterb 28166–75: der Gotes sun Hat uns den wec vur geleit Der zu der ewigen selde treit. Er sprichet: "swer durch mich niht lat Allez daz er besezzen hat, Der mac niht wesen ein junger min. Wer ouch hat den vater sin Und muter lieber danne mich, Ist daz er drabe niht bricht sich, Er mac min junger niht gewesen."

130. Passnl K217,20–25: nicht lange er bi den vrunden bleib, wand in in sinen iungen tagen sin herze druf begonde iagen, daz er die werld solde vlien und sich von den luten zien, durch got in armut genesen.

phrosyne, who wants "to live in true chastity and in purity of heart,"[131] flees home to avoid the marriage her father has arranged for her, disguises herself as a man, and enters a monastery. Anthony, who wants to "escape the filth" of the world after the death of his parents,[132] gives away his inheritance. For Euphrosyne and Anthony the threat of entanglement in the secular world provokes their active exfiliation.[133]

Although exfiliation offers many opportunities for intergenerational conflict—between Euphrosyne, for instance, who wants to remain a virgin, and her father, who has arranged a marriage for her—it is remarkable how seldom such conflict actually materializes. Sometimes the child's guardians support the course he has chosen: when Lanzelet decides to leave home his foster mother provides him with a fine horse and splendid armor because she "realized that he wanted to leave the country for no other reason than glory."[134] In other cases parents' brief resistance merely illustrates their love and anxiety for their departing child: when the Schüler zu Paris decides he must set out to win fame and fortune "this caused both [of his parents] sorrow and heartfelt pain. They were afraid that some misfortune might befall him who was so dear to them."[135] But in the end he departs—presumably with their blessing, since "he took with him whatever he wanted of silver and gold."[136] Most striking are those cases where the narrative successfully maneuvers around what seems like an unavoidable conflict. After Alexis has already committed himself to a life of pious chastity, his father arranges a marriage for him. But Alexis does not refuse, since "he did not want to trouble his father nor force his will on him."[137] After the ceremony Alexis dutifully leads his bride to bed—since, once again, "he did not challenge his father's authority."[138] Only then does he inform his wife

131. Väterb 27937–39: Ir wille was, mohte ez wesen, In rehter kuscheit genesen An des herzen wize.

132. Väterb 319–23: Er dahte . . . Wie er den unflate Uz der werlde entwiche.

133. The scriptural injunction: SaeldH 7167–76; StUlrc 165–68. —Others who leave family and friends to serve God: AvaJoh 195–202; BMärtr 17904–6; ObSrvt 264–65; PhMarl 4834–37; VlSrvt 292–316. —Others who flee marriage: AlxusA 237–300; AlxusB 90–145; AlxusF 275–637; BMärtr 702–821; Ioland 175–98, 443–61; JnaMrt 6, 19, 65; KAlxus 208–51; MarBrt 18–88; StEuph 574–96; Väterb 30707–89, 39206–54. —Others who give away their inheritance: BMärtr 3221–53, 10401–10, 25869–75, 27991–96; JnaMrt 72–73; KSilvr 716–39; Passnl K7,65–87, K192,91–193,17, K293,22–294,1.

134. Lanzlt 349–51: Dô diu künegîn daz bevant, daz er gerne rûmte dez lant, durch niht wan umb êre.

135. SlPrsC 100–107: Daz was leit in beiden Und tete in ime herzen we. . . . Si vorchten, daz sinem zarten libe Mochte geschehen ungemach.

136. SlPrsC 111–12: Er nam van silbir und van golde Mite ime, swaz er wolde.

137. AlxusB 75–76: er wolde den vater niht betrüeben noch sînen willen an im üeben.

138. AlxusB 88: er enstrâfte niht des vater munt.

that he plans to leave the next day to become a beggar in a distant country. Even though Alexis is committed to a life of ascetic piety completely at odds with the plans of his father, the text goes out of its way to suppress any hint of conflict between father and son, insisting at every stage on Alexis's obedience.[139]

One must keep in mind that, with very few exceptions (Helmbrecht is one), the heroes of the MHG child narratives are models in every regard and that, again with very few exceptions (the mother of Iolande is one), their parents or foster parents are models as well. As model children are expected to obey their parents, so model parents are supposed to love their children; and all are expected to subscribe to the same religious and social values. If the ideality of both the children and their guardians is to be maintained, then it is inconceivable that there should be much occasion for conflict between them. This ideal is so strong that stories in which conflict seems inevitable usually find ways of evading it. Where the parents resist the child's exfiliative desire, as in the *Schüler zu Paris C*, they do so only out of love, not out of fundamental opposition. And where children, like Alexis, are determined to follow a path radically different from the one their parents had in mind, they get their way without ever actually confronting the authority they are compelled to thwart. Thus parents show themselves loving and children show themselves obedient even when they pursue courses that are clearly irreconcilable.

Of course there are some MHG children—among them famous figures like Parzival, Gregorius, Helmbrecht, and the maiden in *Armer Heinrich*—who differ openly with those who raised them. These struggles, however, come about not because the children or the parents have somehow gone wrong, but because each is committed to a cultural ideal that cannot easily be reconciled with the other. In *Parzival* the son's commendable desire to realize his knightly vocation cannot be reconciled with his mother's love, which wants to protect him from the dangers of combat. In *Iolande* the praiseworthy desire of the daughter to realize her religious vocation cannot be reconciled with the legitimate authority of her parents to arrange a marriage. In *Flore und Blanscheflur* the son's perfect love for a

139. The child's guardian offers no resistance to his departure: ETrist 185–258; PrLanc 1:39,20–42,11, 1:117,15–124,35; UAlexr 1421–62; WilOrl 2899–3037; WolfdB 9,1–38,4. —Parents or guardians offer only token resistance: Englhd 320–35; FlorBl 2567–663; Jakobr 309–20; StdabA 60–106; Wglois 1274–410. —Conflict seems inevitable but is nevertheless evaded: AlxusA 185–230; Blnsdn 1.60–128; Bussrd 240–70, 504–25; KAlxus 160–99; Kudrn 401,1–487,4; MarBrt 12–29; Melrnz 186–251; Nchtgl 83–95; Passnl K472,64–473,22; Väterb 27964–8417, 30707–42, 32496–505, 35817–69, 39139–75; VorNov 70–112; WilÖst 804–930.

Christian slave cannot be reconciled with the prudent concern of his parents, the king and queen of pagan Spain, for the future of their kingdom. In every case the conflict arises not from childish willfulness or parental stubbornness, but because parents and children are devoted to irreconcilable cultural ideals.[140]

Many of the phenomena discussed above resemble those we nowadays consider characteristic of adolescence. They are not characteristic of adolescence in MHG texts, however, since MHG writers do not acknowledge such a stage of life. First, the physiological preconditions are missing. For us adolescence falls between puberty and adulthood, but, as was shown above, MHG writers allow no time between those two milestones. Second, the psychological attributes of modern adolescence are missing. Dr. Spock expresses a widely held view when he explains that adolescents will display "rebelliousness" and "rivalrousness with parents"[141]—even though there is not a great deal of evidence "to support the contention that [adolescence] is a period of emotional storm and stress and general rebelliousness"[142] and even though "studies across racial, cultural, and socioeconomic groups [find] that most teenagers feel close to their parents, not distant."[143] The popular expectation of struggle between parents and adolescent children finds no analogue in MHG narrative, however. As was just shown, MHG texts go out of their way to avoid intergenerational conflict, even when it seems inevitable.

Nor is there any evidence that MHG children engage in the process of identity formation, including role experimentation and vocational choice, which experts and nonexperts expect of modern adolescents.[144] Identity formation plays no role in MHG childhood for the simple reason that the children's identities are already formed at birth. Their identities are intrinsic, a consequence of the nature, MHG *art*, with which they are born. Parzival is destined to be a knight because he has inherited "inborn bravery

140. Others who struggle with their guardians to realize their knightly vocation: Greg 1479–824; WolfdA 306,2–316,4; PrLanc 1:117,24–119,19; Helmbr 224–648. —Others who struggle with their guardians to realize their religious calling: ArmHnr 557–902; AlxusF 275–420; BMärtr 8765–937, 10370–401, 22981–94, 34436–95; Jüdel 130,71–131,5; Judenk 216–58; Passnl K301,28–303,11, K515,87–517,66, K592,53–593,17; Rennew 22832–78. —Others who struggle with their guardians over love: Eneit 260,7–284,34, 341,39–345,4; TandFl 928–4056. —Even the mother of Iolande, surely one of the least attractive MHG parents, has her defenders: Wyss, *Legendenepik*, 263.
141. Spock, *Baby and Child Care*, 501.
142. Gallatin, *Adolescence*, 147.
143. Steinberg and Belsky, *Infancy, Childhood*, 499.
144. Gallatin, *Adolescence*, 223–41.

and the nature of the lineage of Gahmuret," his father.[145] Iolande shows at an early age that she is destined for a religious life: "no matter how young she was, she trod worldly things under her feet with vigor."[146] Flore, conceived and born the same day as Blanscheflur, is destined to love her: from the moment of their birth, "when they lay in their cradles, their gestures revealed that they loved one another."[147] It is absurd to talk about identity formation or experimentation with roles or vocations in connection with such heroes and heroines. Their identities, that is, their natures, are fixed from birth. Even the peasant's son Helmbrecht, who seems more like a rebellious adolescent than any other MHG figure, claims that he has "inherited" a knightly disposition from his godfather, a knight, and from a courtier his mother slept with when she was pregnant with him.[148] Helmbrecht does not claim that he must try out life as a knight to "find out who he is" but that knighthood has been part of his nature from birth.[149]

Affiliation: Making New Ties

As children grow up ties are not only broken but also made. At the same time Wolfdietrich's relation to his father becomes progressively weaker, his ties to Berhtung multiply. Berhtung rescues the infant, later he receives him into his home and assumes the roles of mentor and foster father. Wolfdietrich thinks Berhtung actually is his father. Wolfdietrich's relation to his

145. Parz 174,24–25: Gahmuretes art und angeborniu manheit.
146. Ioland 146–47: dy werilt trat sy bit gewalt zen vûzen alse junc sy was.
147. FlorBl 602–7: dô se in den wagen lâgen . . . ir gebærde des verjach daz se ein ander minneten.
148. Helmbr 1378: von dem erbet mich daz an.
149. Since my earlier discussion of these issues (Schultz, "Adolescence") has occasioned some comment (Hanawalt, *London*, 8; Reyerson, "Montpellier," 354), I would like to note two points. First, I did not claim that "adolescence" should never be used in connection with the Middle Ages, only that there is nothing in MHG texts that resembles what we nowadays usually mean by the term. Second, I suggested that any claim concerning adolescence in the past, if it is to be credible, must be based on an informed and explicit definition of what is meant by the term (535–36). Adolescence is understood in too many different ways (by anthropologists, psychologists, ordinary people) and in everyday usage carries with it too many unexamined assumptions to be useful in scholarly writing without precise specification. If, with an eye to medieval phenomena, one were to define adolescence as a stage of life that falls after a person has left his or her parents' home but before that person has attained full adulthood, then there is little doubt that one would be able to find groups or texts that recognize such a stage of life in the Middle Ages. If, however, in a given time and place, such a stage exists only for some people (males but not females, apprentices but not peasants), then one will want to consider whether adolescence is really the best term for it. If adolescence is to qualify as a "stage of life," commensurate with infancy, childhood, and adulthood, then everyone ought to pass through.

mother follows a different course. Their ties are broken in early childhood and Wolfdietrich forgets she ever existed, but just as he is about to come of age she appears at Berhtung's and they become reacquainted. Here broken ties are mended. When Wolfdietrich comes of age he not only rediscovers old bonds; at the same time he contracts a whole new set of relationships with those around him by becoming a knight and by assuming the role of king. The reestablishment of ties with his mother, the various bonds he forms as a child with Berhtung, and the new relationships he assumes on coming of age represent three kinds of affiliation: refiliation, childhood affiliation, and adult affiliation. I will discuss the first two in this chapter. Adult affiliation, which includes the rites of passage that mark the end of childhood, will be considered in the next.

After Wolfdietrich has been in the charge of Berhtung for quite a while, his mother, now a widow, appears at the castle gates. Her other sons have accused her of having borne an illegitimate child, Wolfdietrich, and have cast her out of her own home. When she arrives in search of refuge, Berhtung tells Wolfdietrich to welcome his mother—which surprises Wolf-dietrich since "he thought that Berhtung's wife was his mother."[150] The next morning he challenges his foster father to disclose the truth of the matter and Berhtung sends him to the queen. "I am your mother," she explains, "and you are my little child";[151] then she hands Wolfdietrich a document that tells the whole story. When he has read it, "he laid his head in his mother's lap [and] they both cried and lamented greatly. He embraced her and kissed her [and] their clothes became wet"—with tears, presumably.[152] The tearful embrace of Wolfdietrich and his mother offers a striking image of *refiliation*—the reestablishment of ties of filiation that had been broken.

Refiliation can restore ties that have been obscured from ignorance or from distance. Like Wolfdietrich, Willehalm von Orlens grows up under the mistaken impression that he is the son of his adoptive parents—until a squire comes along and tells him otherwise.[153] Willehalm can no longer be reunited with his natal parents, since both are dead, but the discovery of their identity does restore him to his position as heir to his ancestral lands. Dietleib, on the other hand, knows his genealogical status perfectly well— but he misses his father, Biterolf, who abandoned wife and children when

150. WolfdA 281,3: er wânde ez wær sîn muoter daz Berhtunges wîp.
151. WolfdA 300,4: ich bin dîn muoter und du mîn kindelîn.
152. WolfdA 305,1–3: Dô neigte er sîner muoter daz houbet in die schôz. dô wart ir beider weinen und ouch ir jâmer grôz: er halstes unde kustes, ir kleider wurden naz.
153. WilOrl 2830–76.

Dietleib was two. So he leaves home, crosses most of Europe, and ends up at the court of Etzel, where, eventually, father and son are reunited. Even before they learn each other's identities—which both have concealed with pseudonyms—Biterolf and Dietleib "frequently exchanged friendly glances even though they had done nothing to deserve them" because, as we are told somewhat earlier, "wherever you see a blood relative, your heart will bear you to him, even if you have no knowledge of him."[154] "Nature prompted their reaction," writes Ulrich von Etzenbach of a similar situation.[155] The natural law according to which relatives are always drawn to one another helps to motivate what amounts to a law in MHG narrative: natal filiations that are unknown or hidden will ultimately be revealed both to the individuals directly involved and to those around them, and the individuals will be restored not only to their lineages but also to their rightful places in society. In most cases the revelation occurs before the end—often right at the end—of the hero's childhood.[156]

There are less dramatic forms of refiliation as well, in which children whose identities are perfectly well known simply return home. After the Virgin has been married to Joseph she leaves the Temple, where she spent most of her childhood, and returns to her parents in Nazareth for several eventful months.[157] Eventually, of course, she does leave her parents' home, and in this she is typical. Whether refiliation is a matter of knowledge, as in the case of Willehalm von Orlens, or merely a matter of geography, as in that of Mary, it does not result in a permanent return home. After Willehalm learns his parentage he does not retire his to ancestral Hainault but sets off for England, of which in the end he becomes king. After Mary returns to her birthplace at Nazareth she does not stay there permanently but soon sets out with Joseph for Bethlehem. It is generally the case in

154. BitDlb 4082–84: swie siz niht hæten versolt, si wehselten doch dicke vil güetliche blicke; 3322–24: swâ ieman sippefriunt siht, wart ers mit künde niht gewar, in treit iedoch daz herze dar.

155. WilWnd 6433: diu natûre seite in daz.

156. Ancestry is revealed before the end of childhood: WilOrl 2830–59; WWilhm 283,8–20, 284,1–5. Ancestry is revealed at the conclusion of childhood: AplTyr 15120–206; BMärtr 7801–948; ELgAur 703,9–12; Greg 1739–55; GTrojk 1826–1907, 2204–11; JngTit 5128,3–4; JWeltc 13752–86; KTrojk 5058–343; Melrnz 2253–515; Parz 140,9–141,9; PrLanc 1:129,37–130,20; Rennew 17653–962; Väterb 37756–38002; WolfdA 282,1–283,3, 292,1–308,4. —Relatives are drawn to one another even though they are unaware they are related: ELgAur 702,13–15; GTrist 3240–45; KTrojk 3194–239; MaiBfl 212,35–213,38, 219,10–11; Rennew 14612–826; Väterb 37696–99, 37712–26; WilWnd 5210–88, 5732–58; WolfdB 168,3–169,1, 188,3; WWilhm 272,21–30, 290,16–18, 291,2–3, 291,27–30. —Gregorius, Lancelot, Lanzelet, and Wigamur must wait until after they have come of age before they learn all the important facts of their ancestry.

157. Passnl H12,94–13,4; PhMarl 1524–27; WlMarl 2621–46; WrMarl 2009–22.

MHG narrative that childhood leads away from parents, birthplace, and childhood home, not back to them. This is true even of cases of refiliation, where the child's return to his or her origins receives considerable attention.[158]

Wolfdietrich's discovery that the refugee queen is actually his mother is all the more dramatic in that, until then, he thought Berhtung and his wife were his parents. His confusion testifies to the close bond that exists between Wolfdietrich and his foster parents. This bond is paralleled by another, since Berhtung is not only Wolfdietrich's foster father but also his master or teacher, a title by which he is called on several occasions.[159] The roles of foster parent and teacher are varieties of *childhood affiliation*, postnatal attachments that are formed in caring for and educating children but that do not last into adulthood except in a much different form.

Given the number of orphans in MHG narrative, as well as the high incidence of abandonment, abduction, and other sorts of exfiliation, it is hardly surprising that there is a great demand for foster parents. Some foster parents are clearly deputies of natal parents—like Benigna, in whose care Beaflor's father places her when she is twelve, since her own mother has died. Other foster parents replace the natal parents—like Jofrit, who adopts Willehalm von Orlens at birth. Willehalm takes Jofrit to be his real father, and Jofrit makes Willehalm his heir: "I fully intend to consider you my child and to make subject to you the people, possessions and lands of which I am called lord."[160] The most graphic adoptions occur when the foster mother feigns pregnancy, then claims that the adopted child is her own. When the abandoned infant Albanus is brought to the king of Hungary, the king "told the queen (since they had no heir) to lie in bed and say that she had delivered a son until the news got out, since in this way they could provide the kingdom with an heir."[161] All in fact believe that Albanus is the child of the king and queen.[162]

158. The childhood stories of Hagen and Charlemagne (Kudrn, KrlGal, StrKrl) are exceptions. —Refiliation: Exdus 245–62; GuFrau 2955–63; Jakobr 567–99; Ksrchr 2805–42, 2875–3930; Kudrn 136,2–162,4; Melrnz 2253–515; Passnl H82,18–21; Pilat 346–51; RWeltc 8976–9007; StUlrc 228–32; Väterb 32745–33227; VBüMos 33,1–11.

159. WolfdA 297,3, 397,2, 307,4.

160. WilOrl 2998–3002: ich han des gûten mût Das ich dich wil ze kinde han Und wil dir machon undertan Lúte, gůt unde lant Des ich herre bin genant.

161. Alban 2,23–28: der cuninc sprach du ze der cuningen dad si læge uf hir beitte (wande si ingeinen eirve inheitte) inde spræche dad si eines sunes læge biz dad mære alsus uzquæme. wande bit sustanen sachen mahten si ir riche einen eirve machen.

162. The child knows its guardians are not its biological parents: GuFrau 120–26; JngTit 677,1–679,4, 686,1–687,4; JWeltc 19974–86; Ksrchr 1442–81; Lanzlt 189–401; Parz

Given the number of foster parents in MHG narrative, it is gratify-
ing to discover that they are, virtually without exception, in every way
the equal of real parents. Beaflor's foster father "showed her much greater
devotion than her own father, from [whose sexual advances] she just barely
escaped."[163] And Willehalm's adoptive mother, "Elise, raised him so tenderly that there never was a mother who treated her child better."[164] In
Friedrich von Schwaben Ziproner invokes Elise as a standard in order to
praise her own foster mother: "I have heard of an extraordinary princess,
renowned far and wide for her excellence, [who] reared the child Willehalm
von Orlens with devotion devoid of any falsity: it is said that her equal has
not been born. Even in comparison with her I will praise my mother."[165]
Note that Ziproner refers to her foster mother simply as "mother," a conflation of surrogate and natal parents that is not uncommon. When Tristan
kisses his foster father "as a child should [kiss] his father" the narrator observes: "that was right and proper: he was his father and he his child."[166]
Not only do foster parents equal real parents, they become real parents.[167]

Children also form affiliations with their nurses, their teachers, and

---

344,20–345,18, 477,7–8; UWilhm 16,14–19,2, 29,22; Väterb 37295–330; WilÖst 1252–54, 1336–58;
WilWnd 5387–464; WolfdB 262,3–263,4; WTitrl 25,1–4, 29,1–32,1, 38,1, 39,1–2; WWilhm 5,20–
24, 23,4–9. —Foster parents are taken for biological parents: AplTyr 14930–15206; Greg
1069–100, 1137–58; GTrist 1933–54, 2037–42, 2178–90; GTrojk 1419–33; KTrojk 590–93; Passnl
H313,73–314,40; PrLanc 1:21,4–5; Rennew 9954–10247, 11606–7, 11665; WilWnd 5049–104;
WolfdA 280,1–307,1–4. —It is not clear what the child assumes: RWeltc 8962–68; Schnkd 29–
30. —Other feigned pregnancies: GTrist 1894–954; ELgAur 216,16–20; Passnl H314,20–36;
MaiBfl 188,30–190,9.

163. MaiBfl 40,9–12: er was ir getriuwer vil . . . danne ir rehter vater was, von dem si
kûme genas.

164. WilOrl 2670–74: Elýse . . . Zoh ez so zartecliche Das es nie mûter kinde bas Erbot.

165. FrdSwb 7444–51: Ich hab von ainer fürstin gehôrt usserkorn . . . an tugenden weit
erkannt: Die zoch von Orlenntz das kind Wilham Mit trúwen öne falschen galm. . . . Born
sol nit sein ir genoß. Dawider prys ich die mûter mein.

166. GTrist 3945–47: als ein kint sinen vater sol; daz was vil billich unde wol: er was sin
vater und er sin kint.

167. Foster parents said to equal or surpass biological parents: GTrist 1933–54, 2178–90,
3945–55; GTrojk 1440–53, 1560–61, 2283–300; GuFrau 126–33; JngTit 691,2–4; Ksrchr 1454–55,
1462–63; KTrojk 574–99, 5370–419; MhMarg 125–26; Parz 392,11; PrLanc 1:20,31–32, 1:40,30;
RWeltc 8962–66, 9171–74; WTitrl 96,3–4, 115,1–2. —The vocabulary of filiation is used for instances of affiliation: BitDlb 3393–94; FrdSwb 6897–913, 7437–51, 7653–54;
Greg 1515, 1536, 1625, 1659, 1732, 1804; GTrist 2046, 2384, 2051, 2192, 2590, 2604, 2606, 4362–
86; GTrojk 1459–64, 1500, 1545, 1653, 1656, 1665, 1672, 1692, 1702, 2242, 2267; HnrKgd 3611–12;
Ksrchr 1454–56, 1462–63, 1465; KTrojk 5385–91; MaiBfl 18,6–7, 19,13–14, 19,22–24, 40,5–12;
Parz 177,14. —The only exceptions to the general excellence of foster parents occur in the case
of Tarsia (AplTyr 15231–320) and when noble children are reared in lower-class households:
Greg 1285–358; KrlGal 5,30–33, 5,62–6,40; WilWnd 5049–185. But this is not always the case:
the shepherd and his wife who raise Paris are excellent in every regard. —Stepmothers, in
which *Friedrich von Schwaben* is particularly rich, can be good (FrdSwb 167–644, 4353–56) or
bad (FrdSwb 6887–913, 7654–713; TößSwb 101,28–102,3, 103,13–16).

those who rescue them, and here too the relations are excellent. Until she was fifteen Margaret was in the care of her nurse, whose supervision she accepted "as a very good daughter should. If she could have had her heart's desire she would never have parted from her [nurse] until death took her from her."[168] Parzival's teacher Gurnemanz "tended him in such a way that a devoted father could not have treated his children any better."[169] Paris's rescuer hears the abandoned infant crying for hunger in the woods and brings him to his wife, who "raised him as if he were her own child."[170] In every case the new attachment, whether nursing, teaching, or rescuing, is likened to the ties that bind a child to his biological parents.[171]

The large number of foster parents, nurses, teachers, and rescuers in the MHG childhood narratives and the consistency with which they are said to perform their roles every bit as well as natal parents turns them into the equivalent of parents. Parents, of course, are required for generation and thereby establishing the crucial ties of lineage. But their essential function is exhausted at birth. Nurture can be provided just as well by others—which is a good thing, considering how often MHG parents are unable to care for their own children. Thus after birth the essential bond for a MHG child is not to parents but to nurturers, who may or may not be the child's parents. Parental nurture is the ideal and, as the citations in the previous paragraphs make clear, sets the standard. In practice, however, parents are only one of a number of kinds of nurturer, all of them equally admirable. Thus Ziproner can address her birth mother, who raised her for eleven years, and praise her recently deceased foster mother, who raised her for nine, calling them both "mother": "Mother," she says, "I cannot keep silent about the loss I suffered concerning my devoted mother."[172] Even addressing the woman who bore her, Ziproner does not hesitate to equate biological and foster parents, using the term "mother" to create a single class of nurturer.

While MHG writers celebrate the ties that bind children to their nur-

168. WlMarg 160–64: als ein vil guote tohter sol. waer es gestanden an ir, sô was daz wol ir herzen gir daz sie nimmer von ir kaeme ê ez ir der tôt benaeme.

169. Parz 165,9–12: solh was sîn underwinden, daz ein vater sînen kinden, der sich triuwe kunde nieten, möhtez in niht baz erbieten.

170. GTrojk 1433: [den] Zoch sy als er wer ir kind.

171. For other nurses or teachers see chapter four. —Rescuers: Exdus 225–68; Greg 939–1050; GuFrau 1807–26; Jüdel 133,71–134,50; Jüdenk 480–547; Ksrchr 1420–81; KTrojk 542–69; MaiBfl 55,21–26; RWeltc 8948–66; StrKrl 168–78; VBüMos 32,16–33,5; WilÖst 1116–269; WolfdA 84,1–120,4.

172. FrdSwb 7437–40: Mûter, ich kan nit gedagen . . . Die verlust die ich genommen han An meiner getrúwen mûter.

turers and other adults, they waste few words on children's ties to those their own age. Gregorius is said to have gone "with his playmates to where it was appropriate for them to play";[173] and Margaret tends sheep "with those of her own age, who were her playmates."[174] Like the schoolmates discussed in chapter four, these playmates exist only as an undifferentiated mass, helping to constitute a particular setting but not entering into individual relations with the protagonist. Even references of this kind are rare and, with few exceptions, are restricted to noncourtly settings. Although Herod knows that "a child likes to be with other children," few others seem to have noticed.[175]

Although they are treated more fully elsewhere, brief mention must be made of the institutional affiliations MHG heroes and heroines contract in the course of their childhood. At Mark's court, Eilhart's Tristrant sustains relations not only with the king, but also with the steward, to whom Mark entrusts him; the marshall, who is enjoined to treat him better than anyone else; and the retinue in general, who are asked "to be good to him and protect him from any distress."[176] In school, the Judenknabe does not only learn from his master, but participates fully in the communal life: he "went to church with the others as was customary" and "ran into the churchyard to play" with his classmates.[177] In his monastery the Zwölfjähriges Mönchlein not only learns what he is taught but "kept diligently to the rule of the order"—that is, he followed the common discipline.[178]

Growing Away

Whatever our anxieties about the treatment of Baby M, it is obvious that her childhood, even shuttling back and forth between two homes, is a great deal more stable than that of most MHG children. Beaflor's mother dies when she is twelve, her father makes sexual advances, she flees alone in a ship and is deposited on the coast of Greece. While the texts represent a

173. Greg 1286–88: Grêgôrius mit sînen spilgenôzen kam dâ si spilnes gezam.
174. WzMarg 206–7: mit ir eben alten die ir gespilen warent.
175. SwrzPr S60,61–62: er wizze wol. dc ain kint gerne ist bi den andern. —Playmates: BitDlb 2033–36; ELgAur 578,7–8, 673,8–11, 809,12–16; GuGrhd 2896–905; KndJsu 2663–67, 2702; KTrojk 612–13; Lanzlt 4067–75; Passnl H50,53–57; StElis 710–59; WlMarl 1565–66; WTitrl 25,4–28,4.
176. ETrist 303–39; H334–37: er bat daß ingesind, daß sie im gůt wären und in vor allen schwären wölten behütten.
177. Judenk 50–51: daz kint quam nach gewonheit zur kirchen mit den andern; 115–17: daz kint zu kirchove lief, . . . spilen mit den kinden.
178. ZwöMön 46: er hielt mit vlîze den orden.

range of attitudes towards dislocation, there are two that warrant special mention. They can be illustrated by the circumstances under which the two MHG Tristan romances move their hero from his first home to Cornwall, where his childhood concludes.

According to Gottfried, Tristan is abducted from the home of his foster parents and then abandoned on the coast of Cornwall. He has no idea where he is, and there is no one in sight—so he prays, and in the course of his prayer describes his situation. "Now I look around me in all directions and see no living being anywhere about. I am afraid of this vast wilderness: wherever I turn my eyes I seem to see the end of the world. Above all I am afraid that wolves and other animals will eat me no matter where I turn." [179] A bit later Tristan imagines the misery back home: "Oh dear mother," he cries out, "I know for sure that you are torturing yourself with laments. Father, your heart is filled with misery." [180] The outburst is heartfelt but mistaken, since those Tristan apostrophizes are not his mother and father, as he believes, but his adoptive parents—his outburst reminding us that he is as ignorant about his identity as he is about his location. Tristan's isolation is complete: he is utterly alone, he does not know who he is, he does not know where he is, and he is afraid that he will lose his life.

Tristan's situation can stand as an emblem for the acute dislocation that is the frequent consequence of exfiliation in the MHG childhood narratives. Like Tristan, many children are confused about where they are or where they are headed. Shortly after he sets out for King Arthur's, Meleranz "knew for sure that he had ridden astray." [181] As Wilhelm von Österreich sets sail to search for his beloved he tells the crew: "we must travel I don't know where." [182] Others, again like Tristan, are isolated from society. Parzival "was hidden in the wilderness of Soltane and raised there, cheated of the kingly way of life" to which he was born. [183] Still others do not know their true identity. Lanzelet tells Johfrit: "I have absolutely no idea who I am or where I'm headed." [184] Others are exposed to mortal danger just like Tristan. Gregorius was abandoned to the waves in a little vessel

179. GTrist 2500–2513: nu warte ich allenthalben min und sihe niht lebendes umbe mich. dise groze wilde die vürht ich: swar ich min ougen wende, da ist mir der werlde ein ende. . . . über daz allez so vürht ich, wolve unde tier diu vrezzen mich, swelhen enden ich gekere.

180. GTrist 2604–6: a süeziu muoter, wie du dich mit clage nu quelest, daz weiz ich wol; vater, din herze ist leides vol.

181. Melrnz 336–37: der junge man wol weste daz er irre reit.

182. WilÖst 820–21: wir muzzen . . . varn ich [en]waiz wa hin.

183. Parz 117,30–118,2: der knappe alsus geborgen wart zer waste in Soltâne erzogen, an küneclîcher vuore betrogen.

184. Lanzlt 527–28: dar zuo hân ich vermisset gar, wer ich bin und war ich var.

where "the wild winds tossed him which ever way God commanded, into life or into death."[185]

While Gottfried's Tristan is abducted and abandoned, the hero of Eilhart's *Tristrant* leaves home of his own volition. The idea is his tutor's, who suggests, once Tristrant has grown strong enough, that he travel abroad. The hero then asks his father for leave: "I want to observe foreign countries," he tells the king. "Not very many people have come to know me except those who are at your court. It might not be bad for me if I had to endure hardship and also if I saw in my youth what the customs are in other realms."[186] Tristrant's father grants the request at once. In this brief scene Tristrant, his tutor, and his father all seem to be of one mind on the desirability of foreign travel, from which they expect the following advantages: it will make the young hero better known, it will teach him to endure hardship, and it will enable him to learn the customs of other countries.

The view that a person profits from leaving home is relatively common. The hunters in Gottfried's *Tristan* observe that "life in foreign countries is good for many people and teaches them much that is valuable."[187] The Schüler zu Paris recalls "a saying he had heard frequently, that a child raised at home often seems like an ox"—a recollection that causes him to set out in pursuit of fame and fortune.[188] The principle that education is best acquired away from home is institutionalized in the practice of fosterage, according to which, in the words of Hugo von Trimberg, "many a noble child was sent from one country to another so that he might learn in his youth from the teaching of a worthy lord the sort of admired behavior that would enable him to acquire a good name."[189] The teachings of Chris-

185. Greg 926–28: daz [kint] die wilden winde wurfen swar in got gebôt, in daz leben ode in den tôt. —Others isolated from society or ignorant of where they are headed: BitDlb 2526, 2356–62; Bussrd 556–685; FlorBl 1501–1894, 2567–950; Jakobr 375; Kudrn 67,1–106,4; Passnl H82,2–17; Pilat 308–47; Wglois 1411–15; Wigmur 421–22; WolfdA 155,1–120,4. —Others ignorant of their identity: ELgAur 701,4–5; Greg 1332, 1402–3; GTrojk 1834–42; KTrojk 590–96; Parz 140,3–8; Passnl H314,53–56; PrLanc 1:21,4–5; Rennew 13106–19; Väterb 37322–30; Wigmur 367–404; WilOrl 2822–70; WilWnd 5238–45; WolfdA 280,1–305,4. —Others exposed to mortal danger: BMärtr 822–96, 9017–181; ELgAur 137,27–38, 372,24–37, 424,13–425,21, 744,16–18; GTrojk 1328–72; Hlgnlb 68,38–69,4, 135,31–136,20; KrlGal 7,20–35; Ksrchr 1407–29; KTrojk 435–529; Kudrn 68,1–72,4; MaiBfl 43,13–44,4; Passnl K115,85–116,61, K303,84–305,1, K323,74–332,73; StrKrl 158–75; VBüMos 32,11–18; WolfdB 154,2.

186. ETrist H207–19: ich wil besehen fremde land. mich haben nit vil lút erkant, wann die in dinem hoff sind. . . . eß dörft mir nicht wesen laid, ob ich nun hett arbait und ouch in miner jugent besehe, weß man pfläge in fremden richen.

187. GTrist 3126–27: unkünde ist manegem herzen guot und leret maneger hande tugent.

188. SlPrsC 85–88: Do gedachte er an ein wort, Daz er ofte hete gehort, Daz ein heimgezogen kint Dicke ist uzen als ein rint.

189. Rennr 539–43: Dô wart manic edel kint gesant Von einem lande in daz ander lant, Daz ez zuht und êre Nâch frumer herren lêre Sölte lernen in sîner jugent.

tianity and of chivalry both contain mechanisms that encourage people to leave home. "One can still read in Matthew, 'Whoever leaves all that he has or might have in God's name—wife, children, father, mother, fields, house, reputation, vineyards—God will repay him a hundredfold, here with grace and there with eternal life.'" [190] The ideology of knighthood disdains "the one who lies about for the sake of comfort" [191] and honors the one who sets out to win renown. These principles and practices are realized narratively in stories that inevitably lead children away from parents and home and out into the world. The trajectory of MHG childhood is relentlessly exogamous. [192]

The value attached to leaving home within the fictional world of MHG narrative seems to accord with practices and values of the hegemonic classes of the Middle Ages. The historical St. Elizabeth, just like the literary one, was sent by her parents, the king and queen of Hungary, to the court of her future husband in Thuringia when she was only four. Fosterage was a practice of the medieval nobility, who must have expected some benefit from shipping their children off to other courts to be raised. Scholars too advocated life abroad—like Bernard of Chartres and Hugh of St. Victor, who held living in a foreign country to be one of the preconditions for the study of philosophy. [193] The exfiliation recommended in the MHG texts is a relatively mild kind: parents send their children off to be educated or the children themselves decide it is time to leave home and do so with the blessing of their parents or guardians. This sort of exfiliation is regarded as thoroughly beneficial, as it seems to have been not only in literary texts but in the culture at large.

We too believe that children have to leave home, at least emotionally. Freud tells us that from puberty on "the human individual must devote himself to the great task of detaching himself from his parents, and only after he has done so can he cease being a child and become a member of the social community." [194] Dr. Spock tells us that "youths have got to separate

190. SaeldH 7165–76: man noch in Matheo list . . . "swer in Gottes namen lat daz er han moht ald daz er hat, wip, kint, vatter, mûter, aker, hus er, reben . . . dem wirt ez wider hundert valt von Got ingnaden hie gegeben und dar zů dort daz ewig leben."

191. Greg 1683: der verlît sich durch gemach.

192. On the advantages of leaving home: Englhd 306–8, 322–25, 508–13; ErnstB 72–87; HvKemp 50–51; Kudrn 575,3; TandFl 618–21; UWilhm W26,17–27; WilOrl 2866–69, 2918–28. —For a stunning analysis of the exogamous imperative in Ulrich's Lanzelet see Schimd, "Mutterrecht."

193. Bindschedler, "Bildungsgedanke," 33–35.

194. Freud, Vorlesungen, 349: Von dieser Zeit an muß sich das menschliche Individuum der großen Aufgabe der Ablösung von den Eltern widmen, nach deren Lösung es erst aufhören kann Kind zu sein, um ein Mitglied der sozialen Gemeinschaft zu werden.

themselves emotionally from their parents in order to find out who they are and what they want to be."[195]

Whereas we stage this separation in familial and psychological terms as the drama of adolescence, MHG narratives stage separation in personal and spatial terms as a series of attachments, separations, and new attachments. Sometimes exfiliation proceeds smoothly and resembles our notions of a normal childhood: the child grows up (natural), is sent to school (passive), and decides it is time to leave home (active). Sometimes it proceeds traumatically: the child is orphaned, abducted, isolated, ignorant of his identity, exposed to great danger. The two degrees of separation engender two themes: the value of leaving home on the one hand, and the trauma of radical dislocation on the other.

Over the last twenty-five years psychologists have studied intensively the quality of infants' attachment to their caregivers, their response to separation from those to whom they are attached, and the degree of anxiety they experience when placed in strange situations as an index of the strength of their attachments.[196] The tremendous amount of attention that exfiliation receives in the MHG childhood narratives suggests that MHG writers share our concern with attachment and separation, while the presence of extreme and dangerous forms of dislocation suggests that for them too the instability of childhood attachments represents a locus of cultural anxiety. Noble children in medieval Germany were after all likely to experience considerable dislocation, both natural (death of parents and caregivers) and cultural (fosterage, oblation). In spite of the shared concern with attachment and separation, however, there is one profound difference. Whereas we assume that unstable ties in childhood will leave permanent psychological scars, the MHG childhood narratives show that they do not. Thus the narratives offer welcome, if only literary, comfort to the anxieties of exfiliation. Those children who lose track of their relatives will inevitably find them. Those who do not know their true identity will always be told. Those who are separated from their parents before they come of age will always find nurturers ready to care for them every bit as well as their parents would have. Although the MHG childhood narratives are filled with disruption and danger, they offer as well the promise of stability and comfort.

195. Spock, *Baby and Child Care*, 503.
196. Kagan, *Nature*, 50–64.

6. Adulthood: Coming of Age or Growing Up

On July 7, 1984 three teenagers, 15, 16, and 17 years old, attacked a gay man in Bangor, Maine. They chased their victim down the street, called him names, beat and kicked him when he fell to the ground, then threw him off a bridge into a stream, where he drowned. The attackers were soon apprehended, confessed their part in the murder, and were arraigned. Before the trial could begin, however, the judge had to determine whether the accused should be tried as juveniles or adults. According to state law in Maine, those under eighteen can be tried as adults if the offense with which they are charged is particularly grave, if it was committed in a violent, premeditated, or willful manner, or if the sentence they would receive if convicted as adults is more likely to deter them from further crime than the sentence they would receive as juveniles.[1] These provisions show the state of Maine to be of two minds concerning the boundary between childhood and adulthood, at least with regard to the criminal liability of its teenagers. On the one hand, they assume the boundary is fixed: ordinarily those accused of murder are considered adults at age eighteen. On the other hand, they treat the boundary as flexible: certain kinds of acts (violent, premeditated, or willful) or certain kinds of actors (those who will be deterred from further crime) may cause the perpetrators to be considered adult even before they reach that threshold.

MHG texts also acknowledge both fixed and flexible thresholds between childhood and adulthood—although, not surprisingly, the criteria are different from those employed by the state of Maine. Many MHG children cross the threshold by performing certain established rites of passage. Flore comes of age when he is knighted, Blanscheflur when she is married. Others, however, assume adult roles during childhood. When she is nine Iolande announces that she will not marry since she has resolved to devote her life to Christ. Although Iolande is still a child when she commits herself

1. *Maine: Revised Statutes*, Title 15, Chapter 503, §3101, 4, D–E.

to lifelong virginity, she has nevertheless made a commitment that is appropriate for an adult. Therefore Iolande's commitment to perpetual virginity, which occurs during childhood, no less than Flore's assumption of knighthood, which concludes his childhood, should be considered an adult affiliation. Both represent the assumption of adult roles. Both are appropriate to adults and continue into adulthood. In this they differ from childhood affiliations—with foster parents or teachers, for example—which must be abandoned or renegotiated when a child comes of age.

The examples of Flore and Iolande illustrate not only that adult affiliations can be made during childhood but also that secular and religious affiliations are often opposed to each other. When Iolande commits herself to Christ she announces thereby her refusal to take a mortal husband. She refuses, that is, to perform the secular rite, marriage, and to make the secular affiliation, to a husband and to the status of wife, by which a MHG maiden ordinarily comes of age. The opposition of secular and religious is so profound that I have organized this chapter accordingly and will treat first the secular affiliations and then the religious ones.

Love and Friendship

According to Konrad Fleck, "God, who often works miracles, had so arranged things"[2] that Flore, son of the pagan king and queen of Spain, and Blanscheflur, daughter of the queen's captive Christian confidante, are both born on the same day. Even in the cradle the infants' smiles "declared that they loved one another."[3] At age five "they began to understand how one should be subject to love."[4] When they go to school "they read all the books on love,"[5] learn what the books tell them, and act accordingly. They sit in a lovely orchard, kiss each other and embrace, and speak about the joys and sorrows of love. It is abundantly clear that Flore and Blanscheflur have fallen in love and that they play their parts very much like adults. In their earliest childhood they have contracted an adult affiliation, one that remains strong until they die at age 100: "They lived a great many years in such devoted love that they never became even the tiniest bit less fond of each other."[6]

2. FlorBl 566–67: nû hâte ez got alsô beschart, der . . . dicke tuot wunders vil.
3. FlorBl 606–7: ir gebærde des verjach daz se ein ander minneten.
4. FlorBl 615–17: dô begundens sich verstân wie man sol wesen undertân der minne.
5. FlorBl 712–13: nû begunden sie lesen diu buoch von minnen allezan.
6. FlorBl 7841–45: mit sô getriuwen minnen . . . lebten sie vil manic jâr, daz sie einander umb ein hâr sît nie wurden leider.

Like the love of Flore and Blanscheflur, so the love of other MHG children tends to observe the same conventions as love between MHG adults. In most cases it's love at first sight: when the twelve-year-old Meleranz first sees Tydomie, "Venus set him on fire at once with her scorching brand. His heart and body burned with the fire of love."[7] The surveillance or *huote* that adult lovers must often endure appears in exaggerated form as the sequestration of maidens: Siegfried goes to Worms to win Kriemhild as his bride, but he lived there "for one entire year and in the whole time he never saw the lovely maiden" since she is not ordinarily permitted to appear in public.[8] The dialectic of service and reward also plays a role. When Schionatulander declares his love to Sigune she hardly knows what he is talking about, but she does know enough to reply: "Your youth has not yet properly earned me. First you must serve me from behind your shield. Be prepared for that."[9] As Sigune's response reminds us, love is one area in which MHG females enjoy a relatively high degree of autonomy, and this is no less true of children than it is of adults. Like Sigune, Amelie and Flordibel do not hesitate to demand service from their suitors.[10] Others, like Thysbe or the heroine of the *Nachtigall*, think up and instruct their lovers how to carry out the plans that enable them to satisfy their desire.[11] In secular narrative the variety of roles available to a female is greatest after she has affiliated herself with a lover but before she has become attached to a husband.[12]

Although the love of MHG children resembles the love of adults in many ways, the extreme youth of some of those who "grew up in love"[13] does generate a theme peculiar to the childhood narratives, that of child love. Here I refer not to any children who are in love (Meleranz, Kriem-

7. Melrnz 838–41: Vênus zunt in an der stunt mit ir heizen vackel an. herze und lîp ime bran von der minne glüete.

8. Niblgn 138,1–3: Sus wont' er . . . in Guntheres lande volleclîch ein jâr, daz er die minneclîchen die zîte niene gesach.

9. WTitrl 71,3–4: mich hât dîn jugent noch niht rehte erarnet. dû muost mich under schiltlîchem dache ê dienen: des wis vor gewarnet.

10. TandFl 565–68; WilOrl 4099–4101, 4445–46, 5139–200.

11. PyrThs 109–62; Nchtgl 83–143.

12. Love at first sight: Bussrd 104–48, 201–39; Eneit 9991–10060, 10942–90; KrlGal 35,25–37,28, 59,19–60,12, 61,9–62,2; KTrojk 698–803; PrLanc 3:474,12–17; SlPrsC 272–358. —A youth seeks a particular maiden: GuGrhd 1731–60, 3009–48; WilÖst 657–930; WolfdB 9,1–38,4, 81,1–92,1. —For sequestered maidens see chapter five. —Heroes who perform love service: Englhd 1842–66, 1966–71, 2196–97, 2356–63; JngTit 744,3–745,4; Melrnz 1237–47, 1637–52; TandFl 655–761; WilÖst 3380–83. —Maidens who take the initiative in matters of love: Bussrd 240–65; Englhd 883–1267, 1880–915, 2327–97, 2914–43; Melrnz 752–1586, 2721–42, 2816–969; MOswld 1003–192, 2483–582; Parz 345,27–347,6, 368,23–372,12; PrLanc 3:398,9–400,4, 3:436,3–439,13, 3:474,4–475,15; Rother 1515–45, 1918–30, 2289–98, 2315–522; SlPrsC 188–301; TandFl 1349–96.

13. GuFrau 87: si wuohsen in der minne.

hild), who might be called "young lovers," but to those cases where the extreme youth of the lovers is emphasized (Sigune, Flore), whom I will call "child lovers." MHG writers indicate in a number of ways that child love is a literary phenomenon. Wolfram names the source: he has Schionatulander reveal that he "got to know about love from stories."[14] Ottokar demonstrates the artificiality of the convention: in reporting the marriage of Guta, daughter of Rudolf von Habsburg, and Wenzel, son of Ottokar of Bohemia, which had been arranged for political reasons, he observes that the children "didn't waste much time pining away for one another; their minds were too dull to feel what Schionatulander felt for his lady, the radiant Sigune, in the years of their childhood."[15] Rudolf von Ems invokes the literary tradition at the same time he tries, disingenuously, to distance his protagonists from it: "But surely you, Lady Love, and you too, Childhood, are at odds with one another, as master Walther von der Vogelweide has told us. He has claimed in one of his songs that you are completely inimical to each other."[16]

Nearly a century after Freud wrote "that the child brings germs of sexual activity with him into the world"[17] and that "the child long before puberty is capable of mature love,"[18] we are no longer so sure that children and love are, in fact, inimical. But the MHG writers are not thinking of in-

14. WTitrl 68,1: jâ erkande ich . . . minne von mæren.
15. ORmchr 17990–97: si liezen wênic sich belangen senlichen nâch einander: als Schionatulander tet nâch sîner froun, der klâren Sigoun, in ir kintlichen jâren, darzuo disiu wâren bî ze kranken witzen.
16. WilOrl 4466–71: Nu sint ir doch an andern gram, Vro Minne, und ŏch dú Kinthait, Als úns maister Walther sait Von der Vogel waide, Der sanch das ir baide Warent gar an ander gram. The reference is to Walthr 102,8: minn unde kintheit sint ein ander gram. —Love is inimical to childhood: FlorBl 119–23, 614–20, 792–94; JngTit 185,1–186,3; ORmchr 75750–92; Rennew 19186–99; WTitrl 48,1. —Determining which pairs exemplify child love and which are merely children in love depends less on the ages of the lovers, which are often impossible to determine, than on explicit mention of the theme of child love: FlorBl 599–843; GuGrhd 3009–16; GuFrau 77–116; JngTit 709,1–712,1, 806,2–4; Melrnz 1485–97; PyrThs 37–39; Rennew 3138–39, 4990–91; WilÖst 1623–87; WTitrl 46,1–73,1, 83,2–131,4. In three cases it is possible to determine the age at which child love begins. Five: Flore and Blanscheflur realize they are in love (FlorBl 614–20). Before six: Pyramus and Thysbe (PyrThs 37–39). About ten and thirteen: Amelie and Willehalm von Orlens (WilOrl 3941–42, 4101, 4445–46). —It is worth comparing these with the ages given for falling in love in other cases, where child love is not an issue. Twelve: bourgeois maiden (SlPrsC 224–28); Meleranz (Melrnz 170–71); Hugdietrich decides to woo Hildburg (WolfdB 25,1–2). About thirteen: Hugdietrich woos Hildburg (WolfdB 26,1–2); Partonopier (PartMl 394–99). About fifteen: young nun (Sperbr 66–69); Beaflor (MaiBfl 13,26–29, 31,15–18). Sixteen: Schüler zu Paris (SlPrsC 96–99). Almost nineteen: Charlemagne (KrlGal 49,25–26). Not more than twenty: youth (Nchtgl 37–38).
17. Freud, *Drei Abhandlungen*, 133: Es schien uns vielmehr, daß das Kind Keime von Sexualtätigkeit mit zur Welt bringt.
18. Freud, *Aufklärung der Kinder*, 22: das Kind ist lange vor der Pubertät ein . . . fertiges Liebewesen.

fantile sexuality. They are thinking of the power of love. They are thinking of children not as subjects but as objects. By having Flore and Blanscheflur fall in love "when they lay in the cradle"[19] Konrad Fleck can demonstrate the general principle that "the god of love is so powerful that he makes children wise, the young old, [and] the inexperienced hoary with age."[20] This is a commonplace of medieval literary love theory. Although MHG writers acknowledge the artificiality of child love and assert that it is contrary to the nature of children, they are happy to sacrifice the children to demonstrate the power of love.

Precisely because love is contrary to the nature of children, those who love are to that extent like adults. In this way love is like the other heroic signs that show children to be special because they are like grownups. To be sure, some young lovers behave foolishly: Engeltrud refuses to reveal her love until Engelhard has nearly died of despair; Tandareis is so distracted by love he cuts his hand with a bread knife. But they are hardly more foolish than adult lovers like Gawan or Orgeluse. It is the nature of love, after all, not only to make the young wise, but also to make the wise foolish. Even the very wise: when Aristotle succumbs to the charms of Phyllis, "love turned him into a child."[21] Thus, even though Engeltrud or Tandareis behave foolishly, in this they are no different from adult lovers. There are other cases, however, where child lovers display not the foolishness of lovers but the foolishness of children. When Schionatulander tells Sigune of his love, she asks, "must I keep it with my dolls?"[22] After Flore and Blanscheflur went to school and "began to read books about love,"[23] they go into an orchard and diligently practice what they have learned. This is not like the awesome precocity of the Virgin, who spoke like a thirty-year-old when she was only three, or of Malefer, who carried six men on his back when he was twelve. Sigune or Flore are at best childishly cute, at worst foolish. Love is one of the most unstable elements in the MHG childhood narratives: it can turn children into adults or it can reveal them to be merely foolish children.

Love is not only unstable, it is also destabilizing, causing children to transgress against the usual boundaries between childhood and adulthood. Partonopier fights heroically at the head of the troops of the French king

19. FlorBl 602: dô se in den wagen lâgen!
20. FlorBl 610–13: so gewaltic ist der minnen got daz er kint machet wîs, die jungen alt, die tumben grîs.
21. ArPhlS 352–53: diu minne . . . macht in zeinem kinde.
22. WTitrl 64,3: muoz ich si behalden bî den tocken?
23. FlorBl 712–13: nû begunden sie lesen diu buoch von minnen.

before he has been knighted. Engeltrud has sex before she is married. Meljanz takes up arms against Lippaot before he has properly come into his inheritance. Hilde leaves her father's home before she has been married. In these cases love not only causes children to act like adults in the heroic sense, it causes them to undermine the very distinction between childhood and adulthood. Males who fight before they are knighted, females who have sex before they are married, kings who command before they have been invested all transgress against the rites of passage—knighting, marriage, inheritance—that ordinarily distinguish childhood from adulthood. Love is destabilizing not only because it is unpredictable—sometimes it causes children to act like adults, sometimes like foolish children—but even more because it undermines the distinction between childhood and adulthood. It is in the very nature of love to cause "the young person to become like the old, and the old to become like the young,"[24] and thus it is in the very nature of love to undermine the integrity of childhood and adulthood as distinct, distinguishable categories.

Love is the principal bond that causes MHG children to form close attachments to other individuals of their own age, but it is not the only one. Friendships also occur—although, as has already been mentioned, the sort of relations we would expect among playmates and schoolmates are hardly to be found. There are, however, a number of cases in which youths form attachments that, like the love affairs just discussed, continue to play an important role in adulthood. Herzog Ernst and his lifelong friend Wetzel were raised together, as were Achilles and Patroclus.[25] In the *Jakobsbrüder* and in Konrad von Würzburg's *Engelhard* the bonds of friendship formed in childhood are the principal subject of extended narratives.[26]

Secular Rites of Passage

After the love of Flore and Blanscheflur becomes obvious, Flore's parents separate the two by selling Blanscheflur into slavery. Flore sets out to find his beloved and, after many adventures, locates her in a tower in Babylon, where she is being held pending her imminent marriage to the emir. Flore makes his way into the tower and into Blanscheflur's bed, where the two

24. GuFrau 103–5: ez wirt von ir gewalte der junge als ouch der alte, der alte als ouch der junge.
25. ErnstB 124–27; KTrojk 6472–83.
26. Other friendships: PhMarl 4244–47; StdabA 10–11; StdabB 14–40.

are soon discovered. Although they are sentenced to death, their intense devotion to each other so moves the onlookers that they intercede on the lovers' behalf, eventually earning them not only the emir's pardon but his favor as well. Once pardoned, Flore asks the emir to give him Blanscheflur in marriage, which he agrees to do, knighting Flore on the same day. The following day news arrives that Flore's father has died, the newlyweds set off at once for Spain, and, on their arrival, they are crowned king and queen. The three events crowded together at the end of *Flore und Blanscheflur*, knighting, marriage, and inheritance, are the three rites of passage in MHG narrative. They mark the threshold between childhood and adulthood. Thus, whereas Flore and Blanscheflur are called *kint* until they gain the emir's pardon, when they leave for Spain the narrator can say of Flore: "Now he is completely a man."[27]

Clearly the emir regards knightly investiture as the essential rite of passage for secular males. He has just pronounced the lovers man and wife when he suddenly decides that "he would not let Flore cross the sea unless he had knighted him first and that Flore would only then consummate his marriage to Blanscheflur."[28] Flore has not asked to be knighted—indeed, he has never betrayed the slightest interest in knighthood. But the emir obviously cannot imagine Flore's consummating his marriage to Blanscheflur unless he has satisfied what, in this case, is a purely formal requirement, so he stages a magnificent celebration on the day of the wedding, at which he knights Flore and 100 others along with him. The emir assumes that unless a young man of noble birth has been knighted he is still under age and has no business engaging in any kind of adult male behavior, such as getting married.

In other texts the connection between knighting and manhood is stated explicitly. As Vivianz lies dying in the arms of his uncle, Willehalm, he recalls the ceremony in which he was knighted, "when with your help I became a man and assumed the dignity of the shield."[29] For Vivianz the ceremony when he "assumed the dignity of the shield"—that is, when he was knighted—is the moment when he "became a man." It is the same for Wigamur, who, when he was knighted, "became his own man according to knightly custom"[30] and for the hero of Ulrich's *Willehalm*, who was

---

27. FlorBl 7021, 7224, 7249, 7341, 7389; 7774: er ist nû v_lleclîche ein man.
28. FlorBl 7501–7: Der amiral beriet sich dô daz er Flôren niht alsô lieze varn über sê, er machet in ze ritter ê . . . und er danne . . . ze briute Blanscheflûr næme.
29. WWilhm 66,7–9: dô ich . . . wart ein man mit iuwer helfe und ich gewan schiltes ammet.
30. Wigmur 1339–40: also ward nach ritterlichen sÿtten Weygamur sein selbs man.

raised "with care until he completed the years of childhood and assumed the dignity of a knight."[31] For many MHG heroes knightly investiture is not followed immediately by marriage or kingship but by a period of itinerant fighting, which some have called "youth."[32] But this period is not part of childhood: Wigalois may ride off on adventure before becoming a husband and a king, but he "became a man" beforehand,[33] at the time he was knighted.[34]

Vivianz's dying words reveal not only the close connection between knighthood and manhood but also the importance of Willehalm's role in making him a knight; it was "*with your help*," he tells Willehalm, that "I became a man." When a youth becomes a knight he requires the "help" of an adult male, often a king, who will knight him: thus Galaffers knights Charlemagne (*Karl und Galie*); when Charlemagne has become emperor he knights Willehalm (Ulrich's *Willehalm*); and after Willehalm has come of age he knights Vivianz (Ulrich's *Willehalm*, recalled in Wolfram's *Willehalm*). Knighting establishes a masculine genealogy in which filiation occurs at the moment an adult male, already "his own man," declares that another male is now "his own man." Knightly filiation does not transmit noble blood or ancestral attributes but rather the relative freedom to act enjoyed by an adult male fighter. As usual, love confuses these relations: Partonopier and Lancelot are knighted not by men but by women and are filiated thereby into a knighthood of love.[35]

31. UWilhm W52,22–24: Karl in mit vlîze zôch, biz er von kindes jâren quam und ritters orden an sich nam.
32. Duby, "Youth." For those who have adopted Duby's view: Peters, "Sozialgeschichte," 404–24.
33. Wglois 1658: sus wart her Gwîgâlois ze man.
34. When Zarncke cites Vivianz's words in the *Mittelhochdeutsches Wörterbuch* he glosses *man* as *ritter*, "knight." For the nineteenth-century lexicographer as for Vivianz *ritter werden* and *man werden* are simply equivalent (Benecke, Müller, Zarncke, *Wörterbuch*, 2:30,48b). —Knighting is explicitly equated with the end of childhood: GuGrhd 3545–49; Melrnz 1243–44; TandFl 218–22; ORmchr 20971–75; Wglois 1659–60; Wigmur 1398–1401; WolfdD 3.7,1–9,2 (but see 3.61,3–4); WWilhm 67,16. —On the equivalence of knighthood and manhood: Bumke, *Höfische Kultur*, 318–19; Bumke, *Ritterbegriff*, 108. —Peters argues cogently that Duby's thesis concerning "youth" is based on literary rather than historical phenomena ("Sozialgeschichte," esp. 416–36).
35. Knighting by kings or emperors, sometimes the hero's own royal father: Eneit 6265–93; Englhd 2434–43; ErnstD 101–8; FlorBl 7501–31; KrlGal 53,12–56,42; Lohgrn 2407; Melrnz 2677–720, 3030–174; PrLanc 1:135,1–6, 2:792,17, 3:3,18–21; TandFl 2040–41. —Knighting by high nobles: Frndst 40,1–41,3; ORmchr 57996–58010; Rennew 2674–76; Wigmur 1398–405; WolfdB 270,1; WWilhm 63,7–25. —Knighting by high ecclesiastics: GuGrhd 3593–603; Greg 1625–48; JngTit 455,2; MaiBfl 83,26–84,3; ORmchr 70395–418. —Knighting by queens: GTrist 12736–42; JngTit 700,1; PartMl 12333–37, 12364–625; Parz 97,25–30; PrLanc 1:129,16–21, 1:146,30–147,2; WTitrl 39,1. —On knighting by women: Heinzle, *Stellenkommentar*, 66.

But noble blood does play a role. In the Middle Ages elaborate knightly investiture ceremonies were performed—indeed, could only be afforded—for the sons of the highest nobility, a class to which the heroes of MHG narrative texts belong almost without exception. The fact that MHG secular heroes are regularly knighted at lavish festivals—when Fivianz is knighted, "a thousand knights or more" come to Willehalm's court, where they find music, feasting, jousting, and "great joy up here in the castle and on the field" down below[36]—adds to the glory of the investiture. Conversely, a knighting ceremony heightens the splendor of a festival. One day when Arthur was about to hold court and "was considering how he could make this court particularly magnificent, he saw his nephew Karados. He made him a knight then and there" along with thirty other *juncherren*.[37] Knighting ceremonies are at least as much a celebration of courtly life as they are milestones in the life of the new knight: "Courtly society itself was the event and also the addressee of the ceremony."[38] By investing a young knight at a festival, which is for courtly society the moment of its greatest collective self-affirmation, that society acknowledges and celebrates his new position as an adult member of the highest nobility. Those who are knighted at such ceremonies are shown to be nobles even more than they are shown to be knights.[39]

In most cases becoming a knight leads directly to the first public demonstration that the hero is now "his own man." Before he is a knight young Charlemagne has to stand by and watch as 200 French knights ride off to help defend the Spanish king Galaffers, at whose court they have found refuge.[40] A year later, however, just before a second battle, Charlemagne is knighted[41]: now he is the one who leads the French into battle, and he is the one who kills the enemy commander in single combat. When Charlemagne is knighted he is changed—literally overnight—from a helpless bystander into a heroic commander and the greatest warrior in sight. In other less

36. UWilhm A328,27: tvsent ritter oder mer; A331,18–19: nv waz grozzv́ fróde hie vf der bvrg vnd in dem plan.

37. RpParz 50,13–18: alse sich der künig versan, daz er den hof rich wolte han, er sach sinen neven Karadote . . . den macht er ritter zuo der stunt.

38. Orth, "Rittererhebung," 161: Die höfische Gesellschaft selbst war das Ereignis wie auch der Adressat der Zeremonie.

39. Investiture at festivals: Eneit 6265–93; Englhd 2418–35; FlorBl 7518–67; GuGrhd 3397–708; JngTit 1125,1–1151,1; Ksrchr 11378–80, 13933–34, 16445–50; Kudrn 172,1–193,4; MaiBfl 81,18–96,12; Melrnz 2703–3774; Niblgn 27,1–42,1; ORmchr 67879–976; Rother 5005–63; Wglois 1622–716; WilOrl 5650–884; WilWnd 239–348, 8214–40; WolfdB 269,3.

40. KrlGal 38,20–28.

41. KrlGal 53,12–57,34.

dramatic cases investiture is followed by a bohort at which the new knight displays his jousting skills before a courtly audience: after his knighting, Wigalois "became a man with knightly deeds on the field."[42]

Many texts elaborate the basic elements of knightly investiture. *Karl und Galie* devotes over 150 lines to the "splendid and noble arms" in which Charlemagne is knighted,[43] thereby celebrating the tools of the knightly trade. When Tristan knights his companions he exhorts them to practice "humility, loyalty, [and] liberality,"[44] thereby articulating a knightly ideology that includes moral as well as martial values. When Titurel is knighted "the bishop pronounced for him the blessing of the sword."[45] Involving the clergy in the knighting ceremony establishes a religious affiliation: "Today," writes Peter of Blois in the late twelfth century, "knights receive their swords from the altar so that they will profess themselves sons of the church."[46] When Mai is knighted he is accompanied by "one hundred squires who seemed to him worthy of assuming the office of the shield and the status of knight along with him,"[47] and who are thereby obligated to him. Each of the elements mentioned—rich arms, knightly ideology, clerical involvement, numerous companions—heightens the significance of knightly investiture as a moment of courtly self-realization and class affirmation.[48]

42. Wglois 1659–60: sus wart her Gwîgâlois ze man. —Knighting ceremonies followed by the demonstration of knightly skills: Eneit 171,16–20, 173,39–174,24; Englhd 2444–51; ETrist 455–532; GuGrhd 3626–67, 4945–52; GTrist 5053–60; KrlGal 56,45–57,29; Kudrn 180,1–186,3; Lohgrn 2411–30; Niblgn 33,3–36,4; ORmchr 67950–71, 69339–42; Rennew 2810–29; Rother 5041–54; TandFl 2005–241; UWilhm W332,14–23; WilOrl 5788–813; WilWnd 309–20; WolfdD 3.7,1–9,2. —On Charlemagne's first deeds as a knight: Beckers, "Karls erster Zweikampf."

43. KrlGal 54,64: wapen edell ind fiere.

44. GTrist 5050: diemüete, triuwe, milte.

45. JngTit 455,2: der bischof im vor sagende was swertes segen.

46. Peter of Blois, *Epistolae* (quoted in Bumke, *Höfische Kultur*, 332): Sed et hodie tirones enses suos recipiunt de altari, ut profiteantur se filios Ecclesiae.

47. MaiBfl 82,39–83,3: hundert knappen . . . die in des wol dûhten wert . . . daz si mit im nâmen schildes amt und rîters reht.

48. Knighting mentioned only briefly: BMärtr 22995–97; Eracl 2392–95; ErnstB 111–23; ETrist 516–32; FlorBl 7401–31; Greg 1641–48; KrlGal 46,51–57; PartMl 18728–35; Passnl K592,53–593,17; PKonPr S239,29–30; PrLanc 2:792,17; UAlexr 2200; WilÖst 7896–910; WolfdB 268,1–269,4. —Knightly clothes and armor: FlorBl 7526–31; GuGrhd 3581–92; Greg 1641–48; JngTit 1135,1–1137,4; KrlGal 54,12–56,42; Kudrn 171,3–4, 173,2–4; LAlexr S425–29; MaiBfl 84,4–5; Melrnz 3048–74; Niblgn 30,1–31,2; ORmchr 69335–38; PrLanc 1:125,2–14; Rennew 2681–779; Rother 5041–44; TandFl 2028–39; UWilhm A330,6–331,9; Wglois 1631–41; Wigmur 1311–38; WilOrl 5767–85; WWilhm 63,10–64,4. —Instruction in knightly ideals: GTrist 5018–45; JngTit 1143,1–1147,4; MaiBfl 83,29–38; PrLanc 1:120,3–123,31; Rennew 2576–91. —Ecclesiastical involvement: GuGrhd 3563–600, 4932–44; GTrist 5012–26; Lohgrn 2402–12; Magzog 43–46; MaiBfl 83,25–84,3; Melrnz 3121–49; Niblgn 32,1–33,1; ORmchr 8115–16, 67939–43, 69327–34, 70395–418; PrLanc 1:134,35–135,4; Rennew 2661–74; TandFl 2044–47;

Although MHG writers are, for modern tastes, remarkably casual about numbers—often omitting them, sometimes treating them inconsistently—they do occasionally indicate the ages at which their heroes are knighted. The youngest are eleven, the oldest twenty-four, but most of those for whom ages are given are knighted when they are between fifteen and nineteen.[49] These numbers are close to those attested historically. When the sons of Frederick Barbarossa were knighted at Mainz in 1184, at a festival that made a deep impression on their contemporaries, one was eighteen, the other a year and a half younger.[50] Other historical figures seem to have been knighted between the ages of fifteen and twenty or perhaps a bit older.[51]

Although, as the examples just mentioned make clear, there are similarities between literary and historical knighting, two important differences should be kept in mind. First, historically, knightly investiture was never universal, even among the highest nobility. While some dynasties, the Hohenstauffen and the Babenberger for instance, liked to celebrate the knighting of their sons, other princely houses never felt such a need. There never was an obligation to celebrate knightly investiture.[52] In MHG literary texts, on the other hand, knighting is nearly universal. Sometimes, as in the *Crone* or *Herzog Ernst B*, it is mentioned only in passing.[53] Sometimes, as in *Parzival*, it is confused.[54] But, with hardly an exception, all male children in MHG narrative who enter secular adulthood are knighted.

UWilhm A331,30–332,17; WilOrl 5761–90; WilWnd 8216–17. —Companions knighted (number, if stated, in parentheses): ErnstB 111–36 (1); ErnstD 101–09 (1); ETrist 521–22 (60); FlorBl 7510–11 (100); GuGrhd 3588–92 (12); GTrist 4550–54, 5046–52 (30); JngTit 451,1 (200), 1135,4 (100); Klage 4014–16 (100); Kudrn 178,4 (600); Lohgrn 2403–10 (600); Melrnz 3045–46 (200); Niblgn 30,1–2 (400); ORmchr 67884–88 (24), 67904–05 (50), 69327–45 (25); PrLanc 1:133,29–31; TandFl 2028–31 (100); UWilhm A328,12–15 (100); WilOrl 5767–87 (about 100); WilWnd 290–91, 8220–22; WWilhm 63,8–9. —On the knighting ceremony: Bumke, *Höfische Kultur*, 318–41; Bumke, *Ritterbegriff*, 101–18. Recent literature: Bumke, "Bestandsaufnahme," 421 n. 38.

49. Ages at knighting in MHG texts: Eleven: Erec 9462–85. Eleven or older: WolfdD 3.6,1. Thirteen: Orendl 173–75. Thirteen or older: WolfdD 3.6,2. Fifteen: BMärtr 22995–97; ELgAur 724,16–17; FlorBl 6968–71; GrshPr 450a,24–25; Melrnz 171, 2274–77, 2516–17; Passnl K593,14–15; PrLanc 2:785,20–12, 2:828,8–13. Seventeen: GTrist 2131, 4122, 4551. Eighteen: PrLanc 1:117,24–25; StLudw 8,16–17, 24,13–17. Nineteen: KrlGal 49,25–26, 46,6. Over twenty: Wglois 1320. Twenty-four: Rother 5002; Frndst 12,2, 16,3, 35,5, 39,3; WilWnd 6969–74, 7916–20, 7935–36.

50. Bumke, *Höfische Kultur*, 278.

51. Hofmeister, "Puer, iuvenis," 297–301. —Lambrecht's Alexander and Ulrich's Lanzelet come of age by receiving arms, not by knighting, both at age fifteen: LAlexr S410; Lanzlt 300–01.

52. Bumke, *Höfische Kultur*, 335.

53. Crone 421–24; ErnstB 111–23.

54. Bumke, "Parzivals 'Schwertleite' "; Groos, "Parzival's 'swertleite.' "

This includes not only famous heroes like Siegfried, Tristan, and Lancelot but also Gregorius, who is raised in a monastery school, Flore, who never shows the least interest in knighthood, and the son of Guter Gerhard, who is a rich merchant.[55]

Literary knighting also has a different meaning. In the historical Middle Ages knighting ceremonies were organized by ruling families for their own sons or for the sons of important vassals[56]: the festivals thus served to demonstrate the wealth and power of particular dynasties. Sometimes this is the case in MHG narrative: Siegfried, Tristan, and Willehalm von Orlens are all knighted at ceremonies mounted by their fathers, foster fathers, or close relatives, ceremonies that might redound, that is, to the glory of their lineage. But almost as many MHG heroes are knighted at ceremonies organized by those with whom they have no family relationship. It is the personal excellence of Wigalois, Charlemagne, Flore, or Engelhard that inspires sovereigns to whom they are not known to be related to organize lavish festivals around their investiture. This changes the meaning of the event. To be sure, the festival at which Arthur knights Wigalois represents a display of sovereign wealth and power no less than the festival Barbarossa organized around the knighting of his sons. But whereas Barbarossa, by placing his sons at the center of the celebrations, used the occasion to make a claim about dynastic continuity (in other words to project his own power in another way), Arthur, by placing Wigalois at the center of things, uses the occasion to make a claim about class coherence. He suggests that any noble youth who promises to be an excellent knight deserves a lavish investiture ceremony. In this the textual representation of knightly investiture parallels the historical designation of all knights, from the emperor down to those just barely able to procure their own armor, as *milites* or *ritter*[57]: in both cases the real distinctions of power and the real interests of particular lineages are disguised by the fiction that all participate in the status and institutions of the larger class of noble knights.[58]

55. Most of the exceptions fall into two classes. First, a number of texts set in ancient Greece: Konrad von Würzburg's *Trojanerkrieg*, the *Göttweiger Trojanerkrieg*, Rudolf von Ems's *Alexander*, Seifrit's *Alexander*. Second, a number of heroic epics: Ulrich von Türheim's *Rennewart*, *Biterolf und Dietleib*, *Wolfdietrich A*.

56. Of the 22 German instances of historical knighting listed by Erben (*Schwertleite*, 5–8, 13, 13 n. 95) from the twelfth and thirteenth centuries, it is impossible to tell who organized the event in 5 cases. Of the remaining 17, 8 were knighted by their fathers, 3 by an uncle or brother, 3 by the emperor, 2 by bishops, and one by himself.

57. Bumke, *Ritterbegriff*, 88–148; Fleckenstein, "Abschließung," 367–68; Fleckenstein, "Rittertum und höfische Kultur," 422–27.

58. On the relation between arming, knighting, and class: Bumke, *Ritterbegriff*, 88–118;

As the ceremony of knighting is the principal rite of passage for the young heroes of MHG narrative, so the ceremony of marriage is the principal rite of passage for young heroines. Blanscheflur's marriage comes immediately after she has been saved from imminent execution, when Flore asks the emir to unite him and his beloved. The emir obliges at once with the words: "I give you [Flore] this lady in marriage, and to you, lady, I give him as husband."[59] A celebration follows at which the young couple are the center of attention, and the next day they depart for Spain. It is only after they return to Spain, however, that Flore "took Blanscheflur as his wife—because, until he brought her home, he had not once touched her physically in the way, surely you all must know, that one touches a wife."[60] With the emir's words, marking the public union of Flore and Blanscheflur, and their first sexual relations, which mark the private consummation of their union, Blanscheflur comes of age. She assumes the public and private roles of an adult woman.

The relation between marriage and adulthood for females is expressed in MHG by a lexical identity: *wip* means both "wife" and "woman." Thus to become a *wip*, "wife," is inevitably to become a *wip*, "woman." *Wip* designates as well a "woman who has had sexual relations," as opposed to a *maget*, "virgin," and it is possible to be called a *wip* after having had sex even if one is not married. Nevertheless, the lexical identity of "woman," "wife," and "sexually active woman," all of them *wip*, does powerful ideological work, representing as natural and inevitable the proposition that a sexually active woman *is* a wife *is* a woman. This identity means that the line from *Flore und Blanscheflur* I translated above as "the way one touches a wife" could just as well have been translated as "the way one touches a woman" or as "the way one touches a sexually active woman": they are the same.

Since marriage and the beginning of female sexual activity coincide lexically, it is not surprising that marriage and physical maturity coincide chronologically. In the very rare cases where MHG texts mention signs of female physical maturity (the only references are to the growth of breasts),

---

Bumke, *Höfische Kultur*, 64–71, 318–22. —Although larger numbers of knights were invested in the mass investitures that became more and more common in the thirteenth century, the literary representation remains an idealization in relation to these too: it is surely more glorious to be knighted in a ceremony at which one is the center of attention—as Flore is, for instance, even though 100 others are knighted along with him—than in a ceremony where one is part of a group of 249 others. Ulrich von Liechtenstein is the only protagonist of a MHG text to be knighted under the latter circumstances (Frndst 39,4–41,3).

59. FlorBl 7490–91: ich gibe iu dise frouwen zê und iu, frouwe, in ze man.

60. FlorBl 7835–70: [er] nam sî dô ze wîbe: wan er sî mit sîme lîbe dâ vor nie beruorte, unz er sî heim gefuorte, in die wîs, ir wizzent wol, alsô man bî wîbe sol.

such mention comes immediately before marriage.[61] One discovers a similar coincidence if one compares the age of marriage in literary texts with the ages of puberty in medieval medical texts. In the relatively few cases where MHG writers bother to record the age at which a maiden is married, she is said to be between twelve and fifteen.[62] Medieval medical treatises place the age of menarche, the only sign of puberty with which they are concerned, between twelve and fourteen, occasionally fifteen.[63] In other words, the age at which maidens marry in MHG literary texts corresponds to the age of puberty in medieval medical writings. By this measure as well, marriage and maturity coincide. Finally, there is ample historical evidence that many noble women married within the same range of ages: the English princess Matilda was twelve when she married Henry the Lion; Adelheid von Frauenberg is said to have been married by fourteen; Elizabeth of Hungary was married at the same age.[64] Studies of the German nobility in the fourteenth and fifteenth centuries show that one-third to one-half of the daughters who married did so when they were between twelve and fifteen.[65]

MHG marriage has a public and a private aspect. Publicly, the maiden is given to her husband by her father or guardian: she is the object of a transaction between two men. King Louis takes his daughter Alise by the hand and says to the man she is to marry: "Rennewart, I want to give you this maiden."[66] Then, as is often the case, he asks his daughter for her consent: "Daughter Alise, do you want him?" And she responds: "Lord

61. See chapter five n. 75.

62. Twelve: Kudrn 199,1–4. In thirteenth year: Passnl KIII,14–17. Thirteen: BMärtr 579–80; Wglois 3760–63, 4316. In fourteenth year: Passnl H83–11,1; TößSwb 50,19. Fourteen: StElis 325–33, 1457–75. Less than fifteen—but more than eleven: WilWnd 110–17, 7007–9. Fifteen: BMärtr 11819–20; Passnl K327,68–69; FlorBl 6970–71; WlMarl 1787–93. At least fifteen: MaiBfl 13,26–29, 31,15–18; Ioland 2362–63 (although she is nine when her family begins to ask her whether she wants to marry [Ioland 175–93]). Only Euphrosyne, at eighteen, is substantially older: Väterb 27827–32.

63. Amundsen and Diers, "Menarche," 363–69; Post, "Menarche," 83–87.

64. Bumke, Mäzene, 88; TößSwb 50,19; Arnold, Kind, 24.

65. Herlihy, Households, 106; Borst, Alltagsleben, 442; Koebner, "Eheauffassung," 138–39. —According to anthropologists and social historians, the (northern and western) "European marriage pattern" differs from that found in Mediterranean cultures in many ways, among them the relatively late age at which the partners marry (Goody, Family and Marriage, 8, 128–29, 189; Mitterauer, Jugend, 28–29). This may have been true for men: in the twelfth and early thirteenth centuries many noble men were in their thirties or even forties when they married for the first time (Freed, "Source Collections," 98). But it does not seem to have been the case among the women of the medieval nobility, whether in literature or in life. Indeed, the desire of the nobility to produce male heirs and to keep their wealth within the lineage puts them under pressures very much like those that formed the extra-European marriage pattern.

66. Rennew 5078–79: dise maget . . . Rennewart, die wil ich dir geben.

father, I am of such a mind that I say yes in good faith."[67] Some couples
are married with the help of ecclesiastics: "A patriarch gave Partonopier
and Meliur to one another, and a bishop."[68] Others get along without the
benefit of clergy until the morning after they consummate the marriage,
when they go to church to hear mass, and still others are married without
any ecclesiastical involvement at all. The varying degree of clerical participation is not surprising in a period during which the church was becoming
more and more involved in the marriage ceremony.[69]

The public aspect of most marriages is heightened by placing them in
the context of a courtly festival. When Larie is married, the partying lasted
"twelve whole days"; there were knightly games and feasting, music and
dancing; those in attendance "saw a surfeit of joy there every day."[70] By
incorporating marriages into festivals, MHG texts guarantee that the individuals being married are incorporated into society at the moment of its
greatest glory. The public union is customarily followed by a private one,
to the pleasures of which MHG texts like to allude with a coy directness.
"No one should ask me whether they might have been happy that night,"
the narrator says of Wigalois and Larie. "Yes indeed, their delight was such
that it is beyond compare. They embraced each other with heartfelt love
until daybreak."[71]

67. Rennew 5087–89: "Alyse tohter, wilt du in?" "herre vater, ich han den sin daz ich
mit triwen spreche ja."

68. PartMl 17398–99: si gap ein patriarche sâ zein ander unde ein bischof.

69. Public joining of spouses: AplTyr 17085–88; Bussrd 1033; Englhd 493–95; Erec 2123–
25; FlorBl 7486–95; Häsln 499; KAlxus 174–75; Lohgrn 2307–10, 6811–13; MaiBfl 87,3; Melrnz
12213–38; Niblgn 614,4–616,4; TandFl 16345–46; Treuep 156–78; Väterb 30752–55; Wglois
9420–42. —Clergy involved: AlxusA 205–9; AlxusB 79–80; AplTyr 13393–401, 18385–88; Erec
2123–25; Häsln 498–99; KAlxus 170–75; MaiBfl 86,18–87,5; Melrnz 12250–61; Rennew 5096–
142, 32116–50; RnfrBr 10384–90; Väterb 35854–57. Nuptial mass in detail: ORmchr 75467–
576. Couple attends church the morning after: GuGrhd 4945–72; Lohgrn 2402–3, 6823–70;
Niblgn 644,1–645,4; RnfrBr 11188–97; TandFl 16670–74; Wglois 9484–519. —Marriage without church or clergy: AplTyr 2212–17; Bussrd 1010–67; Englhd 4993–5013; ETrist 2802–07;
FlorBl 7481–500; GTrist 12532–75; Helmbr 1503–34; StElis 1457–79; Treuep 156–221; Väterb
30743–55, 39170–74; WolfdB 233,1–255,4. —Marriage coincides with coronation or political affiliation: AplTyr 18389–99; Eneit 13120–32; GTrist 12532–75; Kudrn 179,1–2, 547,3–549,2, 665,1–
2, 1608,4, 1666,4–1667,1; MaiBfl 87,11–18; Melrnz 12274–83; Niblgn 645,3–4; PartMl 17370–95.
—On the relation of literary models to historical marriage practice: Masser, "Gahmuret,"
119–22.

70. Wglois 9797: volleclîche zwelf tage; 9774–75: dar zuo si vreuden überkraft sâhen alle
tage dâ.

71. Wglois 9478–83: niemen darf des vrâgen ob si die naht iht wæren vrô. jâ si, deiswâr,
ir vreude was sô daz der niht gelîchen mac. mit herzeliebe unz an den tac si sich under-
viengen. —Marriages at festivals: AlxusA 213–25; AlxusF 427–62; AplTyr 2182–211; Bussrd
497–544, 1010–67; Eneit 13100–220; Englhd 4990–5003; Erec 1887–2221; ETrist 2807; FlorBl
7501–770; GTrist 12532–75; GuGrhd 4880–5098; Häsln 334–501; Helmbr 1487–613; KrlGal
209,29–210,57; KAlxus 176–79; Kudrn 172,1–193,4, 547,1–559,4, 1608,1–1695,4; Lohgrn 2311–

The two parts of a MHG marriage, one public and contractual, the other private and sexual, parallel the two elements of a Christian marriage, consent (contractual and preferably public) and consummation (private and sexual), that played such a large role in the twelfth-century debate over what makes a marriage valid. Whereas Gratian held that sexual relations were required, others, notably Peter Lombard, held that consent alone made a marriage binding, a view that was adopted by Pope Alexander III and became the standard teaching. One can find suggestions of both positions in MHG texts. According to the *Väterbuch* Margaret Reparata allowed herself to be married publicly, but then she ran off just before she was to be led to the marriage bed, disguised herself as a man, and entered a monastery.[72] For Margaret sex rather than the public ceremony seems to be the crucial threshold. Not surprisingly, the Franciscan preacher Berthold von Regensburg takes the more orthodox view. He regards a marriage between two seven-year-old children as binding even if they have never lain together, even if they have never kissed, and even if they have never caressed each other; he is careful to specify, however, that they must have been married "in accordance with the wishes of both of them."[73] For Berthold, consent constitutes marriage. Although one can find passages in MHG texts that recall the theological debates, MHG writers show little interest in problematizing the distinction. In most cases consummation follows immediately on the public union, and even in those rare instances, like Flore and Blanscheflur, where there is a considerable delay, the difference between the two events is of little consequence.[74]

While the church worked to resolve the theological issues surrounding marriage, the medieval nobility continued to pursue its own goals. For them marriage was "primarily an instrument of dynastic politics," one

523; MaiBfl 69,10–96,13; Melrnz 11473–12671; Niblgn 579,1–689,4; PartMl 17400–443; Rennew 4933–5064; StElis 615–44, 1476–79; TandFl 15817–17420; Treuep 173–221; Väterb 30752–55, 35817–33; WilWnd 187–348; WolfdB 233,1–255,4. —Marriages with consummation: AplTyr 2231–56, 13406–14, 18292–340; ETrist 2808–52; GTrist 12576–675; GuGrhd 4345–46, 5022–58; Lohgrn 2351–90, 6814–30; Niblgn 629,1–4; MaiBfl 92,34–93,37; Melrnz 12322–32; Rennew 5152–64, 32259–347; RnfrBr 10738–11171; TandFl 16639–57; Treuep 179–93; WilWnd 327–32; Wglois 9458–83.

72. Väterb 35854–917.

73. BertvR 1:313,13–14: mit ir beider willen.

74. The consensual theory of Peter Lombard and Alexander III is somewhat more complicated than my explanation makes it seem. See Brundage, *Law, Sex,* 187–94, 234–39, 262–70, 331–37. —Although Berthold follows the majority view, against Gratian, in insisting that consent is necessary and sufficient for valid marriage, with regard to the minimum age at which consent can be given he stands with Gratian (seven) against the majority (twelve for girls, fourteen for boys) (Brundage, *Law, Sex,* 238, 357).

through which they could guarantee the generation of legitimate heirs and establish affiliations with other lineages.[75] "In most cases," as they pursued these ends "no consideration whatsoever was given to the desires of the daughters who were to be married."[76] This is certainly the case for the historical noblewomen whose unions are mentioned in vernacular accounts. The marriage of Elizabeth of Hungary was arranged when she was an infant and hardly in a position to have an opinion on the subject. The relatives of Adelheid von Frauenberg "gave her to a noble lord, as is the custom of the world,"[77] even though she is so opposed that she prays to be stricken with leprosy in order to thwart their plans. Ottokar chronicles more than fifteen marriages, every one of which is negotiated by the head of a noble house for political or dynastic ends. Some are supposed to bring peace: "with the marriage" of the daughter of the margrave of Brandenburg to the Hungarian crown prince in 1261 "all hostile acts, which had been done by both parties, were supposed to cease."[78] Other marriages are meant to win allies: in order to lure Heinrich von Kärnten away from Albrecht of Austria, Wenzel II "promised him his eldest daughter as a reward."[79] While it is possible that the maidens were more involved in choosing their husbands than these accounts suggest, and while there is evidence of historical marriages where love did play a role, it is surely noteworthy that Ottokar can write thousands of lines about marriage and not once treat a maiden bride as anything other than a silent pawn. It seems that the daughter of Hilary of Poitiers describes the situation of most noble maidens without exaggeration when she says of her father: "He has the power to give me to anyone he wishes."[80]

Under such circumstances it is not surprising that a husband might be chosen that a daughter dislikes and that, in literary contexts at least, she will resist marrying him. Aglye, whose father has arranged a marriage to suit his political interests, refuses to cooperate: "You should know that the son of the king of Marroch will never lie with me, no matter how much they all think they are still going to celebrate at my expense. They will have to

75. Bumke, *Höfische Kultur*, 534: Für den Laienadel war die Ehe primär . . . ein Instrument der dynastischen Politik.
76. Bumke, *Höfische Kultur*, 546: die herrschende Praxis, die auf den Willen der zu verheiratenden Töchter in den meisten Fällen überhaupt keine Rücksicht nahm.
77. TößSwb 50,10: nach der welt gewonhait do gabent sy ir fründ ainem edlen herren.
78. ORmchr 7636–39: mit der hîrât sold al vîntliche tât, diu beidenthalben was getân, zwischen in ein ende hân.
79. ORmchr 85921–22: der lobte im ze miete die eltist tohter, die er hiete.
80. BMärtr 186–87: er hatt wol gewalt mich zegeben wem er will. —On courtly marriage practice: Bumke, *Höfische Kultur*, 534–47; Rösener, "Höfische Frau," 219–21.

bury me first."[81] Nor is it surprising, considering the authority that fathers and aspiring husbands expect to wield, that maidens are put under great pressure to marry against their will or not to marry as they wish. When Hilde elopes with Hetel, her father pursues them with a large army and wounds Hetel in battle.[82] Even women whose fathers have died and who exercise political power in their own right are not safe from this sort of pressure: when Condwiramurs rejects the suit of Clamide he raises an army and attacks her until he "devastated [her] citadels and lands"[83] and placed her under seige. This typical romance situation represents a very powerful pressure to marry.

While it is not surprising that young women are pressured to marry or that they resist taking the husbands to whom they have been promised, it is remarkable, considering the pressure, how often they succeed in getting their own way. Aglye remains steadfast in her refusal to wed the son of the king of Marroch and eventually marries her beloved, Wilhelm von Österreich. Condwiramurs refuses to surrender to Clamide's seige and marries Parzival, the man of her choice. There are, in fact, very few cases where a secular heroine actually does marry someone she did not choose herself. And even in these cases she usually turns out to love the man she is obliged to marry anyway. Although Enite is not consulted when her father arranges her marriage to Erec, she turns out to be more than willing—indeed, her desire for Erec is so great "that they probably would have played a very intimate game" even before the wedding, "if it could have been kept secret."[84] MHG writers seem to attach considerable importance to consent after all—but they do so, one suspects, less out of devotion to the marriage doctrines of the church than to the conventions of medieval literary love, which they wish to incorporate into the institution of marriage.

In many cases the partners also succeed in gaining the approval of the parents who opposed them. Although Hilde's father pursues her with a large army, in the end he is easily placated, attends Hilde's wedding and coronation, and reports to his wife when he returns home that he cannot imagine a better match.[85] For the most part then, MHG texts present an ideal of marriage in which the desire of the children is reconciled with the

81. WilÖst 9512–16: wizz mir geligt nymmer bi des kûnges sun von Marroch, swie daz si alle wænent noch hohzit mit mir haben! man must mich e begraben.
82. Kudrn 447,1–525,4.
83. Parz 194,14–16: mir hât der künec Clâmidê . . . verwüestet bürge unde lant.
84. Erec 1853–56: ez wære wætlîch, und hetez nieman gesehen, daz dâ wære geschehen ein vil vriuntlîchez spil.
85. Kudrn 560,1–4.

authority of the parents: even if MHG daughters do not choose whom they marry, at least they love the men they must take as husbands; and even if they thwart their parents' plans, they are reconciled with them in the end. In this regard, at least, the literary representation of marriage clearly idealizes historical practice.

Of the three events that mark Flore and Blanscheflur's coming of age, the last is Flore's assumption of his father's throne. On the morning after he and Blanscheflur are married, two messengers arrive in Babylon looking for their "young lord."[86] They announce that Flore's father has been dead for six months and that the princes of the country think it's high time for Flore to return home if he hopes to find things still in order. Flore sets out "like a kingly hero" and, on his arrival in Spain, is received joyously by the population: "They praised God very greatly because, as it seemed to them, things had turned out well: their rightful, ancestral lord would rule over the country that had been held for him for so long."[87] The transformation is clear: Flore is no longer the "young" lord, dependent on his father's authority; having assumed that authority, he is now the "rightful" lord. In inheriting his father's kingdom Flore assumes his father's role in the world and comes of age.

Although there are other texts that make the connection between inheritance and coming of age, inheritance actually plays a surprisingly small role in MHG narrative. In some stories there are possessions that the hero might have inherited, but for one reason or another this possibility has been precluded: in *Eraclius* the patrimony has been sold (along with Eraclius himself!) and the proceeds given to the poor; in Ulrich's *Willehalm* the sons have been disinherited and sent abroad to fend for themselves. In other cases inheritance is possible, but the possibility is ignored: Meleranz and Wilhelm von Österreich are the heirs apparent to France and Austria, but the entire interest of the narratives is on their adventures and conquests abroad, not on the line of succession back home. This is true even in those works, like the prose *Lancelot* or Gottfried's *Tristan*, where the hero *does* come into his patrimony: this inheritance is always of less interest than the lands and honors that the hero acquires on his own.[88]

---

86. FlorBl 7655: ir junkherren.
87. FlorBl 7770: als ein küneclîcher degen; 7786–90: sie dûht ez wære wol ergangen, und lobten got vil verre daz ir rehter erbeherre des landes solte walten, daz im lange was behalten.
88. Inheritance linked to coming of age: Alban 3.13–27; Parz 803,2–23; PrLanc 1:25,29–32; WilOrl 3021–22; WolfdA 309,1–2. —Inheriting political dominion: Alban 3.19–27; BMärtr 24679–88; Bussrd 1054–65; Frndst 35,6–8; GuFrau 147–74; Hlgnlb 253,21–22; JngTit 954,4,

Condwiramurs, the Gute Frau, Tydomie, and Osann[89] also inherit, although inheritance for women is different than for men. It is, for instance, never explicitly linked to coming of age. And yet, in some sense at least, the women clearly have come of age, since they exercise political authority over lands they have inherited. In every case, however, their dominion is compromised since they are under attack by a spurned suitor and must wait for the hero to rescue and marry them. Thus, although a woman can be said to come of age when she inherits, her inheritance, and thus her majority, is only secure once she has married. But then, although the inheritance is secure, it is no longer hers, since, at marriage, it passes out of her control and into that of her husband. The morning after Parzival defeats Kingrun, Condwiramurs "gave him her lands and her fortresses, since he was the love of her heart."[90]

Like knighting and marriage, male inheritance is represented in idealized fashion in most MHG texts, where it generates little interest or conflict. In real life it was taken more seriously. Ulrich von Liechtenstein doubtless reflects historical practice more closely than other writers when he reports: "Meanwhile my father had died and I had to return home like many another whose forebears leave him property."[91] Questions of inheritance play a large role in legal texts like the *Schwabenspiegel*,[92] doubtless because, in the historical Middle Ages, such questions often led to conflict. After the death of Albert I, his son "Frederick, the dauntless prince, displayed a manly spirit" and continued his father's struggle to keep Bohemia "in the possession of the kingdom."[93] The absence of conflict over inheritance, like the universality of knightly investiture or the romantic and generational concord at marriage, represents a cultural ideal of a harmonious and coherent society, an ideal of noble life that is often celebrated in MHG literary texts.

1106,2–4; Klage 3756–64, 3996–4016; Kudrn 188,2–190,2; LAlexr V559–64; Niblgn 39,1–2, 42,2–43,4; RAlexr 3299–309; RBarlm 334,11–338,38; SAlexr 823–924; StrKrl 227–74; UAlexr 2193–204; WilOrl 3113–33, 5896–909; WilWnd 103–46.

89. FrdSwb 1881–932.

90. Parz 202,26–28: dô gap im bürge unde lant disiu magetbæriu brût, wande er was ir herzen trût.

91. Frndst 35,6–8: indes lac min vater tot—do muost ich heim als maniger tuot, dem sine vordern lazent guot.

92. Schwsp La15, La38, La161, La186, La324, Le48b, Le49a, Le49b, Le51, Le52, Le53, Le64.

93. ORmchr 95115–18: Fridrich der furste unverzeit menlichen muot . . . liez an im sehen; 92226–27: daz er doch daz lant behielte in gewer dem rîch.

Saintly Affiliations

Iolande displays her religious commitment at an early age. "In the days of her childhood," we are told, "the tender maiden held vigils, prayed, fasted, and beat herself with switches."[94] When her mother takes her along on a visit to a convent Iolande begs the children who were showing her around "to bring the habit and place it on her, [since] she wanted to remain a nun there."[95] They are horrified and call the abbess, and Iolande has no choice but to return home with her mother. Sometime later a Dominican friar pays a visit to her parents and asks Iolande about her earlier resolve: "Do you still have the intention which you formed so early in your childhood when you wanted to become a nun?"[96] She says her intention is the same, then asks him to choose the community she should enter. When he does so, "the friar's word bound her heart to the convent from that moment, so that she never wavered in her resolve."[97] Each of these actions represents a commitment on Iolande's part—first to a life of pious discipline, then to a religious vocation, and finally to a particular convent. Although Iolande is not yet an adult, her commitments are adult affiliations: it is not merely appropriate but admirable for adults to live a religious life. And although Iolande is not a saint, her affiliations are saintly, since they reveal her disdain for the world and her commitment to God. As in the case of most pious children in MHG narrative, saintliness becomes evident early in childhood.

In some cases the religious affiliation is established even before the child is born: Jesus reminds the Zwölfjähriges Mönchlein, who had been pledged to a monastic life before birth, that "your chaste mother gave you to me body and soul before you ever received mortal life in the vast kingdom of the world."[98] In other cases affiliations have been established in the prenarrative past: at the very outset of her story Agnes rejects the gifts of a rich admirer "since another suitor has come ahead of you and I have

---

94. Ioland 215: in hiren kindeldagen; 205–8: wachen, beden, vasten . . . bit rŭden sich dy zarde slŭch.

95. Ioland 230–33: bit hôen vlîze sy des bat, dat sy den orden brehten und hir den ane lehten, sy woilde nunne blîven dâ.

96. Ioland 554–57: has du den willen noch . . . den du sô vrŭ begundes dragen bî dînen jungen kindeldagen, dâ du ein nunne woldes sîn?

97. Ioland 644–47: des brŭders wort hir herze bant zŭ deme klôstre van der zît, dat sy . . . van deme willen ny engetrat.

98. ZwöMön 238–41: dîn reiniu muoter hât dich mir mit lîbe unt mit sêle ergeben, ê du gewunne ie menschen leben ûf disem ertrîche breit.

pledged myself to him," that is, to Christ.[99] In narratives like these the protagonists' commitment to holiness is not an event in the story but rather a precondition for the events of the story that follows.[100]

Other religious affiliations occur within the narrative. When "he was only seven years old," the hero of *Mönches Not*, "a small child, was sent to the forest to a monastery,"[101] that is, he was committed while still a child to a religious life according to the characterisic medieval practice of oblation. Other texts report ages for oblation ranging from three to thirteen.[102] If one excepts the mystical paragons in the *Schwesternbücher*, oblation leads to a profound religious commitment in only about half the cases.[103] For the others, oblation means they are kept ignorant of the world. Because of the isolation in which she grows up, the heroine of the *Sperber* "did not recognize the people or the customs they practiced outside" the convent and can be tricked into sexual relations with a passing knight.[104] The literary evidence, in which oblation is nearly as likely to lead to erotic adventures as to religious commitment, recalls the discussion among medieval churchmen concerning the wisdom of placing children in monastic houses before it could be known whether they really had a religious vocation. This concern led some orders to discourage the practice, although the church continued to regard oblates as bound for life. Secular law codes, on the other hand, regulate the conditions under which they might leave. The *Schwabenspiegel*

99. Hlgnlb 67,18–20: wan ein ander liphaber hât dich vorkomen, und deme habe ich mich vertrûwet.

100. Promised to God before birth: StLudw 52,31–53,4. —Preexisting holiness: BMärtr 3214–19, 4859–60, 8760–69; Hlgnlb 161,38–39; Ioland 158–74, 194–218; KAlxus 150–51, 164–65; Passnl H11,22–32, K6,65–7,64, K111,18–39, K111,65–112,78, K217,6–9, K293,1–3, K301,1–27, K354,66–75, K354,83–355,50, K396,44–69, K505,10–12, K618,22–59; StElis 703–5, 896–97; StUlrc 145–52; Väterb 248–55, 30631–35, 35797–816, 39127–33; WerMar 1554–60, 1583–98, A1409–44, A1847–64; WlMarg 125–39; WzMarg 130–72. —Married to Christ: BMärtr 610–45, 1429–36; Ioland 175–87; JnaMrt 19, 65; MHMarg 178–85, 211–16; Passnl K112,14–78, K113,8–40, K113,70–73, K114,64–65, K116,36–39, K116,63–65; PhMarl 932–1015, 1080–83, 1404–5; Väterb 28021–24, 28036–43; VrJngf Dorothy 144, 296–305; WlMarg 527–37; WlMarl 1893–990; WzMarg 246–53. —Devotion to the Virgin: ArmSch 91–112; MarBrt 4–11; ScholM 8–27; TKdlbg 59–89, 150–61.

101. MönNot 14: ez was wan siben jâr alt; 9–13: Ein kleinez kint wart . . . gesant Ze einem klôster in einen walt.

102. Three: TößSwb 48,10. Four-and-a-half: Irmgrd 20. Five: TößSwb 33,23. Six: TößSwb 90,20; ZwöMön 24–29. Seven: AdlSwb 183,63[2]; MönNot 14. Not more than eight: KrbSwb 118. Nine: KrbSwb 105, 109. Under ten: EngSwb 24,26. Ten: AdlSwb 172,40[2]; Irmgrd 13. Eleven: TößSwb 87,5. In twelfth year: UlmSwb 141. Thirteen: TößSwb 82,23, 100,19. *In kintlichen tagen:* TößSwb 83,20. *Kint:* UlmSwb 135.

103. Oblation leads to piety: ELgAur 819,1–15; Hlgnlb 99,15–100,6; HnrKgd 3575–96; JnaMrt 15; ZwöMön; the cases from the *Schwesternbücher* listed in the previous note. Oblation does not lead to piety: Gänsln 20–26; MönNot 9–18; Sperbr; VorNov 29–32.

104. Sperbr 64–65: [si] Weder liute noch site erkande, Des man ûzerhalben pflac.

allows children who were given to monastic houses before they were seven to return to the world before they are twelve if maidens, fourteen if youths, without forfeiting any of their secular prerogatives.[105]

The most dramatic religious affiliations come with conversion, of which there are two forms. Some children—the Jewish boys in *Jüdel* and *Judenknabe*, the Indian prince Josaphat—convert from other religions to Christianity. Other children, who are born Christian, experience conversion when they abandon the comparatively worldly ways of their parents for a more demanding asceticism. Alexis leaves his wife on their wedding night, telling her "that he had entrusted his chaste pure life to God's mercy and [that] he wanted forever after to be a wandering pilgrim"; his course soon leads him to Edessa, where "he sat down among the lepers [and] lived from alms along with them."[106] Like Alexis, many MHG saints express their commitment to God as a commitment to lead a chaste life and, again like Alexis, affiliate themselves with an ascetic vocation—pilgrim, beggar, hermit, monk.[107]

Although there are cases of genuine childhood conversion, in general MHG texts prefer to keep the drama of conversion out of childhood. Some include the conversion but ignore the drama. One of the lives of Margaret says simply that "very early the child turned her back on all heathen practices and idols and on everything her father believed."[108] Her conversion is a simple matter of fact, one that requires neither elaboration nor explanation. Others include the drama but move it to the end of childhood, even if the religious commitment was made earlier. When Alexis goes to school

105. Schwsp La27. —On oblation: Boswell, "*Expositio*," 25–26; Boswell, *Kindness*, 243–49.

106. AlxusF 547–50: daz er sîn kiusche reinez leben in gotes gnâde hæte ergeben und er ouch iemer wolde sîn ein ellender bilgerîn; 656–67: zen werltsiechen er gesaz. daz almuosen er mit in nôz.

107. Saints convert to Christianity: BMärtr 13425–45, 13468–72, 22974; ELgAur 347,3–5, 423,17–18, 462,18–22, 596,14–29, 724,12–726,12, 788,20–26; GrshPr 450a,10–20; Hlgnlb 253,18–19; JnaMrt 3; Jüdel 130,46–70, 132,69–72, 134,31–50; Ksrchr 1906–17; LBarlm 7179–405; KPantl 166–277, 366–75; Passnl K471,48–472,58, K592,18–33, K594,18–19; PKonPr S239,26–28; RBarlm 169,27–177,36; StMarM 75–80, 102–3, 153–58; StVeit 62–65; VrJnfr Margaret 51–62. —Secular figures convert out of personal devotion to a Christian: FlorBl 7791–829; KrlGal 37,3–9, 71,32–72,12, 76,50–52, 208,47–209,14; PartMl 10111–233. —Those who become beggars or hermits: AlxusA 271–326; AlxusB 133–68; AvaJoh 195–206; BMärtr 17904–6; JnaMrt 20, 72–73; Passnl H348,56–69, K94,6–9, K217,20–25; Väterb 393–422, 8933–36, 39206–54. —Those who enter religious orders: BMärtr 3249–60, 10369–82, 10411–19, 21074–76; ELgAur 582,9–19; HnrKgd 3595–96; GrMarl 386–94; Hlgnlb 99,15–17; Ioland 219–306, 545–704, 1715–2610, 5635–839; KSilvr 458–77; MarBrt 82–87; Passnl K193,10–13, K399,92–400,15; PhMarl 499–514; Väterb 8906–9, 33566–632, 35891–917; ZwöMön 35–37.

108. WlMarg 136–39: daz kint vil zîtlîche flôch allen heidenischen site und diu abgot dâ mite und swaz ir vater geloubte.

and reads about chastity "his heart became so inflamed by God that at once
he put on the pure garment that maidens wear eternally." [109] What is in his
heart, however, only becomes visible to the world when he abandons his
bride and becomes a beggar in a distant country. This is the general rule:
if conversion occurs during childhood it is not dramatic, and if it is dramatic it is pushed to the end of childhood. Although there are exceptions,
MHG writers do not seem to consider dramatic conversion an activity for
children.

Although many conversions occur at the end of childhood, conversion
itself is not one of the rites of passage, since there is nothing in its nature
that requires it to happen at any particular time of life: Iolande turns to
God as a young child, Francis just as he enters manhood, Augustine not
until he is well into his thirties. The conversion of Alexis is caused by and
therefore coincides with his marriage, but this causal coincidence does not
mean that conversion itself marks the beginning of adulthood: we know
that Alexis has reached the end of childhood because he was expected to
marry, not because he refuses to marry.

The most decisive turning from the world comes not with the end of
childhood but with the end of life, and for saintly children death brings the
heavenly reward they have earned by their exemplary lives. When Vitus is
martyred, along with his nurse Crescentia and his master Modestus, "each
of them gave up the spirit, which our Lord received and admitted them
to the glory which other martyrs also enjoy." [110] When the Zwölfjähriges
Mönchlein dies, Jesus addresses him: "Arise, beloved, spotless soul. Since
you are of such perfect excellence, you are saved; today you shall be with
me, crowned in my father's kingdom." [111] The religious heroes and heroines
are all "of such perfect excellence" that their "spotless souls" are transported
at once to heaven. It is the ultimate sacred affiliation. [112]

109. AlxusF 197–200: Sîn herze wart sô gar enzunt von gote, daz er an der stunt an sich
nam daz reine kleit, daz meide tragent in êwikheit.
110. Passnl K304,94–305,1: ir ieglich gab uf sinen geist, die unser herre wol entpfie und
sie zu den eren lie, die andere marterere ouch haben.
111. ZwöMön 280–85: wol uf reiniu sêle trût . . . sît du sô vollekomen bist an edelkeit,
dû bist genesen, dû solt noch hiute bî mir wesen, gekrœnet in mînes vater rîch.
112. Martyrs: BMärtr 847–96, 1241–47, 8056–131, 9120–81, 12213–63; HgMarg 1452–1654;
Hlgnlb 40,9–24, 60,2–4, 135,40–136,20; JnaMrt 3, 6, 22, 32, 38, 38, 39, 46, 51, 56, 61, 65, 82, 89,
90, 92; Passnl K116,30–66, K294,46–80, K304,34–305,1, K332,29–73; StMarM 551–644; Väterb 38058–118; WzMarg 981–1162. —Others who die and are saved: ArmSch 1135–33, 1204–30;
ScholM 382–443.

Disdaining the Secular Rites

For most of Iolande's childhood she is locked in a struggle, primarily with her mother, over whether or not she will marry. The first hints of the struggle occur when Iolande is a little over nine and "they asked her if she wanted to get married. 'No,' she said, 'it cannot be that a mortal man could ever become mine.'"[113] Later, when Iolande learns that a marriage has been arranged for her, she calls out: "No, that cannot be. Neither heart nor tongue will ever commit me to any man except the one I have chosen myself. I am provided for. [Christ], who has chosen me as his bride, is a thousand times better than the man you have assigned me."[114] When she is told that her parents will forfeit a large sum if she does not marry, she is unmoved. And when her mother threatens to shut her in a room with the man to whom they have promised her, she is unafraid: "Even if I were locked up securely with a hundred men, as long as I had God's help I would surely come out untouched."[115] In the end Iolande's parents are defeated. They can find no way to get her to marry, since she refuses to abandon her commitment to the life of a nun. For Iolande, as for other pious children in MHG narrative, their sacred calling requires them to refuse the secular rites of passage.

Many saints' lives, especially those of female saints, dwell at length on the struggle to avoid marriage. Margaret Reparata is so upset at the prospect that, on the day of her wedding, she throws herself on the ground, praying to God that he "might remove her from the filthiness of the world, so that the chaste fabric of her heart might remain undefiled by the world and she might spend all her years in chastity until her death."[116] Later in the day she runs away from home, disguises herself as a man, and enters a monastery. The lives of other saints, most of them males, recount the saints' refusal to accept their inheritance. When Nicholas's parents die "his heart and mind were greatly troubled about how he might dispose of his

---

113. Ioland 177–81: man sy vrâgen des began, aver sy wolde nemen man. "nein," sprach sy, "des enmach nyt sîn, dat unmer moge werden mîn kein man, der mûze sterven."

114. Ioland 813–20: nein . . . des enmach nyt sîn. der munt und ôich dat herze mîn gelovent zwâre nummer man dan als ich selven erkoren han. ich bin berâden: . . . der mich ze brûde erkoren hat, der is noch bezzer dûsentfalt dan er, den ir hat mir gezalt.

115. Ioland 3817–21: sô lanc ich got ze helfen han . . . wêre ich bit hundert manne noch besluzzen vast, ich soilde doch wol unbevlecket kumen dan.

116. Väterb 35841–49: Und sprach ir gebet an Got Daz siner truwe gebot Ir zu helfe queme Und sie da beneme Der werlde unvlat, Daz ires herzen kusche wat Unbesult in erden blibe Und daz sie alle ire zit vertribe Mit kuscheit untz an den tot.

father's inheritance, which was considerable, so that it might be put to good use. He shared his wealth with God, taking pity on orphans and the poor and offering them a generous hand."[117] Having given to the poor, Nicholas next gives dowries to the daughters of a neighbor to save them from prostitution; soon he is made bishop, and by then his public life is well under way.[118]

Apparently the parents and relatives of Margaret and Nicholas believe them ready to come of age: otherwise they would hardly have arranged Margaret's marriage or allowed Nicholas to dispose of his inheritance. Therefore we can conclude that the saints have reached an age at which their childhood should be over. And yet, even though they are old enough to come of age, they refuse to do so. The refusal is deliberate. If Margaret married she would assume the role of an adult woman in the world, and if Nicholas kept his father's fortune he would assume his father's role in the world. Marriage means sex, inheritance worldly property. They represent what Margaret calls the "filthiness of the world," Abraham of Kidunaia the "bonds and false pleasures of the world."[119] Whereas for Flore and Blanscheflur coming of age represents fulfillment and liberation, for Margaret and Abraham it represents contamination and bondage. It is hardly surprising, given such an understanding, that young saints refuse to come of age.

In many stories young saints are not put in a position where they must refuse to come of age, since the whole question is ignored. The stories of the most famous prophets—Moses, John the Baptist, Jesus—skip from early childhood to manhood. The years when they might have come of age are of so little interest that they are missing altogether. The stories of many future clerics, like Ulrich, move from home to school to minor and then major ecclesiastical positions without troubling to announce just when it

117. Passnl K7,74–85: mit bekummertem mute was do sines herzen sin, wa er solde legen hin und machen gar bederbe sines vater erbe, des vil was unde genuc. . . . deme [gote] teilte er mite ouch sin gut, an weisen unde an armen, die er sich liez erbarmen und bot sine milde hant.
118. Others who refuse or try to refuse marriage (besides the martyrs listed in note 112): AlxusA 186–299; AlxusB 65–139; AlxusC 51–78; AlxusF 264–633; BMärtr 1442–58; ELgAur 426,14–20; Hlgnlb 161,21–162,5; KAlxus 160–241; Passnl H10,90–12,88; PhMarl 890–1499; TößSwb 87; Väterb 39139–213, 27797–28337, 30707–81, 35817–917; WerMar 1539-A1877; WlMarl 1787–2726. —Others who refuse their inheritance: ELgAur 21,14–35, 220,22–26, 789,31–34; Passnl K192,79–193,5, K293,24–294,1; BMärtr 3221–60, 10405–17, 18709, 25869–938, 27991–96; StKatM 511–45; Väterb 308–92. —Martin is the only MHG saint who confronts knighthood, which he accepts unwillingly (GrshPr 450a,24–27; Passnl K593,6–13; PKonPr S239,29–30). In one account Alexis is instructed in knighthood, but nothing more is said on the subject (AlxusA 175–86).
119. Väterb 30824–25: der werlde clobe Und . . . ir valschen wunne.

is that their heroes become adults. We are not even told when Ulrich, a "priest" who is "chosen bishop," [120] is ordained. The stories of Dominican nuns in the *Schwesternbücher* begin when the protagonist enters the convent, but once she is there no distinction is made between childhood and adulthood—even in the nearly twenty cases where the heroine enters as a child (ages three to thirteen). Even in the relatively detailed life of Mechthild von Waldeck, who entered the convent when she "was not more than eight years old" and who is said to have been "a right pure person from the days of her childhood on," [121] there is no way of distinguishing the pious acts and mystical events of her childhood from those that occurred later in her life. [122]

Religious narratives can be indifferent to the secular rites of passage because their protagonists are not subject to earthly time. Thus they do not change. When Margaret "was scarcely a day old, her heart constantly burned for the love of God like the flame of a fire." [123] Werendraut von Büren was "a completely innocent and pure person from the days of her childhood until her death." [124] If a life is all of one piece with regard to its salient characteristic, in this case saintliness, then there is no reason to break it up by the introduction of irrelevant articulations, like secular coming of age. Saints' lives unfold according to a heavenly timetable rather than an earthly one. When the infant Ulrich dislikes his nurse's milk this is explained as a "miracle" that "God worked in him because he saw the

120. StUlrc 256: phaffen; 324: ze bisschoffe irwelt.

121. KrbSwb 118: was nicht mer denn acht jar alt; und was ein recht lauter mensch von iren kintlichen tagen auf.

122. Kartschoke considers Ulrich's childhood over when he goes to school at St. Gall, but he does not explain why (*Geschichte*, 355). —Ordination is also overlooked in the lives such famous ecclesiastics as Gregory, Jerome, Nicholas, and Remi (BMärtr Gregory, Remi, Nicholas; Passnl Jerome, Nicholas). So far as I know, Cunibert, Boniface, Servatius, and Silvester are the only future saints said to have been ordained, and in no case does ordination coincide with coming of age: Cunibert is made bishop while still a child; Boniface and Silvester are ordained at thirty (JnaMrt Cunibert 80; BMärtr Boniface 10420–22; KSilvr 458–77). For the others see BMärtr 27991–92; ObSrvt 280; VlSrvt 317–54. The minimum canonical age of ordination for a priest was always 25, for a bishop 30 (Metz, "Droit canonique," 32). —The hero of *Der Scholar und das Marienbild* is ordained at age fifteen, but his story cannot be considered representative of saints' lives: he dies right after he is ordained, and he is not a saint (ScholM 33, 377–47). —I know of only one case in which, after a maiden's entry in the convent, the fact that she is a child receives any serious attention (UlmSwb 141–42) and of only one other that includes a childhood episode (EngSwb 7,36–810). —On the absence of regular chronology in the *Schwesternbücher*: Ringler, *Viten- und Offenbarungsliteratur*, 336, 350, 359.

123. WzMarg 130–37: Do sy was kume tages alt. . . . ir hercze . . . nach gottes minne ze aller zitt bran sam des fres flam.

124. KrbSwb 105: die was gar ein unschultiger reiner mensch von iren kintlichen tagen uncz an iren tod.

future in store for him."[125] Ulrich's future glory is known to God when Ulrich is still a newborn. This is true even in the case of a saint like Francis, who experiences a dramatic conversion just when he enters manhood. God provoked his conversion with an illness, we learn, "because he *had known for a long time* how the noble captain was destined to lead the army of the barefooted [the Franciscans] through the Red Sea of the world towards that rich country where they would all find clothes and shoes as they deserved."[126] Francis's conversion may happen to coincide with the end of his youth, but that is merely fortuitous: its timing is determined by the wisdom of God.[127]

This does not mean that saints do not grow up. When Bernard is young he is called *kint*, and after he is twenty-two he is called *man*.[128] This only makes sense if Bernard, like other males in MHG narrative, grows from a *kint* into a *man*. Bernard is praised for the chastity he showed "from childhood into old age."[129] Again, this only makes sense if there are parts of Bernard's life that can be called *kintheit* and *alter*. To the extent that saints are mortals like the rest of us they are bound to grow up, beginning as children and becoming men and women: their biological participation in the world is unavoidable. But their participation in the secular world is limited: although they may be expected to marry or inherit property, they will refuse to do so, since they do not want to assume the roles of secular men and women. Thus it is that saints grow up but do not come of age.

Childhood and Adulthood, Secular and Religious

For the three teenage murderers in Bangor, it was of the greatest consequence that the judge decided to try them as juveniles: as such the stiffest sentence they could receive was confinement in a correctional facility until they turned twenty-one. Had they been tried and convicted as adults they would have been sent to prison for a minimum of twenty-five years. Clearly the state of Maine sees a big difference between the acts of children and the acts of adults: it is the acts of adults that really count. MHG texts also attach

125. StUlrc 82–83: got abe mit im ein wunder tet wander kunftigiv dinc an im sach.
126. Passnl K515,94–516,3: wand er vor lange weste, wie der edele houbetman solde . . . uber daz rote werldemer leiten der barvuzen her an daz riche lant hin zu, da si kleidere unde schu aller vunden uf ir recht.
127. The constancy of piety: BMärtr 4859–60; Passnl K241,16–19, K293,2–3.
128. Passnl K395,72, K395,78, K395,84, K396,7, K396,37, K401,40, K406,18, K406,46.
129. Passnl K395,5: inz alder von der kintheit.

great importance to the difference between the acts of children and those of adults, although they do not have a judge to tell them which are which. Instead they recognize a few rites of passage, which mark the threshold between childhood and adulthood, as well as a number childhood ties that remain unaffected by the transition to adulthood. As must have become clear by now, secular and religious texts differ in the importance they attach to the distinction between childhood and adulthood. In concluding this chapter I would like to note three aspects of this difference: one lexical, one structural, and one cultural.

MHG has two related expressions that approximate English "to come of age": *ze sinen tagen komen* and *ze sinen jaren komen*, literally, "to come to one's days" or "years." Berthold von Regensburg refers inclusively to "grown-up people, who have come to their days." [130] In secular contexts the MHG expressions are associated with the rites of passage. With bearing arms: Wigamur is raised by a sea creature "until he came to his days, when he should have borne the arms of a man." [131] With marriage: the priests in the Temple invoke God's commandment that "all the maidens who had come to their years should be given to men in marriage." [132] And with inheritance: "Claudas swore that he planned to return their lands when the children had come to their years." [133] In saints' lives, however, "coming to one's years" is not associated with the arrival of adulthood but with an earlier access of wisdom or piety. With formal education: when Dominic "came to his years he was sent to school." [134] Or with saintliness: "When the child" Euphrosyne, who must be considerably less than twelve, "came to her years, she strove with complete diligence to walk in the paths of righteousness." [135] The secular usage, where "coming to one's years" coincides with coming of age, serves to emphasize the distinction between childhood and adulthood, while the religious usage, where one can "come to one's years" at any time during childhood, serves to efface that difference. [136]

130. BertvR 1:12,8–9: gewahsen liute . . . die zuo ir tagen komen sint.
131. Wigmur 348–50: untz er kam zu seinen tagen, das er solt haben getragen . . . mannes were.
132. PhMarl 894–96: daz man ze manne solde geben die megde alle in êlîch leben, die komen waeren zuo ir tagen.
133. PrLanc 1:25,29–32: Claudas . . . schwůr . . . das er den kinden . . . alles ir lant wold wiedder geben, wann sie zu yrn jaren kemen.
134. ELgAur 499,13–14: Do er zů ioren kam do wart er gesendet . . . zů schůlen.
135. Väterb 27763–66: Do daz kint zu jaren quam, Mit allem vlize sich an nam Da ez wanderte . . . rehte wege.
136. Some maintain that there is a difference between *ze sinen tagen* and *ze sinen jaren komen*. However, they are interchangeable in almost every context, as can be seen from the following list, where I have distinguished them by "t" (*ze sinen tagen*) or "j" (*ze sinen jaren*).

This lexical evidence corroborates a number of observations that have already been made concerning the structure of the MHG childhood narratives. In secular texts the transition to adulthood is nearly always marked by a rite of passage, the importance of which is heightened by the idealized form in which these rites appear: lavish knightly investiture for all, marriage that reconciles the desires of the bride with those of her parents, inheritance without conflict. Very few affiliations (primarily love) remain untouched as children cross this threshold. In religious texts, on the other hand, the rites of passage are refused by young saints, who want nothing of worldly adulthood, or else the rites are simply ignored. At the same time religious protagonists form a larger number of adult affiliations during childhood (general piety, monastic life, conversion), all of which remain stable from childhood into adulthood. As a consequence of these differences, childhood is much more clearly articulated from adulthood in secular texts, where everything changes on coming of age, than it is in religious ones, where much remains the same as saints move gradually into adulthood. Here again one sees that secular texts stress the distinction between childhood and adulthood while religious texts do not.

Just because religious texts do not mark the transition between childhood and adulthood with the enthusiasm of the secular texts does not mean they are unaware of the difference. Saints are called *kint* when young, *man* or *wîp* when older; they too pass through *kintheit* and enter *alter*. But the biological and societal distinction between childhood and adulthood is not so important in their lives as is the spiritual distinction between worldliness and saintliness. Thus a writer will offer evidence that a saint has been devoted to God from birth or will focus on the moment when a saint turns from the world toward God. These are matters of primary importance. The change in worldly status, from child to adult, is distinctly secondary.[137]

In secular texts, on the other hand, the distinction between childhood and adulthood is of the greatest importance. By clearly marking, celebrating, and idealizing the transition between childhood and adulthood,

---

Bearing arms: Lohgrn 734–35/t; WolfdA 245,3–246,4/j. Marriage: ELgAur 673,7–8/j; FrdSwb 8055–60/j; Hlgnlb 242,35–36/t; Passnl H10,88–11,9/j; Rennew 4058–60/j; Rennr 435–43/t; SaeldH 6916–22/t; Schwsp La55/t; SwrzPr F96,33–36/t; WerMar D1987–90/j. Inheritance/ lordship: BMärtr 27991–96/j; Rennew 11656–62/t; Schwsp Le45/t, Le49a/t, Le57/t. Wisdom/ piety: ELgAur 423,18/j; GrshPr 450a,10–15/j; Passnl K354,60–63/j. Schooling: BMärtr 4831–32/t; ELgAur 499,13–14/j; StdabA 12–13/j. Standing in legal disputes: Schwsp La13/t, Le49a/ t, Le50a/j. General: GuFrau 40–47/j; Ioland 984–97/t; KTrojk 13574–75/j; Melrnz 1476–80/j; Rennew 10056–57/t; RWeltc 9186–96/t; StDrth 95–99/t; StFran 410–12/t.

137. On the significance of Christianity in undermining the distinction between child and adult in Rome: Wiedemann, *Roman Empire*, 200.

secular texts give a distinct shape to childhood, a shape that it only has in secular contexts. In this way secular culture claims childhood—at least childhood that is distinct and different from adulthood—as a peculiarly secular phenomenon. When religious texts suppress the distinction between childhood and adulthood they make a point: that saintly constancy is more important than the articulations of worldly life. When secular texts celebrate this distinction they make their own point: that secular culture, that is, noble, courtly culture, has the power to shape its own life.[138]

138. See Bourdieu (*Outline*, 165; "Rites") on the role of rites of passage in maintaining the symbolic order and thus the real power of those who occupy the dominant position in the social structure.

7. Genres: Different Children's Stories

Most everyone, it seems safe to say, assumes that Moses was a Jew—most everyone, that is, except Sigmund Freud. Freud believed that Moses was an Egyptian. The argument Freud advances in support of this unorthodox view depends in large measure on an investigation by his disciple Otto Rank into "the myth of the hero's birth."[1] Rank found that the hero is usually abandoned shortly after his birth, as Moses is by his mother, that he is rescued and raised in a second family, as Moses is by Pharaoh's daughter, and that he returns to his natal family when he comes of age, as Moses returns to the Israelites and leads them out of Egypt. Since Rank is concerned with the "myth" of the hero, he has no reason to question the terms of the narratives he studies. For him, therefore, Moses is the child of Israelite parents, as the story claims: Moses is a Jew.[2] Freud qualifies Rank's scheme, however, by attaching a rider that applies to historical rather than purely fictional personages. "In all cases that can be evaluated," Freud claims, although he does not bother to give any examples, "the first family, the one from which the child is exposed, is the invented one, while the later family, into which the child is taken and in which it is raised, is the real one."[3] Thus the historical "Moses is an Egyptian," since the family in which he was raised is Egyptian; but he "is supposed to be turned into a Jew by means of the saga,"[4] by means, that is, of the fictional first family of the mythical scheme. For Rank the Biblical story of Moses' childhood falls into a large class of childhood narratives that he calls "the myth of the hero's birth." For Freud it falls into a special subclass of this group that applies to heroes who are also historical personages. The difference is merely a difference

1. Rank, *Der Mythus von der Geburt des Helden.*
2. Rank, *Geburt des Helden*, 16–20.
3. Freud, *Moses*, 111: Und nun führt vielleicht der neue Gesichtspunkt zur Klärung, daß die erste Familie, die, aus der das Kind ausgesetzt wird, in allen Fällen, die sich verwerten lassen, die erfundene ist, die spätere aber, in der es aufgenommen wird und aufwächst, die wirkliche.
4. Freud, *Moses*, 112: Moses ist ein . . . Ägypter, der durch die Sage zum Juden gemacht werden soll.

of narrative classification, but the difference is important: it determines whether Moses is born a Jew or an Egyptian.

Such problems of classification are not unknown in Middle High German. Does Gregorius, for instance, belong with Ulrich and the other clerical saints because a large part of his childhood is spent in a monastic school? Or does he belong with Parzival and the other knights because, although he has been taught none of the necessary skills, he ends his childhood by setting out to become a knight? The answers to these questions, as to those concerning Moses' parentage, hinge on the ways in which one defines the different classes of childhood narrative. This chapter is devoted to describing those classes: the genres of childhood.

Since I am not looking for subtle distinctions but instead for a modest number of clearly differentiated genres, each of which can accommodate a reasonable number of narratives, I have deliberately employed relatively crude criteria: extent (do they tell all of childhood or only part?), focus (do they emphasize the beginning of childhood or the end?), articulation (do they show distinctive breaks within childhood?), and themes (do they thematize education, virginity, love?). In what follows I discuss first the narratives that tell part of childhood, then those that begin at birth and continue to adulthood.

Scenes from Childhood

Among the MHG childhood narratives, there is one genre, the *childhood of the prophet*, that relates the beginning of childhood but not the end. Based on scriptural accounts, these narratives restrict their compass to that of their source: Moses' birth, abandonment, and adoption; John's conception, birth, and departure for the wilderness; the story of Jesus from conception to age twelve and the visit to the Temple. Within this limited compass they are concerned above all with the marvels that reveal the hero's divine nature. In Adelbrecht's *Johannes Baptista* "the large number of miracles" that accompany John's birth convince the onlookers that "God has chosen him among those of this world."[5] The childhood of the prophet is the first genre of childhood narrative to occur in MHG texts, around 1100 in the *Mittelfränkische Reimbibel*. It continues to be written—in Old Testament paraphrase, universal history, independent texts, sermons, and

5. JohBap 100: der fil manigen wnder; 104–5: uf dirre erde hat in got erwelt.

legendaries—until the end of the period under investigation.[6] In spite of the authority of the figures and the frequency with which their stories are recounted, Moses, John, and Jesus are the only child heroes whose stories are told in narratives of this type.

Only a few of these texts restrict themselves to the Bible stories. Most feel free to draw, frequently to base themselves, on apocryphal compilations. The *Vorauer Bücher Mosis* tell how the infant Moses destroys Pharaoh's crown, on which a pagan god is represented, an incident that derives ultimately from the Jewish historian Flavius Josephus.[7] The stories of Jesus' childhood in the *Marienleben* of Walther von Rheinau and Bruder Philipp are based on the *Vita beate virginis Marie et salvatoris rhythmica*, itself a compilation of apocryphal and legendary material.[8] Even though MHG writers did not hesitate to incorporate nonscriptural material into the childhood of the prophet, they nevertheless did not dare to expand the chronological scope of the hero's childhood. Bruder Philipp raises a "great lament" that he could not "find anything written about Jesus after he turned twelve until the time that he introduced holy Christianity with his teaching."[9] Neither he nor any other writer tried to fill in this gap, nor the similar gap in the lives of Moses and John the Baptist, with a continuous narrative.[10]

They did not invent narrative to close the gap because they were thinking in typological rather than biographical terms. When Frau Ava narrates the flight into Egypt she supplements the biblical account with the information that "when the child rode into the country, not a single idol remained whole there."[11] She was inspired to do so by Isaiah 19.1, "the idols of Egypt quail before him," one of the regular readings for the Christmas season, which she evidently took as an Old Testament prefiguration, necessarily fulfilled in the New Testament life of Jesus.[12] While this is a typological relation in the strict sense, the childhood of the prophet also

6. Moses: Exdus 197–268; JWeltc 6173–906; RWeltc 8877–9185. —John: AvaJoh 9–220; Passnl H345,52–348,85; GrshPr 445a,3–445b,10; SaeldH 955–1002, 2366–406. —Jesus: AvaJes 1–430; MfRmbl 135–208; Passnl H28,37–56,2; PhMarl 1616–5359; SaeldH 633–2355; WerMar 2427-A4468; WlMarl 2815–6825.

7. Wells, *Vorau* Moses, 123–24; Hamilton, "Baudouin," 139–49.

8. Päpke, *Marienleben*, 43–44; Masser, *Bibel- und Legendenepik*, 106; Masser, "Marien- und Leben-Jesu-Dichtung," 147.

9. PhMarl 4896–906: Hie hebet sich mîn grôze klage . . . daz ich niht geschriben vinde von Jêsû . . . dar nâch dô er was worden alt zwelf jâr unz an die zît daz er die heiligen kristenheit ane huop mit sîner lêre.

10. On the gap in the scriptural accounts of Jesus' life: SaeldH 2353–55; WlMarl 6690–731.

11. AvaJes 379–80: dô daz chint in daz lant räit, nehäin apgot ganz dâ nebeläip.

12. Masser, *Bibel, Apokryphen*, 189–90.

allows a less strict, biographical typology. When Moses destroys the idol-laden crown, a priest tells Pharaoh: "If this [child] grows up, he will destroy your idols."[13] The priest understands the child's act as a prefigurative sign of the deeds the adult will perform. Such childhood acts do not inaugurate a continuous narrative of individual growth but prefigure, across the gap in the biographical chronology, the events of adulthood. They do not stand in a linear relationship to adulthood but in a typological one. In a general sense, this is true of the genre as a whole: the childhood of the prophet does not introduce a childhood narrative but prefigures an adult narrative.

While the childhood of the prophet concentrates on the beginning of childhood and most of the other genres are obsessed with its end, there are a small number of texts that recount an incident from the middle of childhood and its immediate consequences. Among these the only coher-ent group comprises five stories about miracles of the Virgin: the *Jüdel*, the *Judenknabe*, *Thomas von Kandelberg*, *Der Scholar und das Marienbild*, and Heinrich der Klausner's *Armer Schüler*. The heroes of these stories are young scholars devoted to the Virgin: the Jüdel, a young Jew sent to a Christian school, wipes a cobweb off an image of the Virgin, and soon after has a vision and converts. For one reason or another the heroes come into conflict with their fathers, teachers, schoolmates, or bishops: the rela-tives of the Jüdel, outraged at his conversion, throw him into an oven. The Virgin rewards the young heroes for their devotion by coming to their aid when they most need help: she protects the Jüdel from the flames until a bishop arrives, leads the child from the oven, and baptizes him along with many of his relatives.

The stories do not make much of the potential maternal relationship between the Virgin and the child heroes, focusing instead on issues of service and reward: the Virgin tells the Jüdel, "no one who ever offered any service to me or my son was ever without our help no matter what the need."[14] Nor do the stories emphasize the children's purity and free-dom from sin so much as their weakness and foolishness: the Virgin actu-ally laughs when she hears the "childish words" and the "foolishness" of the Armer Schüler, a "silly fool" who is "simple as a calf."[15] And yet, this "foolish child was wiser than the graybeards" because he placed com-

13. VBüMos 33,23–26: sol dirre werden alt. . . . er zestoret dir dinev apgot.
14. Jüdel 132,78–81: der meinen svn oder mir. Ie dehæin dinest enbot. daz des zedehæiner not. vnser helfe vergaz.
15. ArmSch 691–94: Dô lachte di reine, Dô si hatte wol gehort Sîne kintlîche wort Unde sîne alwêrekeit; 240: Der alwêre tôre; 72: Einveldic als ein kalp.

plete trust in the Virgin.[16] The didactic point is clear: if foolish children know enough to serve the Virgin, surely adults should know enough to do the same.[17]

Coming of Age

The prophetic childhood narratives, limited to early childhood, and the miracles of the Virgin, limited to the middle, occur in relatively small numbers of texts. There are a large number of narratives, however, that focus on the end of childhood and the transition to adulthood. These coming-of-age narratives include some of the most popular genres, that of the martyr and that of the bride.

The *childhood of the martyr* pays little or no attention to the child's birth and early childhood, focusing instead on the struggle that precedes martyrdom: the *Passional* begins telling of Vitus when "he was twelve years old [and] the news spread concerning him that he was a Christian."[18] The struggle of the child martyr is always structured as one between a young Christian and various pagan authorities: Vitus must contend with his father and the emperor Diocletian. In an effort to get the children to abandon their faith, the authorities offer lavish rewards and threaten cruel punishments, but the children remain steadfast: Diocletian promises to adopt Vitus as his son if he gives in and to make a mockery of his life if he does not, but Vitus "was not the slightest bit frightened since he was accustomed to trust in Jesus Christ with all his heart."[19] The saints' steadfastness provokes their persecutors to more extreme measures, which the writers describe in loving detail: Diocletian has Vitus thrown into prison along with his tutor, Modestus, then he tries to have them burned, eaten by a lion, and, along with Vitus's nurse, Crescentia, hanged. In nearly every case God intervenes on behalf of his servants: he breaks the chains of Vitus and

16. ArmSch 388–89: Sus was daz alwêre kint Wîser denn di grîsen sint.
17. Other passages in which these stories are interpreted in terms of service and reward: ArmSch 624–37, 701–8; Judenk 158–69, 372–81, 556–68; ScholM 1–3; TKdlbg 177–80. —There are a few other *Mären*—the *Halbe Decke*, *Berchta*, and *Das gebratene Ei*—that offer scenes from childhood, but they have little else in common. The story of Obilot, who figures largely in book seven of *Parzival*, is unique: a substantial narrative that takes place in the middle of her childhood is incorporated into a much larger text.
18. Passnl K301,28–30: er was ot zwelf iar alt, do von im vloc daz mere, wie er ein cristen were.
19. Passnl K304,15–17: hievon er nichtesnicht erschrac, wand er mit allem herzen pflac keren an Iesum Cristum.

his companions, shields them from the flames, tames the lion, and sends violent storms to thwart the emperor. When God's power and the martyrs' unshakable faith have been sufficiently demonstrated, the saints are allowed to die and gain their hard-earned reward: Vitus, Modestus, and Crescentia "gave up their spirits, which our Lord received, and admitted them to the glory that the other martyrs enjoy as well."[20]

The childhood of the martyr occurs in sermons and in a few independent texts, but it is most likely to be found in the great legendaries, the *Buch der Märtyrer*, the *Passional*, and the *Elsässische "Legenda aurea,"* as well as in lesser collections. Margaret is far and away the most popular, with at least six independent texts devoted to her legend as well as accounts in most of the collections.[21] The stories of Agnes, Dorothy, Pancras, Pantaleon, and Vitus also occur in multiple versions.[22]

The stories of the female martyrs differ from those of the males in a number of regards. First, for the maidens the struggle always begins as a contest about marriage: they refuse a powerful heathen who wants to wed them, often claiming that they are already married to Christ. Margaret tells Olybrius: "another has taken me in marriage and I will suffer death for his sake before I part from him."[23] Second, the episodes of the story proceed directly from this initial refusal, giving the narratives of the maidens a more coherent structure than those of the male martyrs, which comprise a series of more loosely related episodes. From Olybrius's first sight of Margaret the two are locked in a struggle between his desire and her faith. Third, desire for, voyeuristic display of, and violence against the female body invariably play a role. Olybrius "ordered the beautiful maiden to stand naked before him so that he might look at her with carnal gaze"; then he has her beaten with iron rods "so hard that the skin broke and blood poured forth and watered the earth."[24] Although the gender-specific issues of marriage

20. Passnl K304,94–305,1: ir ieglich gab uf sinen geist, die unser herre wol entpfie und sie zu den eren lie, die andere marterere ouch haben.

21. HgMargl; Marglg; MHMarg; StMarM; WlMarg; WzMarg; BMärtr 11799–12280; ELgAur 423,16–425,32; HoffPr 120,4–24; JnaMrt 46; Passnl K326,1–332,86; VrJngf.

22. Agnes: BMärtr 577–912; ELgAur 135,19–139,13; Hlgnlb 67,8–69,34; JnaMrt 6; Passnl KIII,1–119,52. —Dorothy: StDrth; VrJngf. —Pancras: JnaMrt 32; Passnl K293,1–294,80. —Pantaleon: BMärtr 13391–682; ELgAur 787,4–95,10; KPantl. —Vitus: BMärtr 8755–9222; ELgAur 371,10–373,6; Hlgnlb 134,13–136,36; JnaMrt 39; Passnl K301,1–305,13; PKonPr M246,1–249,120; StVeit. —Also: JnaMrt Celsus 3, Theodosia 22, Celsus 38, Felicula 38, Agapitus 56, Seraphia 61, Fausta 65, Barbara 89, Eulalia 90, Secunda 51, Dioscorus 92; Passnl Agatha K176,1–185,37, Juliana K187,1–191,98.

23. MHMarg 212–15: wan mich hât ein ander zuo im gemahelôt: durch den sô lîde ich den tôt ê ich von im entwîche.

24. MHMargl 253–56: er hiez die maget wol getân vor ime nackot stân daz er sî mohte

and chastity are crucial in the stories of the virgin martyrs, they are gradually overshadowed by the more general defense of the faith in the face of persecution. Margaret's last words to Olybrius are not about marriage and virginity but about Olybrius's refusal to believe: "I am greatly amazed," she tells her persecutor, "that you still do not want to recognize my creator."[25]

Among the child martyrs, only Vitus is not on the threshold of adulthood. He is defined as "a blessed child"[26] or as "a little child,"[27] and Diocletian's cry, "Woe is me that I shall be overcome by a child,"[28] depends for its effect on the fact that it is a child, weak by nature, who, with God's help, has vanquished an emperor. The other child martyrs are represented as older. Pancras, about fourteen,[29] "was beautiful and young and was just beginning to grow into manliness."[30] Margaret, at fifteen,[31] "was both beautiful and young and was just entering that time of life that brings pleasure."[32] Her story requires her to be of marriageable age. Thus the stories of the child martyrs, with the exception of Vitus, are concerned not with the overall course of childhood but with the sort of commitment a child makes on becoming an adult. The martyrs all insist, at the cost of their lives, on maintaining the commitment to Christianity they have already made, rather than entering into secular manhood or marriage as they are pressured to. When they ought to come of age, they forfeit their earthly adulthood and are rewarded with eternal glory.

Whereas the virgin martyrs would rather die than marry, most secular maidens are quite happy to take mortal men as husbands. When, as is often the case, their stories are interested only in the events leading up to their marriage they too are coming-of-age narratives. The *childhood of the bride* has three versions, distinguished by whether the heroine acquires her husband as a result of the courtship pattern, after a single episode of knightly combat, or according to arrangements made by her parents or guardians.

---

beschouwen mit fleischlîchen ougen; 297–302: dô hiez der ubele man die maget slahen an mit slegen sô harte daz sich daz fleisch zarte und daz daz bluot nîder flôz und daz ertrîche begôz.

25. MHMarg 559–61: mich nimt michel wunder dîn daz dû den schepfâre mîn noch niht erkennen wil. —On "the construction of sexual assault" (22) in hagiographical texts: Gravdal, *Ravishing Maidens*, 21–41.

26. Passnl K301,1: Vitus was ein selic kint.

27. Ksrchr 6469: sanct Vît was ain wênigiz kindelîn.

28. Hlgnlb 136,9–10: wê mir, daz mich ein kint uberwinden sal!

29. JnaMrt 32; Passnl K294,10–11.

30. Passnl K294,13–15: er was schone unde iunc und nam alrest den ufsprunc an ufwachsender manheit.

31. BMärtr 11819–23; Passnl K327,68–69; WlMarg 151–56; WzMarg 1144–49.

32. Passnl K327,85–87: [si] was beide schone unde iunc und nam alrest den uzsprunc in lusticlicheme lebene.

The *courtship-pattern bride* appears first as a name, offered as the only suitable partner—although distant and dangerous to woo—for a prince in need of a bride: in *Kudrun* Hilde is recommended to Hetel, even though her father is known to kill anyone who proposes marriage. In spite of the danger, the prince decides to court the princess, either in person or through messengers: Hetel chooses the safer course and sends a delegation of knights disguised as merchants. When the suitor or his emissaries arrive at court, the princess takes an interest in them: Hilde invites one of Hetel's messengers to her chambers since she has been captivated by his singing. The princess learns of the suitor's intentions and, almost invariably, casts her lot with him: when Hilde learns that Hetel "has withdrawn his attention from all other women for [her] sake alone," she replies: "If he is my equal in birth I would like to lie with him." [33] With the help of trickery or brute strength and usually with the cooperation of the princess, the suitor or his deputies manage to get her out of her father's custody and bring her home. Once there she marries the prince. [34]

The courtship pattern is responsible for the marriages of some of the most celebrated MHG heroines: not only Hilde but also her daughter Kudrun, both Isoldes, Kriemhild, Paug in the *Münchner Oswald*, Hildburg in *Wolfdietrich B*, and the heroine of *König Rother*. [35] The historical marriage of Elizabeth of Glogau to Otto III of Bavaria is recounted by Ottokar more or less according to this scheme. [36] While the courtship pattern is a large hypotactic structure, capable of organizing numerous episodes into a single narrative framework, it is concerned with only a small part of the heroine's childhood, the events leading directly to her marriage. A few texts do mention briefly earlier parts of her life [37] but even in these cases, marriage is the overriding concern. Although the courtship pattern is organized around the actions of the hero and his agents, the heroine is not merely the passive object of their exertions: Hilde is actively involved in arranging her escape. [38]

33. Kudrn 404,4: er hât durch dich einen genomen von allen frouwen sîn gemüete; 405,2: kome er mir ze mâze, ich wolte im ligen bî.
34. On the structure of Hilde's marriage: Loerzer, *Eheschließung*, 37–77.
35. Kudrn 617,1–619,4, 630,1–667,4; ETrist 1344–2852; GTrist 8350–12674; Niblgn 44,1–70,4, 281,1–305,4, 333,1–335,1, 607,1–630,1, 644,1–647,4; MOswld 29–3219; WolfdB 9,1–255,4; Rother 16–2938.
36. ORmchr 88712–89045.
37. Kudrn 197–98, 573–77; ETrist 1020–50, 1192–220; GTrist 7165–95, 7715–27, 7955–8141; Niblgn 2,1–19,4.
38. On the marriage in *König Rother* and its relation to similar narratives: Fromm, "Rother," 354–71. —On the courtship pattern: Andersson, *Preface*, 56–78; Curschmann, *Spiel-*

While the courtship-pattern bride figures in a relatively long series of adventures, the *knightly-combat bride* is won in a single knightly contest. Whoever desires Iblis, the heroine of Ulrich von Zatzikhoven's *Lanzelet*, must fight her father at a particular spot in a magical forest.[39] As Lanzelet approaches this spot, he and Iblis see each other and fall in love. Lanzelet fights and kills Iblis's father, after which he turns to her with the tender greeting: "I have won you by my victory."[40] He asks her to overlook his responsibility for her father's death, which she does "since love commanded her to do so,"[41] and then the two ride off and consummate their union. Although the knightly-combat episode is generally much shorter than the courtship pattern, the role the maiden plays in it is basically the same: she turns up when the hero needs her, already of marriageable age, she is won by his efforts, and she marries him. Marriages of besieged princesses, like Condwiramurs, are somewhat longer versions of this same pattern. Narratives of brides won by knightly combat appear primarily in courtly romances written in the decades around 1200: Enite in Hartmann's *Erec*; Iblis, Galagandreiz's daughter, and Ade in Ulrich's *Lanzelet*; Belacane and Condwiramurs in Wolfram's *Parzival*; Larie, the heroine of Wirnt von Gravenberg's *Wigalois*; and, later in the century, Elsam in *Lohengrin*.[42]

The most modest version of the childhood of the bride is the *arranged marriage*. At the beginning of the *Treueprobe*, a rich merchant in Verdun decides to marry his daughter, Irmengard, to Bertram, the son of his close friend. After the fathers have sealed the deal with a handshake, the children are called and Irmengard "was pledged to the youth as his lawful wife."[43] Bertram embraces her, she weeps copiously, thereby demonstrating her modesty, and that evening they go to bed, where "the youth and the very beautiful maiden came to an understanding in no time."[44] Like Hilde and Iblis, Irmengard enters the narrative only to be married. While the historical arranged marriages reported in MHG texts all take place, unless the fathers of the partners change their minds,[45] very few of the fictional

---

mannsepik, 50–53; Fromm, "Rother," 355–56; Kuhn, *Tristan, Nibelungenlied*, 19–27; Siefken, *Überindividuelle Formen*, 21–41.

39. Lanzlt 3870–919.
40. Lanzlt 4570: ich hân erworben iuch mit sige.
41. Lanzlt 4594: wan ez ir diu liebe gebôt.
42. Erec 308–1497, 1887–2221; Lanzlt 667–1231, 1365–2249; Parz 16,2–44,30, 179,13–203,11; Wglois 3617–823; Lohgrn 341–850, 2038–402. —On this type of episode: Schultz, *Round Table*, 66–77.
43. Treuep 159–60: dem knappen si gesworen wart zeim elichen wibe.
44. Treuep 190–91: der knapp und diu vil schœne maget versüenet wurden an der stunt.
45. ORmchr 60124–63, 79094–81450; StLudw 47,34–49,36.

arranged marriages are actually celebrated. Usually they are frustrated by circumstances (Rüdiger's daughter) or by the maiden's active opposition (Amelie).[46]

These three sorts of marriage have different literary and historical roots and are characteristic—primarily, although not by any means exclusively—of three different narrative genres. The courtship-pattern marriage evidently descends from mythological and folktale patterns, from heroic tales of robbing and winning brides. It occurs most commonly in heroic epic and in so-called *Spielmannsepik*, where it is one of the defining features of the genre. The knightly-combat marriage is a version of the standard knightly-combat episode: the knight accepts a challenge, defeats an opponent, and wins something he desires—fame, freedom, in this case a wife. It is to be found primarily in romance, as one of a series of more or less equivalent episodes. The arranged marriage is doubtless closest to the historical practice among the medieval German nobility. It occurs most frequently in chronicles and religious narratives, although it may also appear in heroic epic and romance.

Structurally, none of the three forms of marriage treats the maiden as anything more than an object of exchange: in the courtship pattern she is captured, in knightly combat she is won, and in the arranged marriage she is negotiated away by her guardians. Nevertheless, as these patterns actually occur in the fictional texts, there is an evident attempt to transform the female object of a marriage transaction into the female subject of a love relationship. In courtship-pattern and knightly-combat marriages, she desires the union for which, structurally, she is destined: Hilde wants to lie with Hetel, Iblis loves Lanzelet. In the arranged marriage, her opposition can frustrate the plans: Amelie prevents the marriage her father has negotiated with the king of Spain. In the first two cases she collaborates with the marriage plot, in the third she opposes it: in either case the outcome coincides with her desires. Only in the genre ostensibly closest to history, the chronicles, are the wishes of the bride completely ignored.[47]

46. Arranged marriages: Bussrd 226–33, 497–544; Eneit 3937–4025; GuGrhd 1731–60, 3882–962, 3110–4460; Helmbr 1293–613; Lohgrn 339–40; Niblgn 1678,1–1686,4; ORmchr 7606–8224, 12862–79, 13605–13, 13926–67, 17733–18115, 19931–20216, 41061–185, 60124–69, 60231–37, 67706–68234, 69592–615, 74605–75868, 85915–23, 86528–34; SaeldH 6816–7452; StLudw 47,34–49,3; TößSwb 50,9–11; WilOrl 10209–404; WilÖst 2137–807, 9007–10264. —Marriages are arranged for many saints, but they are almost always frustrated. See below under "virgin saints." On the arranged marriage of Kriemhild: Masser, "Gahmuret," 119–22.

47. On the differences between literary and historical models of marriage: Masser, "Gahmuret."

While the childhood of the bride tells how a child comes of age by assuming the social position of an adult married woman, there is a small group of *Mären* that tell of children's *erotic naïveté*. Three—*Dulciflorie*, the *Sperber*, and the *Häslein*—tell the story of a maiden who grows up isolated from the world and who can therefore be tricked into having sexual relations with a knight without knowing what she is doing. Having been chastised by her guardian for her behavior, she insists on taking back the love she gave the knight, which leads to another sexual encounter. Two—the *Gänslein* and Zwingäuer's *Des Mönches Not*—tell of young monks whose ignorance, even after spending a night in bed with a woman, allows the first to believe that women are geese, the second that he is pregnant. The point of the stories seems to be laughter at the expense of the children, whose ignorance is so profound, and at the expense of their guardians, whose surveillance is so ineffectual. At the same time they illustrate how the incommensurability of various discourses of sexuality renders it difficult for adults and children, laypeople and religious to understand each other. Two other *Mären* share with those just mentioned the themes of sequestration and first sexual experience. Here, however, the children know what they are doing, and here it is the maiden who takes the initiative: she comes up with the plan that enables her to escape the surveillance of her parents and meet with her lover. In the *Nachtigall* they meet in an orchard, are discovered, and marry. In *Pyramus und Thisbe* their meeting is thwarted by animals and confusion and leads to their tragic deaths.[48]

Later Childhood

Although love plays a role in many of the childhood narratives mentioned so far, it is usually subordinate to other concerns: marriage or first sexual experience. In other genres of childhood love plays the major role, and in these cases the chronological scope of the stories increases to accommodate it. Stories of lovers begin earlier in childhood than those of martyrs or brides and thus, although they invariably culminate in marriage and adulthood, they are concerned with more than the way in which their protagonists come of age.

The *childhood of the enamored maiden* begins in the middle of the heroine's childhood, when the hero, also still a child, arrives at her father's

48. For a suggestive analysis of this sort of narrative see Schnyder, "'Mönches Not.'"

court: Amelie is seven when Willehalm von Orlens arrives in London and is made her companion.[49] Heroine and hero fall in love, and eventually they confess their love, often after considerable anguish and at considerable risk: when Willehalm first tells Amelie he loves her, she has no idea what he's talking about; he falls ill and nearly dies before she finally declares herself ready to return his love. If the hero is not yet a knight, the heroine insists that he become one before she will join him: Amelie tells Willehalm, "I want you to be knighted and to do service as my knight this bright summer"; "if you return here to me before winter, I will go with you wherever you want."[50] For one reason or another, the lovers' plans are thwarted and they are separated: Amelie and Willehalm are captured while trying to elope, and Willehalm is exiled. During their separation the hero is busy distinguishing himself as a knight, while the heroine must remain at home: Amelie laments the absence of her beloved "with mind and heart, with lamentable pains, [and] with agonizing distress, which she suffered both in body and spirit to such an extent that her physical strength was nearly extinguished from the agony."[51] Often the heroine must resist pressures that she marry someone else: Amelie's father wants her to marry the king of Spain but she refuses so resolutely that the Spaniard loses interest. While the lovers' separation can last for the larger part of a romance, eventually it ends in marriage: Amelie and Willehalm are reunited and married through the efforts of her aunt and are eventually reconciled with her father as well.

The childhood of the enamored maiden is a relatively common one in MHG narrative. The stories of Alize in Wolfram von Eschenbach's *Willehalm* and of Alise in Ulrich von Türheim's *Rennewart* follow the pattern, as do those of Obie in Wolfram's *Parzival*, Aglye in Johann von Würzburg's *Wilhelm von Österreich*, Engeltrud in Konrad von Würzburg's *Engelhard*, as well as of Meliur and Igla in his *Partonopier und Meliur*. Other maidens who grow up according to this scheme include the heroines of *Karl und Galie, Tandareis und Flordibel, Reinfried von Braunschweig*, and the *Bussard*.[52]

The childhood of the bride and that of the enamored maiden account for most of the stories of secular maidens in MHG. Both ignore birth and

49. WilOrl 3771.
50. WilOrl 5152–55: So wil ich das du laitest swert Und dise liehten sumerzit . . . Mit dienste min ritter sist; 5189–92: Vor dem winter . . . So kum du wider her ze mir, So var ich, swar du wilt, mit dir.
51. WilOrl 10414–29: Do clagte in diu gûte Mit sinnen und mit herzen, Mit clagelichem smerzen, Mit wetûnder arebait Die si an libe, an mûte lait So sere das ir von der not Des libes kraft was vil nach tot.
52. On this pattern as it is realized in *Willehalm von Orlens* and *Tandareis und Flordibel*: Cormeau, "'Tandareis,'" 33–36.

early childhood and both are embedded in narratives that focus primarily on the adventures of the hero rather than those of the heroine. They differ, however, in a number of ways, all of which accord the enamored maiden greater importance. The narrative of the enamored maiden usually begins when she is younger and, as a consequence, we know more about her childhood. She falls in love with her future husband when he is also still a child, unlike the case in stories of the bride, where the hero is already an adult when he first meets his future spouse. Thus the enamored maidens are more nearly equal to their partners in age and in status than the brides. They are also much more equal participants in the action. Whereas Hilde offers modest help in bringing about her abduction, Amelie requires Willehalm to perform knightly service before she will grant her love. The greater freedom of the enamored maiden is a consequence of the thematic focus of the genre, which is on the love between the children, not, as in the childhood of the bride, on the hero's cleverness or prowess. This love is represented with all the conventions of medieval literary love: suffering and illness, protestations of devotion and exchange of letters, and constancy in separation. This too amounts to an increased role for the maiden, since medieval literary love is the secular realm where female autonomy is greatest.

Of the several different patterns for youths who fall in love, one, the *childhood of the enamored youth*, belongs here. Like the childhood of the enamored maiden, it begins somewhere in the middle of childhood: Engelhard is introduced when he is old enough to leave his parents' home in search of fame and fortune. The hero and heroine come into contact and fall in love: Engelhard arrives at the Danish court and is eventually assigned to serve the king's daughter, Engeltrud, with whom he falls in love. For one reason or another the lovers get into difficulty: Engelhard must become grievously ill from love before Engeltrud admits that she returns his passion. The hero becomes a knight and the lovers are separated, although not always in that order: in the case of Engelhard, he is knighted by the Danish king, then rides off to prove his knightly mettle, which Engeltrud had made a condition of granting her love. The heroes of Pleier's *Meleranz* and *Tandareis und Flordibel* follow the pattern of the enamored youth, as do Schionatulander and Tschinotulander in Wolfram's *Titurel* and Albrecht's *Jüngerer Titurel*, Partonopier and Anshelm in Konrad von Würzburg's *Partonopier und Meliur*, and the hero of the *Bussard*.

Until the enamored youth comes of age he and his beloved are more or less equal. Not only are they close in age and degree of amorous involvement, they are also close in status: both are children and often both are serving at court. Once the hero comes of age, however, it seems to be the same old story: the narrative follows him, an adult male fighting to win his bride, while she, a child, stays home and receives little attention. Yet things are not quite the same, for the relative parity of their early life transforms other elements of the story. Because she is a lover and not just a bride, her childhood is more extensive, more interesting, and more adult, since love is adult. She is a major actor, whose love is the equal of his and whose role in determining the course of the action is significant. Her waiting at home is more than just passing time. It gives his adventures meaning and it has its own more passive heroism, as she suffers the pain of separation and resists attempts to marry her to those she does not love. His role is changed as well. He is no longer the captor, carrying off the bride he has won or been granted by negotiation. He is now a lover, constrained by his love and by his beloved, by his obligation to rescue her and by the tasks she assigns him.

Comprehensive Childhood

Of the childhood narrative genres that follow children from birth to adulthood, the *childhood of the clerical saint* is the most tranquil. All the clerical saints are born into wealthy Christian families who raise them with care. Early in life the saints reveal their pious dispositions, but they do so in relatively sober acts of asceticism or charity rather than in dramatic cures and the like: even "in his childhood," according to the *Passional*, Dominic "fled the comforts of this world," preferring to sleep on the floor rather than in a bed.[53] The young saints are sent to school, where they excel in the study of the Bible: in school Dominic's "heart, his mind, and his reason all drew him completely according to God's will to Scripture, where he was well instructed about God and the foundations of faith."[54] In the lives of many clerical saints there follows an amorphous stretch, in which the young man demonstrates his holiness in various ways and at the end of which he seems to have become an adult. However, since for most of them there is no crisis on coming of age and since in many cases ecclesiastical rites of passage are absent, it is often impossible to determine just when the child does become an adult. Dominic is a comfort to the weak and a champion of virtue; he

53. Passnl K354,66–67: in siner kintheit ez vloch hie der erden gemach.
54. Passnl K354,83–87: vernumft, herze unde sin truc ez al zu male hin nach gotes willen in die schrift. got und des gelouben stift lernter wol darinne.

honors the aged, teaches the young, and sells all that he has to support the poor and hungry; eventually the bishop learns of his excellence and makes him a canon. Then one day he comes to a place where heresy is widespread and he begins his preaching.

There are many saints who grow up according to the peaceful scheme just outlined. Some, like Jerome and Bernard, become monks. Others, like Ambrose and Ulrich, become secular clerics. Among those who become secular clerics are some, like Nicholas and Gregory, whose childhood comes to a more dramatic conclusion: when their fathers die they recoil at the prospect of possessing earthly wealth, so they give away their inheritance. Although Ulrich and Silvester receive independent treatment, all the other accounts of clerical saints appear in the verse legendaries from the end of the thirteenth century, the *Buch der Märtyrer* and the *Passional*, and in the *Elsässische "Legenda aurea,"* the prose legendary from the middle of the fourteenth.[55]

It is appropriate that the childhood of the clerical saint should be particularly at home in the great legendaries, since these are establishment figures. Instead of dramatic miracles and spectacular martyrdom, they display diligent piety and conscientious study. They are destined to be administrators, occasionally champions, of the institutional church, the kind of organization necessary for the production and dissemination of vast ordered hagiography like the *Passional* or the *Legenda aurea*.

Like the clerical saints, those who grow up according to the *childhood of the virgin saint* grow up relatively peacefully. They too are born into pious families. They too lead pious lives and shine in school or other institutional settings: Mary joins the company of the Temple maidens, where, according to Wernher's *Maria*, she distinguishes herself for her beauty, her embroidery, her piety, and her humility. Only when the virgin saints reach the end of their childhood do things become more dramatic, when their guardians decide it is time for the children to marry and the children refuse: Mary

55. Ambrose: BMärtr 4791–851; ELgAur 283,12–25; Passnl K241,14–242,21. —Benedict: Passnl K217,1–218,5; JnaMrt 20. —Bernard: Passnl K395,1–400,9; ELgAur 536,1–537,25. —Dominic: Passnl K353,1–355,61; ELgAur 499,1–19. —Erhard: ELgAur 104,17–21. —Gregory: BMärtr 3200–63; Passnl K192,1–193,15; ELgAur 220,13–26. —Jerome: BMärtr 21065–129; Passnl K505,1–69; ELgAur 656,12–657,11. —Nicholas: BMärtr 25833–988; ELgAur 20,25–21,15; Passnl K6,16–7,87. —Remi: BMärtr 21257–84; ELgAur 115,13–116,4; Passnl K93,1–94,9. —Silvester: BMärtr 27975–96; KSilvr 101–477. —Ulrich: ELgAur 799,4–26; StUlrc 63–245. —Martin of Tours (ELgAur 724,9–17; GrshPr 450a,8–27; Passnl K592,1–593,17; PKonPr S239,24–29) and Peter Martyr (ELgAur 303,1–25) are unusual among the clerical saints in that they are born to pagan families and their conversion occasions some conflict, in Martin's case since he must serve as a knight.

tells the priests at the Temple, "I do not ever intend to take a husband for worldly ends! Yea, I have promised my soul unsullied to God."[56] Sometimes the young saint actively resists marriage, and sometimes the obedient child allows the marriage to take place, only to run off before the marriage can be consummated. The saints' struggle to preserve their virginity is all the more notable in that it comes at the end of such an uneventful and obedient childhood, suggesting that only a virtue as compelling as chastity could cause these dutiful children to contemplate disobedience.

The childhood of Mary is told in a number of texts devoted to her life, beginning with Priester Wernher's *Maria* and including the *Marienleben* of Bruder Philipp, Walther von Rheinau, and others; her story also appears in the *Passional* and in the *Elsässische "Legenda aurea."*[57] Although Mary is surely the most illustrious of the virgin saints, there are at least as many accounts of the childhood of the popular Alexis, most of them in independent texts.[58] The legendaries also contain stories of Euphrosyne, Brigid, Abraham of Kidunaia, and Margaret Reparata.[59] The stories of Elisabeth Bechlin and, in a somewhat unorthodox form, that of Princess Elizabeth, both in the *Tößer Schwesternbuch*, follow the same pattern.[60]

Both the virgin martyrs and the virgin saints display their pious devotion by refusing marriage, but the stories of the martyrs focus almost exclusively on this moment of crisis, while those of the virgin saints extend backward to birth and forward into adulthood. The former are independent coming-of-age narratives, the latter are introductory portions of much longer biographies. In both cases the child must struggle to realize a religious commitment. But the martyrs must struggle openly against hostile and powerful heathen authorities to defend the Christian faith itself, while the virgin saints struggle within a Christian context, often privately, to realize an authorized but especially demanding spirituality. The former die for their steadfast faith, the latter are able to realize their chaste ideal. Both kinds of narrative teach Christian virtue. But the stories of the virgin martyrs are principally concerned with the heroic defense of the faith,

56. WerMar 1590–95: ich niemer enwil deheinen man gewinnen ze werltlîchen dingen! . . . ja hân ich got entheizen mîne sêle unbewollen.

57. WerMar 1029-A1877; PhMarl 369–1499; WlMarl 713–2726; GrMarl 283–434; MarlKg 1.1–264; Passnl H8,39–12,88.

58. AlxusA 140–299; AlxusB 44–139; AlxusC 37–78; AlxusF 38–633; ELgAur 426,4–20; KAlxus 120–241; Väterb 39099–213; Hlgnlb 161,13–162,5.

59. BMärtr Brigid 1429–57; Väterb Euphrosyne 27746–28425, Abraham 30605–781, Margaret Reparata 35787–917.

60. TößSwb 87, 99–102.

while those of the virgin saints are more specifically concerned with the individual pursuit of chastity. In every regard the childhood of the virgin saints is more peaceful and more personal.

Except for the enamored youths mentioned above, nearly all the secular males figure in narratives that begin at birth and continue without major interruption until their heroes come of age at knighting. The *childhood of the knight* has three varieties, which differ in the degree of dislocation their heroes experience: the stay-at-home knights, the fostered knights, and the autonomous knights.

The *stay-at-home knight* spends his entire childhood at one place. Lambrecht's Alexander is born at home—to the accompaniment of earthquakes, storms, and an eclipse. He is carefully educated at home by a team of six masters, including Aristotle. After he tames the ferocious horse Bucephalus, his father proclaims him his heir, and then Alexander requests arms: "I am now fifteen years old," he says, "and have come of age, so that I can properly bear arms."[61] The king is glad to provide them, and soon "the child was armed and mounted according to knightly custom."[62] This same pattern, according to which a youth is born, educated, and comes of age in one place, can be found in the Alexander romances of Rudolf von Ems, Ulrich von Etzenbach, and Seifrit and, with much less attention to education and much more to knightly investiture, in the childhood of Siegfried in the second *aventiure* of the *Nibelungenlied*.

There are a number of other future knights or princes who grow up in one place, but only after having to endure radical dislocation as infants: Lanzelet, Lancelot, and Malefer are abducted; Gregorius and Albanus are abandoned. After this initial shock, however, they stay put and are nurtured with care. Although a certain amount of confusion surrounds their coming of age—Lanzelet is armed and leaves home, although he lacks training in crucial knightly skills; Lancelot insists that Arthur knight him but then subverts the ceremony—all except Albanus and Malefer indicate their eagerness to come of age, and in every case, even that of Gregorius, they do so with the active participation of those who raised them.[63]

Whereas the stay-at-home knight leaves home at the end of his child-

---

61. LAlexr S410–13: nû bin ih funfzehen jâr alt . . . und bin sô komen zô mînen tagen, daz ih wol wâfen mac tragen.

62. LAlexr S430–31: Dô daz kint nâh rîterlîchen site wol gewêfent was und geriten.

63. I have placed Albanus and Gregorius in the category of the stay-at-home knight because their childhoods seem to resemble that of Lanzelet more than any other: both suffer infant dislocation; both are carefully nurtured and grow up without leaving their childhood homes.

hood, the *fostered knight* leaves home in the middle and comes of age at another court. The childhood of the fostered knight thus falls clearly into two parts, of which the first is spent at the court of the hero's parents: according to Ulrich von dem Türlin, Willehalm begins his life at his father's court at Narbonne. For one reason or another the young hero is sent or taken to another court: Willehalm's father disinherits all his sons and dispatches Willehalm to the court of Charlemagne. On his arrival the child is made a member of the court, where he remains until he is knighted: when Willehalm arrives at Charlemagne's "the king received him tenderly and accepted him as his very own child: he was cared for solicitously in the imperial chambers until the day [eight years later] when he received the office of the shield."[64]

Although the childhood of the fostered knight reproduces what is assumed to have been a common pattern of childrearing at medieval courts, the genre does not occur in courtly romance. It first appears in a chronicle (Dietrich in the *Kaiserchronik*),[65] later in *Herzog Ernst B* and *D*, but primarily in heroic texts: *Wolfdietrich B*, Ulrich's *Willehalm* (Willehalm and Fivianz), Stricker's *Karl*, and *Karl und Galie*.[66]

The narratives vary greatly in length (from forty lines to over three thousand), in the ways they motivate the child's departure from home (Ernst: for education; Dietrich: as a hostage; Charlemagne: for his safety), and in the sort of education the children receive at their second home (Wolfdietrich is instructed; Charlemagne and Fivianz learn by observation).[67] Nevertheless, they all share one crucial feature: when the hero leaves his natal home, he is not thereby freed from adult supervision but rather transferred from the authority of his parents to that of the head of the court to which he is sent or taken. The hero continues to learn and grow at this second home, although just how this happens is usually left vague, and he is knighted there.[68]

Many of the most celebrated MHG heroes grow up according to

64. UWilhm W29,16–25: do er in des rîches hof nu quam, der küneg in lieplîche enpfie. . . . er nam in im ze kinde gar: in des rîches kamer man sîn pflac mit flîze biz an den tac, daz er enpfie schiltes amt.

65. Ksrchr 13895–934, 14183–84.

66. The story of Fivianz is told discontinuously: UWilhm 316,2–318,27, 324,4–25, 327,30–332,25.

67. WolfdB 264,1–266,4; KrlGal 44,44–49; UWilhm 324,4–25.

68. The knighting of Stricker's Charlemagne is not narrated, although it is clear from various allusions that he must have been knighted in Spain before he turned eighteen (StrKrl 206–11, 227–44). —It is unclear whether Ernst B is knighted in Greece or, as seems more likely, back at home.

another bipartite scheme, the childhood of the *autonomous knight*. Like the fostered youths, they spend the first part of their childhood at home under the supervision of their parents: Eilhart's Tristrant is born by caesarean section, given to a nurse, then entrusted by his father to a tutor, who provides a detailed education. Like the fostered youths, the autonomous knights leave home in the middle of their childhood: at his tutor's suggestion Tristrant seeks permission to visit foreign lands, which his father grants. Unlike the fostered knights, however, once the autonomous knights leave home they are more or less on their own: Tristrant heads for Cornwall and once there decides to conceal his identity. The heroes make their way, often by circuitous routes, to a great court where their heroic natures are recognized and where they come of age: Tristrant arrives at the court of King Mark where he "grew in excellence and acquired great renown until he was worthy to be knighted whenever he wanted."[69] This occurs when Morold arrives in Cornwall and Tristrant wants to fight him. The childhood of the autonomous knight occurs primarily in courtly romance: Wolfram's *Parzival*, Gottfried's *Tristan*, Wirnt's *Wigalois*, *Wigamur*, and the courtly heroic epic *Biterolf und Dietleib*.

The crucial difference between the childhood of the fostered and the autonomous knight lies not in the status of the child once he reaches a second home (the autonomous Tristrant has the same status at Mark's court that the fostered Willehalm has at Charlemagne's) but in the independence that the child enjoys between homes (Tristrant chooses to become a member of Mark's court while Willehalm was sent to Charlemagne by his father). This autonomy is manifest in several ways. The young heroes make their own decisions: Parzival, Wigalois, and Dietleib decide on their own to leave home. They are isolated: Parzival, Wigalois, and Wigamur ride off alone; Tristan is left alone on the Cornish coast; Tristrant and Dietleib lead small bands of retainers. And they determine their goals: Parzival and Wigalois choose Arthur's court, Tristrant chooses Mark's, Dietleib seeks his father, Tristan heads for civilization. Whether by choice or by compulsion, as the autonomous knights leave home they find themselves in situations where they must assume responsibility for their lives.

Two traits occur frequently in the knightly childhood narratives, regardless of which subclass they fall into. The first is anonymity. Those who suffer dislocation at birth—Lancelot, Malefer, Albanus, Gregorius, Tristan,

69. ETrist H346–50a: also wůchß der júngeling zů eren und zů grössem lob in deß kúngeß Marcken hoff, biß er dar zů tögte, daß er wol niemen mochte daß swert, wenn er wolt.

Wigamur—invariably lose track of their true lineage; Lanzelet and Parzival do not even know their own names. Those autonomous knights who do know who they are—Tristrant, Wigalois, Dietleib—choose to keep this information secret when they leave home. As these youths move out into the world, the people they encounter do not know who they are. Thus whatever distinction they achieve results neither from the solicitude of their parents or guardians nor from public knowledge of their exalted lineage, but from the recognition that their own attributes and abilities command. Their successes are their own.

Movement is the second characteristic common in the knightly childhood narratives. Many infants are displaced. All the fostered and the autonomous knights move in the middle of their childhood. Even the stay-at-home knights are affected by this impulse: they are the one group in which the decision to come of age and leave home is most likely to originate with the child, as if, having grown up in one place, they, even more than the others, can't wait to leave. The mobility that is one of the adult knight's chief attributes is a defining characteristic of the knightly childhood as well. Even as children they are already knights errant. Like their anonymity, the errancy of the young knights represents a degree of independence, harbinger of the autonomy they will enjoy once they have come of age as secular adult males.

Many future knights fall in love. Some, the enamored youths, whose childhoods follow a pattern close to that of the enamored maidens, have been discussed above. Others, however, fall in love within the framework of one of the knightly schemes just described. The hero of *Willehalm von Orlens* grows up according to the pattern of the autonomous knight. An orphan, he is adopted, raised, and educated with great care by the duke of Brabant. When he discovers that he is not the duke's son, he decides to depart for the court of the English king, where he soon falls in love with the king's daughter, Amelie. Although she spurns him at first, eventually she agrees to marry him if he will return to Brabant to be knighted, which he does. In other texts love has an even greater effect. The childhood of Flore conforms to the structure of the autonomous knightly childhood, but here love has completely displaced knighthood as theme and motivation: it dominates Flore's infancy and education; it motivates his departure from home and his knighting. The childhood of Wilhelm von Österreich is also based on the autonomous pattern, but in this case love explodes the scheme: well into the second part, Wilhelm is separated from his beloved for a long series of exploits—prophetic, allegorical, amorous, courtly, military—near the end of which, almost as an afterthought, he is knighted.[70]

When a future knightly hero falls in love as a child the relation of childhood to adulthood is altered. In the stories where young love is absent, the childhood narrative serves as a general introduction to the adult narrative: attributes are demonstrated that play a role later, like strength or prowess. Occasionally some of the episodes of childhood have subsequent ramifications (Parzival and Jeschute; Dietleib and Gunther), but knighting establishes a clear break between the events of childhood and those of adulthood. When a young knight falls in love, however, that love—not love in general but his love for a particular partner—dominates both his childhood and the rest of the narrative. This is even more true of the enamored youth, discussed above, whose story contains even less of childhood before he falls in love. Thus the childhood of the enamored knight or the enamored youth functions less like a biographical introduction to the story of the hero's knightly adventures than the first episode in an integral narrative of the hero's love.[71]

Although the childhood narratives of most secular heroines conform to the partial genres of the bride or the enamored maiden, there are some texts that tell the *childhood of the princess protagonist* from birth to adulthood: Wolfram's *Titurel*, Albrecht's *Jüngerer Titurel*, *Flore und Blanscheflur*, *Mai und Beaflor*, the *Gute Frau*, and *Apollonius von Tyrland* (Tarsia). In these cases the heroine's story resembles one of the patterns of knightly childhood mentioned above. Sigune and the Gute Frau are fostered out to other courts. Beaflor and Tarsia begin like fostered children but end like autonomous ones: fleeing incest or murder, they are on their own until they marry. The princess protagonist must endure dislocations just like a future knight: her parents die, she is sent to other courts or countries, she is enslaved, she must flee home and make her way on her own. But there is one sort of dislocation that she never suffers (except Tarsia): unlike many young knights, she is never so disoriented at birth that she grows up ignorant of her identity. And there is one sort of attachment that she never lacks (again except Tarsia): unlike many young knights, she never comes of age without falling in love. The narratives thus reproduce the familiar gender differentiation: while maidens in MHG narrative are not usually accorded as much independence as youths (hence less disorientation), love is the one

70. On the substitution of love for knighthood in *Flore und Blanscheflur*: Klingenberg, "*helt* Flore."

71. On the structural consequences: Karnein, "Minne," 116–18.

sphere in which females can exercise an autonomy equal to or greater than that of males (hence its presence in childhood stories where the female is the protagonist).

Whereas most MHG narratives tell of children who are exemplary for their virtue, there are a few that recount the *childhood of the sinner*. Pilate and Judas are child murderers.[72] Mary of Egypt runs away from home to become a prostitute.[73] The young oblates in the *Vorauer Novelle* take up the study of sorcery. The stories of the child sinners are composed of familiar elements. All but Mary suffer some early dislocation: the illegitimate Pilate is nursed by his lowly mother in a mill, then moved to his father's court. Wherever they end up after this dislocation, the children all receive careful nurture: Pilate's father, the king of Mainz, "raised him well, along with his legitimate son."[74] However, this careful nurture is wasted on the child sinner: "Pilate, having no regard for life or property, killed his brother in anger."[75] The crime, sin, or fault causes the children to leave home: Pilate's father sends him to Rome as a hostage. Once they have reached the new location they repeat the sin that drove them from home: Pilate kills a prince at the Roman court. The moral is clear: the sinful nature is impervious to the nurture that has such a beneficial effect on the heroic nature. The fact that the childhood of the sinner is composed of the same elements as the other genres of childhood only serves to make the strength of the sinful nature more apparent.[76]

A number of texts recount the *childhood of the refiliated son*. These are stories in which youths, usually still infants, become separated from their parents: the sons of Faustinian are shipwrecked; Wilhelm von Wenden sells his sons into slavery; the sons of Eustace are carried off by animals; and the sons of the Gute Frau are lost when their father is swept away by a swollen river.[77] The children grow up apart from their parents but are reunited be-

72. Pilat 308–550; Passnl H81,47–84,31, H312,76–316,81.

73. BMärtr 5205–22; JnaMrt 23; Väterb 34411–520.

74. Pilat 358–59: mit sînem êlîchem sone Týrûs in . . . wol zô.

75. Pilat 397–99: Pŷlâtus durh unmût ne ahtiz lîb noh daz gût, dem brûdere er den lîb nam.

76. On the resistance of the sinful nature to admirable nurture see chapter four. —The two stories of Pilate differ in their treatment of the hero's nature. According to *Pilatus* Pilate has some justification for his hostility and the greater strength of the hero: the legitimate son relies on friends and relatives to get ahead and Pilate is able to kill him because he is stronger (Pilat 871–99). According to the *Passional* Pilate has the lesser strength and wicked nature of the baseborn: the legitimate son is stronger, while Pilate, whose "base lineage made him weak" (Passnl H82,50: sin vnart machte in . . . swach), kills his half brother treacherously.

77. Ksrchr 1235–481, 2058–4038; WilWnd 2192–358, 5049–882, 6219–8240; BMärtr 7461–956; Väterb 36956–38002; GuFrau 1634–826, 2907–80.

fore they come of age. Since the whole point is to show how children who
have been separated from their parents, and usually from each other as well,
are reunited, they run counter to the general rule according to which the
MHG childhood narratives lead their protagonists away from their parents. The refiliation of the children makes sense in the context of the larger
narratives, however, since these are, to a greater or lesser extent, religious
in character: the separation and reunion of children and parents illustrate
the way God tests and rewards his servants. As the wife of Eustace says
when she is reunited with her sons: "the great God of heaven is so full of
mercy, he can repay us well for whatever we have suffered."[78]

A different tale of refiliation is told in the story of Hagen in *Kudrun*,
who is carried off by a griffin from his father's court, and in that of Paris
in Konrad von Würzburg's *Trojanerkrieg*, who is abandoned at birth and
raised by a shepherd couple. These are childhood narratives of a more usual
sort: stories of individual heroes, told continuously, and prefaced to narratives of their adult adventures. Like those mentioned above, however, they
are circular, returning their heroes to the homes from which they began,
rather than linear, leading the heroes away from home and parents and into
the world.

The End Justifies the Means

According to Freud, the biblical story of Moses' birth and abandonment
turns an historical figure who was born an Egyptian into a mythical figure
who is born a Jew. If Freud's claim about Moses' parentage is true, then
the need for such a transformation is obvious, since it is inconceivable that
the deliverer of Israel could have been of other than Jewish birth. Moses'
career as an adult requires that he be born a Jew. This principle, that a
certain adulthood requires a certain childhood, is true in the MHG childhood narratives as well. In concluding this chapter I would like to note a
number of ways in which the hegemony of adulthood affects the genres of
childhood.

If one sets out, as I did, to group the MHG childhood narratives
according to the most obvious structural and thematic criteria, one will
find that one has grouped together those stories whose protagonists grow

78. BMärtr 7904–7: der hoche Got vonn himelreich der ist genadenn also vol, der mag
uns ergeczenn wol das uns zelaid ist geschehenn. —Similar lessons: Ksrchr 3024–28; Väterb
37938–49.

into a particular vocation: prophet, virgin saint, bride, knight, and so forth. Some vocations, those of bride and knight, can be reached by several routes, but no one who is raised as a child martyr ever becomes a bride, and no one who grows up as a knight ever becomes a prophet. It is not merely that the different genres conclude when the child enters the appropriate adult role, but that childhood itself differs—structurally and thematically—according to the adult role that the child is going to assume. The end of childhood determines the course of childhood: the bride does not need an education, the clerical saint does. For many adult vocations, the events of early childhood are irrelevant, so they are ignored. Here the prophets are the exception that proves the rule: although their stories are limited to the beginning of childhood, the miracles and prophecies of which they consist are oriented unmistakably to adulthood. Thus the nature of the generic categories themselves teaches a lesson about the knowledge of childhood in MHG narrative: the end of childhood, adult vocation, determines the course of childhood itself. This of course is precisely the opposite of the modern assumption, that the events of childhood determine the kind of adult one becomes.

Since adult vocations distinguish between religious and secular, it is not surprising that the genres of childhood distinguish rigorously between religious and secular as well. The only children who fall somewhere between the two camps are those few who do not fit easily into any of the regular genres: Elizabeth of Hungary, Martin of Tours, the maiden in *Armer Heinrich*, Gregorius. The religious genres differ from the secular ones primarily in their attitude to coming of age, as discussed in the last chapter. Whereas the principal secular genres are defined by the rites of passage with which they end (brides, knights), the religious genres either ignore these rites (prophets, clerics) or refuse them (martyrs, virgin saints).

Doubtless it is also adult arrangements that are responsible for the distinction among the genres of childhood between female and male. The female genres all revolve around issues of love (enamored maiden, princess protagonist) or marriage (bride). The male genres may tell of love (enamored youth, enamored knight), but most ignore these issues (prophet, clerical saint, knight, refiliated son). Those genres that include both females and males focus by definition on sex and marriage (erotic naiveté, virgin saint), or else have a special category for females that does the same (virgin martyr), or else make sex the defining issue for the one maiden included (the prostitute sinner Mary of Egypt). In every case females are restricted to stories about sex, love, or marriage. The stories of males may include these themes but they are much more likely to be concerned with other issues instead or in addition: birth, education, precocious signs of prowess or piety.

These thematic differences correspond to structural ones. The major genres of female childhood either ignore the early part of childhood (bride, enamored maiden, virgin martyr) or pass over it quickly (princess protagonist, virgin saint) to focus on the end. The stories of youths are much more likely to begin at birth, and it is only among the genres restricted to males that one finds those that omit the end of childhood (prophet) or ignore coming of age (clerical saint). Both thematically and structurally MHG childhood distinguishes strictly according to gender: for maidens it is restricted to the themes of sex, love, and marriage and to the years just before adulthood in which these themes become important; for youths childhood is both more extensive, often beginning at birth, and more varied, treating a whole range of themes. It is another victory of culture over nature, depriving maidens of the years they must have lived through to focus instead on the moment, of obsessive interest to phallocentric culture, when they might become sexually active. Here too the end "justifies" the means.

8. History: Two-and-a-Half Centuries of Childhood

Let us assume what is currently the most widely held view, that the New Testament gospels were written in this order: Mark, Matthew, Luke, John.[1] And then let us look chronologically at what each of the gospels has to say about the childhood of Jesus. The first evangelist, Mark, ignores the subject altogether, beginning his narrative only with Jesus' baptism by John. The second, Matthew, does tell us about Jesus' childhood, beginning with the appearance of an angel to Joseph; he briefly mentions the nativity, then tells at greater length of the Magi, the Flight into Egypt, and the Slaughter of the Innocents, pausing often to document how each event represents the fulfillment of an Old Testament prophecy. Luke, the third evangelist, offers a more elaborate story. He tells of the appearance of Gabriel to Mary, of the Roman census, the manger, the shepherds, the chorus of angels, and the presentation in the Temple. He doubles the number of nativity stories by incorporating that of John the Baptist and extends the account of Jesus' childhood up to age twelve and the visit to the Temple. The fourth evangelist, John, seems at first glance to return to the practice of the first: he skips childhood and begins his narrative with Jesus' baptism. Actually, however, John has not ignored Jesus' childhood but rewritten it: the narrative of biological origin has been transformed into a poem of cosmological origin, the hymn to the Word with which the fourth gospel begins.

When one considers the gospels chronologically one finds a clear pattern in the changing representation of Jesus' childhood: it is ignored by Mark, exploited for typological ends by Matthew, expanded and elaborated by Luke, and refigured as a cosmological hymn by John. First childhood is absent, then it looks backwards, then it is magnified, and finally it is transfigured.

The childhood of Jesus has a history in MHG as well. It first appears about 1100 in the *Mittelfränkische Reimbibel* and then in more than a half

---

1. Alter and Kermode, *Literary Guide*, 377–78.

dozen other texts before the end of the period under investigation. In the *Reimbibel* and in the slightly later account of Frau Ava the childhood of Jesus seems to have been part of a much larger narrative of salvation history. When it appears again toward the end of the century the childhood of Jesus takes two forms. Konrad von Fußesbrunnen's *Kindheit Jesu* is devoted, as its title indicates, exclusively to the "childhood of Jesus." Wernher's *Maria* incorporates the story of Jesus' birth and infancy in a life of the Virgin. When the childhood of Jesus is told again in the decades around 1300—in a Königsberg manuscript, in the *Passional*, and in accounts by Walther von Rheinau and Bruder Philipp—it is always as part of a life of the Virgin. The MHG history of the childhood of Jesus falls, then, into three distinct periods: between 1100 and 1130 it is woven into salvation history, between 1170 and 1200 it stands alone or is incorporated into the life of the Virgin, between 1280 and 1310 it occurs only in a Marian context. First childhood is subordinate to history, then it enjoys a moment of narrative autonomy, ultimately it is part of maternal biography.

Just as the four evangelists had reasons for their differing treatment of Jesus' childhood, so did the writers of the MHG accounts. These reasons, however, will only become apparent if one knows something of the history of MHG childhood in general. This chapter is devoted to tracing that history.[2]

1100–1150: The Age of the Prophets

Writing in MHG began without childhood. The first texts—Williram, the *Ezzolied*, the *Annolied*—make their appearance shortly after 1050 and do so with tremendous authority. They are not concerned with childhood, however, but with the great issues of Christian salvation. If they contain narrative, it is the narrative of salvation history that dominates. In time this vernacular religious tradition begins to adapt narrative books of the Old and New Testaments and, along with them, a number of childhood narratives. Thus it is that, when stories of childhood first appear in MHG, around 1100, they do so within the context of salvation history. And it is within this context that they remain for about forty years.

The oldest extant MHG childhood narrative is the one just mentioned, the story of the childhood of Jesus in the *Mittelfränkische Reimbibel*

2. All the dates in the following for which a source is not given are from VL. Whenever I have relied on another authority for dating I have cited it.

(around 1100). Thus the first MHG childhood narrative represents what I have called the childhood of the prophet, as do all those that follow until 1140: the story of Moses in the *Altdeutsche Exodus* (1100–20), of John the Baptist and Jesus in the works of Frau Ava (before 1127), of Moses in the *Vorauer Bücher Mosis* (1120–40), and of Jesus in *Von Christi Geburt* (1120–40). It should not be surprising that the first MHG children are prophets. Their stories occur in religious texts centrally concerned with salvation history, a kind of historical thought in which typological relations play a crucial role. It is hardly surprising that narratives suffused by typological relations should favor a sort of childhood narrative that, as I argued in the last chapter, engenders the same.[3]

Although the childhood of the prophet is the first kind of childhood narrative to appear in MHG, it did not have the influence one might have expected. Indeed, over the next two centuries it occurs only in other accounts of the childhoods of the very same prophets in whose service it made its first appearance: Moses, John the Baptist, and Jesus. Considering both the chronological priority of these accounts and the religious authority of these figures, one might have expected that the childhood narratives of other heroes, above all religious heroes, would be fashioned to conform to the same pattern, but this is not the case. The future of the MHG childhood narrative lay not with typology alone but with other models of childhood that incorporated prefigurative elements into more extensive, chronologically more complete accounts.

1150–1200: Importing Childhood

These other models were introduced into MHG, almost without exception, from French and Latin sources in the second half of the twelfth century. Here the pathbreaker was Lambrecht, whose *Alexanderlied* (1150–60), based on the Old French *Alexandre* of Alberic de Pisançon, is the first German text to contain a more or less complete narrative of its hero's childhood from birth until adulthood—in this case the childhood of the stay-at-home knight. Before the end of the century three other MHG texts containing knightly children were adapted from French: Eilhart von Oberg's *Tristrant* (about 1170), the first of the autonomous knights; *Graf Rudolf* (1170–90),

---

3. On salvation history and early MHG literature: Kuhn, "Frühmittelhochdeutsche Literatur," 143–45; Vollmann-Profe, *Geschichte*, 81–83, 86–88; Wehrli, *Poetologische Einführung*, 243–63.

of which the surviving fragments include a detailed program of courtly education; and Ulrich von Zatzikhoven's *Lanzelet* (1194–1205),[4] another stay-at-home, but this time with infant dislocation. Although it is difficult to compare these texts with their sources—only the very beginning of Alberic's *Alexandre* has survived; the sources for *Tristrant* and *Graf Rudolf* as well as the "French book"[5] on which Ulrich claims to have based his romance have all vanished—one can assume from what remains of Alberic and from what is known about the Tristan and the Lancelot traditions that the German writers preserve the general outline of the French originals. That means that the model of knightly childhood introduced into Germany between 1150 and 1200 was a model that had been developed, in its general outline, in France. This, of course, is not surprising: France was in many ways the model for Germany in the twelfth century, both in matters of chivalry and in those of chivalric narrative.[6]

Four other knights should be mentioned whose stories—less extensive, less coherent, less influential, and not based on French models—were written in this period. The *Kaiserchronik* (mid-twelfth century), based on Latin sources, contains a very brief account of the childhood of Dietrich.[7] *Herzog Ernst A* (1160–87),[8] which survives only in fragments, must have told the story of its hero's childhood if, as is widely assumed, it followed the same basic plot as the later *Herzog Ernst B*. Dietrich and Ernst, the first fostered knights in MHG, are the only such children to be sent to courts in Greece. *Orendel* (ca. 1190) contains a very few lines on the childhood and knighting of its hero. *König Rother* (1152–65)[9] concludes with a brief account of the birth of the hero's son, Pepin, and a more lengthy account of the lavish festival at which he is knighted.[10] Pepin's knighting is the first and only substantial representation of such a festival before that organized for Siegfried in the *Nibelungenlied*.[11]

4. Wehrli, *Geschichte*, 295.

5. Lanzlt 9324: welschez buoch.

6. Comparing Lambrecht with his source, one finds that he has added information about Alexander's eyes and rearranged his education somewhat (Alberic, *Alexandre*, 62, 88–105; LAlexr V132–37, V171–214). —On Eilhart's sources: Wolff, VL, 2:413. On *Lanzelet* as *enfance*: Pérennec, "*daz welsche buoch*," 37–41.

7. Ksrchr 13895–934, 14183–84.

8. Szklenar (VL, 3:1177) dates *Ernst A*, at the earliest, between 1160 and 1170, Wehrli (*Geschichte*, 223), at the latest, 1187.

9. Szklenar, VL, 5:89; Bumke, *Mäzene*, 92, 336.

10. Rother 4758–81, 4991–5063.

11. On Dietrich's illegitimacy: Stackmann, "Dietrich," 139–40. On the *Kaiserchronik* Dietrich in general: Knape, "Typik," 17–21, 24. —It is hard to agree with Bumke's reference to "detailed descriptions of a knighting ceremony" in Lambrecht's *Alexanderlied* and Veldeke's *Eneit* (*Ritterbegriff*, 111 n. 102: die ausführlichen Beschreibungen einer Schwertleite). Neither

König Rother is of considerably greater interest for the story it tells about Pepin's mother. This is the first MHG childhood narrative of a maiden and the first example of the childhood of the bride, in this case a bride won according to the courtship pattern. Around 1170 the courtship pattern appears again, in the stories of Paug in the *Münchner Oswald* and Isalde in Eilhart's *Tristrant*. A few years later the stories of three other brides are told, all won in a single episode of knightly combat. Lavinia marries the hero of Heinrich von Veldeke's *Eneit* (begun before 1174, completed after 1184),[12] which is based on the Old French *Eneas*. Enite marries the hero of Hartmann von Aue's *Erec* (1180–90), adapted from Chrétien de Troyes's *Erec et Enide*. Iblis marries the hero of Ulrich von Zatzikhoven's *Lanzelet*.

This is a heterogeneous group. Although Eilhart, Veldeke, Hartmann, and Ulrich have French sources, *Rother* derives from German oral tradition[13] and *Oswald* from the life of a seventh-century Northumbrian saint and king.[14] Half of the brides are won according to the courtship pattern, half in a single episode of knightly combat. Furthermore, where one can compare the MHG texts with their sources, one sees that the German writers did not hesitate to make changes, at least in detail: Veldeke decreases the importance of love and increases that of marriage;[15] Hartmann makes Enite more of a child.[16] Nevertheless, in spite of the differences, all these stories share one feature: they limit themselves to the period of a

---

Lambrecht, who devotes only twelve lines to Alexander's arming (LAlexr V357–68), nor Veldeke, who praises but does not portray any of the investiture of Barbarossa's sons (Eneit 13221–52), offers a "detailed description" in the manner of the *Nibelungenlied* or even of *König Rother.* —On Ernst's education: Curschmann, *Spielmannsepik*, 38; Rosenfeld, *Ernst*, 11–12. —I have here followed the majority opinion and assumed that *Ernst A* and *Ernst B* tell essentially the same story (Wehrli, "Ernst," 142; Sklenar, VL, 3:1179; Rosenfeld, *Ernst*, 10). If the later version is not a reliable guide to the earlier (Curschmann, *Spielmannsepik*, 36, 77), at least with regard to the childhood of the hero, and if the childhood of Ernst was absent in *Ernst A* but present in *Ernst B*, then *Ernst B* would belong to the important group of texts from the early thirteenth century, discussed below, that add childhood narratives to stories that previously did not contain them.

12. Bumke, *Mäzene*, 113–18.
13. Vollmann-Profe, *Geschichte*, 129–30.
14. Curschmann, *Spielmannsepik*, 9–14; Curschmann, VL, 6:770.
15. He radically shortens the lovers' speeches of doubt and impatience (*Eneas* 9839–10090; Eneit 333,15–335,18) and composes a lengthy description of their marriage and the events surrounding it (*Eneas* 10091–122; Eneit 335,26–347,12).
16. Chrétien claims that Enide is not only beautiful but intelligent (*Erec*, 537–38, 1271); Hartmann ignores this. Chrétien emphasizes the grief of the parents (*Erec*, 1438–58), Hartmann that of the daughter, who wept "ardently, as was appropriate for a child" (Erec 1456–58: vrouwe Enite urloup nam, als einem kinde wol gezam, vil heize weinende). Chrétien has Enide returning the hero's glance "as if they were competing" (*Erec*, 1481: qu'il feisoit li par contançon); Hartmann has her look at her companion often, but "timidly" (Erec 1489: bliuclîchen).

maiden's life just before she is married. While Lanzelet is of interest from birth, Iblis is of interest only when she is marriageable. Lanzelet grows up. Iblis gets married.

Although it survives only in fragments, there is no reason to doubt that the Trierer *Floyris* (around 1170)[17] retains the basic outlines of its French source. If so, then it was not only the first MHG tale of child lovers but also the first MHG narrative to tell the story of a maiden's childhood from birth.[18]

At the same time children make their first appearances in secular narrative they appear as well in a rather diffuse group of stories that might be called pious tales, narratives in which religious aspects play a large role, even though their protagonists are not saints. The *Kaiserchronik* contains a lengthy account of the three sons of Faustinian, the first appearance of the childhood of the refiliated son.[19] The story is derived from the fourth-century *Recognition of Clement*, of which it is the first vernacular adaptation.[20] The fragmentary and anonymous *Albanus* (before 1190), based on a Latin source,[21] contains a childhood narrative similar in many ways (incest, abandonment, rescue) to that in the roughly contemporaneous *Gregorius* of Hartmann von Aue, apparently based on the Old French *Vie de Saint Grégoire*.[22] The German adaptor of *Albanus* may have added the scene in which the infant is found and brought to the king of Hungary.[23] Hartmann seems to have added the description of Gregorius's education and the eloquent defense of knighthood that Gregorius makes in his dialogue with the abbot.[24] These additions make the story of Gregorius more like those of Alexander and Tristrant, where education also receives considerable attention and where the heroes are also determined to become knights. The heroine of Hartmann's *Armer Heinrich* (1190–97), for which no source is known, is unusual in many ways: her father is not a noble but a rich peasant; her story, although it does not begin at birth, begins earlier than the stories of most female children; and, although she does marry in the end,

17. Ruh, *Höfische Epik*, 1:53.
18. Van Dam, 1VL, 1:627. On the various proposals for dating: Winkelman, *Brücken-pächterepisode*, 13–14. —Although both van Dam (1VL, 1:628) and de Smet ("Trierer Floyris") believe that the writer of the *Trierer Floyris* treated his source rather freely, there is no reason to suppose that he altered the general outline to any significant degree.
19. Ksrchr 1235–4038.
20. Ohly, *Sage und Legende*, 74–84.
21. Morvay, VL, 1:107
22. Cormeau and Störmer, *Hartmann*, 123; Herlem-Prey, "Neues zur Quelle."
23. Morvay, *Albanuslegende*, 75–77.
24. Schottmann, "Gregorius," 87–90, 93–94; Herlem-Prey, "Dialog," 67, 72–73.

the narrative is concerned not primarily with her marriage but with her desire to sacrifice her life to cure her lord, Heinrich, of leprosy.[25]

The pendant to these pious children can be found in *Pilatus* (1170–80), where the hero commits two murders before he comes of age. This account, based on one of the few Latin versions of the Pilate legend to include a childhood narrative,[26] differs from all others, Latin and vernacular, in presenting the murderous protagonist in a comparatively favorable light.[27]

The production of childhood narratives of saints, which monopolized writing about children in the first third of the twelfth century, seems to have ceased by 1140 and to have picked up again only in the final third. When it reappears, it does so in entirely new contexts and with many new characters. While the religious children of the early part of the century were all prophets whose stories were incorporated into narratives of salvation history, those from the last third of the century are saints of many different kinds, whose stories occur in texts that focus on the biography of a single individual: sermons and saints' legends.

Twelfth-century sermons recount the familiar stories of the prophets: John the Baptist and the twelve-year-old Jesus in the Temple.[28] They introduce the lives of the child martyrs: Agnes, in an extremely condensed version; Margaret, in a brief summary; and Vitus, in a surprisingly detailed account.[29] And they tell of the anomalous Martin of Tours, once in skeletal abbreviation and once in greater detail.[30] This last, in the *Grieshabersche Predigten I*, is of some interest since it motivates Martin's knighting with unusual clarity, thus displaying the same interest in the end of a knight's childhood that one finds in the stories of Alexander or Gregorius.[31]

25. I have appropriated and expanded the category of pious tale from Hanns Fischer, who, of the texts I consider, includes only *Armer Heinrich* in his list (*Märendichtung*, 52–53). —On the relation between *Albanus* and *Gregorius*: Morvay, *Albanuslegende*, 158–63. On Gregorius's childhood, especially his crucial discussion with the abbot: Dittmann, *Gregorius*, 223–31; Cormeau, 'Armer Heinrich' und 'Gregorius', 55–64; Hirschberg, "Gregorius," 246–54. —If one accepts Tobler's argument ("*gemahel*") that the maiden in *Armer Heinrich* is Heinrich's betrothed or spouse throughout, then she becomes somewhat less anomalous.

26. Ohly, *Sage und Legende*, 58; Schönbach, review of Tischendorf, 167.

27. Schönbach, review of Tischendorf, 195; Harms, *Kampf mit dem Freund*, 116. On the nature of this Pilate see chapter seven, note 76.

28. GrshPr 445a,3–445b,10; MtdtPr 304–5.

29. LpgzPr 280,6–27; HoffPr 120,4–42; PKonPr M246,1–249.

30. PKonPr S239,25–30; GrshPr 450a,8–27.

31. "The early history of the vernacular sermon," writes Kartschoke, "remains one of the most problematic chapters in German literary history" (*Geschichte*, 243: Eines der noch immer schwierigsten Kapitel der deutschen Literaturgeschichte ist die Frühgeschichte der volkssprachlichen Predigt), and questions of dating are anything but resolved. While some place the *Grieshabersche Predigten I* and the *Speculum Ecclesiae* in the middle of the century or

One should not conclude from the sermons mentioned above that twelfth-century sermons in general are especially interested in childhood, for they are not. It is in fact much more common to find sermons for saints' feast days that lack childhood narratives, even when such narratives are ordinarily part of the legends for the saints in question. In the *Hoffmannsche Predigtsammlung* a sermon for the feast of St. Nicholas mentions two regular features of the saint's legendary childhood, that as an infant he stood up in his bath and that on two days of the week he nursed only once.[32] Here, however, the prophetic acts of infancy are not the first episodes of a biography but the first items on a list, which continues with the miracles of adulthood. Konrad's *Predigtbuch* begins with four sermons for Christmas, but only one recounts the biblical story of Jesus' birth, and it does so only as an introduction to an allegorical "expositio" of its meaning.[33] Even where childhood narratives do occur in sermons their function is as much hortatory as narrative. After Zechariah regains the power of speech and names his infant child, the Grieshaber story of John the Baptist mentioned above is interrupted to draw this lesson: "Thereby you can be certain, dearly beloved, that John can help you to complete grace with God, since at such a young age he helped his father regain his speech with nothing more than his name."[34]

Independent saints' lives reappear with Priester Adelbrecht's *Johannes Baptista* (before 1170), which, like the earlier accounts of John's childhood, is based primarily on scriptural sources.[35] The stories of two child martyrs are told in fragmentary texts, the *Margaretenlegende des XII. Jahrhunderts* (1170–80)[36] and *S. Veit* (around 1170).[37] The latter is the only MHG account of Vitus's life that begins with the saint's birth, early care, and baptism. Since its source has not been established, it is impossible to tell whether this more complete beginning represents a chronological extension by the German writer, which would be unique among MHG saints' lives, or merely

earlier (Mertens, VL, 3:256, 9:51–52), others place the latter, at least, after 1150 (Morvay and Grube, *Bibliographie*, 10). I have followed Vollmann-Profe (*Geschichte*, 156) and grouped the sermons together after the middle of the century.

32. HoffPr 116,2–6.
33. PKonPr S5,37–9,42.
34. GrshPr 445a,28–33: Dabi mvget ir wol wizzen. Mine vil lieben daz er iv nv̊ wol gihelfen mac aller gnaden vmb got. do er do also chinder sinem vater siner sprache niwan mit sinem namen wider half.
35. Geith, VL, 1:62; Vollmann-Profe, *Geschichte*, 197.
36. Bartsch, in Marglg, 295. Williams-Krapp (VL, 5:1242) takes no stand on the reliability of this dating; Kartschoke (*Geschichte*, 341) disputes it.
37. Ehrismann, *Geschichte*, 2.1:155; Rosenfeld, *Legende*, 42.

a faithful translation of an unusually complete Latin model. Albert von Augsburg's life of Ulrich of Augsburg, *Das Leben des Heiligen Ulrich* (late twelfth century), a faithful translation of a Latin *vita* of 1030,[38] introduces a new genre, that of the clerical saint.

Two impressive texts, Priester Wernher's *Maria* (1172)[39] and Konrad von Fußesbrunnen's *Kindheit Jesu* (1190–1200), are based on the *Gospel of Pseudo-Matthew*, a Latin compilation of apocryphal writings, probably from the fifth or sixth century,[40] that tells the story of Mary's birth and childhood and of Jesus' birth and childhood up until after the return from Egypt. Wernher, who follows the general outline of Pseudo-Matthew, tends toward the homiletic: he does not hesitate to expand his source with additional material from the Bible and the liturgy, from hymns, sermons, and popular legend,[41] nor does he hesitate to interrupt his account frequently to draw lessons for his audience. Konrad, who devotes his entire narrative to Jesus' life from birth until some time before age twelve, tends towards the secular: he dedicates more than a third of his text to an elaborate account of the Flight into Egypt, dwelling in particular on the hospitality shown Jesus and his parents in a robber household, like writers of courtly romance, who are also much interested in social ritual. Konrad's *Kindheit Jesu* is one of the few lengthy MHG texts devoted exclusively to the narration of its hero's childhood.[42]

At the beginning of the twelfth century the childhood of Jesus was inevitably woven into larger narratives of salvation history. At the end, it stands on its own. In the course of the century childhood has become autonomous. The development is not uniform: even at the end of the century Wernher's childhood of Jesus is incorporated into the life of his mother, saints' lives appear often in sermons, and the childhood of the bride is always embedded in the larger narrative of how the hero wins his wife. Nevertheless, by the end of the century the childhood of the saint is found not only in salvation history or sermons but also, with greater autonomy, as the first part of an independent biography—as in Albert's life of Ulrich. The childhood of the knight, of which there are quite a few by the end of

---

38. Geith, introduction to StUlrc, 9.
39. WerMar 5799–801; Bumke, *Mäzene*, 135.
40. Masser, *Bibel- und Legendenepik*, 88–89.
41. Masser, *Bibel, Apokryphen*, 87–89, 270–83.
42. Two manuscripts of Wernher's *Maria* add, after the return from Egypt, a brief account of various miracles that the adult Jesus performed. However, according to Masser (*Bibel- und Legendenepik*, 92), manuscript D, which does not contain these miracles, represents the original.

the century, also introduces an independent narrative: it tells a continuous story from birth to maturity, comes to a clear conclusion with knighting, and displays a relatively high degree of structural completeness and contextual independence—that is, of narrative autonomy. The legends of Vitus and Margaret, devoted entirely to childhood, are, like the *Kindheit Jesu*, completely independent childhood narratives. Although it would be inaccurate to speak of a uniform development from dependent to autonomous childhood narratives in the course of the twelfth century, it is clear that the proportion of narratives that are continuous, complete, and relatively independent increases throughout the period. Childhood has ceased to be merely an occasion to demonstrate a prophet's future role in salvation history and has become a topic of interest in its own right.

This interest is clearest in the case of secular males. The secular youths, who are all future knights, are rigorously distinguished from the secular maidens, who are all brides. This generic distinction means that the youths get more attention, since their stories are told from birth to adulthood, while the maidens are of interest only when they get married. Childhood is male. Furthermore, even within the genre of the childhood of the knight the stories of the twelfth-century youths are remarkably uniform. First, love plays no role: even famous lovers like Tristrant or Lanzelet remain untouched by this emotion until after they have come of age. Second, education receives a great deal of attention: Lambrecht musters a troop of six masters to teach his hero everything from writing and music to warfare and law; the fragments of *Graf Rudolf* describe a comprehensive courtly curriculum; Eilhart devotes 18 percent of Tristrant's childhood to education, nine times the percentage Gottfried devotes to Tristan's.[43] Third, each young knight brings his childhood to its conclusion with great determination: Alexander insists on receiving arms at age fifteen; Tristrant resolves to fight Morold and gets his uncle to knight him; Lanzelet himself decides to leave the isle where he was raised and set off on his own. This decisiveness contrasts with the more passive attitude of many later MHG knights, including such great heroes as Siegfried, Tristan, and Charlemagne, toward their coming of age. In the second half of the twelfth century the childhood of the knight is uniform, pedagogic, and vigorous. It is an age of discipline and determination, the heroic age of the knightly child.

The vigor of the model seems to have affected other noble youths as well. The most obvious is Gregorius, whose education receives detailed at-

43. Eilhart has 328 lines of childhood (ETrist 99–350, 455–532), 58 for education (126–84). Gottfried has 3322 lines of childhood (GTrist 1746–5068), 68 for education (2054–2122).

tention, who praises knighthood as a noble vocation, and who is no less determined than Alexander to come of age. That most of these features were added by Hartmann to the story he found in his source suggests that he considers education and inevitable knighthood to be essential parts of childhood for a noble youth, even when that youth is raised in a monastery. The twelfth-century idealization of the noble youth may also explain the unique and surprisingly heroic representation of the half-noble protagonist in *Pilatus*. Perhaps it even explains Konrad's *Kindheit Jesu*, one of the very few lengthy narratives devoted entirely to childhood. Although Konrad relates the most sacred of all childhood stories, he "probably wrote for a courtly audience"[44] and he dwells with particular interest on the kind of ceremony in fashion at courts. That the childhood of Jesus moves in the course of the twelfth century from dependence in the *Mittelfränkische Reimbibel* to autonomy in *Kindheit Jesu* may, paradoxically, indicate that it has moved from a sacred to a courtly context, where male childhood is a subject of particular interest.

1200–1250: The Golden Age of Secular Childhood

In the first half of the thirteenth century the particular interest in knightly childhood expands to become a general interest in secular childhood. During a period in which religious children disappear almost completely, secular children continue to be imported from France, new children are conceived in Germany according to the established patterns, and still others appear representing entirely new models of childhood narrative. The first half of the thirteenth century, which witnessed what Ingeborg Glier calls "an 'explosion' of German literature with regard to genres and types that is without precedent,"[45] is also the most productive period for the secular childhood narrative, both in the number of texts written and in the degree of innovation they display.

As in the fifty years before 1200, so in the fifty years after, stories of young knights and young brides continue to be translated from French into German without major alteration. Tristan and Isold make their second appearance in Gottfried von Straßburg's *Tristan und Isold* (1200–20), based

---

44. Bumke, *Geschichte*, 381: Der Dichter . . . hat wahrscheinlich für ein höfisches Publikum gedichtet.
45. Glier, *Geschichte*, 8: eine "Explosion" der deutschen Literatur nach Gattungen und Typen, die ohne Beispiel ist.

on the *Roman de Tristan* of Thomas. The childhood stories of Charlemagne and his beloved Galie are given lengthy treatment in *Karl und Galie* (1215–20), which claims to be adapted from a French book.[46] The narrative does correspond to the pattern of Old French *enfances*, common in France but not in Germany, according to which a young hero is exiled from his native country, makes his name abroad, and returns to reclaim his patrimony.[47] However, it offers an account of Charlemagne's childhood that differs substantially from all other extant versions.[48] Lancelot's childhood dominates much of the beginning of the prose *Lancelot* (before 1250), "in principle a word-for-word translation" of the French *Lancelot en prose*.[49] Finally, part of Blanschandin's childhood survives in a fragment of *Blanschandin* (ca. 1250), adapted from the French *Blancandin et l'Orgueilleuse d'Amour*.

Although these six children share the same French ancestry as many of those whose stories were adapted before 1200, they vary the earlier patterns. The young knights no longer realize the model of disciplined, vigorous childhood with the consistency of the earlier youths. Lancelot and Charlemagne do not receive an elaborate education; Blanschandin is not taught knighthood. Tristan and Charlemagne do not initiate their own coming of age. Lancelot does not remain untouched by love until after he is knighted. The stories of the brides change as well, no longer being strictly limited to the events surrounding their marriage. Isold's education is detailed. Galie falls in love with Charles before he has even seen her, then she gets her father to arrange his knighting. These changes represent three developments that will transform the world of secular childhood in the thirteenth century. First, there is a tendency to expand childhood: the stories of Isold and Galie begin earlier than those of twelfth-century brides. Second, child love attracts interest: Lancelot and Galie fall in love before they come of age. Third, gender distinctions become blurred: careful education is not required of all knightly youths nor forbidden to all courtly maidens; both youths and maidens fall in love.

The tendency to expand childhood can be seen most clearly in those texts where German writers adapt written sources. Wolfram von Eschenbach's *Parzival* (1200–10) is based principally on Chrétien de Troyes's *Conte du Graal*. Yet where Chrétien begins his hero's childhood just before he rides away from his mother's home to become a knight, Wolfram precedes

46. KrlGal 1,9–10.
47. Wolfzettel, "*Enfances* (I)," 325–26.
48. Beckers, VL, 4:1015; Horrent, *Enfances*, 182–98.
49. Steinhoff, "Artusritter," 273: eine im Prinzip wortgetreue Übersetzung der altfranzösischen Vorlage.

this event with an account of Parzival's birth, his mother's decision to raise him in the woods, and something of his early childhood there. Wolfram thus transforms a partial childhood narrative into a complete one. Stricker's *Karl der Große* (after 1220) is a modernization of the twelfth-century *Rolandslied* of Pfaffe Konrad. Yet where Konrad has nothing to say about the childhood of his protagonists, Stricker adds a brief account of Charlemagne's childhood, which he put together using scraps of the legends of Bertha and Charlemagne.[50] Rudolf von Ems's *Willehalm von Orlens* (1235–43)[51] claims to be based on a French romance,[52] which is no longer extant. Yet if one compares it with Philippe de Beaumanoir's *Jehan et Blonde*, which descends from the same source, it seems that Rudolf added his hero's early childhood to a partial account, just as Wolfram did in *Parzival*.[53]

Childhood narratives seem also to have been added to older material in texts for which there are no known written sources—although, given that fact, the additions are harder to demonstrate conclusively. The author of the *Nibelungenlied* (1180–1210) is thought to have invented the courtly childhood of Siegfried that fills the second *aventiure*[54] and, as a deliberate pendant to it, the appearance of the young Kriemhild in the first.[55] The latter represents an expansion of the traditional courtship pattern, in which the bride enters the narrative only when she is already of marriageable age. *Kudrun* (midcentury) now begins with the story of Hagen's childhood, generally assumed to be a late invention meant to place him in a genealogical context and, perhaps, to explain his fierceness.[56] Here too the traditional

---

50. Geith, *Carolus Magnus*, 171–72; Horrent, *Enfances*, 202–5; Schnell, "Strickers 'Karl,' " 58–61; von der Burg, *Strickers Karl*, 162–70.

51. Brackert, *Rudolf*, 241–42; Bumke, *Mäzene*, 251, 268.

52. WilOrl 15601–30.

53. Brackert, *Rudolf*, 65–67; Lüdicke, *Willehalm*, 73–102, 115–22; Wachinger, "Rezeption Gottfrieds," 66. —Those who have compared Wolfram's treatment of Parzival's childhood to his source have noted many changes besides the one mentioned in this paragraph: he shortens "noticeably" Parzival's encounter with the knights (Green, "Parzival's Departure," 380); he scales down the mother's parting advice so it is more suitable for a child (Richey, "Independence," 355); he takes the hero's knighting out of the hands of Gornemant and places it in those, less expert, of Iwanet (Bumke, "Schwertleite," 238–40; Groos, "swert-leite," 248–53); he makes the young hero less foolish (Bumke, "Schwertleite," 237; Richey, "Independence," 352), more courtly and less single-mindedly oblivious to those around him (Huby, "Entwicklung," 265–66); he omits those details that undermine clarity and rationality (Huby, "Bearbeitungstechnik," 41). —Although much has been made of the relations between Rudolf's *Willehalm* and Gottfried's *Tristan* (see below, note 79), in the expansion of the childhood of his hero he stands closer to Wolfram.

54. Andersson, *Preface*, 112–17, 138; de Boor, introduction to Niblgn, XXXVII.

55. Haug, "Höfische Idealität," 37–39; Wachinger, *Studien*, 84–85.

56. Campbell, "Hagen"; Hoffmann, *Kudrun*, 25, 290; Hoffmann, "Hauptprobleme," 186–87; Kuhn, "Kudrun," 211.

childhood of the bride has been expanded backwards, most likely by the writer of the text we know: we are told of the birth and something of the childhood for both Hilde and Kudrun.[57] Although these expansions are very brief, Hilde and Kudrun are nevertheless the only MHG brides won according to the courtship pattern whose childhood narratives begin at birth. According to Hermann Schneider, the writer of *Wolfdietrich A* (ca. 1230)[58] "thoroughly recast the older source and enriched it, above all with a captivating story of the hero's childhood"[59]—although before accepting this claim one should consider that other scholars have detected parallels in German, French, folkloric, legendary, and historical texts.[60] If these speculations are accurate, then in all three texts older Germanic heroic tales were elaborated by the addition or expansion of childhood narratives (relatively courtly ones in the *Nibelungenlied* and *Kudrun*) at the moment that the tales first achieved written form in the first half of the thirteenth century.[61]

At the same time some writers were adapting and expanding previously existing stories, others were composing new narratives from scratch. And when they did so they were careful to include childhood narratives. Both Wirnt von Gravenberg and Heinrich von dem Türlin drew freely on elements of the French and German romance tradition to compose, respectively, *Wigalois* (1210–15)[62] and *Diu Crone* (ca. 1230).[63] Wirnt gives Wigalois a regulation knightly childhood and Larie a childhood of the bride won in knightly combat—but in the new expanded mode of the thirteenth cen-

57. Kudrn 197–199, 573–77.

58. Wisniewski, *Dietrichdichtung*, 153; Heinzle, *Geschichte*, 158–59.

59. Schneider, *Heldendichtung*, 358: Die ältere Vorlage hat er gründlich umgeschmolzen und sie vor allem durch eine entzückende Kindheitsgeschichte des Helden bereichert.

60. Baecker, "Wolfdietrich," 34–44; Scheludko, "Versuch einer Interpretation," 2–21; Schneider, *Heldensage*, 346–58; Schneider, *Wolfdietrich*, 22–26, 180, 183–333.

61. On the childhood of Hagen in *Kudrun*: Hoffmann, *Kudrun*, 25–28, 290; Loerzer, *Eheschließung*, 20–26; Schröder, "Hetel und Hilde," 52–61; Siefken, *Überindividuelle Formen*, 18–19, 44–54. —On Kudrun's marriage: Grimm, "Eheschließungen," 56–69; Loerzer, *Eheschließung*, 111–16.—Loerzer (*Eheschließung*, 78–79) and Siefken (*Überindividuelle Formen*, 77) believe that the childhood of Kudrun was modeled on that of a young hero since there was no traditional narrative pattern for the childhood of a maiden. It is hard, however, to imagine any writer would need literary models to think up the meagre elements of Kudrun's childhood (birth, careful attention, maturity) or to get them in the right order. And in any case, there had in fact been a number of texts with complete childhood narratives for maidens before the middle of the century: Wolfram's *Titurel*, *Dulciflorie*, *Flore und Blanscheflur*, *Gute Frau*. —If *Herzog Ernst A* did not contain a childhood narrative for its hero (see note 11), then *Herzog Ernst B* (after 1208), which does contain such a narrative, would be another example of an early-thirteenth-century text to have added childhood to its source.

62. Neumann, "Wigalois," 194.

63. Cormeau, *Zwei Kapitel*, 49–54, 97–99, 100–123; Cormeau, "Leserdisposition," 123–24; Cormeau, *Zwei Kapitel*, 221–24.

tury: although she herself does not appear until of marriageable age, we do learn about her life up to that point from an account by another character.[64] Heinrich begins *Diu Crône* with a very brief childhood of Arthur.

As Wirnt and Heinrich draw on various romance traditions, so other writers draw on other traditions to compose childhood narratives. Ulrich von Türheim combines material from various heroic sources—Wolfram's *Willehalm*, the Old French Guillaume d'Orange cycle, perhaps a Latin life of William[65]—to compose his *Rennewart* (1243–50),[66] a continuation of Wolfram's *Willehalm*. It brings Rennewart's childhood to a regulation conclusion with his knighting,[67] then provides a lengthy childhood of Rennewart's son Malefer and a brief childhood of Malefer's son Johannes. Rudolf von Ems bases his *Alexander* (1230–50) on Latin texts, principally the *Historiae Alexandri Magni [regis Macedonum]* of Quintus Curtius Rufus.[68] But for the first 5000 lines, which include the childhood of Alexander, he follows the *Historia de preliis*, a tenth-century adaptation of a late-classical Alexandrian account of Alexander's life usually referred to as the Pseudo-Kallisthenes, and draws on a third Latin source, the twelfth-century *Alexandreis* of Walter of Châtillon, to augment the long speech of instruction that Aristotle gives Alexander.[69] Rudolf is the first MHG writer to use Latin sources to write the childhood of a secular figure.[70]

The determination with which MHG writers of the first half of the thirteenth century provide their texts with complete childhood narratives may reflect the tendency towards completeness, the fondness for the *summa*, that has been said to characterize the thirteenth century.[71] Writers and audiences seem to have wanted the complete story of the hero or heroine from birth on: if the sources left part of the biography out, the writers of the thirteenth century filled it in. The age seems to have desired genealogical completeness in particular.[72] Many of the same texts that show

64. Wglois 3626–823.
65. Bumke, *Geschichte*, 258.
66. After 1243: Heinzle, *Geschichte*, 42. Before 1250: Bumke, *Geschichte*, 259.
67. Rennew 2497–831.
68. Fechter, *Lateinische Dichtkunst*, 140–41.
69. Hübner, "Alexander," 33–34; Wisbey, "Aristotelesrede"; Brackert, *Rudolf*, 244–45.
70. On the fight between Malefer and his father: Harms, *Kampf mit dem Freund*, 109–13. —Although the absence of a knighting ceremony in Rudolf's *Alexander* might reflect the respect for earlier ages that Brackert believes Rudolf gained from his familiarity with Latin historical sources (Brackert, *Rudolf*, 167), it is difficult to detect this sensitivity to historical difference in Rudolf's description of Alexander's knightly education, which includes chess and falconry (RAlexr 1862–69). —On Alexander's childhood: Schouwink, *Fortuna*, 126–33.
71. Kuhn, "Aspekte" [Akademievortrag], 24; Kuhn, "Aspekt" [Minnesangs Wende], 186; Wehrli, *Titurel*, 13.
72. Hoffmann, "Hauptprobleme," 186–87.

an increased interest in children—Wolfram's *Parzival*, *Kudrun*, *Wigalois*, Rudolf's *Willehalm* and *Alexander*—show an interest in these childrens' parents as well. Duby has noted a parallel development at the very end of the twelfth century in France among the authors of genealogies of noble houses: where a family's memory of its ancestry dies out the author invents a founding father.[73] Bumke notes that those princely houses that cultivate the writing of genealogies are precisely the ones who are active as the patrons of courtly literature.[74] The desire for childhood narratives one finds in MHG texts of the early thirteenth century seems to reflect a general desire for completeness, biographical and genealogical.

The strength of this desire is illustrated most vividly in two cases where the addition of a childhood narrative actually detracts from the narrative as a whole. The brief childhood narrative that Stricker added when he wrote *Karl* is so little integrated into the work itself that no notice is taken of the remarkable fact that Charlemagne is supposed to have spent most of his childhood under the protection of Marseiles, his future enemy.[75] The brief childhood of Arthur with which Heinrich begins the *Crone* is in fact misleading: the narrator pretends to be going to tell us a story about Arthur's youth, but the childhood narrative is only a bridge between the prologue and the depiction of the Arthurian festival with which the romance really gets underway.[76] That childhood narratives are incorporated into texts that would actually be more coherent without them indicates the degree to which such stories were considered the natural beginning for narrative texts in the first half of the thirteenth century.

If MHG texts of the first half of the thirteenth century show an increased desire for childhood, they show as well a heightened interest in the desire of children: this is the great age for stories of child love. Most are based on French sources. Konrad Fleck's *Flore und Blanscheflur* (ca. 1220) is an expanded adaptation of the "version aristocratique" of *Floire et Blancheflor*.[77] It is the only extended narrative to be devoted entirely to child love. Rudolf von Ems's *Willehalm von Orlens*, mentioned above for its expansion of the hero's childhood, tells at length of the child love between Willehalm and Amelie, which Rudolf seems to have taken from his source. The anonymous *Gute Frau* (ca. 1230), which claims an otherwise unknown French source,[78] begins with a story of child love, but then moves on after 200 lines

73. Duby, "Kinship," 143–44.
74. Bumke, *Mäzene*, 51.
75. Haake, "Rolandslied," 282–83, 293.
76. Crone 249–55.
77. Ganz, VL, 2:746.
78. GuFrau 1–14; Mackinder-Savage, VL, 3:329.

to knightly deeds, religious poverty, separation, and reunion: child love serves as little more than an introduction to a text that is about something else altogether. Its anomalous presence is testimony to the popularity of narratives of child love in the first half of the thirteenth century.[79]

The desire for child lovers is so strong that adults are turned into children to satisfy the demand. In writing *Aristoteles und Phillis [B]* (dated variously 1200–50) [80] the German author took the figure of Alexander, who appears in all non-German versions of the story as a grown man,[81] changed him into a schoolboy, and thereby made "the child Alexander" [82] the child lover of Phyllis. In writing *Titurel* (after 1217) [83] Wolfram took Sigune and Schionatulander, two lovers who had already appeared in *Parzival*, changed them back into children, and invented a love story for them. Wolfram not only turns lovers into children, he also turns children into lovers. Whereas in Chrétien's *Conte du Graal* the Pucele as Petites Manches gets the reluctant Gauvian to fight on her behalf by presenting him with an injustice done her that must be redressed,[84] Obilot, her counterpart in *Parzival*, attains the same end by approaching Gawan as a lover ready to reward her knight's service with her love.[85] Wolfram has has transformed the precocious maiden from a youthful plaintiff into a child lover. Whereas in the Old French *Aliscans*, Aelis falls in love with Rainouart only after he has left her father's court to fight with Guillaume,[86] in *Willehalm* Wolfram explains that Rennewart was made the companion of Alize much earlier, as soon as he arrived at court, and that their love grew out of this contact.[87] Wolf-

---

79. On the structure of the childhood narratives in *Willehalm von Orlens*: von Ertzdorff, *Rudolf*, 311–35. —Although there are certain similarities between Rudolf's *Willehalm* and Gottfried's *Tristan* (Lüdicke, *Willehalm*, 85–88), they are not so striking that, at least with regard to the hero's childhood, one can regard *Willehalm* as an "Anti-*Tristan*" (Brackert, *Rudolf*, 33) or assume that Rudolf's audience would have understood *Willehalm* as a "critical parody" of *Tristan* (Haug, "Rudolfs 'Willehalm,' " 93). Willehalm's education, as Brackert himself points out (221), is actually quite different from Tristan's. The way Willehalm learns his true parentage is altogether unique. His request to leave home to further his courtly and knightly education is closer to Eilhart's *Tristrant* or even *Parzival* than to Gottfried. Once Willehalm gets to England and falls in love, his childhood has nothing at all in common with Tristan's. See also Heinzle, *Geschichte*, 45. —The anomalous status of child love in the *Gute Frau* is evident in the fact that even relatively detailed investigations of the text ignore it completely (Röcke, "Minne," 147–58).
80. Ca. 1200: Rosenfeld, "Aristoteles," 323; Rosenfeld, VL, 1:434. 1230–50: Jefferis, "Aristoteles," 171. Frosch-Freiburg (*Schwankmären*, 96 n. 1) believes Rosenfeld's dating is too early, although she does not offer an alternative.
81. Rosenfeld, "Aristoteles," 333.
82. ArPhlB 2.47: alexander daz kint.
83. Bumke, *Wolfram*, 13.
84. Chrétien, *Conte du Graal*, 5297–328.
85. Parz 369,1–372,12.
86. *Aliscans*, 3851–62.
87. WWilhm 284,13–16.

ram has moved the beginning of their love back into their childhood and transformed them thereby into child lovers.[88]

The interest in child love is but one aspect of a certain sentimentality that enters the secular childhood narrative just before 1200 and becomes pronounced during the first half of the thirteenth century. Whereas previously childhood had consisted of little more than birth, education, and signs of future vocation, now one finds these elements augmented by various small signs of childishness. Children begin to cry: Parzival when he hears the birds sing, Tristan when he is abandoned in Cornwall.[89] Others play with toys: the maiden in *Armer Heinrich* gets hair ribbons and rings, Sigune, Obilot, Dulciflorie, Amelie, and Willehalm's daughter have dolls, Amelie also has pet birds.[90] Writers express a nostalgia for the childishness of children: when Tristan's education begins, Gottfried laments that he must abandon the undisciplined freedom of early childhood.[91] At the same time the attachment of parents or foster parents to their children becomes more tender: the mothers of Gregorius and Parzival, the parents of Flore, and the foster parents of Tristan and Lancelot react to the departure of their children with a grief quite unknown to the parents or guardians of Alexander, Tristrant, and Lanzelet.[92] When children fall in love with one another the stories delight in observing the "childish" way in which they deal with the adult emotion: Sigune and Amelie don't understand what love is the first time they hear the word and ask naive questions; Flore and Blanscheflur spend their lunch break practicing what their school books teach them about love. It is only during the first half of the thirteenth century that a substantial number of stories of child love are written, and it is only during that period that any of these stories have a happy outcome.

88. On the versions of *Aristoteles und Phillis*: Frosch-Freiburg, *Schwankmären*, 100–104. —Although most scholars believe Wolfram invented *Titurel* out of the characters he created in *Parzival* (Wehrli, *Titurel*, 7, 10), Ruh ("Liebessprache," 502) follows Mohr in arguing that Wolfram based the story on a tale that was known to his public. —On the relation of Obilot to the French model: Ertzdorff, "Obilot," 129; Mohr, "Obie," 9–17. —Wolfram makes other changes in the childhood of Rennewart: he omits the fearsome master who taught Rainouart before he was abducted, although the master does appear in *Rennewart* (Rennew 17806–17), and he adds something about Rennewart's courtly education by the merchants who sold him to the French king (WWilhm 283,21–22; Mergell, *Quellen*, 54). The considerable attention paid to the growth of Rennewart's beard after Alize kisses him is also Wolfram's invention; in the source Rainouart has the beginnings of a beard throughout (Lofmark, *Rennewart*, 151–56).
89. Parz 118,14–28; GTrist 2482–86.
90. ArmHnr 335–38; WTitrl 30,1–3, 64,1–3; Parz 372,15–18; Dulcfl 366–71; WWilhm 33,24; WilOrl 3820–24.
91. GTrist 2068–86.
92. Greg 783–822; Parz 128,16–30; FlorBl 2916–50; GTrist 2375–400; PrLanc I:117,23–24, I:118,3–30, I:124,19–22, I:125,28–30, I:130,31–131,1.

They serve then as the most distinctive instance of the sentimental interest in childhood that enters MHG narrative during this period.[93]

While writers like Wolfram or Rudolf sentimentalize children's ignorance of love, others eroticize it. The heroines of the *Sperber* (1200–1250) and the fragmentary *Dulciflorie* (shortly after 1210) have been raised in seclusion, so they don't know what's at stake when they agree to let a passing knight take their love, if he can find it, in exchange for a sparrow hawk he is carrying. While the *Sperber* begins when its heroine is nearly an adult, *Dulciflorie* accommodates the thirteenth-century desire for completeness and begins with the heroine's birth and early education.[94]

Interest in childhood is not limited to literary texts but can be observed in didactic texts as well. The first such texts, *Winsbecke* (1210–20),[95] *Winsbeckin*,[96] and the *Welscher Gast* of Thomasin von Zerklaere (1215), appear in the second decade of the thirteenth century, the *Magezoge* in mid-century. It seems that the interest in secular education evident in Lambrecht's *Alexanderlied* or Gottfried's *Tristan* was great enough to inspire independent, nonfictional treatment. Although these early didactic texts are alert to all sorts of ways in which children might go wrong, in general they seem quite hopeful about the prospects of educating children—at least in comparison with didactic writers from the end of the century. "The tone," writes Gärtner about the *Magezoge*, "is optimistic and the teachings are for the most part formulated in a positive manner. The conviction that virtue is teachable predominates."[97] It seems then that the increased interest in childhood displayed by MHG narratives texts after the turn of the century is part of a more general interest in and positive attitude towards childhood that can be observed in vernacular didactic writing as well.

Surprisingly, at the same time secular writers are fascinated with child-

93. When Rudolf recounts the sacrifice of Jephthah's daughter he elaborates the father's love in a way the Bible does not (RWeltc 19512–88). The sentimentalization of childhood continues in the second half of the century. Ulrich von Liechtenstein praises those who comfort crying orphans (Frndst 2nd Büchlein 215–18). When Jans Enikel recounts the sacrifice of Isaac or the abandonment of Moses he elaborates parental love and grief even more than Rudolf (JWeltc 3733–4044, 6281–440).

94. Niewöhner (*Sperber*, 166–70) argued that both *Sperber* and *Dulciflorie* descend from a lost verse narrative of the twelfth century. Rosenfeld accepted this thesis at one point (1VL, 4:230), but seems now to have doubts about it (VL, 2:243). Frosch-Freiburg (*Schwankmären*, 33, 40–41) denies the possibility of charting filiations with any precision.

95. Wehrli, *Geschichte*, 456. According to Bumke (*Geschichte*, 334) it is impossible to date either the *Winsbecke* or the *Winsbeckin*.

96. The handbooks remain silent about the dating of the *Winsbeckin*.

97. Gärtner, VL, 5:1154: der Ton [ist] zuversichtlich, und die Lehren sind überwiegend positiv formuliert. Es herrscht die Überzeugung, daß Tugend lehrbar sei.

hood, writers of religious texts have hardly a thing to say on the subject.
The stories of saintly children are quickly enumerated. A sermon in the
St. Pauler Predigten (before 1230) contains an account of John the Baptist's
conception and birth.[98] The childhood of Moses is recounted in Rudolf's
Weltchronik (ca. 1250). The story of St. Margaret is told twice, once in the
Wallersteiner Margareta-Legende (before 1218 or after 1235)[99] and again in
the *Margareta* of Wetzel von Bernau (1200–50).[100] The disinterest in saintly
children is so pervasive that even an ambitious saint's life like the *Sanct
Francisken Leben* of Lamprecht von Regensburg (ca. 1238) gets by with
only a general reference to its hero's childhood—this even though the "sinful lack of discipline"[101] in which Francis is said to have grown up would
seem to invite narrative elaboration. The equally ambitious *Heiliger Georg*
of Reinbot von Durne (1230–50), although it mentions the saint's father
and brothers, his father's death and the brothers' knighting,[102] feels no need
to say anything more about George's childhood.

Although the first half of the thirteenth century produced few stories
of young saints, pious tales—religious stories whose heroes are not saints
—continued to be written. The *Jüdel* (before 1225) tells the story, already
mentioned in a twelfth-century sermon and told again at the end of the
thirteenth in the *Passional*, of a Jewish schoolboy who converts to Christianity and is rescued from death by the Virgin.[103] The *Vorauer Novelle*
(before 1250)[104] tells of two oblates who turn to the study of magic; after
they grow up one of them dies and the other repents. Considering the de-
cidedly secular cast of vernacular writing about childhood in this period
it is not surprising that the most substantial pious tales of the early thirteenth century are those that demonstrate the religious vocation of a secular ruler. Otto II of Freising's *Laubacher Barlaam* (before 1220) and Rudolf
von Ems's *Barlaam und Josaphat* (1222–32)[105] are both based on the same
source. Although the childhood narratives are similar in outline, Rudolf
gives his hero an education closer to the medieval European courtly norm:
a team of masters teaches him manners, modesty, reading, and kingly liberality.[106] Otte's *Eraclius* (shortly before 1230), based, at least for the hero's

98. StPlPr 116,2–117,16.
99. Bumke, *Mäzene*, 239; Williams-Krapp, VL, 5:1242.
100. Bumke, *Geschichte*, 396.
101. StFran 408: sündeclîcher frîheit.
102. StGeor 105–35.
103. Eis, "Fragment," 552, 554.
104. Heinzle, *Geschichte*, 173; questioned by Bumke, *Geschichte*, 403.
105. Bumke, *Geschichte*, 395.
106. RBarlm 24,37–25,3.

childhood, on Gautier d'Arras's *Eracle*, also tells the story of a pious sovereign. Although Otte, in adapting Gautier's childhood narrative, stresses the religious aspects and reduces the courtly elements, he nevertheless increases the relative importance of childhood: his childhood narrative is a third longer than the French, even though, on the whole, his version is shorter.[107]

That religious texts have so little to say about childhood in the first half of the thirteenth century probably has less to do with childhood than with the general situation of MHG religious writing in the period. New forms of spirituality, of which the increasingly important role of lay piety and the newly founded mendicant orders are the most obvious manifestations, seem to have made the old religious genres obsolete and to have required something else. "In the entire area" of religious writing, according to Hugo Kuhn, "German writers of the thirteenth century had to begin anew."[108] In the second half of the century this new beginning will bear fruit. But in the first half religious writing about children is rare.

1250–1300: Disillusion and the Return of the Saints

Secular children lose their special fascination in the second half of the thirteenth century, at the same time interest revives in religious children, above all in young saints. It is among them the one must look for innovation. This does not mean that secular childhood narratives cease to be written in substantial numbers between 1250 and 1300, for they are. But by the end of the century secular childhood has lost its hegemonic position and, for the only time in the history of MHG childhood, one finds negative representations of children.

By the middle of the century the adaptation of childhood narratives from French sources has nearly ceased. And it has ceased altogether for those future knights who can manage to control their amorous impulses until they are adults. The narratives of knightly children who do not fall in love are no longer adapted from French sources but compiled from German or classical ones. The substantial story of young Dietleib in *Biterolf und Dietleib* (1260–80) is related to that of young Detlef in the *Thidrek-*

---

107. Feistner, *Eraclius*, 104–5, 116. —On the Greek and Latin sources of the Barlaam and Josaphat legend as well as the medieval French versions: von Ertzdorff, *Rudolf*, 192–200.
108. Kuhn, "Aspekte" [Akademievortrag], 11: Hier überall mußte also das 13. Jahrhundert auf deutsch neu beginnen.

saga—although the author of the MHG text felt free to combine heroic and courtly motives to fashion figures altogether his own.[109] *Wigamur* (ca. 1250 or 1250–1300)[110] begins with an extended childhood narrative, clearly inspired by *Lanzelet, Parzival*, and *Wigalois*.[111] Ulrich von dem Türlin's *Willehalm* (1260–80)[112] includes brief childhood narratives for its hero and, from the hand of an anonymous continuator, for his nephew, Fivianz, both invented from elements contained in Wolfram's *Willehalm*.[113] Two stories that descend from Germanic traditions appear in new versions, providing a revised childhood for Herzog Ernst in *Herzog Ernst D* (1250–1300) and a substantially different childhood for Wolfdietrich in *Wolfdietrich B* (ca. 1250).[114] Most of these texts exhibit a tendency toward normalization. *Wigamur*'s devotion to its famous models is unmistakable. The young heroes in Ulrich's *Willehalm* and *Wolfdietrich B* receive much more orthodox fostered childhoods than do those in their sources. They as well as Herzog Ernst D receive more carefully detailed knighting ceremonies. It seems that the writers of these texts were eager to make their heroes' childhood, especially their knightly investiture, conform more closely to the standard format than did the related texts on which they drew.[115]

MHG writers who based their texts on Latin sources were also concerned to give their heroes an orderly childhood, a goal that forced them to consult and combine several texts. Since the principal source for Ulrich von Etzenbach's *Alexander* (1270–90),[116] the *Alexandreis* of Walter of Châtillon, does not include the story of Alexander's childhood, Ulrich adds

109. Curschmann, "Dichtung über Heldendichtung," 19–21; Curschmann, VL, 1:881; Hoffmann, *Heldendichtung*, 179.

110. Bumke, *Geschichte*, 232.

111. Bumke, *Geschichte*, 232; Classen, "Wigamur," 204–05; Ebenbauer, "Wigamur," 29.

112. Schröder (*Arabel-Studien*, 1:7) dates *Willehalm* in the beginning of the 1260s, Bumke (*Mäzene*, 201) after 1269.

113. Heinzle, *Geschichte*, 153; Rosenfeld, 1VL, 4:610; Suchier, *Quelle*, 36–37.

114. Wisnieswki (*Dietrichdichtung*, 153) dates *Wolfdietrich B* around 1250, Heinzle (*Geschichte*, 159) says merely thirteenth century, Hoffmann (*Heldendichtung*, 150) suggests the first half, and de Boor (*Geschichte*, 3.1:179) the end of the century.

115. On the basis of a few parallels between *Biterolf* and *Wigalois*, critics writing on the former have claimed that it is somehow modelled on the latter (de Boor, *Geschichte*, 3.1:174; Hoffmann, *Heldendichtung*, 179; Spechtler, "Biterolf," 257–60). While Wigalois and Dietleib do both leave home to seek their fathers, this is the only distinctive feature they share, and it actually plays a very small role in *Wigalois*: both narrator and hero forget it the moment Wigalois leaves home. See van der Lee, *Vatersuche*, 179–83. —Classen ("Wigamur," 204–10) argues that the childhood of Wigamur is a parody of its models, intended to make us laugh; Ebenbauer ("Wigamur," 28–44) that, by so thoroughly isolating Wigamur from his "family," it sets the stage for a demonstration that birth is nearly everything, individual accomplishment almost nothing.

116. Behr, "Böhmerhof," 419–21.

one, basing it on the *Historia de preliis* and incorporating a part of the *Alexandreis* originally unrelated to childhood.[117] Since the principal source for Konrad von Würzburg's *Trojanerkrieg* (1280–87),[118] the *Roman de Troie* of Benoît de Sainte-Maure, has nothing to say about the childhood of Paris or Achilles, Konrad adds childhood narratives for both, drawing on the fifth-century Latin prose *Excidium Troiae* and on Statius's *Achilleis*.[119] A second MHG account of the Trojan War, the anonymous *Göttweiger Trojanerkrieg* (probably 1270–1300), also begins with the story of Paris's childhood, although it only tells part of the childhood of Achilles.[120] It too seems to have been based on several sources, including the *Excidium Troiae* and Dares's *Historia de excidio Troiae*.[121] The sources for the stories of Paris and Achilles in Jans Enikel's *Weltchronik* (1277–1290) are unknown. Where one can compare the Latin sources with the MHG childhood narratives it is evident that the German writers expanded them considerably. For Alexander's childhood Ulrich turns 300 lines of Latin prose into more than 1500 lines of MHG verse.[122] For Paris's childhood Konrad takes a 100-line flashback in the *Excidium Troiae*[123] and expands it to well over 5000 lines of verse. For Achilles's childhood Konrad had only about twenty lines of very scanty information from the *Excidium*[124] and a few retrospective hints from Statius.[125]

While the writers of the second half of the thirteenth century display considerable enterprise in fashioning substantial childhood narratives from a few distinctive details in their sources, their young heroes display somewhat less. Earlier heroes—Tristrant, Gregorius, Lanzelet, Lancelot, Parzival, Rennewart, Wigalois, Willehalm von Orlens, and Blanschandin—all demonstrate their eagerness to leave home and get on with their knightly careers. After 1250 only Dietleib exhibits this sort of determination. Ulrich von dem Türlin's Willehalm and Fivianz, Ernst D, Wolfdietrich B, Konrad

117. Behr, "Böhmerhof," 413–19; Toischer, *Alexandreis*, 322–48, 365.
118. Brandt, *Konrad*, 71.
119. Brandt, *Konrad*, 174–76; Cormeau, "Quellenkompendium," 304–7; Knapp, *Hector*, 20, 54–58.
120. GTrojk 14943–80, 15064–71, 15659–80, 16273–482.
121. Steinhoff, VL, 3:200.
122. *Historia de preliis*, 129,1–135,25; UAlexr 173–1730.
123. *Excidium Troiae*, 1,1–6,26.
124. *Excidium Troiae*, 10,21–11,9.
125. Statius, *Achilleis*, 1.38–41, 1.116–18, 1.149–57, 1.174–76. —On the sources available in the Middle Ages on the Trojan War: Brandt, *Konrad*, 174; Knapp, *Hector*, 14–18. —The differences between Statius and Konrad are so profound that it is hard to know what Knapp has in mind when he says that, in recounting Achilles's upbringing, Konrad "basically follows Statius" (*Hector*, 54: Im wesentlichen folgt er dabei Statius).

von Würzburg's Paris and Achilles, and the Paris of the *Göttweiger Trojaner-krieg* all stay put or move about according to the will of others and begin their knightly careers only when someone else decides that it is time for them to do so. This diminution of knightly spirit reflects a change in the kinds of sources used. In general, knightly children derived from French courtly traditions display noticeably more eagerness to come of age than those whose childhoods derive from Germanic or Latin ones, even in the first half of the century: Siegfried, Herzog Ernst B, Rudolf von Ems's Alexander, Wolfdietrich A, the Hagen of *Kudrun* exhibit less enterprise than heroes with French antecedents. After 1250 the MHG childhood of the knight is derived exclusively from Latin and Germanic sources and thus reflects the more docile knightly children usually found there.

At the same time knights become more docile, lovers remain vigorous and plentiful. But they age: the very young lovers (child lovers) who were so popular in the first half of the century are succeeded by slightly more mature lovers (young lovers) in the second. Although they are not yet adults, they are no longer so young that any special mention is made of their childishness. Konrad von Würzburg's *Partonopier und Meliur* (1277), a relatively faithful paraphrase of the French *Partonopeu de Blois*,[126] tells not only the story of the eponymous lovers but also that of Anshelm and Igla. *Mai und Beaflor* (1270–80) claims to be based on a prose chronicle,[127] but this is unknown to modern scholarship. In other cases, writers took advantage of the creative autonomy they had enjoyed since the beginning of the century to compose their own narratives, often drawing on a number of traditions. Der Pleier put together *Tandareis und Flordibel* and *Meleranz* (1240–70) by combining structures of Greek romance or French lais with elements taken from previous MHG narratives.[128] The writer of *Reinfried von Braunschweig* (after 1291) drew freely on a wide range of German and Latin sources to create the story of Yrkane and her love for Reinfried.[129] In two different texts Konrad von Würzburg makes courtly young lovers out of those who, in other versions of these tales, display little of this refined emotion. He mentions a Latin source for *Engelhard*[130] (1255–60)[131]—apparently a version of the popular legend of Amicus and Amelius[132]—but

126. Brandt, *Konrad*, 156.
127. MaiBfl 3,3–24.
128. Kern, *Pleier*, 216–63, 278–311.
129. Ohlenroth, "Reinfried," 68.
130. Englhd 208–16, 6492–95.
131. Brandt, *Konrad*, 68–69; Brunner, "Phantasien," 275.
132. Oettli, "Quellengeschichte," 6–7.

whereas other versions emphasize the devotion of the two male friends, Konrad elaborates the love between one of the youths and Engeltrud.[133] Similarly, in writing the *Trojanerkrieg* (1280–87), Konrad transforms the story of Achilles and Deidameia he found in Statius's *Achilleis*—a tale of disguise, passion, and rape[134]—into a narrative of young love of nearly 4000 lines.[135]

Even though these writers allowed themselves great freedom to mix and match, their narratives all end up sharing one distinctive structural trait: they either skip the birth and early childhood of their protagonists (except Beaflor; for Meleranz these years are dispatched in twenty lines) or they separate the early years from the years of young love by 7000 lines of other material (Achilles). Having detached early childhood, they begin when the heroes leave home (Meleranz, Engelhard, Partonopier, Achilles) or when the lovers first encounter one another (Tandareis, Flordibel, Engeltrud, Mai, Meliur, Anshelm, Igla, Deidameia, Yrkane). In other words, these narratives of young love run counter to the tendency, so pronounced in the first half of the century, to write complete childhood narratives. By suppressing early childhood and beginning with a love that is not specially marked as childish, the narrative of young love functions more like the first part of a story of adult love and adventure than like a traditional childhood narrative.

In addition to the longer narratives, there are also a number of short texts, *Mären*, about lovers: three versions of the *Schüler zu Paris* (*A*: thirteenth century; *B* and *C*: ca. 1300), which end tragically, and two versions of the *Studentenabenteuer* (*A*: mid-thirteenth century; *B* by Rüdeger von Munre: ca. 1300), which emphasize their heroes' cleverness. These texts introduce two new kinds of child protagonist to MHG narrative: the stu-

133. Könneker, "Erzähltypus," 245–46; Oettli, "Quellengeschichte," 2–3.

134. Statius, *Achilleis*, 1:252–396, 560–674.

135. KTrojk 13402–17321. —The thirteen-year-old Partonopier is "a child in years" (PartMl 558: ein kint der jâre) when the story begins and is later called a child in two specific circumstances for very specific ends: the king of France invokes the weakness of children in an effort to dissuade him from fighting (PartMl 4872); Irakel refers to the foolishness of children to excuse him for having looked at Meliur (PartMl 8908, 8928, 11467). Otherwise Partonopier is not called a child after his love affair with Meliur gets underway, and his love is not thematized as child love. —*Engelhard* shares distinctive motives with both *Willehalm von Orlens* and *Tandareis*. Willehalm and Engelhard are near death before their beloved finally promises her love on the condition that the hero first be knighted and display his knightly prowess (WilOrl 5139–200; Englhd 2327–79). Tandareis and Engelhard reveal their love when, distracted by the presence of their beloved, they accidentally cut themselves while slicing bread (TandFl 1042–1217; Englhd 1966–2076). On the relation between *Willehalm* and *Tandareis*: Cormeau, "Tandareis," 32–36. —On the love of Achilles and Deidameia: Cormeau, "Quellenkompendium," 312–14.

dent and the city maiden. The appearance of students in fiction, among the most popular figures in short narrative texts,[136] is doubtless related to the increasing likelihood of encountering students in everyday life.[137] The appearance of city children too must be related to historical developments, in this case the increasing importance of cities as sites of literary production. It is all the more remarkable then that, as children, these new figures fall into the same category as the resolutely courtly Tandareis, Flordibel, and Meleranz: they are lovers who are no longer very young children.

Two texts seem to resist the fashion and keep alive the earlier interest in child love: Albrecht's *Jüngerer Titurel* (1260–73 for the relevant parts), which tells of the child lovers Sigune and Tschinotulander, and *Aristoteles und Phyllis [S]* (ca. 1287), which recounts the love of the schoolboy Alexander. Yet these texts are not quite so devoted to the older tradition as it might seem. In *Jüngerer Titurel* child love occurs only in those strophes that Albrecht took from Wolfram's *Titurel*. When he invented a childhood narrative on his own, for Titurel, the young hero prefers the love of God to earthly love and is explicitly said to have remained chaste for many years in spite of the interest women showed in him.[138] In *Aristoteles und Phyllis [S]*, although Alexander is called *kint* when he is sent to school,[139] as soon as he falls in love he becomes a *jungelinc* and "the young lord."[140] When the same story was told in the first half of the century Alexander is still called *kint* at the end of the story.[141] Thus even though *Jüngerer Titurel* and *Aristoteles und Phyllis [S]* bring stories of child love from the first half of the century into the second, at the same time each betrays the diminished interest in child love one finds after 1250.[142]

Although writers of the second half of the thirteenth century are particularly interested in stories of young love, they do continue to compose tales of erotic naiveté. The *Häslein* (ca. 1300) is very close in plot to the earlier *Sperber*, although the heroine has been changed from a young nun to a village maiden. In the *Gänslein* and in Zwingäuer's *Des Mönches Not* (both 1250–1300) a young monk plays the role of innocent. Tales of erotic naiveté,

136. Fischer, *Märendichtung*, 121–22; Stehmann, *Studentenabenteuer*, 118–20.
137. Schirmer, *Motivuntersuchungen*, 126.
138. JngTit 197,1–4, 252,1–258,4.
139. ArPhlS 39, 47, 54, 65, 76.
140. ArPhlS 109: dem jungelinge; 101, 172: der junge herre.
141. ArPhlB 2.47.
142. On the changes Albrecht has made in the figure of young Schionatulander: Ebenbauer, "Tschionatulander," 379, 387–88. —On the many small changes that Albrecht makes in the strophes he adopts from Wolfram: Ragotzky, *Wolfram-Rezeption*, 124–26; Schröder, *Wolfram-Nachfolge*, 77–79.

which appear at the beginning of the thirteenth century with *Sperber* or *Dulciflorie* and disappear at the end with *Häslein*, change in meaning with the change in literary context. In the first half of the century they are the humorous and exploitative pendant to the stories of child love. Childish ignorance plays a role in both, but it is turned into a joke in the former and sentimentalized in the latter. This ignorance is possible both at court (*Dulciflorie*) or in a monastery (*Sperber*). In the second half of the century the stories of child love have matured into stories of young lovers. Now the crucial issue is first love: it is managed competently in the romances of young love and foolishly in the tales of erotic naiveté. Since all the young people at court have become proficient young lovers, erotic naiveté has been banished to the village and the monastery. As the century progresses the single issue that calls forth different responses changes from ignorance of love (which can be sentimentalized or laughed at) to first love (which can be managed well or foolishly). The tales of erotic naiveté have become the foolish, noncourtly pendant to the courtly tales of young love.[143]

If one compares the kinds of secular childhood narrative written between 1150 and 1200 with those written a century later, between 1250 and 1300, one notices that an important shift has taken place. In the first half century the principal stories of secular youths are taken from French sources: they all tell of future knights who are carefully educated, know nothing of love, and are eager to come of age. In the same period, the childhood narratives for secular maidens, whether they depend on French or German sources, are also of a single type: the maidens enter the narrative only just in time to get married. Between 1150 and 1200 the world of secular childhood is quite simple: there are only two genres, that of the knight and that of the bride; gender distinctions are clear, so that youths become knights and maidens become brides; and children remain chaste, since neither youths nor maidens know anything of love until just before marriage. The only exceptions to these rules are the child lovers of the

143. On dating of *Des Mönches Not*: Fischer, *Märendichtung*, 205. —There is some disagreement over whether *Sperber* is actually the direct source for *Häslein*: Janota (VL, 3:544–55) and Niewöhner (1VL, 3:544–55) deny direct dependence, Frosch-Freiburg (*Schwankmären*, 34–42) assumes it. —As is often the case in texts concerning religious, it is not altogether clear that the young monks should be considered children. Both are called *jungelinc* and one is called *kint* even at the end of the story, although mostly they are called "monk" (Gänsl 30; MönNot 31, 534). Given the ambiguity I have decided to include them, especially since they so clearly belong with the stories about maidens. —In spite of these similarities, however, Frosch-Freiburg (*Schwankmären*, 23 n. 3) is surely right to challenge Niewöhner's assertion (*Sperber*, 67–68) that *Gänslein* is little more than *Sperber* with the sex of the main characters switched. Except that they both concern the sexual innocence of young religious, the two stories have hardly a thing in common.

Trierer Floyris, who, although isolated in the twelfth century, are harbingers of things to come.

The chaste youths of French ancestry and the chaste maidens of French and German ancestry who dominate the scene during the second half of the twelfth century continue to play an important role in the first half of the thirteenth, but not after that: their illustrious line dies out in midcentury with *Blanschandin* and *Kudrun*. In any case, they had had serious competition since shortly after 1200 from the descendants of the *Trierer Floyris*. These child lovers, based for the most part on French models, establish themselves both in the traditional long form of romance and in the new, shorter *Märe*, where the only children to be found are those involved in erotic adventures. As might have been predicted, the arrival of eros throws everything into turmoil, and the first half of the thirteenth century, in many ways the golden age of the MHG secular childhood narrative, is at the same time the period in which the genre system is most confused.

By 1250, however, things have sorted themselves out and a somewhat different system of secular childhood narratives begins to emerge. The only secular youths of the old type, chaste young knights, are those whose stories depend on German and classical Latin traditions. All the other secular children—that is, all maidens, and all youths in texts from the tradition of French courtly romance, in *Mären*, and in some texts based on Latin sources—represent a new type, the young lover. The young lovers are the slightly older brothers and sisters of the child lovers who had so upset things in the first half of the century. These slightly older lovers, however, are able to find a place in the new, more stable system of childhood genres that dominates the second half of the thirteenth century. There are, once again, only two principal groups: the first comprises the chaste young knights who grow up knowing nothing of love; the second comprises both youths and maidens who fall in love before coming of age.

Eros has rearranged not only genre but also gender. In the second half of the twelfth century the two genres of childhood reinforce a strict correspondence of sex and gender: there is a childhood for males, according to which youths become knights, and a childhood for females, according to which maidens become wives. In the second half of the thirteenth century, however, genre differences do not correspond so neatly to sex and gender distinctions: there is the familiar childhood of the knight, which includes only youths who know nothing of love, and there is the childhood of the young lover, which includes enamored youths and enamored maidens. The distinction is no longer between males (knights) and females (brides) but between nonlovers (males) and lovers (males and females). Among lovers the difference between male and female is less pronounced than it is between future knights and brides: the stories of lovers are more likely to begin at the same age, and education, once the distinctive prerogative of secular youths, plays a very minor role. Thus the system of genres has been rearranged so that differences of sex no longer correspond to differences of role and so that, among lovers, gender differences have been reduced.

Love also affects the relation of childhood and adulthood. In the second half of the twelfth century youths are distinguished from adults by their ignorance of love. This ceases to be the case in the first half of the thirteenth century, when a significant group of MHG children are overcome by desire: on the one hand this makes them more like adults, since love is an adult emotion; on the other, they show themselves to be children by the childish ways they handle their amorous feelings. By the second half of the century, however, the lovers have grown up somewhat: they are now older and better able to manage their love affairs. In other words, they have become more like adults. This approximation of childhood and adulthood gives rise to a group of romances in which a single love story dominates the entire narrative and in which the fact that the hero is a child for the first part and an adult knight for the second is of secondary importance. Love has reduced the distinction between childhood and adulthood. Thus a shift in the genres of childhood, from young knights and brides to young knights and lovers, not only undermines the categories of gender but destabilizes the category of childhood itself.

In the second half of the thirteenth century, and especially toward its end, one finds negative portrayals of children in secular texts for the first and only time in the entire history of MHG narrative. The most famous of these is certainly the protagonist of Wernher der Gartenære's *Helmbrecht* (1240–1300, perhaps around 1280).[144] But he is not alone. The narrator of *Reinfried von Braunschweig* laments that nowadays "there is no child so small that he does not want to squander his time in mockery, abuse, cursing, swearing, insults, games, gluttony, and all sorts of loose living."[145] This opinion is shared by the writers of didactic texts. Konrad von Haslau's *Jüngling* (1275–90) begins with the observation that "young people nowadays are lax in discipline,"[146] concludes with a description of spoiled children,[147] and ends each section with the same refrain: the youngster who fulfills Konrad's dire

144. Heinzle, *Geschichte*, 78; Ruh, in Helmbr, xvi–xvii; Schindele, "Helmbrecht," 139.
145. RnfrBr 12670–74: ez ist kein kint sô kleine, ez welle sîne zît verzern in luoder schelten fluochen swern, spot spil und frezzenîe und aller luoderîe.
146. Jünglg 4: nu sint die jungen an zuhten laz.
147. Jünglg 1097–228.

predictions should pay him a penny, or sometimes more. Konrad's dyspep-
tic tone is taken up and elaborated at much greater length by Hugo von
Trimberg in his *Renner* (completed 1300), which resounds for over 24,000
lines with laments for the decline of virtue and courtesy among the young.
At the beginning of the century the father in *Winsbecke* presents his son
with a series of positive virtues to which he should aspire. Near the end
of the century Konrad and Hugo present young people with a series of
mistakes they are likely to make—if they have not already done so. Konrad
and Hugo expect less.

By the end of the thirteenth century the attitude toward secular children in MHG narrative seems to have been touched by a subtle but notable
change. As in the first half of the century, there are still stories of young
knights and of young lovers in considerable number, but something of the
earlier enthusiasm has been lost, both on the part of the youthful protagonists and on the part of those who write their stories. The young knights
no longer insist on setting off on their own, eager to prove their heroic
prowess; instead they wait at home or go where they are told until someone else decides it's time to knight them. They have become docile. The
young lovers are no longer seized by love in the cradle but much later;
often their early childhood is ignored altogether. They have become young
adults. The children in didactic texts are no longer presented with a set of
positive virtues to which they are encouraged to aspire but with a collection of mistakes that they are assumed to have already made. They are given
a negative model. Finally there is young Helmbrecht, the only protagonist
of a secular text to disdain the good advice of his father and take up a life
of crime.

On the one hand, the children seem less admirable: the knights are
passive and Helmbrecht is a criminal. On the other hand, the writers seem
less enthusiastic about childhood: they ignore the early years of the lovers
and they teach virtue by a negative model. This is only a matter of degree:
there are still a large number of secular childhood narratives produced and
nearly all the children represented are paragons. Yet, comparing these texts
with those from the first half of the century, one cannot help but notice a
slight dissolution of the earlier optimism, an incipient disillusion with children. Apparently the pessimistic tone that colors much MHG writing in
the thirteenth century[148] did not leave the world of childhood unaffected.

As noted above, writing about young saints declined appreciably dur-

148. Kuhn, "Aspekt" [*Minnesangs Wende*], 176–79, 192.

ing the first part of the thirteenth century. It is not until the second half of the century, especially the last third, that saints' legends with childhood narratives begin to appear again in substantial numbers. This is a consequence not of any particular interest in childhood itself but of the accelerating production of saints' lives in general: since the Latin sources for these German legends sometimes included childhood narratives, so did the vernacular versions.

Of course, individual legends continued to be written. The ever popular Margaret is represented by Hartwig von dem Hage's *Margaretenlegende* (late thirteenth century), *Die Marter der heiligen Margareta*, in which Margaret's status as child receives uncommon emphasis,[149] and perhaps by *Sante Margareten Marter*.[150] The equally popular Alexis appears in four texts: *Alexius F* (1250–1300), Konrad von Würzburg's *Alexius* (1260–75), *Alexius B* (end of the century), and *Alexius A* (ca. 1300). Of these, two are particularly interesting: *Alexius F*, which expands the childhood narrative considerably to include substantial passages on hereditary traits, education, and the obligations of children and parents;[151] and *Alexius A*, one of the very few MHG narratives for which there is good evidence that it was written by a woman, which projects back into Christian Rome the medieval practice of sending youths away to other courts to be educated in knighthood. In addition to *Alexius*, Konrad von Würzburg also wrote lives of *Silvester* (1260–74) and *Pantaleon* (1275–80),[152] neither of which has much of interest to say about its hero's childhood.[153]

Along with the renewed production of saintly childhood narratives came a renewed interest in lives of the Virgin, of which none had been written since Wernher's *Maria*, more than a century earlier. The first part of the *Grazer Marienleben* (after 1280), based, like Wernher's *Maria*, on the *Gospel of Pseudo-Matthew*, is unique among the MHG lives of the Virgin: it was originally an independent text devoted to Mary's childhood up to age thirteen, but ignoring her coming of age and marriage.[154] As

149. MhMarg 262, 460, 688.
150. The dating of the last two is problematical. The former has been placed in the twelfth century (Haupt in MhMarg, 152), after 1235 (de Boor, *Geschichte*, 3.1:533) and 1250–1300 (Williams-Krapp, VL, 5:1241), the latter in the twelfth (Bartsch, in StMarM, 459–65) and in the thirteenth or fourteenth centuries (Vogt, "Margaretalegenden," 264–65).
151. AlxusF 45–78, 92–136, 264–422.
152. de Boor, "Chronologie," 252–53.
153. On *Alexius A*: Jackson, *Legends*, 49–50; Wyss, *Legendenepik*, 231–33. —On Konrad's *Alexius*: Jackson, *Legends*, 105–8. —Wyss (*Legendenepik*, 254) claims that Konrad modelled his account of Silvester's childhood on schemes that he knew from courtly romance, although, as far as I can tell, there are more differences than similarities.
154. Masser, "Grazer Marienleben," 550–51.

an independent but partial childhood narrative it resembles Konrad von Fußesbrunnen's *Kindheit Jesu*. The single manuscript of the *Marienleben der Königsberger Hs. 905* (late thirteenth century), based on a ninth-century revision of Pseudo-Matthew,[155] has lost a gathering and, along with it, all of Mary's and much of Jesus' childhood. The *Marienleben* of Walther von Rheinau (before 1300),[156] although generally dismissed as an uninspired translation,[157] brings two important innovations. It is the first of a number of German works to be based on the *Vita beate virginis Marie et salvatoris rhythmica*, an influential compilation of apocryphal and legendary material written before or about 1250.[158] It is also the first MHG text to contain both a complete and continuous story of Mary's childhood, from conception to marriage (Wernher is discontinuous,[159] the *Grazer Marienleben* partial), and the story of Jesus' childhood, from conception to age twelve (Wernher has only infancy, the *Grazer Marienleben* nothing). This model, inherited from the *Vita rhythmica*, dominates the writing of MHG lives of the Virgin for the rest of the period under consideration.

The tendency to combine extensive biographies of several biblical figures that one encounters in the late-thirteenth-century lives of the Virgin and Jesus is evident as well in *Der Saelden Hort* (end of thirteenth century).[160] It tells the lives of Jesus, John the Baptist, and Mary Magdalene, each of whom gets a childhood narrative.

The most important innovation in MHG hagiography occurs not in the independent saint's life but in the appearance of the vernacular legendary. Earlier in the thirteenth century an older form of Latin legendary, which united a disparate assortment of previously composed saints' lives in their original form, was superseded by a new form, in which the lives were edited and abbreviated to create a collection of relatively brief legends in a uniform style arranged according to the church calendar. By far the most influential (although not by any means the only one) of these *novae legendae* was the *Legenda aurea* (*Golden Legend*), composed in the 1260s by Jacob of Voragine, which survives in over one thousand manuscripts and was an important source for nearly all the later German legendaries.[161]

155. Hinderer, in MarlKg, 108; Masser, *Bibel, Apokryphen*, 113.
156. Masser, *Bibel- und Legendenepik*, 106.
157. Päpke, *Marienleben*, 43–44; Masser, *Bibel- und Legendenepik*, 106; Masser, "Marien- und Leben-Jesu-Dichtung," 147.
158. Masser, *Bibel, Apokryphen*, 47.
159. Masser, *Bibel- und Legendenepik*, 93.
160. Bumke, *Geschichte*, 390.
161. Steer, "Geistliche Prosa," 307–8; Williams-Krapp, *Legendare*, 12.

The *Väterbuch* (1265–80),[162] devoted to the lives of various Church fathers, hermits, and penitents, combines old and new techniques. Although many of the lives skip childhood, the most prominent—those that are longer, those that begin and end the collection—do include childhood narratives. For the lengthy first *vita*, that of Anthony, which is clearly intended to provide an impressive opening for the collection, a childhood was compiled from various parts of the *Vitae patrum*,[163] an ancient collection, attributed to Jerome, that is the principal source for the *Väterbuch*. The comparatively lengthy legends with which the *Väterbuch* concludes also contain substantial childhood narratives, adapted and elaborated from various sources: those of Euphrosyne and Abraham of Kidunaia from the *Vitae patrum*,[164] that of Alexis from the *Legenda aurea*,[165] those of Zosimus and Mary of Egypt from a Latin life of Mary by Hildebert of Lavardin, who is responsible for adding childhood narratives for both figures to the accounts he found in his own source.[166]

The *Passional* (before 1300), compiled by the writer of the *Väterbuch* according to the new style, comprises three parts: the first tells the life of Mary, including her childhood, those of Jesus and Pilate, and a number of miracles; the second contains lives of other New Testament figures; the third and longest part is a collection of nearly 75 saints' lives, of which about 20 percent begin with childhood. The principal source for the *Passional* was clearly the *Legenda aurea*, although the German writer felt free to rearrange the material he found there and to incorporate material from other texts. He does not seem to have included childhood narratives unless he found them in his sources, but he did elaborate his material in adapting it, and this elaboration affects the childhood narratives as much as anything else: the section of the childhood of Jesus based on Konrad's *Kindheit Jesu* is expanded by about one third.[167] For the most part he did not invent new incidents but merely provided reasons and details, often inventing direct speech where it was merely summarized in the *Legenda aurea*.[168] The childhood of Judas is expanded by the information that his parents, in abandoning him to the waves, were following the example of Moses: thus

162. Helm and Ziesemer, *Literatur des Ritterordens*, 52; Steer, "Geistliche Prosa," 315.
163. Haupt, *Buch der Väter*, 78; Helm and Ziesemer, *Literatur des Ritterordens*, 58; Hohmann, *Väterbuch*, 25.
164. Haupt, *Buch der Väter*, 88; Hohmann, *Väterbuch*, 35–47.
165. Hohmann, *Väterbuch*, 35, 36.
166. Kunze, *Maria Aegyptiaca*, 56–58, 69–71.
167. Masser, *Bibel, Apokryphen*, 100.
168. Tiedemann, *Passional*, 95, 117.

the model is named.[169] In telling the incident in which Judas murders his royal foster brother, the narrator adds a discussion of the inevitable superiority of noble birth: here the general principle is given that explains the action.[170] The childhood narratives of clerical saints are all expanded so that their piety leads them to excel at the study of Scripture in school, which in turn causes them to resolve to lead a chaste and godly life.[171]

A still unpublished collection of short Latin legends from before the twelfth century is the principal source for the *Buch der Märtyrer*[172] (before 1300, perhaps as early as 1250–75),[173] the least impressive of the three late-thirteenth-century verse legendaries. Its verse is comparatively crude and its plots relatively simple. Except for saints like Agnes and Vitus, whose entire legends take place before they come of age, childhood receives scant attention: that of Mary of Egypt is dispatched in eight lines, that of Jerome in twelve.[174]

The *Jenaer Martyrologium* (end of the thirteenth century) is an historical martyrology, that is, a list of saints whose feasts fall on each day of the year. Occasionally, however, bits of biographical information are attached in sufficient quantity to the names listed to make up a brief *prose* saint's life.[175] Because the basic list is so extensive, the *Jenaer Martyrologium* includes many saints whose lives had not previously appeared in German, some of which mention childhood—Albinus, Theodosia, Felicula, Secunda, Agapitus, Thecla, Hilarion, Romanus, Eulalia.[176] A few stories contain details of interest: foundlings who speak miraculously to reveal their true paternity;[177] an attempted abortion;[178] a child bishop.[179] The legend of the virgin martyr Barbara, appearing for the first time in German, is told at considerable length—almost forty lines.[180]

Although the *Jüdel* had appeared before 1225, it is only towards the end of the century that miracles of the Virgin concerning children appear

169. Passnl H313,51–66.
170. Passnl H314,57–315,6.
171. Passnl K7,26–64, K192,26–49, K241,78–87, K354,76–97, K396,36–52, K505,10–63. —On the childhood of Jesus: Masser, *Bibel, Apokryphen*, 98–105. On Pilate: Schöndorf, review of Tischendorf, 196. On Elizabeth of Hungary: Oessenich, "Elisabethlegende," 185. On Alexis: Jackson, *Legends*, 50. On Mary of Egypt: Kunze, *Maria Aegyptiaca*, 83–84.
172. Kunze, "Hauptquelle," 46.
173. Knapp, "Bruchstücke," 439; Kunze, VL, 1:1094.
174. BMärtr 5209–16, 21065–76.
175. Williams-Krapp, *Legendare*, 22.
176. JnaMrt 15, 22, 38, 51, 56, 65, 72–73, 82, 90.
177. JnaMrt 44, 80.
178. JnaMrt 52.
179. JnaMrt 80.
180. JnaMrt 89.

in any number. Three of them are part of the *Passional*: *Ein Scholar, Marias Bräutigam, Der Scholar und das Marienbild*, and the *Judenknabe*, which is based principally on the *Jüdel*.[181] Two others occur as independent texts: the *Armer Schüler* of Heinrich der Klausner and *Thomas von Kandelberg* (both end of the century).[182] The heroes of these stories (like the Jüdel) represent a kind of child not previously seen in MHG religious narratives. They are not future saints and prophets—or even future rulers, like Eraclius and Josaphat—but schoolboys or students of whose adult life we learn scarcely a thing. They do not come from rich and powerful families but, with the possible exception of the Scholar, Marias Bräutigam, from poor or marginalized backgrounds. Their stories are not set in the heroic age of the early Christians but in contemporaneous medieval settings. Their piety does not manifest itself in the steadfast defense of their chastity or their faith in the face of torture and other hardships but in their profound devotion to the Virgin. The sympathy that the Virgin shows in return for their foolishness and helplessness suggests that the sentimental attitude toward children evident in secular narrative in the first half of the century is not entirely without a parallel in religious texts.

More remarkable are two other, longer texts from this period: Bruder Hermann's *Leben der Gräfin Iolande von Vianden* (after 1283) and the anonymous *Leben der heiligen Elisabeth* (1300 or shortly thereafter). Although Iolande is said to suffer more than St. Agnes and Elizabeth more than St. Margaret,[183] they in fact have little in common with such venerable saints. They are not ancient martyrs but recent historical figures, and the texts in which they appear are the first vernacular biographies of such figures. They do not perform dramatic miracles or suffer cruel martyrdom but display their piety in an intense but nevertheless more human form: Iolande struggles to enter the convent of her choice, Elizabeth to realize her pious ideal in the context of a secular court. They seem to represent the shift noted by students of hagiography from a generally earlier form of sanctity, "the result of contemplation of the infinite mystery of a totally 'other' and nearly inaccessible God," toward a generally later form, based on "an imitation of Christ . . . in whose footsteps one must follow to attain eventual eternal bliss."[184] Indeed, the mere fact that the childhood of the future saint, Elizabeth, so closely resembles that of the future prioress, Iolande,

181. Rosenfeld, VL, 4:892.
182. Richert, VL, 3:758; Rosenfeld, ıVL, 4:454.
183. Ioland 4254–63; StElis 1001–7.
184. Vauchez, "Saint," 324. —See also Goodich, *Vita perfecta*, 207; Vauchez, *Sainteté*, 619–20.

indicates the extent to which models of piety have become less awesome and more human. Perhaps it is this same humanizing tendency that causes Jans Enikel, when he recounts the sacrifice of Isaac or the abandonment of Moses in his *Weltchronik* (1277–1290), to elaborate the parents' love and grief to an extent not found in any other MHG version.[185]

The same religious ferment that led to the greatly accelerated production of saints' lives led also to the flourishing of the vernacular sermon. However, the sermons of the second half of the thirteenth century contain very few childhood narratives. Berthold von Regensburg (active 1240–72), one of the great preachers of the German Middle Ages, has many things to say *about* children—on their baptism, education, discipline, feeding, and the like[186]—but he does not relate childhood narratives, partly, perhaps, because he does not write German sermons for saints' feast days, where such narratives usually occur. The more disparate collection that goes under the name of the St. Georgener Prediger (before 1300)[187] is no more interested in childhood narratives than Berthold. Thus a sermon for the feast of the birth of the Virgin ignores the opportunity to tell the story of her birth in favor of an explication of Esther 8.16. Another collection, attributed to the Schwarzwälder Prediger (around 1280), does write sermons for saints' feasts but only one of them, for the feast of Alexis, begins with a childhood narrative: it is taken from the *Legenda aurea* and is dispatched in four sentences.[188]

In spite of the virtual disappearance of children from sermons towards the end of the thirteenth century, the period is clearly one in which the number and variety of religious childhood narratives grew in a way it had not since the last third of the twelfth century. Two developments deserve note, each of which parallels more general trends in religious life. First is the impulse to collect, systematize, and regularize saints' lives, which parallels the increasing institutionalization of the church. This impulse is seen in the vast legendaries, especially the *novae legendae*, which present lives of similar proportions, but also in texts that combine the lives of several saints like Walther's *Marienleben* or *Der Saelden Hort*. Second, some religious childhood narratives exhibit a less awesome, more human dimension, which parallels the increased importance of lay religious devotion in the period. One sees this in stories about poor but pious scholars and in the

185. JWeltc 3733–4044, 6281–40.
186. BertvR 1:31–36, 2:57–59.
187. Heinzle, *Geschichte*, 216; Steer, "Geistliche Prosa," 327.
188. SwrzPr F96,29–41.

lives of historical women like Iolande and Elizabeth. Unlike the interest in secular children at the beginning of the century, however, the flourishing of religious childhood narratives at the end does not indicate a particular interest in children as such. There does not seem to be any great impulse to add or expand childhood narratives. Where a given saint's childhood appears in the Latin source, then it will appear in the German adaptation; it may be expanded (*Passional*), but only as part of the general elaboration of the source.

1300–1350: Perfunctory Childhood

To a certain extent the first half of the fourteenth century resembles the second half of the thirteenth. Secular children continue to appear in only two types, knights and lovers, and religious texts maintain their hegemony. And yet there are two striking changes. The first is quantitative: the number of secular childhood narratives written in the fifty years after 1300 is half that written in the fifty years before. The second is qualitative: of this radically reduced number, most are derivative, cursory, fragmentary, or partial.

The most coherent and vigorous group of secular childhood narratives are those of the lovers. Child lovers, who had practically vanished from sight in the second half of the thirteenth century, return for a final appearance early in the fourteenth. Johann von Würzburg's *Wilhelm von Österreich* (1314),[189] which draws on elements from many previous romances,[190] comes closest of all the fourteenth-century secular texts to maintaining the earlier pattern: like *Willehalm von Orlens* it tells the story of the hero from birth, the heroine from an early age, and traces their love from childhood through separation to reunion over the course of a long romance. Johann does vary the pattern, however: education receives little attention, perhaps because Wilhelm is "wise by nature,"[191] and childhood lacks the usual closure, since Wilhelm's perfunctory knighting comes after a long series of adventures. Johann also introduces new elements: the protagonists exchange many love letters, and, not long after they are united, they both die tragic deaths. The *Märe Pyramus und Thisbe* (1300–50), unlike its indirect source, Ovid's *Metamorphoses*, turns its protagonists into child lovers and sets their tale, as in *Wilhelm von Österreich*, at court. Like *Wilhelm* and the nearly con-

189. WilÖst 19574–81.
190. Glier, VL, 4:826; Mayser, *Studien*, 17, 28–31, 94.
191. WilÖst 632: von natur wis.

temporaneous *Schüler zu Paris A* and *B* considered above, it thematizes the deleterious effects of surveillance and ends tragically.[192]

Older lovers have better luck when they too make their final appearance shortly after 1300. They figure in two *Mären* that concern students and take place in cities. In *Frauenlist* a poor but clever student gains the love of a rich married woman with artful speeches. In the *Bussard* the student, son of the king of England, and his Parisian girlfriend, daughter of the king of France, elope, then suffer separation and madness before they are reunited and married. The only tale of young love not to take place in a city, *Nachtigall A*, may have been written later in the century.

While the stories of lovers continue old traditions, those of the knights and maidens present a sorrier picture. The second part of the prose *Lancelot*, translated from French (ca. 1300), includes the disjunct account of Galaad's childhood and the story Parceval's knighting. *Wolfdietrich D* (ca. 1300) [193] contains yet another version (fragmentary) of Wolfdietrich's childhood, this time with a slightly more courtly education.[194] The *Rappoltsteiner Parzifal* (1331–36), which incorporates Wolfram's *Parzival* in a narrative two-and-a-half times as long, makes a few changes in the original—bowdlerizing the scene in which Parzival is born and introducing some foolishness to his instruction by Gurnemanz [195]—and adds the strange story of Gawan's son, who makes a dramatic appearance at age five to stop a fight between his father and his uncle, is abducted we never learn where or by whom, and reappears after he is already a knight.[196] Seifrit's *Alexander* (1352) is, like the prose *Lancelot*, essentially a literal translation, in this case of the *Historia de preliis*.[197] The most rough-and-tumble MHG Alexander narrative, it shows little interest in idealizing its hero.[198] Like Johann, Seifrit wastes hardly a word on his hero's education: while Lambrecht devoted about 100 lines to

---

192. On the love letters in *Wilhelm*: Brackert, "Minnebriefe," 14–15. —Mayser (*Studien*, 32) claims that Gottfried's *Tristan* was the model for Wilhelm's education, but this seems unlikely. The two texts do share a number of features—the heroes both master reading and courtly skills—but this can be said of almost any MHG prince who receives a court education. More striking are the differences: Tristan is taught knightly skills, which are ignored in the case of Wilhelm, and Wilhelm knows university subjects, which are not mentioned in connection with Tristan. —On the relation of *Pyramus* to Ovid and to its MHG context: Hart, *Pyramus*, 37–38; Schirmer, VL, 7:930; Ziegeler, *Erzählen*, 274–75.
193. Wisniewski, *Dietrichdichtung*, 153.
194. WolfdD 3.2,1–5,4.
195. RpParz XLVII, XLVIII.
196. RpParz 215,25–225,15, 251,7–252,39, 275,26–276,34.
197. SAlexr 9027–28; Buntz, *Alexanderdichtung*, 31.
198. Hübner, *Alexander*, 45.

the subject, Rudolf von Ems about 500, and Ulrich von Etzenbach about 400, it is dispatched by Seifrit in 17.[199]

The early fourteenth century also contains an unusually large number of unorthodox stories of maidens. The prose *Lancelot* tells of the maiden of Challot, who falls in love with Lancelot, then dies when he does not return her love. Heinrich von Neustadt's *Apollonius von Tyrland* (1305–15) takes from its Latin source the story of Tarsia. It is the only detailed account of the life of a secular maiden from birth to marriage in which love plays no role and the only such story in which the protagonist, like many males, is ignorant of her true identity, suffers radical dislocation (abandonment, abduction, attempted murder, slavery), and survives by her wits. *Friedrich von Schwaben* (after 1314, but perhaps much later)[200] tells the story of Angelburg, whose stepmother has transformed her first into a deer by day, then into a dove before the curse is broken by Friedrich, who restores her to her ancestral lands and marries her. The text also tells of Ziproner, Friedrich's daughter by an interim wife, who leaves her mother to live with Friedrich and Angelburg. Ziproner plays an important role in the story, but not according to any of the usual schemes. Finally one should mention Ottokar von Steiermark's *Steirische Reimchronik* (1301–09), which reports over fifteen historical marriages, some at great length. Not one of the first-time brides is anything more than a silent pawn in the political strategies of her male relatives.

Of the texts mentioned above, almost all were written in the first two decades of the century, which means that by 1320 the secular childhood narrative has nearly vanished from MHG texts. And of the texts that were written, only the small group of young lovers preserves the traditions of secular childhood that had been nurtured for 150 years. The stories of young knights are fragmented, copied, or distorted. The stories of future brides do not fit into any of the familiar patterns. It seems that the disillusionment with secular childhood that one can detect at the end of the thirteenth century leads to the dissolution of secular childhood early in the fourteenth.

While the production of secular childhood narratives declines precipitately early in the fourteenth century, stories of saintly children continue to be written at a relatively constant rate until the end of the period under

199. SAlexr 599–615.
200. Ziegeler maintains *Friedrich* could have been written in the fifteenth century (Sappler, "Friedrich," 144 n. 6).

consideration. A few of those written in the years around 1300, *Das Leben der heiligen Elisabeth*, *Alexius A*, and *Der Saelden Hort*, were discussed above. The development of the religious childhood narrative after the turn of the century parallels that before: the lives of familiar saints are written again, lives of saints which have not previously been told in MHG are introduced, and new forms for the sacred childhood narrative are developed.

The childhood of the popular Alexis receives its most abbreviated treatment (35 lines) in *Alexius C* (early fourteenth century) and that of the equally popular Margaret receives another, rather unremarkable, treatment in the *Passienbüchlein von den vier Hauptjungfrauen* (1300–50). Quite remarkable, on the other hand, is the *Marienleben* of Bruder Philipp (1300–10). With over 100 known manuscripts and fragments as well as 22 manuscripts of a prose adaptation, it is the best transmitted, and therefore presumably among the best known, German verse text of the Middle Ages.[201] It owes this popularity to the strength of the cult of the Virgin and to its literary quality.[202] Philipp ignores almost half the material in his source, the *Vita rhythmica*, while adding material from the gospels as well as elaborations of his own invention, thereby transforming what was a rather incoherent collection of episodes and miracles into a coherent narrative enlivened with a host of engaging details, details that add particularly to the story of Jesus' childhood.[203]

Other saints appeared for the first time in MHG, or at least for the first time in independent texts, of which four begin with childhood narratives. A life of Katherine of Alexandria, *Katharinen Marter*, contains one of the more detailed accounts of her childhood, elaborating her mastery of school subjects and her dispersal of her parents' fortune.[204] Unfortunately, most of the childhood narrative is missing from a life of Euphrosyne, *Sand Eufrosin leben* (1300–50), from what is considered the most polished life of Dorothy, *Von sent Dorothea* (1300–50),[205] and from Nikolaus von Jeroschin's life of Adalbert, *Sent Adalbrechtes leben* (1327–31). The prose *Leben des heiligen Ludwig* of Friedrich Köditz (1310–23 or after 1331), noteworthy as the vernacular biography of a twelfth-century historical figure, Ludwig IV of

---

201. Gärtner, VL, 7:588; Masser, "Marien- und Leben-Jesu-Dichtung," 145.
202. Masser, *Bibel- und Legendenepik*, 108.
203. Gärtner, VL, 7:594; Gärtner, "Philipps 'Marienleben,'" 202–3; Masser, "Marien- und Leben-Jesu-Dichtung," 146; Masser, *Bibel- und Legendenepik*, 110; Päpke, *Marienleben*, 33–41.
204. StKatM 546–51.
205. Busse, in StDrth, 25–29; Williams-Krapp, VL, 2:213.

Thuringia, actually tells less about the childhood of its ostensible subject than about that of his wife, Elizabeth of Hungary.

The major innovation in MHG sacred narrative in the first half of the fourteenth century is the appearance of prose legendaries. The first of these may be a still unedited collection of at least 26 lives written in the 1320s and intended for reading in a Dominican convent in Switzerland.[206] Twenty years later Hermann von Fritzlar wrote his *Heiligenleben* (1343–49), in which the legends are so short that only a few saints—Agnes, Aquinas, Vitus, Alexis, and Elizabeth—get childhood narratives at all, and even these are abbreviated. Much more important than either of these was the *Elsässische "Legenda aurea"* (around 1350), the first of several prose adaptations of the work of Jacob of Voragine. Among the many lives of saints who had not yet appeared in German are some that include childhood narratives: Erhard, Peter Martyr, Servatius, Kilian, Maximilian of Cilli, Ottilia. Although the German translator allowed himself certain liberties with his Latin source, he did not make substantial changes in the childhood narratives. The *Elsässische "Legenda aurea,"* one of the most impressive prose monuments of the fourteenth century, was the standard legendary in the German-speaking southwest for about 100 years.[207]

The *Elsässische "Legenda aurea"* contains not only childhood narratives of saints but also a Marian miracle concerning coming of age; it is an abbreviated version of *Ein Scholar, Marias Bräutigam*, which had appeared earlier in the *Passional*.[208] Another, much lengthier miracle story is told in Kunz Kistener's *Jakobsbrüder* (ca. 1350): the body of a twelve-year-old who dies on a pilgrimage to Compostella is carried there by his traveling companion and restored to life by St. James. The story, for which no source is known, is, like Konrad von Würzburg's *Engelhard*, clearly related to the widespread tale of the friends Amicus and Amelius.[209]

Although religious childhood narratives were written in substantial numbers in the first half of the fourteenth century, the most innovative sort of religious writing in this period, mystical writing, ignores children almost entirely. Whereas earlier preachers often tell brief childhood narratives of saints whose feasts are celebrated on a given day, the mystics will not stoop to mere storytelling. A sermon (1313–22)[210] of Meister Eck-

206. Probst, VL, 1:842–43; Steer, "Geistliche Prosa," 314.
207. Steer, "Geistliche Prosa," 312.
208. ELgAur 582,9–19.
209. Reiffenstein, VL, 4:1158–59.
210. The most likely dates for the German sermons (Langer, "Gottesgeburt," 136).

hart that takes as its text a few lines from Luke about the birth of John the Baptist abandons John immediately to treat more important kinds of childhood and birth: "the soul that wants to be God's child," and "God's greatest desire," which is "to give birth. He is never satisfied unless he gives birth to his son in us."[211] A sermon on the Nativity in the *Paradisus anime intelligentis* (early fourteenth century) moves at once from its text, Isaiah 9.6, to an exposition of the three births of Christ: "the first from the Father in divinity, the second from the Mother in humanity, the third from the Holy Spirit in the soul of the good man or woman."[212] Not even the birth of the Savior can tempt the mystical preacher to tell a story. Biographical texts are no more interested in childhood. Of the 148 lives of Dominican nuns recounted in the *Schwesternbücher* I have surveyed, there is only one that has anything to say about the childhood of its heroine before she enters the convent.[213] Once they are inside, "the appearance of Christ in the form of a child is probably the most frequent vision" they have.[214] Yet he is the only child around: of the seventeen mortals who enter between the ages of three and thirteen, there are only two whose behavior once they enter the convent is in any way related to their youth.[215] Ordinarily the *vitae* ignore life outside the convent entirely, while life within is represented as a series of good works and mystical experiences without any clear chronology. Margareta Ebner seems to express the general attitude of mystics to childhood when, writing of her own life, she refers to the period before her mystical experiences begin: "I cannot describe how I lived for the previous 20 years, because I did not take note of myself then."[216]

While the writers of religious texts in the first half of the fourteenth century do not abandon childhood as completely as the writers of secular texts, they too seem to find the subject less compelling than they previously did. The last religious text to display any imaginative investment in childhood, Philipp's *Marienleben*, was written in the first decade of the

211. EkrtPr 1:177,1–4: Diu sêle . . . diu gotes kint wil sîn. . . . Gotes hœhstiu meinunge ist gebern. Im engenüeget niemer, er engeber denne sînen sun in uns.
212. PrdsAI 19,22–24: die ersten von deme vadere an der gotheit, di anderen von der mudir an der mensheit, di dritten von deme heiligen geist in des gudin menschin sele.
213. EngSwb Alheit von Trochaw 10. I except the lives of Elsbeth Bechlin and Princess Elisabeth, which, according to Grubmüller ("Viten," 187–204), were not part of the original collection.
214. Ringler, *Viten- und Offenbarungsliteratur*, 187: Die Erscheinung Christi in der Gestalt eines Kindes ist die wohl häufigste Vision in den Nonnenviten.
215. EngSwb Irmlein 8; UlmSwb Elsbetlein 141.
216. MEbner 1,13–15: wie aber ich vor lebte wol zwainczig jar, daz kan ich niht geschriben, wan ich min selbs niht war nam. —On Eckhart's teaching concerning the birth of God in us: Langer, "Gottesgeburt," 138–41.

century, only a few years after the *Passional* and the lives of Iolande and Elizabeth. What follows is less than inspiring: a few hagiographical scraps and fragments, the shortest of all the MHG stories of Alexis's childhood, and the cursory accounts of Hermann von Fritzlar. To be sure, the *Elsäs-sische "Legenda aurea"* is a monumental achievement, but it betrays no special interest in childhood: its treatment of the subject is determined by the single Latin source of which it is a translation. In the types of writing where religious writers between 1300 and 1350 are truly innovative, mystical sermons and biographies, they betray not the slightest interest in childhood.

History, Sacred and Secular

Childhood has a history. This is true of the story of Jesus' childhood in the New Testament gospels, just as it is true of the hundreds of childhood narratives written in MHG. A history with as many elements as that of MHG childhood will comprise many different histories—that of the prophet, of the bride, of the Virgin or Alexander. Of these constituent histories, the two most important, those of the religious and the secular childhood narrative, have remarkably different trajectories. To conclude this chapter I would like to note briefly three ways in which these two histories differ: in coherence, in importance, and in independence.

The history of the religious childhood narrative is interrupted twice: by a brief pause in the middle of the twelfth century and a longer one that lasts for the first two thirds of the thirteenth. The composition of secular childhood narratives, on the other hand, is continuous: once such narratives begin to be written around 1150 they are produced in increasing numbers until 1200 and in substantial quantity until just after 1300. Within these 150 years a coherent development takes place. The clear distinctions between male and female and between child and adult that obtain before 1200 are complicated after that date by the arrival of love. After 1250 these distinctions are undermined further; at the same time a slight disillusion with childhood itself becomes evident. The disillusion spreads quickly and shortly after 1300 the secular childhood narrative disappears. This continuous and coherent history stands in marked contrast to the disjunct history of the religious childhood narrative.

Religious and secular childhood narratives differ as well in their relation to the larger traditions of religious and secular writing. The religious childhood narrative is belated. It first appears around 1100, fifty years after religious texts were first written in Middle High German. When it returns in glory in the last third of the thirteenth century it is again belated, the golden age of the secular childhood narrative having occurred in the first half of the century. Religious childhood is not only belated but also optional. It does not seem to have been required in religious narrative between 1200 and 1260. After 1300, although it maintains its position in saints' lives and in the legendaries, it disappears from sermons and never makes its way into mystical biography. Within secular narrative, on the other hand, childhood plays an important role from the start. Indeed, it inaugurates the courtly tradition, appearing at the beginning of the very first secular narrative, Lambrecht's *Alexanderlied*. From then on it remains a vital constituent until the secular tradition itself is restructured early in the fourteenth century with the decline of the extended courtly narrative. While childhood is a belated and optional feature of religious narrative, it is an integral part of MHG courtly narrative from the beginning to the end.

Finally, religious and secular childhood narratives differ in the degree of their dependence on other literary developments. The first religious childhood narratives depend on a tradition of salvation-historical narrative and disappear with that tradition. The second appearance of religious children depends on the general upsurge of vernacular writing. Even at its most vigorous, in the decades around 1300, the religious childhood narrative remains dependent on its sources: religious writers seldom add or subtract from what they find there, nor do they ever invent new childhood narratives from scratch. In the few cases where religious childhood narratives are expanded (*Passional*, Bruder Philipp) it is as part of a general elaboration that affects all parts of the text. Whatever innovations the religious childhood narratives manifest—new forms (legendaries, prose) and new models of piety (imitation rather than awe)—affect childhood only because it is carried along by larger developments in religious writing.

The secular childhood narrative shows more independence. Children succumb to love after 1200 and then age after 1250 quite independent of the general development of secular narrative. Secular writers display considerable freedom in the construction of childhood narratives, elaborating on their sources, combining sources, and making up numerous childhood narratives on their own. Most remarkably, secular childhood receives disproportionate attention in the first half of the thirteenth century: childhood narratives are extended or added where they are missing; childhood is sentimentalized and eroticized. While the religious childhood narrative remains dependent on its sources, the secular childhood narrative elaborates and invents on its own. While the religious childhood narrative remains dependent on the general development of religious and vernacular writing, the secular childhood narrative has a history of its own.

Where the history of the religious childhood narrative is disjunct, belated, and dependent, that of the secular childhood narrative is coherent, integral, and independent. To be sure, the history of the religious childhood narrative is longer: it begins fifty years before that of the secular narrative and is significantly more vigorous at the end of the period. Nevertheless, the religious childhood narrative remains an occasional and dependent part of the long tradition of religious writing, while the secular childhood narrative is an integral and comparatively independent part of the tradition of MHG secular writing. It flourishes between 1150 and 1300, precisely the same century and a half in which courtly culture itself flowers in Germany. Something of an afterthought in the religious tradition, childhood is integral to the self-understanding of secular courtly culture.

9. Obilot's Games: A Different Knowledge of Childhood

When the stately rhythm of *Buddenbrooks* finally brings us to the winter of 1865, Thomas Mann offers a brief chapter in which the disruptive energy of war is juxtaposed to the quiet games of the four-and-a-half-year-old Hanno Buddenbrook. These are games, we are told, "whose fascination and deep meaning grownups are no longer able to understand, games for which nothing more is needed than three pebbles or a piece of wood, possibly wearing a dandelion blossom as a helmet, games that require, more than anything else, the strong, pure, ardent, chaste imagination, still undistracted and undaunted, of that happy age when life is still afraid to touch us, when neither duty nor school dares to lay a hand on us, when we are allowed to see, hear, laugh, marvel, and dream without the world requiring anything from us." [1] What begins as a description of a child's games turns into a description of the "happy age" of early childhood. It is an age of play, with few needs besides a pure imagination and a couple of simple props. It is an age of laughter and dreams, still safe from the demands of the world. It is an age of "deep meaning," which adults are nevertheless unable to comprehend. The rhapsody on early childhood that Hanno's games inspire relies on a knowledge of childhood that was more than a century old by the time Mann wrote *Buddenbrooks* but that is still familiar to us nearly one hundred years later. Today, not only a century after *Buddenbrooks* but also a century after Freud, the belief in the purity, the wholeness, and the endangered difference of childhood remains widespread.

There is no MHG text that, like *Buddenbrooks*, contains an extended general statement on the nature of childhood. And that in itself is sig-

---

1. Mann, *Buddenbrooks*, 297: Diese Spiele, deren Tiefsinn und Reiz kein Erwachsener mehr zu verstehen vermag, und zu denen nichts weiter nötig ist als drei Kieselsteine oder ein Stück Holz, das vielleicht eine Löwenzahnblüte als Helm trägt: vor allem aber die reine, starke, inbrünstige, keusche, noch unverstörte und uneingeschüchterte Phantasie jenes glückseligen Alters, wo das Leben sich noch scheut, uns anzutasten, wo noch weder Pflicht noch Schule Hand an uns zu legen wagt, wo wir sehen, hören, lachen, staunen und träumen dürfen, ohne daß noch die Welt Dienste von uns verlangt.

nifiçant: MHG writers betray little eagerness to define childhood for its own sake. Nevertheless, they wrote a great many stories about children, and these offer a wealth of information about the MHG construction of childhood. In each of the preceding chapters I have drawn on this material to describe one or another aspect of the MHG discourses, institutions, and practices concerning children. Now it is time to look back over those partial analyses, to collect the common themes, and to attempt a more comprehensive description of the MHG knowledge of childhood.

Obilot, who plays a crucial role in the seventh book of Wolfram's *Parzival*, can help provide the categories of that description. We first encounter her in the company of her mother and elder sister, as she is watching the hostile armies of Meljanz, king of Liz, approach Bearosche, the city of which her father, Duke Lippaot, is lord. Although Meljanz was raised by Lippaot after his own father's death, a lovers' quarrel with Obilot's sister has led him to take up arms against his foster father. When Gawan, engaged on an adventure of his own, rides up and camps beneath the city walls, Obilot resolves to enlist the unknown knight in the defense of the city. She approaches him, and, in an eloquent speech, offers her love in exchange for his service. Gawan responds at first that she is too young for love—she is probably between seven and ten—but in the end he agrees to fight as her champion. The next day he does so and captures Meljanz in single combat. After the battle, in front of the assembled court, Gawan turns his prisoner, Meljanz, over to his lady, Obilot; and she, taking advantage of the power she momentarily enjoys, orders that Meljanz and her sister be reconciled. They are, and peace is restored to Bearosche.

The story of Obilot illustrates the four principal themes of the MHG knowledge of childhood. First, childhood is an age of deficiency: as a child, Obilot really is too young to participate in a love-service relationship, just as Gawan says. Second, much of childhood is modeled on adulthood: Obilot's most distinctive acts—her relationship with Gawan, her peace-making—require her to play the role of an adult. Third, childhood is an age of revelation: when Obilot approaches Gawan and when she makes peace she suddenly reveals capacities we had no reason to suspect she possessed. Fourth, childhood is a period of changing relationships: Obilot begins as a young maiden in the company of her mother, becomes the lady whom Gawan champions in combat, and ends by playing a political role of considerable importance.

The story of Obilot can also alert us to two points of difference that must also be accommodated in any description of the MHG knowledge

of childhood. First, MHG childhood is different for males and females: if
Obilot had a twin brother it is not likely that he would offer his love in
return for Gawan's service. Second, secular childhood is different from religious childhood: it is difficult to imagine the pious Iolande propositioning
a passing knight no matter how badly her father needed military assistance.
Finally, the story of Obilot raises the question of the relation between the
knowledge of childhood in MHG texts and that of the culture at large. I
will begin by discussing the four general themes, which I have grouped in
pairs, then the two differences, and finally the vexed question of literature
and life.

The Deficiency of Childhood and the Hegemony of Adulthood

When Obilot first proposes to Gawan that he fight in return for her love,
he responds with an objection based on her age: "You would have to be
five years older before you could grant your love."[2] Obilot is too young.
And, even though she accomplishes a great deal, it is clear on a number
of occasions that Obilot really is too young for the role she has assumed.
There is, for example, the problem of supplying a love token: if Gawan is
going to fight as her champion, he must have a token from her, but she
has nothing to give. Her friend Clauditte, who seems to express the childish perspective that one would usually expect from a maiden of Obilot's
age, offers one of her own dolls,[3] but this is clearly inappropriate. In the
end Obilot must rely on her father, whose "help," she says, "I have never
needed so much as now,"[4] and on her mother, who provides an expensive
dress from which she sends Gawan a sleeve. This he tacks onto his shield
and carries into battle. An adult woman would be able to provide a love
token on her own, but Obilot cannot because she is a child. Although as a
heroine Obilot is surprisingly proficient in some ways, as a child she, like
other MHG children, is deficient.

Children are deficient by nature. Lacking strength they cannot walk or
defend themselves; lacking speech they cry; lacking sense and experience
they are foolish and indiscreet; lacking seriousness they play games and
seek pleasure. Thus the ring game Obilot is playing with her friend Clau-

2. Parz 370,15–16: ê daz ir minne meget gegeben ir müezet vünf jâr ê leben.
3. Parz 372,15–21.
4. Parz 372,28–29: vater, mir wart nie sô nôt dîner helfe.

ditte is a sign of childishness. Young children are pure and nearly free of sin, but even that is the result of lack, the lack of the opportunity to sin. The deficiency of children inheres in the language itself. MHG children are *tump*, lacking in years, wisdom, and experience. Thus when Wolfram refers to the "*tump* capriciousness"[5] that led Obilot's sister to disdain Meljanz's love, he attributes her behavior to the *inevitable* combination of youth, foolishness, and inexperience. The MHG words that designate children—*kneht, knabe, knappe, maget, dierne, juncherre,* and *juncvrouwe*—are also used to designate servants or attendants. Thus when Gawan's *knappen* look around for trees under which to camp[6] there is no way of knowing whether these *knappen* are noble youths serving Gawan in anticipation of becoming knights or merely servants attending their master. The language does not distinguish between youth and servitude.

Perhaps because children are viewed as deficient, MHG writers show little interest in childhood for its own sake. For the first fifty years of the MHG period (1050–1100) no childhood narratives were written, and it took another seventy-five years (until about 1175) before they began to appear in any number. Once writers start composing childhood narratives they remain largely indifferent to early childhood, the years when children are least like adults. Many of the genres of childhood (martyr, erotic coming-of-age, bride, enamored maiden and youth) ignore the early years completely. Others (clerical saint, virgin saint, knight) pass over them quickly. Writers have surprisingly little to say about the nature of the child and they devote little energy to elaborating the specifically childish aspects of their heroic children. Wolfram mentions Obilot's games but shows no further interest in them. The indifference to early childhood was shared by the culture at large, at least in the twelfth century: no one recorded the years of birth of Frederick Barbarossa and Henry the Lion,[7] the two figures who dominated German politics in the second half of that century, or, if someone did, the record was accorded so little importance that it was lost.

The story of Obilot illustrates not only the deficiency of childhood but also the second general theme, its subordination to adulthood. When Obilot departs for her interview with Gawan, she leaves behind the childish games she has been playing with her friend. Acting entirely on her own initiative, although with her father's blessing, she enters into a love-service relation with Gawan, displaying throughout a sovereign command of the

5. Parz 386,17: ir tummiu lôsheit.
6. Parz 352,27–29.
7. Jordan, *Heinrich*, 25.

rhetorical and ritual conventions as well as of the political possibilities of such a relationship. She makes an elegant speech to Gawan seeking his service and, after the fighting, exploits her position as his lady in order to establish peace. The role that Obilot plays with such finesse is not a child's role, however, but an adult one. Gawan indicates as much by switching, as soon as the love-service relationship has been established, from the diminutive with which he first greeted her—he called her "such a tiny little lady"[8]—to an adult form of address: now he calls her simply "lady," as does the narrator.[9] She is accorded the status of an adult on account of the role she plays, that of a woman in a love-service relation. Thus, even though Obilot is clearly a child, for much of the time we witness her she plays the role and enjoys the status of an adult.[10]

What we see here in the case of Obilot is true of MHG childhood in general: that which is worth striving for or writing about is adulthood. The beauty, wisdom, strength, and piety that distinguish MHG child heroes and heroines from ordinary children are the beauty, wisdom, strength, and piety of adults. The eloquence with which Obilot addresses Gawan would do credit to the most accomplished courtly lady. The education MHG children receive is an education for adulthood. They are not taught the skills they will need as children but only those they will need as adults. If Obilot's eloquence in addressing Gawan is the work of the "governess"[11] whom she mentions as having impressed on her the importance of speaking sensibly, then it is clear that the governess has taught Obilot an adult skill. The genres of childhood correspond to genres of adulthood. Each genre—prophet, clerical saint, bride, knight, and so forth—corresponds to a particular adult vocation, which determines the shape of childhood. The weight of adulthood on MHG childhood is so heavy that it displaces other children: unlike Obilot, most MHG children have neither siblings nor friends. As a result, their important relations are with adults: parents, guardians, nurses, tutors, and a whole range of strangers they encounter. The only serious relations children sustain with each other are love relationships—but in falling in love they are understood to be behaving like adults, since "the god of love makes children wise and the young old."[12]

8. Parz 368,29: ein sus wênec vrouwelîn.
9. Parz 370,8, 371,18, 394,2.
10. Schmid argues that Obilot functions, symbolically at least, as a *male* adult responsible for arranging marriages, that is, like the head of the household or the older brother (Schmid, "Obilot," 55–57).
11. Parz 369,9: mîn meisterîn.
12. FlorBl 610–12: so gewaltic ist der minnen got daz er kint machet wîs, die jungen alt.

Taken together, the first two themes suggest a picture of childhood —as an impoverished region, colonized by adulthood—that may seem strange and unattractive to modern readers. Yet it would not have seemed strange to anyone until a century or two ago, since it corresponds to beliefs that dominated Western European thinking on the subject from ancient Greece down to relatively recent times. According to modern scholars, "the Greeks of the classical period were generally not nostalgic for childhood,"[13] which was regarded as a period of life that "is never of value in itself."[14] According to Aristotle "the child is imperfect, and therefore obviously his excellence is not relative to himself alone, but to the perfect man and to his teacher."[15] The Romans, who had a "largely negative picture" of children, also assumed that "childhood is imperfect."[16] Such ideas were still current in the Enlightenment, when the child was regarded as "a person who is not yet complete."[17] Even into the twentieth century, psychologists viewed "the child as a reduced adult, showing on schedule the signs of his fulfillment."[18] From Aristotle's claim that "the child is imperfect" relative to the adult to the psychologists' belief that "the child is a reduced adult," the deficiency paradigm has remained remarkably stable.[19]

Yet it has not remained unchallenged. Beginning in the eighteenth century, people came more and more to regard children as something other than imperfect adults: there was a "growing recognition of the child's special nature."[20] Frequently this special nature has been conceived in nostalgic opposition to the fallen world of adults—as integral, pure, sacred, and irrecoverable. Goethe's Werther looks at children and sees "everything so unspoiled, so whole."[21] The brothers Grimm single out the "purity on account of which children seem so marvelous and blessed to us."[22] Novalis proclaims: "Wherever children are, there is a golden age."[23] Thomas Mann stands solidly in this tradition when he conjures up Hanno Budden-

13. Golden, *Athens*, 4.
14. Deißmann-Merten, "Sozialgeschichte," 269: Kindheit hat nie einen Wert in sich.
15. Aristotle, *Politics*, 1260a.31.
16. Wiedemann, *Roman Empire*, 42, 11.
17. Richter, *Das fremde Kind*, 25: Das Kind . . . erscheint als noch nicht fertiger Mensch.
18. Kessen, *The Child*, 133.
19. For general discussions of the Greek and Roman attitude to childhood see, in addition to the studies cited in notes preceding the last: Eyben, "Sozialgeschichte"; Herter, "Das unschuldige Kind"; Néraudau, *Etre enfant*.
20. Grylls, *Guardians*, 36.
21. Goethe, *Werther*, 30: alles so unverdorben, so ganz!
22. Grimm, *Kinder- und Hausmärchen* [Preface of 1819], 30: jene Reinheit, um derentwillen uns Kinder so wunderbar und selig erscheinen.
23. Novalis, "Blüthenstaub," 457: Wo Kinder sind, da ist ein goldnes Zeitalter.

brook and imagines the "happy age when life is still afraid to touch us." Although we might formulate it somewhat less extravagantly, the contemporary knowledge of childhood is still founded on a belief that the child is not only different but special, on the conviction that the child is "a true human being, valuable to society, requiring special care, and . . . interesting in his own right." [24] Thus a psychologist like Piaget will try to explicate "the self-sufficiency and dignity of the child's mind *in terms of its own logic.*" [25] Or a "weekend historian" [26] like Ariès will dismiss the Middle Ages because they lacked "an awareness of the particular nature of childhood." [27] In doing so he assumes that nowadays we are, in fact, all convinced that childhood has a "particular nature."

It is obvious that the MHG knowledge of childhood conforms to the deficiency paradigm: children are not unspoiled but incomplete, and unless they act like heroes—that is like adults—they deserve little attention. That the writers of the MHG childhood narratives were indifferent to the charms of children's games and apparently unaware of the developmental importance of children's relations with their peers does not mean that the German Middle Ages were especially backward in their attitude toward children. The deficiency paradigm that structures MHG ideas about childhood dominated European thinking on the subject for about 2000 years and is probably shared by much of the world today. In this regard the MHG writers are clearly in the majority camp. We may think them wrong, but it makes little sense to dismiss an understanding of childhood shared by the majority of humanity as a stubborn blindness to the obvious truth of the child's special nature just because the special nature of children seems so obvious to us. If we do so, we simply translate the deficiency paradigm from history into historiography. In both cases something is considered deficient—children on the one hand, an historical knowledge of childhood on the other—that might merely have been considered different. But it makes no more sense to dismiss a knowledge of childhood for its failure to be like our own than it does to dismiss childhood for its failure to be like adulthood.

Nor does the MHG participation in the deficiency paradigm mean Ariès is right when he claims that "medieval civilization failed to perceive" the "difference . . . between the world of children and that of adults." [28] To

24. Kessen, *The Child*, 44.
25. Bruner, *Actual Minds*, 141 (Bruner's italics).
26. The title of Ariès's memoires: *Un historien du dimanche*.
27. Ariès, *Centuries*, 128.
28. Ariès, *Centuries*, 411–12.

lack adult qualities is to be different from an adult, and to prepare for adult tasks is different from being able to perform them. A period of life defined by its lack of adult qualities and adult skills is a period of life defined precisely by its difference from adulthood. One might accept Ariès's claim if it were formulated less extravagantly, since, to judge by the MHG evidence at least, medieval civilization perceived *less* difference between childhood and adulthood than we do. However Ariès could not take credit for the less extravagant version, even if he had written it, since it had already been formulated decades before his book appeared by Norbert Elias, according to whom in the Middle Ages "the distance between adults and children, measured by that of today, was slight."[29] This is certainly true of MHG texts, where childhood has few positive features of its own and where children are admired only when they act adults.[30]

Static Nature and Social Change

As Obilot leaves her game of rings she encounters her father, Lippaot, who is returning from an unsuccessful attempt to gain Gawan's help in defending the city. When Lippaot sees his daughter he asks her where she is headed, and she responds: "I'm going to request the foreign knight's service in exchange for reward."[31] She makes her way to Gawan and, in a series of elegant exchanges, attains her purpose. In doing so she reveals an ability to get famous knights to do her bidding that we had no reason to expect she possessed. She begins the scene, after all, playing with her friend Clauditte, behavior emblematic in MHG narratives of thoughtless childishness, and Gawan is, as she herself states, "the first man with whom I have ever spoken privately."[32] Gawan acknowledges the skill with which Obilot has gotten him to fight on her behalf and, as she and her friend depart, he makes a prediction: "When you grow up, the forest will not be able to provide a sufficient harvest [of lances for knights to break] for the two of you, even if all the trees in it were spears."[33] In making this prediction Gawan assumes that the skill Obilot has just revealed in her dealings with him will remain constant from childhood into adulthood.[34]

29. Elias, *Manners*, 141; see also 175.

30. On the increasing distance between childhood and adulthood from the Middle Ages to the present see also Richter, *Das fremde Kind*, 25.

31. Parz 368,17–18: ich wil den vremden ritter biten dienstes nâch lônes siten.

32. Parz 369,4–5: der êrste man der ie mîn redegeselle wart.

33. Parz 372,5–8: sult ir werden alt, trüege dan niht wan sper der walt als erz am andern holze hât, daz würde iu zwein ein ringiu sât.

34. Mohr does not share my admiration for what he calls Obilot's "teenage-girlish, just-

Since we do not get to see how Obilot behaves after she comes of age, we cannot tell whether Gawan's prediction comes true. And yet it must, since it relies on two principles that are unassailable within the world of MHG narrative. According to the first principle, the individual nature is inborn and immutable. Part of that nature is inherited: it is one's *art*, the nature that one has inherited from one's lineage. MHG children always inherit class, often appearance, and sometimes very particular attributes as well—skill at jousting or susceptibility to love. Obilot may have inherited her mastery of courtly form from her father, whose own skills in this regard are evident in the tact with which he treats Meljanz, at once his lord, his foster son, and his opponent in battle. Another part of one's nature, however, is individual: the heroine, after all, must be greater than her parents. This seems to be true of Obilot, who succeeds in gaining Gawan's help while her father could not.

According to the second principle on which Gawan relies, a child's behavior reveals aspects of her immutable nature. In getting Gawan to fight for her, Obilot reveals that she can command the services of the most celebrated knights, which, in the courtly scheme of things, is testimony to her innate excellence as a woman. Gawan recognizes this revelation of Obilot's nature for what it is and feels confident in predicting her adult behavior on that basis, since the nature of the individual does not change. In the MHG childhood narratives even education can be a kind of revelation. A few words of instruction are all it takes to turn Parzival into a peerless knight, since he is a knight by nature. Here education is merely the catalyst that sparks the realization of that nature. There are cases where education seems to effect real change, and in those cases there is an often unresolved tension between the static nature of the individual and the transformative power of nurture. For centuries religious culture had endeavored to shape and thus change through education children and the adult world of which they would become a part, while in the century around 1200 secular culture embraces education with the even greater enthusiasm of the recent convert. Nevertheless, while Obilot's education may have given her the skill to elicit Gawan's aid, it is her immutable nature that gives her the power.

---

learned love casuistry" (Mohr, "Obie," 14: Die backfischhafte, angelernte Minnecasuistik). Von Ertzdorff, who has a higher opinion of the speech itself, does not share my admiration for its heroine—treating "Fräulein Obilot" with irritating condescension and ascribing the success of the episode not to her but to the "tactful understanding and gentle direction" of Gawan and the "admirable psychological skill" of the poet (Ertzdorff, "Obilot," 139: Dies taktvolle Eingehen und behutsame Lenken; 136: Mit bewunderungswürdigem psychologischem Geschick).

While the nature of the child is stable, the child's position in the world is not, which is the fourth general theme: childhood is a period of changing relationships. When Obilot first appears in *Parzival* it is as the younger of two sisters who, accompanied by their mother, are watching the arrival of Gawan and other knights. Soon she distinguishes herself not only from her mother and her sister but also from her father, when she succeeds in winning Gawan as her champion and as the defender of her father's cause. After the battle she is publicly acknowledged by Gawan as the lady he has served with his prowess, and then, by skillful manipulation of the position she has attained, she establishes peace between the young lovers and thus for the city. Obilot's story carries her out of the company of her mother and into the larger society. At the same time, the larger society takes note of her and acknowledges her more extensive participation. When, at the peak of her career, Obilot receives the homage of Meljanz, just before she orders him to make peace with her sister, this homage is "witnessed by many worthy knights."[35] At the outset Obilot had been a passive spectator, watching what happened at court under the protection of her mother. Now she is a principal actor, and the court has become the audience for the spectacle she directs.

Although the story of Obilot lasts only a few days, the course that it traces—out of dependence on parents, integration into the larger society, and recognition by that society—is the usual course of the MHG childhood narratives. In these stories growing up is not a psychological or a cognitive process nor even primarily a biological one. It is represented instead as a series of changing relations to people, places, and institutions. Children are born with important ties to parents, lineage, and household (not family). As they grow up these ties are augmented or supplanted by others. Some of these displacements correspond to well-attested medieval historical practice, occupy relatively fixed positions in the life of a MHG child, and, in their customary order, can be considered aspects of conscientious childrearing. Children are entrusted to wet nurses and tutors; they are sent to schools or monasteries (oblation) or to other courts (fosterage); they are married or knighted. Other kinds of change are more traumatic. Children are orphaned, abducted, sold into slavery, or martyred; they flee home for their safety or to pursue their knightly or saintly vocation. These changes often expose the children to considerable danger.

While we would expect the amount of disruption in a MHG child-

35. Parz 396,3–4: Obilôte doch sicherheit geschach, dâz manec werder ritter sach.

hood to have catastrophic consequences, in the world of MHG narrative this is seldom the case. The children's internal equilibrium is guaranteed by the immutability of the individual nature, which renders it immune to the effects of external trauma, while their external success is guaranteed by a fictional world that compensates them for the dislocations they experience. As they grow up that world dependably provides nurturers, rescuers, and teachers to replace those they lose. And as they come to the end of their childhood, at the latest, the innate nobility of noble children is always acknowledged and the innate piety of saintly children is always recognized, by God if by no one else, no matter how much these attributes have been obscured or threatened en route. Thus, no matter how great the disruptions they endure, the changing relations of a MHG childhood always lead them to the place that is theirs by nature.

The MHG representation of growing up differs profoundly from the most familiar modern theories of child development, which conceptualize growth as a series of distinct stages. Freud posits oral, anal, and genital stages, followed by the so-called latency period. Erikson elaborates the Freudian scheme by the addition of coordinate psycho-social stages. Piaget describes cognitive development falling into sensory-motor, concrete-operational, and formal-operational stages. In every case, the order of the stages is fixed, each relying on the previous one and assimilating its achievements. Thus Piaget can praise Erikson for incorporating the "Freudian mechanisms" into his system so as "to postulate continual integration of previous acquisitions at subsequent levels,"[36] in support of the premise they all share: stages, here called "levels," building on each other in a given order. According to such schemes the sexual, social, or cognitive nature of the child develops more or less inevitably from stage to stage.

Change comes to the modern child not only according to the fixed schedule of stages but also as a result of experience, and these changes are often thought of as permanent. Freud believes that even the childhood "impressions that we have forgotten" will have left "the deepest traces on our emotional life" and will have "a determining effect upon our entire later development."[37] American parents share this belief: they are unusual, according to Jerome Kagan, "in the depth of their commitment to the view that the psychological qualities of the infant," including "those shaped by

---

36. Quoted in Erikson, *Life Cycle*, 76.
37. Freud, *Drei Abhandlungen*, 75: daß die nämlichen Eindrücke, die wir vergessen haben, nichtsdestoweniger die tiefsten Spuren in unserem Seelenleben hinterlassen haben und bestimmend für unsere ganze spätere Entwicklung geworden sind.

experience, might be preserved for an indefinite time."[38] This belief has determined the nature of much of the research that has been done on childhood around the world: cross-cultural psychologists have often based their studies on the assumption that "childhood experience is . . . the independent variable, behavior in adulthood . . . the dependent or outcome variable."[39]

MHG writers have a much different view of stasis and change in the course of childhood. While we know that natural development means constant change, MHG writers know that the nature of the individual is stable. While we know that experience affects children in ways that are profound and immutable, MHG writers know that the effects of experience, even the most disruptive experience, are superficial and reversible. Even the appearance of new aptitudes is understood by MHG writers as a relatively superficial development: it is not felt to reflect a fundamental change but rather the disappearance of various age-specific obstacles to the full realization of the individual nature. As these obstacles—the deficiencies childhood—disappear, which they inevitably do as the child grows up, then the immutable individual nature—which is defined in adult terms—can be revealed more completely. In the case of heroic children this nature may be revealed in stunning ways at any time during childhood. While for us growing up brings an increase in abilities and aptitudes, for MHG writers it means a decrease in obstacles and deficiencies. While for us childhood is development, for MHG writers it is revelation.

Neither the belief in the immutability of the individual nature nor the penchant for sudden change is unique to the MHG childhood narratives. The belief in static nature can be found in other cultures, including those of ancient Greece and Rome. According to Thomas Wiedemann, "the idea that personality can change was almost completely alien to Greek and Latin biography."[40] Dramatic but external change can be found in many medieval texts, products of an esthetic that delights in unexpected reversals and that favors the external over the internal. This literary world was part of a culture in which the possibility of instantaneous transformation, both historical (the Fall, the Incarnation) and personal (conversion, the wheel of fortune), was an article of faith. While the childhood narratives eschew the profound realignment of conversion and insist on the immutability of the individual nature, those things that do change—aptitudes, location, per-

38. Kagan, *Nature*, 73.
39. Harkness and Super, "Cultural Construction," 221.
40. Wiedemann, *Roman Empire*, 50.

sonal ties—do so suddenly and often dramatically. Given the literary and larger cultural context in which they wrote, we must consider the likelihood that MHG writers really did conceptualize many transformations as more sudden than we do.

Female and Male

Just before the interview in which Obilot succeeds in convincing Gawan to fight against Meljanz, her father attempts unsuccessfully to do the same. In making his case to Gawan, Lippaot explains that Meljanz is taking advantage of the fact that he, Lippaot, has no son. Lippaot does not regret not having a son. In fact, he says, he prefers daughters, and then explains why: "Although she is forbidden to wield a sword, a daughter can provide defense that is just as valuable but in a different way, at least if you and she choose together: by her modesty she will win a son for you who is full of valor; that's what I'm hoping for."[41] Since, according to Lippaot, the chief virtue of a daughter is that she can help him gain a son, it's hard to see why he doesn't want sons in the first place. Nevertheless, in making his strange argument Lippaot does indicate precisely the goal of childhood for a secular maiden: to get married, thereby affiliating a knight, her husband, to her lineage. The goal of childhood for a secular youth is equally clear: it is to wield a sword, to fight. These contrasting goals reflect a profound division between the childhood of maidens and that of youths.[42]

The childhood of maidens is focused exclusively on their sexual, romantic, or potential marital relations with men. Virtually the only word used to designate a child as female is *maget* or "virgin." The term does not name a kind of child (the other being male) but a kind of female (the other being *wip*, women who have had sexual relations). There is no way to designate female sex without also designating sexual status in relation to men. It is the same with the genres of childhood: those that include maidens focus on love (enamored maiden, princess protagonist), marriage (bride, virgin saints, virgin martyrs), or sex (erotic coming of age). Either they ignore early childhood or pass over it quickly, thereby suppressing the

41. Parz 367,24–29: swer sol mit sîner tohter weln, swie ir verboten sî daz swert, ir wer ist anders alsô wert: si erwirbet im kiuschecliche einen sun vil ellens rîche. des selben ich gedingen hân.

42. On "the somewhat obscure verses" (Mohr, "Obie," 14: Die . . . etwas dunklen Verse) in which Lippaut explains his attitude toward daughters: Mohr, "Obie," 14; Schmid, "Obilot," 55.

comparatively long time when the virginity of maidens is not threatened, to concentrate on the relatively short time at the end of childhood when it is. Whether the maidens welcome the interest of men, as the secular figures do, or struggle against it, as the saints do, their stories are always dominated by their relation to men. There are no words for a MHG maiden and no stories worth telling about her, there are, that is, no ways of speaking about her except in relation to male sexuality.

Childhood for males is more varied and more complete. While maidens are called by a single term, there are a number of terms that can be used to designate males—*knabe, junge, jungelinc, degen, kneht*, or *knappe*—all of them signifying a relatively young male, most of them also terms for adult knights. The terms do not designate a kind of child (the other being females) but a kind of male (the other being those relatively older). The genres of childhood that are limited to males (prophet, clerical saint, knight, refiliated son) are much more likely to begin at birth than those that include females. While some of them do tell stories of love (enamored youth, enamored knight), many do not, and all of them are likely to treat other issues: education, adventures, precocious signs of prowess or piety. Thus, although they may sustain relations with females, MHG youths are not limited to these relations.

Whereas we divide an age class (children) into two subclasses according to the single criterion of sex (girls and boys), when MHG wants to indicate the sex of a child it divides the general classes for females and males into subclasses using different criteria: sexual experience for females (they are virgins) and age for males (they are relatively young). As a result, while MHG maidens and youths have certain things in common as children, as females and males they belong to incommensurate classes. On the one hand are virgins of marriageable age, who do or do not get married; on the other are young males, who are born, grow up in a variety of ways, and become adults. This does not mean that maidens are completely subordinate to males. Within the limits that are prescribed, they are allowed considerable freedom to welcome or resist, often successfully, the men who desire them. Nor does it mean that there are no limits on youths: enamored youths must obey the maidens they love, and all youths are subordinate to adult males. It does mean, however, that maidens are defined in a way and limited to an extent that youths are not and that everything they do is only possible within those limits.

There can be little doubt that the relations of female and male in the MHG childhood narratives respond to and reinforce the gender relations

in medieval German culture. Since in a patriarchal society women are defined by their relation to men, all the years in which there are no relations to
men can be ignored. Of course youths are also subordinate to adult males,
as a consequence of their age. But the mere fact of being male renders them
more interesting, so their stories are more extensive and more varied. In
any case, their subordination is one that automatically disappears as they
grow from children into adults. Maidens are subordinate not only by virtue
of age but also by virtue of sex. No matter how old they get or how much
they struggle to distance themselves from men this will never change. As
aged nuns they will still be virgins and brides of Christ. This is the lexical
and structural message of the MHG childhood narratives.

Yet it is more complicated. Between 1100 and 1350 gender relations
were shifting. Canon marriage law, which insisted on monogamy, indis-
solubility, and consent of both partners, strengthened the position of
daughters and wives—although at the same time it became more difficult
for women to control property.[43] Women like Elizabeth of Hungary or
Mechthild von Magdeburg played an important and often very visible role
in religious life—although at the same time vigorous efforts were made to
restrict the role of women in religious orders.[44] The courtly cult of love accorded women a secular cultural power they had not previously enjoyed—
even if it was only a literary fiction.[45] And women do seem to have been
actively involved in the patronage and reception of vernacular literature.[46]
In the MHG narratives written during this period one finds an evident
interest in female agency. Religious maidens from Margaret of Antioch to
Iolande von Vianden succeed in thwarting the efforts that are made to have
them marry. And the secular maidens, with hardly an exception, love the
husbands they marry, often engaging themselves actively to bring about a
union they desire. In some cases the agency of maidens limits the autonomy
of youths and adult men, who are constrained to obey the demands of
those they love.

The situation is complex and contradictory. The texts reproduce, reinforce, and elaborate within the realm of childhood historical arrangements in which women were subordinate to men but in which women
were not completely powerless. As represented in MHG texts, it is natural

43. Brundage, *Law, Sex,* 176–486; Duby, *Knight, Lady, Priest*; Herlihy, *Households,* 80–
82, 98–103; Masser, "Gahmuret," 120–21.
44. Bumke, *Höfische Kultur,* 494–95; Shaher, *Frau im Mittelalter,* 47–50; Southern,
Society and the Church, 310–18.
45. Bumke, *Höfische Kultur,* 503–29, 569–82; Schnell, " 'Höfische' Liebe."
46. Bumke, *Höfische Kultur,* 668–70, 704–6; Bumke, *Mäzene,* 231–47.

and inevitable that male lives are more interesting and more varied than female lives and that maidens only exist in relation to males. Within that limitation, however, maidens do enjoy various forms of agency, authority, and resistance.[47]

Sacred and Secular

When Obilot's father is in need of military assistance Obilot goes to Gawan and offers him her love. Then, after the fighting, she makes peace at Bearosche by ordering her sister to take Meljanz as "her lord and her beloved,"[48] in effect performing a marriage. Events like these are inconceivable in a religious text. When the heroine of *Iolande* is about Obilot's age "they asked her if she wanted to get married." Her response is unequivocal: "'No,' she said, 'it cannot be that a mortal man could ever become mine.'"[49] Virtually the entire narrative is devoted to her efforts to escape the marriage her parents have arranged for her and to realize her intention to enter the Dominican convent to which she has bound herself. She is forced to participate in the social life of the court, is beaten and threatened with rape, but nothing can shake her resolve. Where Obilot is encouraged to offer her love to Gawan and celebrated for marrying off her sister, Iolande struggles steadfastly and, in the end, successfully against all ties to mortal men. The contrast between the behavior of Obilot and that of Iolande reflects a profound division within the MHG knowledge of childhood between the secular and the religious.

As the example of Obilot and Iolande indicates, secular and religious childhoods differ in regard to coming of age. Secular heroes and heroines are eager to grow up, and the major genres of secular childhood (enamored maiden and youth, bride, knight, princess protagonist) all culminate in a ceremony that marks the transition to adulthood. As a result, secular childhood is clearly distinguished from adulthood. Religious heroes and heroines, however, do not want to enter secular adulthood and therefore the genres of religious childhood either ignore coming of age (prophets,

47. Berkvam, studying "nature" in Old French texts, makes a similar but slightly different distinction: "while the *nature* of a boy is related to his lineage and nobility, the *nature* of a girl seems to be rather connected to her femaleness, which transcends social classes and is distinct from her status in life" ("*Nature*," 171).

48. Parz 396,16: zeinem herren und zeinem âmîs.

49. Ioland 177–81: man sy vrâgen des began, aver sy wolde nemen man. "nein," sprach sy, "des enmach nyt sîn, dat unmer moge werden mîn kein man, der mûze sterven."

clerical saints) or else focus on their protagonists' active resistance to the rites of passage (martyrs, virgin saints). As a result, religious childhood is not clearly distinguished from adulthood. Of course religious figures do pass through childhood. But their status is determined not so much by their position in worldly hierarchies as by their place in heavenly ones, and in the heavenly scheme they are just as much saints when children as they are when adults. Therefore the distinction between childhood and adulthood, although it exists, is not articulated clearly and childhood itself is not elaborated. Since the status of secular figures does depend on worldly hierarchies, however, it is important to maintain the secular distinctions, among them the distinction between childhood and adulthood. Therefore the rites of passage, which articulate this distinction, are clear.

At the same time secular writers insist on the distinction of childhood from adulthood, they also exhibit a particular interest in childhood. First, literary history shows childhood to be integral to secular writing in a way it is not to religious. Childhood narratives appear in the very first MHG secular narratives (Lambrecht, *Rother*) and continue to play an important part in the secular tradition until after 1300. Childhood narratives do not appear in religious texts until fifty years after the first such texts were written (1050) and even then the production of religious childhood narratives is subject to several surprising gaps (ca. 1150, ca. 1200–65). Second, secular writers elaborate childhood in a way religious writers never did. While religious writers will mention schooling in passing, secular writers present detailed programs of education, especially in courtly texts written between 1150 and 1250. While religious writers tend to keep important events (like conversion) out of childhood, secular writers expand childhood elements so that they become more important (education) and transfer important events from adulthood into childhood (falling in love). While religious writers include childhood narratives only to the extent they find them in their sources, secular writers between 1200 and 1250 expand the childhood narratives in their sources, add such narratives where they are missing, and include them in texts they compose from scratch. Third, the same period also witnesses an increased sentimentality towards childhood in secular texts. Children begin to cry and to play with toys; parents show a greater tenderness to their children; children fall in love, and the stories delight in observing the "childish" way in which they deal with that emotion. Childhood, an integral part of secular narrative from the start, receives disproportionate attention in the first half of the thirteenth century, something that never happens in religious texts.

The childhood one finds represented in MHG secular texts differs not only from that in religious texts but also from what we know of childhood at medieval German courts. Splendid ceremonies of knightly investiture are nearly universal in MHG narratives, which was never the case in the historical Middle Ages. Splendid marriages at which the bride loves her husband are the rule in MHG courtly texts, while they would have been the exception in real life. The elaborate educational programs one finds in the courtly texts would have been rare if not unheard of at medieval German courts. And one can be pretty sure that there were few historical instances of a love, like that of Flore and Blanscheflur, which begins in the cradle. In all these ways, courtly childhood in literary texts represents a stylization, a ritualization, and an idealization of historical childhood among the nobility in the German Middle Ages.

It is well known that many aspects of life—eating, greeting, clothing, fighting, storytelling, loving—were stylized and elaborated at medieval German courts. This is part of "the tendency to refinement and stylization that appears characteristic of courtly life in the twelfth and thirteenth centuries"[50] and that gave birth to the courtly culture of the high Middle Ages. Sociologists from Norbert Elias to Pierre Bourdieu have argued that the kind of culture one finds at medieval courts is about more than style and refinement. According to Elias "the elaboration of everyday conduct" serves as "an instrument of social distinction."[51] According to Bourdieu "the legitimate culture of class societies [is] a product of domination predisposed to express or legitimate domination."[52] That is, courtly culture distinguishes those who belong to courtly society from those who do not, at the same time it legitimates the hegemonic position that provides its material and symbolic precondition. Courtly culture is about distinction and domination. Or, turning the title of Elias's second volume into the argument it contains: civility *is* power.

The same is true of courtly childhood. Like eating, fighting, love, and the rest, childhood is appropriated by the secular nobility, subjected to a refinement and stylization, and turned into something courtly. It is defined by secular rituals (knighting, marriage), granted its own liberal arts (courtliness, chivalry), and outfitted with other aspects of courtly culture (love, festivals). It is distinguished from noncourtly childhood in the same ways

50. Fleckenstein, *Curialitas*, 469: die Tendenz zur Verfeinerung und Stilisierung, die für das höfische Leben im 12. und 13. Jahrhundert . . . als charakteristisch erscheint.
51. Elias, *Manners*, 106.
52. Bourdieu, *Distinction*, 228.

courtly culture in general is distinguished from noncourtly: by its luxury
(splendid rites of passage, lavish education) and by its discipline (training in manners, chivalry, and the rest).[53] It flourished between 1150 and
1300, the same century-and-a-half that witnessed the flourishing of German
courtly culture. Like courtly life as a whole, courtly childhood "satisfied a
need for princely self-representation."[54] Like courtly literature, it "served
to legitimate and glorify those in a position to pay the high costs of producing it."[55] The simple fact that the nobility can afford to invest so heavily
in childhood is itself a sign of power, at the same time the finished product, courtly childhood, is both an assertion of cultural preeminence and,
for that reason, a legitimation of the very power that enabled it in the first
place. Courtly childhood is a product of power, an assertion of power, and
a tool of power.

What is true of the whole is true of the parts. The importance attached
to the rites of passage affirms the power to enforce boundaries. These
rites not only distinguish those who have undergone them from those
who have not (wives have married, maidens have not) but also those who
may undergo the rite from those who may not (males may be knighted,
females may not)—"thereby instituting a lasting difference between those
to whom the rite pertains and those to whom it does not pertain."[56] The
importance attached to education affirms the power to shape life. One can
shape the mind (through instruction in school subjects) as well as the body
(through training in knightly skills or courtly manners) and in doing so
one shapes not only children but also the society of which they will become adult members. The importance attached to childhood itself affirms
the power to determine what will count in the cultural hierarchy. By transforming something that was generally regarded negatively into a mark
of distinction, courtly culture displays its own ability to set the terms by
which status is measured: "nothing," according to Bourdieu, is "more distinguished than the capacity to confer aesthetic status on objects that are
banal or even 'common.'"[57] Courtly culture turns childhood into an asset,
the possession of which generates profits in the form of enhanced cultural
status. It turns childhood into cultural capital.

53. Bourdieu, *Distinction*, 254–55; Elias, *Power*, 85, 257.
54. Schreiner, "Hof," 86: Kultur entsprach einem Bedürfnis nach fürstlicher Selbstdar-
stellung.
55. Bumke, *Mäzene*, 65: Literatur . . . diente der Legitimierung und der Verherrlichung
derer, die in der Lage waren, die hohen Produktionskosten zu bestreiten.
56. Bourdieu, "Rites," 117.
57. Bourdieu, *Distinction*, 5.

Childhood, Literature, History

If you were to tell the story of Obilot to a friend who is unfamiliar with the conventions of medieval literary love, chances are that your friend would react with amazement. How could a girl of eight or nine approach an adult warrior and negotiate with him about the conditions under which she will grant him her love? How could her father collude in her prostitution and not be castigated? How could a mere child orchestrate a transfer of prisoners that brings peace to the city? This can only be some sort of strange fantasy, completely out of touch with reality. And yet it is not. While it is hard to believe that any historical child would have done many of the things Obilot is said to have done, the MHG childhood narratives, even those that, like the story of Obilot, seem exaggeratedly artificial, can tell us important things about the lives of real children in the German Middle Ages.

The MHG childhood narratives were inevitably part of the larger cultural discourse on childhood in medieval Germany. On the one hand, they would have been meaningless to their contemporary audiences if they had not incorporated common assumptions about childhood. On the other, the textual representation of childhood must have affected the ideas about childhood, even the treatment of children, among those who were familiar with the stories. And yet no one will take the MHG texts for simple reproductions of medieval reality. The texts are rigorously limited by class, significantly determined by literary tradition, and inevitably unsettled by the instability of language and representation in ways so profound that any attempt to read historical childhood out of the literary texts must be highly problematical. Rigorists will throw up their hands. It can't be done. Don't try. They are right, of course: it can't be done with certainty. But then nothing we do with texts can be done with certainty: not text editing, not structural analysis, certainly not psychoanalytic or poststructuralist reading. We accept the uncertainty because we think we can learn something we want to know. In this case, we accept the considerable uncertainty of trying to imagine what the MHG texts can tell us about the lives of real children because we have so few other ways of learning anything about them. The MHG corpus comprises by far the largest body of material we have concerning childhood in medieval Germany. If we refuse out of methodological squeamishness to speculate on what it might be able to tell us about the lives of real children, then we will be left knowing almost nothing about them at all.

From the start I have tried wherever possible to establish a relation between the evidence from the MHG texts and the historical world in which they were written. If they show nothing else these efforts demonstrate that the relation cannot be reduced to a simple formula. Sometimes the texts seem to reproduce what historians believe to be the facts of medieval childhood: fosterage, oblation, arranged marriage, high parental mortality, and many other elements of the narratives correspond to well-attested medieval phenomena. Sometimes the texts contradict the historical evidence: in literature nearly all secular youths are knighted at lavish festivals and nearly all secular maidens love the men they marry, while in real life such knightings and marriages seem to have been much rarer. Sometimes the texts represent things that strike us as impossible: children must have had closer relations with those of their own age than the texts suggest, and they cannot have been as strong or as eloquent as the texts would have us believe. Often the discrepancies between the childhood narratives and historical probability result from the fact that the narratives participate in various literary and ideological traditions: the truncated but miracle-filled stories of the prophets conform to the requirements of a particular genre and the inescapable authority of their scriptural model. In other cases the childhood narratives will have been influenced by other factors: the special status of childhood in secular texts seems to be related to the effort of the secular nobility to describe a cultural ideal and claim a cultural power of its own.

In spite of the many complicating factors, I believe we can assume that where the texts show wide agreement on particular issues—and throughout this study I have been concerned not with the exception but with the rule—then one can be pretty sure these ideas enjoyed wide currency in vernacular culture. They constitute what might be called a vernacular knowledge of childhood, one that is German rather than Latin and that is domestic rather than learned. It seems likely that the vernacular knowledge of childhood among the classes for whom the MHG texts were written will have followed the broad outlines of the MHG knowledge of childhood that I have sketched in this chapter. Probably the German nobility of the thirteenth century did believe that children were deficient, that childhood should be focused on adulthood, that the immutable nature of the individual was revealed during childhood, that no amount of childhood dislocation could prevent the noble nature from attaining its proper place in society, that the childhood of maidens was fundamentally different from that of youths, and that childhood was more important in secular than in religious contexts. Each of these general beliefs is attended by a host of more particular ideas—the insignificance of play, the inevitability of parental love, the inheritance of very specific attributes from one's lineage—that will also have had wide currency.

The vernacular knowledge of childhood will necessarily have affected the lives of real children. Anthropologists and cultural psychologists have amassed a large body of information illustrating how a culture's attitudes and practices enable it to produce the kind of children it wants. Before the age of six, children assimilate culturally specific attitudes to responsibility, success, authority, and casual intimacy and behave "in accordance with the expectations of their culture type."[58] Cultural expectations even affect physical development: "African infants routinely surpass American infants in their rate of learning to sit and to walk but not in learning to crawl" because "African parents provide experiences for their babies that are . . . intended to teach sitting and walking."[59] Examples like these illustrate the claim of Marx Wartofsky that "children are, or become, what they are taken to be by others, and what they come to take themselves to be, in the course of their social communication and interaction with others."[60] Children become what the culture expects them to become. Culture cultures children.

Unless medieval German noble children were able to muster a resistance otherwise unknown among children of the world, then they too must have become the children that they were expected to become. And unless the vernacular knowledge of childhood I have sketched is completely unreliable, it will give us some idea of what medieval German noble children really were expected to become and what they therefore actually became. They knew that they were members of lineages but knew nothing of families in the modern sense; their social world was the household, the court, the monastery, or the school. They knew that, even though parents loved their offspring according to a law of nature, as children per se they had little status—that their behavior was foolish and their play meaningless, that they themselves lacked seriousness. In the first half of the thirteenth century their childish attributes were considered more attractive than at other times, and they probably had a higher opinion of themselves *as children* during those years. In general, however, their only hope for improved status was to become adults or, if they were still too young, to become *like* adults. They knew that their position on coming of age was guaranteed

58. Whiting and Whiting, *Six Cultures*, 179.
59. Rogoff and Morelli, "Perspectives," 345.
60. Wartofsky, "Construction," 190.

by their noble birth, that education, although potentially useful, was not essential to attain adult status, but that training in bookish skills was crucial for clerics. Maidens and youths knew that they were fundamentally different, as children and as adults. Everyone knew that childhood was likely to be disrupted by death of caregivers and by dislocation, but that this would not cause lasting harm because, first of all, nurses, tutors, foster parents, and others would be around to take care of displaced children as well as their parents would have and, second, their ultimate success was guaranteed in any case—even if, for long stretches of their childhood, neither they nor anyone around them knew their true identity. And everyone knew that childhood, clearly articulated from adulthood and elaborated as a distinct stage of life, was primarily a secular, aristocratic phenomenon.

Just as there is variation among literary childhoods, so there will have been variation among historical childhoods, some of it systematic, some of it individual. Nevertheless, medieval German noble children will have had no alternative but to grow up more or less according to the models of childhood that their culture had inherited or invented and provided for them. They will have thought of themselves accordingly, they will have acted accordingly, they will have *been* children according to the possibilities that their culture offered.

There are then two kinds of claims that I want to make. One is narrow but strong: I hope to have described with some precision and comprehensiveness the discourses, the practices, and the institutions of childhood, what I have called the knowledge of childhood, within the largely fictional world of MHG texts. The other claim is weaker but bolder: I believe that the MHG knowledge of childhood I have described provides the best idea we can get of the knowledge of childhood among the German speaking nobility between 1100 and 1350. The second claim carries partly by default, since there are few other sources for this sort of information. But it also relies on the fact that texts are cultural products, that language is not rigorously divided into textual and nontextual, fictional and nonfictional, that, as I have just argued, the textual knowledge of childhood must inevitably have shared a great deal with the broader cultural knowledge of childhood, and that the vernacular knowledge of childhood will have provided the models according to which real children actually became who they were.

Quid Obilot cum Hanno?

Thomas Mann imagines Hanno Buddenbrook at play, and the sight elicits from him a rhapsody on the "happy age when life is still afraid to touch us." Wolfram von Eschenbach imagines Obilot at play and has nothing further to say on the subject. For Mann, Hanno's games represent the fascination of childhood. It is an age of "pure, ardent, chaste imagination," of games whose "deep meaning grownups are no longer able to understand." It is different from adulthood, isolated, intact, pure, incomprehensible. For Wolfram, Obilot's games represent childishness, in which he has no particular interest. He is, however, quite interested in the child Obilot, especially in the skill with which she is able to get Gawan to fight on her behalf. He is interested in the adult competence that Obilot reveals. Whereas for Thomas Mann childhood is worth writing about because it has nothing to do with adulthood, for Wolfram childhood is worthy of attention because it aspires to adulthood.

Mann is so committed to the integrity of childhood that he refuses to allow his fictional child to become an adult: Hanno dies when he is sixteen or seventeen, still without any idea what he would have done had he grown up, still called "little Johann" by the narrator.[61] Hanno dies to preserve the incommensurability of childhood and adulthood. He is sacrificed to Ariès. Wolfram would have nothing but contempt for such a sacrifice. He admires Obilot precisely because she reveals adult qualities: she has mastered the adult rhetoric of love, is able to play an adult role in a love-service relation, and, in recognition of this, is granted the adult title *vrouwe*, or "lady."[62] This, I insist for the last time, does not mean Wolfram has no "idea of childhood," merely that according to his idea of childhood it is natural for children to aspire to adulthood. Obilot is the age of a child—probably less than ten—and she acts like a child by playing children's games. She also acts like a child by behaving in certain ways like an adult. It is characteristic of children, in Wolfram's view, to reveal something of what they will be as adults.

In spite of one's reluctance to confuse literature and life, it is obvious that Hanno's childhood has more to do with bourgeois childhood in turn-of-the-century Germany than it has to do with Obilot's childhood—and that Obilot's childhood has more to do with noble childhood in medieval

---

61. Mann, *Buddenbrooks*, 503, 506, 511, 516.
62. Parz 370,8, 371,18, 394,2.

Germany than with Hanno's. Within certain biological limitations, childhood is culturally constructed. The childhood Mann imagines for Hanno
and the childhood Wolfram imagines for Obilot represent different cultural
formations; they are not the same thing, and we should not be deceived
into thinking they are by the fact that we can call them both "childhood."
They are not the same stage of life with different values attached, but completely distinct stages of life. Obilot has nothing to do with Hanno.

To understand Obilot's childhood we must compare it not to Hanno's
but to those of Isold, Kriemhild, Elizabeth of Hungary, and Iolande von
Vianden. We must situate it in relation to the MHG knowledge of childhood. Only in relation to such a culturally specific knowledge of childhood
does the story of Obilot—or of any other child—make sense. And only
in relation to such an historically specific knowledge of childhood does it
make sense to speculate on childhood in the German Middle Ages. Only
by keeping this in mind can we hope to do justice to the historicity of
childhood.

Bibliography

ABBREVIATIONS USED IN THE BIBLIOGRAPHY

AfdA	*Anzeiger für deutsches Altertum und Literatur*
ATB	Altdeutsche Textbibliothek
Bibl.d.ges.dt.Nat.-Lit.	Bibliothek der gesammten deutschen National-Literatur
Dicht.d.dt.MAs	Dichtungen des deutschen Mittelalters
DTM	Deutsche Texte des Mittelalters
DVjs	*Deutsche Vierteljahrsschrift für Literaturwissenschaft und Geistesgeschichte*
GA	von der Hagen, *Gesammtabenteuer*
GAG	Göppinger Arbeiten zur Germanistik
Germ.Abh.	Germanistische Abhandlungen
MA	Medium Aevum, Philologische Studien
MGH	Monumenta Germaniae historica
dt.Chron.	deutsche Chroniken und andere Geschichtsbücher des Mittelalters
MSB	Bayerische Akademie der Wissenschaften, Munich, Sitzungsberichte, Philosophisch-historische Klasse
MTU	Münchener Texte und Untersuchungen zur deutschen Literatur des Mittelalters
PBB	*Beiträge zur Geschichte der deutschen Sprache und Literatur*
(Tüb)	(Tübingen)
Phil.Stud.u.Qu.	Philologische Studien und Quellen
QF	Quellen und Forschungen zur Sprach- und Culturgeschichte der germanischen Völker
SM	Sammlung Metzler
StLV	Bibliothek des Litterarischen Vereins in Stuttgart
WSB	Österreichische Akademie der Wissenschaften, Vienna, Sitzungsberichte, Philosophisch-historische Klasse
ZfdA	*Zeitschrift für deutsches Altertum und deutsche Literatur*
ZfdPh	*Zeitschrift für deutsche Philologie*

MIDDLE HIGH GERMAN TEXTS

Adam und Eva. In GA, 1:5–16.
Adelbrecht, Priester. *Johannes Baptista*. In Kraus, *Deutsche Gedichte*, 15–23.

Albanus. In Maurer, *Religiöse Dichtungen*, 3:605–13.

Albert von Augsburg. *Das Leben des Heiligen Ulrich*. Ed. Karl-Ernst Geith. QF, n.s. 39. Berlin: de Gruyter, 1971.

Albrecht. *Jüngerer Titurel*. Ed. Werner Wolf and Kurt Nyholm. DTM 45, 55, 61, 73, 77. Berlin: Akademie-Verlag, 1955, 1964, 1968, 1984, 1992.

Alexander, Der wilde. In Kraus, *Liederdichter*, 1–19.

Alexius A. In Gerhard Eis, *Beiträge zur mittelhochdeutschen Legende und Mystik: Untersuchungen und Texte*, 256–303. Germanische Studien, 161. Berlin: Ebering, 1935.

Alexius B. In Max Fr. Blau, "Zur Alexiuslegende II," 174–87. *Germania* 34 (1889): 156–87.

Alexius C. In Massmann, *Alexius*, 77–85.

Alexius F. In Massmann, *Alexius*, 118–39.

Altdeutsche Exodus. In Edgar Papp, *Die Altdeutsche Exodus: Untersuchungen und kritischer Text*, 109–205. MA 16. Munich: Fink, 1968.

Die altdeutsche Genesis nach der Wiener Handschrift. Ed. Viktor Dollmayr. ATB 31. Halle: Niemeyer, 1932.

Amelung, Arthur and Oskar Jänicke, eds. *Ortnit und die Wolfdietriche*. 2 vols. *Deutsches Heldenbuch*, pt. 3–4. Berlin: Weidmann, 1871, 1873.

Das Anegenge. In Dietrich Neuschäfer, *Das Anegenge: Textkritische Studien, Diplomatischer Abdruck, Kritische Ausgabe*, 96–267. MA 8. Munich: Fink, 1969.

Anna von Munzingen. [*Adelhausener Schwesternbuch*] *Die Chronik der Anna von Munzingen*, ed. J. König. *Freiburger Diöcesan-Archiv*, 13 (1880): 153–93.

Aristoteles und Phillis [*B*]. In Hellmut Rosenfeld, "Aristoteles und Phillis: Eine neu aufgefundene Benediktbeurer Fassung um 1200," 326–31. ZfdPh 89 (1970): 321–36.

Aristoteles und Phyllis [*S*]. In Niewöhner, *Neues Gesamtabenteuer*, 234–43.

Ava. *Die Dichtungen der Frau Ava*. Ed. Kurt Schacks. Wiener Neudrucke, 8. Graz: Akademische Druck- und Verlagsanstalt, 1986.

Ava. *Johannes*. In Ava, *Dichtungen*, 10–43.

Ava. *Das Jüngste Gericht*. In Ava, *Dichtungen*, 250–81.

Ava. *Das Leben Jesu*. In Ava, *Dichtungen*, 44–227.

[*Berchta*] *Von Berhten mit der langen nase*. In GA, 3:33–35.

Berthold von Regensburg. *Vollständige Ausgabe seiner* [*deutschen*] *Predigten*. Ed. Franz Pfeiffer (vol. 1) and Joseph Strobl (vol. 2). Vienna: Braumüller, 1862, 1880. Reprint. Berlin: de Gruyter, 1965.

Biterolf und Dietleib. In Oskar Jänicke, *Biterolf und Dietleib, Laurin und Walberan*, 1–197. *Deutsches Heldenbuch*, pt. 1. Berlin: Weidmann, 1866. Reprint. Berlin: Weidmann, 1963.

Blanschandin: Bruchstücke eines mhd. Gedichtes. Ed. Joseph Haupt. *Germania* 14, n.s. 2 (1869): 70–74.

[*Buch der Märtyrer*] *Das Märterbuch*. Ed. Erich Gierach. DTM 32. Berlin: Weidmann, 1928.

[*Der Bussard*] *Der Busant (Magelona)*. In GA 1:331–66.

Busse, Lotte. *Die Legende der heiligen Dorothea im deutschen Mittelalter*. Diss. Greifswald, 1928. Greifswald: Beltz, 1930.

de Boor, Helmut, ed. *Mittelalter: Texte und Zeugnisse*. *Die deutsche Literatur: Texte und Zeugnisse*, vol. 1. Munich: Beck, 1965.

Der deutsche Cato. Ed. Fr[iedrich] Zarncke. Leipzig: Wigand, 1852. Reprint. Osnabrück: Zeller, 1966.

Dulciflorie. In Niewöhner, *Sperber*, 95–105.

Ebernand von Erfurt. *Heinrich und Kunegunde*. Ed. Reinhold Bechstein. Bibl.d.ges.dt.Nat.Lit., 39. Quedlinburg: Basse, 1860. Reprint. Amsterdam: Rodopi, 1968.

Ebner, Christine. [*Engelthaler Schwesternbuch*] *Der Nonne von Engelthal Büchlein von der Genaden Überlast*. Ed. Karl Schröder. StLV 108. Tübingen: Litterarischer Verein, 1871.

Ebner, Margareta. *Offenbarungen*. Ed. Philipp Strauch. In Strauch, *Margaretha Ebner und Heinrich von Nördlingen: Ein Beitrag zur Geschichte der deutschen Mystik*, 1–166. Freiburg: Mohr, 1882. Reprint. Amsterdam: Schippers, 1966.

Eckhart, Meister. *Meister Eckharts Predigten*. Ed. Josef Quint. 3 vols. *Die deutschen Werke*, vols. 1–3. Stuttgart: Kohlhammer, 1958, 1971, 1976.

Eilhart von Oberg. *Tristrant: Edition diplomatique des manuscrits et traduction en français moderne*. Ed. Danielle Buschinger. GAG 202. Göppingen: Kümmerle, 1976.

Elisabeth von Kirchberg. [*Irmegard-Vita*]. In A[nton] Birlinger, "Leben heiliger alemannischer Frauen des XIV XV Jahrunderts [sic]: IV Die Nonnen von Kirchberg bei Haigerloch," 13–20. *Alemannia* 11 (1883): 1–20.

———. [*Kirchberger Schwesternbuch*]. In Roth, "Aufzeichnungen," 104–23.

Die Elsässische "Legenda aurea." Vol. 1, *Das Normalcorpus*. Ed. Ulla Williams and Werner Williams-Krapp. Texte und Textgeschichte, 3. Tübingen: Niemeyer, 1980.

Fleck, Konrad. *Flore und Blanscheflur*. Ed. Emil Sommer. Bibl.d.ges.dt.Nat.-Lit., 12. Quedlinburg: Basse, 1846.

Frauenlist. In Niewöhner, *Neues Gesamtabenteuer*, 87–95.

Freidank. *Fridankes Bescheidenheit*. Ed. H.E. Bezzenberger. Halle: Buchhandlung des Waisenhauses, 1872. Reprint. Aalen: Zeller, 1962.

Friedrich von Schwaben. Ed. Max Hermann Jellinek. DTM 1. Berlin: Weidmann, 1904.

[*Das Gänslein*] *Der Mönch und das Gänslein*. In Franz Pfeiffer, "Zwei alte Schwänke," 95–105. ZfdA 8 (1851): 89–105.

Das gebratene Ei. In Pfeiffer, "Beispiele," 368–70.

Gottfried von Neifen. In Kraus, *Liederdichter*, 82–127.

Gottfried von Straßburg. *Tristan und Isold*. Ed. Friedrich Ranke. 15th ed. Zürich: Weidmann, 1978.

Der Göttweiger Trojanerkrieg. Ed. Alfred Koppitz. DTM 29. Berlin: Weidmann, 1926.

Graf Rudolf. Ed. Peter F. Ganz. Phil.Stud.u.Qu., 19. Berlin: Schmidt, 1964.

Grazer Marienleben. Ed. Anton Schönbach. ZfdA 17 (1874): 532–60.

Grieshabersche Predigten I. "Predigt-Bruchstücke aus dem XII. Jahrhundert." Ed. Franz Karl Grieshaber. *Germania* 1 (1856): 445–54.

Die gute Frau. Ed. Emil Sommer. ZfdA 2 (1842): 392–481.

Hagen, Friedrich Heinrich von der. *Gesammtabenteuer: Hundert altdeutsche Erzählungen: Ritter- und Pfaffen-Mären, Stadt- und Dorfgeschichten, Schwänke, Wundersagen und Legenden.* 3 vols. Stuttgart: Cotta, 1850. Reprint. Darmstadt: Wissenschaftliche Buchgesellschaft, 1961.

[*Die halbe Decke*] *Das Kotzenmaere.* In Lutz Röhrich, *Erzählungen des späten Mittelalters und ihr Weiterleben in Literatur und Volksdichtung bis zur Gegenwart*, 1:93–97. Bern: Francke, 1962.

Hartmann von Aue. *Der arme Heinrich.* Ed. Hermann Paul, 15th ed. Gesa Bonath. ATB 3. Tübingen: Niemeyer, 1984.

———. *Erec.* Ed. Albert Leitzmann and Ludwig Wolff, 6th ed. Christoph Cormeau and Kurt Gärtner. ATB 39. Tübingen: Niemeyer, 1985.

———. *Gregorius.* Ed. Hermann Paul, 13th ed. Burghart Wachinger. ATB 2. Tübingen: Niemeyer, 1984.

Hartwig von dem Hage. *Margaretenlegende.* In Wolfgang Schmitz, *Die Dichtungen des Hartwig von dem Hage: Untersuchungen und Edition*, 259–304. GAG 193. Göppingen: Kümmerle, 1976.

Das Häslein. In de Boor, *Texte*, 1456–63.

Heinrich der Klausner. [*Der arme Schüler*] *Marienlegende.* In Karl Bartsch, *Mitteldeutsche Gedichte*, 1–39. StLV 53. Stuttgart: Litterarischer Verein, 1860.

Heinrich von Neustadt. *Apollonius von Tyrland.* In *Die Werke Heinrichs von Neustadt*, ed. S[amuel] Singer, 1–328. DTM 7. Berlin: Weidmann, 1906. Reprint. Dublin: Weidmann, 1967.

Heinrich von dem Türlin. *Diu Crône.* Ed. Gottlob Heinrich Friedrich Scholl. StLV 27. Stuttgart: Litterarischer Verein, 1852. Reprint. Amsterdam: Rodopi, 1966.

Heinrich von Veldeke. [*Eneit*] *Die Eneide.* In *Heinrich von Veldeke*, ed. Ludwig Ettmüller, 15–354. Dicht.d.dt.MAs, 8. Leipzig: Göschen, 1852.

———. *Servatius.* In *Sente Servas—Sanctus Servatius*, ed. Theodor Frings and Gabriele Schieb, Die epischen Werke des Henric van Veldeken, 1. Halle: Niemeyer, 1956.

Hermann, Bruder. *Leben der Gräfin Iolande von Vianden.* Ed. John Meier. Germ.Abh., 7. Breslau: Koebner, 1889.

Hermann von [Fritzlar] Fritslar. *Das Heiligenleben.* In Franz Pfeiffer, *Deutsche Mystiker des vierzehnten Jahrhunderts*, 1:3–258. Leipzig: Göschen, 1845. Reprint. Aalen: Scientia, 1962.

Herzog Ernst B. In Karl Bartsch, *Herzog Ernst*, 13–186. Vienna: Braumüller, 1869.

Herzog Ernst D. Ed. Hans-Friedrich Rosenfeld. ATB 104. Tübingen: Niemeyer, 1991.

Hoffmannsche Predigtsammlung. In Heinrich Hoffmann [von Fallersleben], *Fundgruben für Geschichte deutscher Sprache und Literatur*, 1:70–126. Breslau: Grass, 1830.

Hugo von Trimberg. *Der Renner.* Ed. Gustav Ehrismann. StLV 247, 248, 252, 256. Tübingen: Litterarischer Verein, 1908, 1909, 1911. Reprint. Berlin: de Gruyter, 1970.

Jans Enikel. *Die Weltchronik.* In *Jansen Enikels Werke*, ed. Philipp Strauch. MGH, dt.Chron., 3.1. Hannover: Hahn, 1891.

Das Jenaer Martyrologium. Ed. Friedrich Wilhelm. *Münchener Museum für Philologie des Mittelalters und der Renaissance* 5 (1932): 1–98.

Johann von Würzburg. *Wilhelm von Österreich.* Ed. Ernst Regel. DTM 3. Berlin: Weidmann, 1906. Reprint. Dublin: Weidmann, 1970.

Das Jüdel. In K. A. Hahn, *Gedichte des XII. und XIII. Jahrhunderts*, 129–34. Bibl.d.ges.dt.Nat.-Lit., 20. Quedlinburg: Basse, 1840.

Der Judenknabe. In Richert, *Marienlegenden*, 187–205.

Kaiserchronik. Ed. Edward Schröder. MGH, dt.Chron, 1.1. Hannover: Hahn, 1892. Reprint. Dublin: Weidmann, 1969.

Karl und Galie: Karlmeinet, Teil I. Ed. Dagmar Helm. DTM 74. Berlin: Akademie-Verlag, 1986.

Katharinen Marter. Ed. Johann Lambel. *Germania* 8 (1863): 142–80.

Kistener, Kunz. *Die Jakobsbrüder.* Ed. Karl Euling. Germ.Abh., 16. Breslau: Marcus, 1899.

Diu Klage. Ed. Karl Bartsch. Leipzig: Brockhaus, 1875. Reprint. Darmstadt: Wissenschaftliche Buchgesellschaft, 1964.

[Köditz] Ködiz, Friedrich. *Das Leben des heiligen Ludwig, Landgrafen in Thüringen, Gemahls der heiligen Elisabeth.* Ed. Heinrich Rückert. Leipzig: Weigel, 1851.

König Rother. Ed. Theodor Frings and Joachim Kuhnt. 3rd ed. Altdeutsche Texte für den akademischen Unterricht, 2. Halle: Niemeyer, 1968.

[*König Tirol*] *Tirol und Fridebrant.* In *Winsbeckische Gedichte*, 76–96.

Konrad, Pfaffe. *Das Rolandslied des Pfaffen Konrad.* Ed. Carl Wesle, 2nd ed. Peter Wapnewski. ATB 69. Niemeyer: Tübingen, 1967.

Konrad, Priester. *Predigtbuch.* In Volker Mertens, *Das Predigtbuch des Priesters Konrad: Überlieferung, Gestalt, Gehalt und Texte*, 179–310. MTU 33. Munich: Beck, 1971.

——— . *Predigtbuch.* In Schönbach, *Predigten*, 3.

Konrad von Fußesbrunnen. *Die Kindheit Jesu.* Ed. Hans Fromm and Klaus Grubmüller. Berlin: de Gruyter, 1973.

Konrad von Haslau. *Der Jüngling.* Ed. Walter Tauber. ATB 97. Tübingen: Niemeyer, 1984.

Konrad von Würzburg. *Alexius.* Ed. Paul Gereke. Konrad von Würzburg, *Die Legenden*, vol. 2. ATB 20. Halle: Niemeyer, 1926.

——— . *Engelhard.* Ed. Paul Gereke, 2nd ed. Ingo Reiffenstein. ATB 17. Tübingen: Niemeyer, 1963.

——— . *Heinrich von Kempten.* In *Kleinere Dichtungen Konrads von Würzburg*, ed. Edward Schröder, 10th ed., 41–68. Dublin: Weidmann, 1970.

——— . *Pantaleon.* Ed. Paul Gereke, 2nd ed. Winfried Woesler. Konrad von Würzburg, *Die Legenden*, vol. 3. ATB 21. Tübingen: Niemeyer, 1974.

——— . *Partonopier und Meliur.* Ed. Karl Bartsch. Vienna: Braumüller, 1871. Reprint. Berlin: de Gruyter, 1970.

——— . *Silvester.* Ed. Paul Gereke. Konrad von Würzburg, *Die Legenden*, vol. 1. ATB 19. Halle: Niemeyer, 1925.

——— . [*Der Trojanerkrieg*] *Der trojanische Krieg.* Ed. Adelbert von Keller. StLV 44. Stuttgart: Litterarischer Verein, 1858. Reprint. Amsterdam: Rodopi, 1965.

Kraus, Carl, ed. *Deutsche Gedichte des zwölften Jahrhunderts*. Halle: Niemeyer, 1894.

──── . *Deutsche Liederdichter des 13. Jahrhunderts*. Vol. 1. Tübingen: Niemeyer, 1952.

Kudrun. Ed. Karl Bartsch, 5th ed. Karl Stackmann. Wiesbaden: Brockhaus, 1965.

Lambrecht. *Alexanderlied*. In Karl Kinzel, *Lamprechts Alexander nach den drei Texten mit dem Fragment des Alberic von Besançon*. Germanistische Handbibliothek, 6. Halle: Buchhandlung des Waisenhauses, 1884.

Lamprecht von Regensburg. *Sanct Francisken Leben und Tochter Syon*. Ed. Karl Weinhold. Paderborn: Schöningh, 1880.

Lancelot, [Prose]. Ed. Reinhold Kluge. 3 vols. DTM 42, 47, 63. Berlin: Akademie-Verlag, 1948, 1963, 1974.

Leben Christi. Ed. Franz Pfeiffer. ZfdA 5 (1845): 17–32.

Das Leben der heiligen Elisabeth vom Verfasser der Erlösung. Ed. Max Rieger. StLV 90. Stuttgart: Litterarischer Verein, 1868.

Die Legende vom zwölfjährigen Mönchlein. In de Boor, *Texte*, 351–55.

Leipziger Predigten. In Schönbach, *Predigten*, 1.

Lohengrin: Edition und Untersuchungen. Ed. Thomas Cramer. Munich: Fink, 1971.

Lutwin. *Adam und Eva*. Ed. Konrad Hofmann and Wilhelm Meyer. StLV 153. Tübingen: Litterarischer Verein, 1881.

Der Magezoge. In Gustav Rosenhagen, *Kleinere mittelhochdeutsche Erzählungen, Fabeln und Lehrgedichte III*, 21–29. DTM 17. Berlin: Weidmann, 1909.

Mai und Beaflor. Dicht.d.dt.Mas., 7. Leipzig: Göschen, 1848. Reprint. Hildesheim: Gerstenheim, 1974.

Margaretenlegende des XII. Jahrhunderts. Ed. Karl Bartsch. *Germania* 24, n.s. 12 (1879): 294–97.

Das Marienleben der Königsberger Hs. 905. Ed. Diemut Hinderer. ZfdA 77 (1940): 113–42.

Die Marter der heiligen Margareta. Ed. [Moriz] Haupt. ZfdA 1 (1841): 151–93.

Massmann, Hans Ferd[inand], ed. *Sanct Alexius Leben in acht gereimten mittelhochdeutschen Behandlungen*. Bibl.d.ges.dt.Nat.-Lit., 9. Quedlinburg: Basse, 1843.

Maurer, Friedrich, ed. *Die religiösen Dichtungen des 11. und 12. Jahrhunderts*. 3 vols. Tübingen: Niemeyer, 1964, 1965, 1970.

Mitteldeutsche Predigten. In Franz Karl Grieshaber, *Vaterländisches aus den Gebieten der Literatur, der Kunst und des Lebens*, 266–343. Rastatt: Birks, 1842.

Mittelfränkische Reimbibel. In Maurer, *Religiöse Dichtungen*, 1:102–68.

Der Münchner Oswald. Ed. Michael Curschmann. ATB 76. Tübingen: Niemeyer, 1974.

Die Nachtigall A. In GA, 2:75–82.

Das Nibelungenlied. Ed. Karl Bartsch, 19th ed. Helmut de Boor. Wiesbaden: Brockhaus, 1967.

Niewöhner, Heinrich, ed. *Neues Gesamtabenteuer: Das ist Fr. H. von der Hagens Gesamtabenteuer in neuer Auswahl: Die Sammlung der mittelhochdeutschen Mären und Schwänke des 13. und 14. Jahrhunderts*. 2nd ed. Werner Simon. Dublin: Weidmann, 1967.

Niewöhner, Heinrich. *Der Sperber und verwandte mhd. Novellen*. Palaestra, 119. Berlin: Mayer & Müller, 1913.

Nikolaus von Jeroschin. *Sent Adalbrechtes leben*. Ed. Ernst Strehlke. In *Scriptores rerum Prussicarum: Die Geschichtsquellen der preussischen Vorzeit bis zum Untergange der Ordensherrschaft*, 2:425–28. Leipzig: n.p., 1863. Reprint. Frankfurt am Main: Minerva, 1965.

Oberaltaicher Predigtsammlung. In Schönbach, *Predigten*, 2.

Der oberdeutsche Servatius. In Friedrich Wilhelm, *Sanct Servatius oder Wie das erste Reis in deutscher Zunge geimpft wurde*, 149–269. Munich: Beck, 1910.

Orendel. Ed. Arnold E. Berger. Bonn: Weber, 1888. Reprint. Berlin: de Gruyter, 1974.

Otte. *Eraclius*. Ed. Winfried Frey. GAG 348. Göppingen: Kümmerle, 1983.

Otto II. von Freising. *Der Laubacher Barlaam*. Ed. Adolf Perdisch. StLV 260. Tübingen: Litterarischer Verein, 1913. Reprint. Hildesheim: Olms, 1979.

Ottokar von Steiermark. [*Steirische Reimchronik*] *Ottokars österreichische Reimchronik*. Ed. Joseph Seemüller. MGH, dt.Chron., 5,1–2. Hannover: Hahn, 1890, 1893.

Paradisus anime intelligentis (Paradis der fornuftigen sele). Ed. Philipp Strauch. DTM 30. Berlin: Weidmann, 1919.

Passienbüchlein von den vier Hauptjungfrauen.

Dorothy: In Busse, *Dorothea*, 15–24.

Margaret: *Büchelin der heiligen Margareta: Beitrag zur Geschichte der geistlichen Literatur des XIV. Jahrhunderts*. Ed. Karl Stejskal. Vienna: Hölder, 1880.

Passional

Parts one and two: *Das alte Passional*. Ed. K. A. Hahn. Frankfurt am Main: Broenner, 1845.

Part three: *Das Passional: Eine Legenden-Sammlung des dreizehnten Jahrhunderts*. Ed. Fr. Karl Köpke. Bibl.d.ges.dt.Nat.-Lit., 32. Quedlinburg: Basse, 1852. Reprint. Amsterdam: Rodopi, 1966.

Pfeiffer, Franz. "Altdeutsche Beispiele." ZfdA 7 (1849): 318–82.

Philipp, Bruder. *Bruder Philipps des Carthäusers Marienleben*. Ed. Heinr[ich] Rückert. Bibl.d.ges.dt.Nat.-Lit., 34. Quedlinburg: Basse, 1853.

Pilatus. In K[arl] Weinhold, "Zu dem deutschen Pilatusgedicht," 272–288. ZfdPh 8 (1877): 253–88.

Pleier, Der. *Meleranz*. Ed. Karl Bartsch. StLV 60. Stuttgart: Litterarischer Verein, 1861. Reprint. Hildesheim: Olms, 1974.

———. *Tandareis und Flordibel*. Ed. Ferdinand Khull. Graz: Styria, 1885.

Pyramus und Thisbe. Ed. Moriz Haupt. ZfdA 6 (1848): 504–17.

Rabenschlacht. In Ernst Martin, *Alpharts Tod, Dietrichs Flucht, Rabenschlacht*, 217–326. *Deutsches Heldenbuch*, pt. 2. Berlin: Weidmann, 1866.

Reinbot von Durne. *Der heilige Georg*. Ed. Carl von Kraus. Germanische Bibliothek, 3,1. Heidelberg: Winter, 1907.

Reinfrid von Braunschweig. Ed. Karl Bartsch. StLV 109. Tübingen: Litterarischer Verein, 1871.

Richert, Hans-Georg, ed. *Marienlegenden aus dem Alten Passional*. ATB 64. Tübingen: Niemeyer, 1965.

Rosenfeld, Hans-Friedrich. *Mittelhochdeutsche Novellenstudien: I. Der Hellerwertwitz; II. Der Schüler von Paris*. Palaestra, 153. Leipzig: Mayer & Müller, 1927.

Roth, F.W.E. "Aufzeichnungen über das mystische Leben der Nonnen von Kirchberg bei Sulz Predigerordens während des XIV. und XV. Jahrhunderts." *Alemannia* 21 (1893): 103–148.

Rüdeger von Munre. [*Studentenabenteuer B*] *Irregang und Girregar*. In GA, 3:43–82.

Rudolf von Ems. *Alexander*. Ed. Victor Junk. StLV 272, 274. Leipzig: Hiersemann, 1928, 1929. Reprint. Darmstadt: Wissenschaftliche Buchgesellschaft, 1970.

———. *Barlaam und Josaphat*. Ed. Franz Pfeiffer. Dicht.d.dt. Mas., 3. Leipzig: Göschen, 1843. Reprint. Berlin: de Gruyter, 1965.

———. *Der guote Gêrhart*. Ed. John A. Asher. 2nd ed. ATB 56. Tübingen: Niemeyer, 1971.

———. *Weltchronik*. Ed. Gustav Ehrismann. DTM 20. Berlin: Weidmann, 1915. Reprint. Dublin: Weidmann, 1967.

———. *Willehalm von Orlens*. Ed. Victor Junk. DTM 2. Berlin: Weidmann, 1905.

Ruprecht von Würzburg. [*Treueprobe*] *Die zwei Kaufleute*. In Niewöhner, *Neues Gesamtabenteuer*, 255–68.

Der Saelden Hort: Alemannisches Gedicht vom Leben Jesu, Johannes des Täufers und der Magdalena. Ed. Heinrich Adrian. DTM 26. Berlin: Weidmann, 1927.

Sand Eufrosin leben. Ed. V. E. Mourek. In "Neuhauser Bruchstücke einer Pergamenthandschrift altdeutscher Gedichte ernsten Inhalts," 158–69. *Sitzungsberichte der königlichen böhmischen Gesellschaft der Wissenschaften: Classe für Philosophie, Geschichte und Philologie*, 1889. Prague: Rivnáč, 1890.

St. Georgener Prediger. Der sogenannte St. Georgener Prediger. Ed. Karl Rieder. DTM 10. Berlin: Weidmann, 1908.

St. Pauler Predigten. Altdeutsche Predigten aus dem Benedictinerstifte St. Paul in Kärnten. Ed. Adalbert Jeitteles. Altdeutsche Handschriften aus OEsterreich, 1. Innsbruck: Wagner, 1878.

S. Veit. In Kraus, *Deutsche Gedichte*, 24–25.

Sante Margareten Marter. Ed. Karl Bartsch. *Germania* 4 (1859): 440–59.

Das Schneekind. In Pfeiffer, "Beispiele," 377–80.

Ein Scholar, Marias Bräutigam. In Richert, *Marienlegenden*, 39–42.

Der Scholar und das Marienbild. In Richert, *Marienlegenden*, 131–48.

Schönbach, Anton E., ed. *Altdeutsche Predigten*. 3 vols. Graz: Styria, 1886, 1888, 1891. Reprint. Darmstadt: Wissenschaftliche Buchgesellschaft, 1964.

[*Der Schüler zu Paris A*] *Die Gesamtabenteuerfassung des Schülers von Paris (G)*. In Rosenfeld, *Novellenstudien*, 394–449.

[*Der Schüler zu Paris B*] *Die Wiener Fassung des Schülers von Paris (W)*. In Rosenfeld, *Novellenstudien*, 270–93.

[*Der Schüler zu Paris C*] *Die Münchener Fassung des Schülers von Paris (M)*. In Rosenfeld, *Novellenstudien*, 207–30.

Der Schwabenspiegel oder schwäbisches Land- und Lehen- Rechtbuch. Ed. F[riedrich] L. A. von Lassberg. Reprint. Tübingen: Fues, 1840. Aalen: Scientia, 1961.

Schwarzwälder Prediger. *Fest- und Heiligenpredigten des 'Schwarzwälder Predigers.'* Ed. Peter Schmitt, Ulla Williams, and Werner Williams-Krapp. Kleine deutsche Prosadenkmäler des Mittelalters, 14. Munich: Fink, 1982.

———. *Predigten des 'Schwarzwälder Predigers.'* Ed. Gerhard Stamm. Kleine deutsche Prosadenkmäler des Mittelalters, 12. Munich: Fink, 1973.

Seifried Helbling. Ed. Joseph Seemüller. Halle: Buchhandlung des Waisenhauses, 1886.

Seifrit. *Alexander.* Ed. Paul Gereke. DTM 36. Berlin: Weidmann, 1932.

Speculum Ecclesiae: Eine frühmittelhochdeutsche Predigtsammlung. Ed. Gert Mellbourn. Lunder germanistische Forschungen, 12. Lund: Gleerup; Copenhagen: Munksgaard, 1944.

Der Sperber. In Niewöhner, *Sperber,* 15–44.

Stagel, Elsbet. [*Tösser Schwesternbuch*] *Das Leben der Schwestern zu Töß samt der Vorrede von Johannes Meier und dem Leben der Prinzessin Elisabet von Ungarn.* Ed. Ferdinand Vetter. DTM 6. Berlin: Weidmann, 1906.

Stricker, Der. *Karl der Grosse.* Ed. Karl Bartsch. Bibl.d.ges.dt.Nat.-Lit., 35. Quedlinburg: Basse, 1857. Reprint. Berlin: de Gruyter, 1965.

Studentenabenteuer A. In Wilhelm Stehmann, *Die mittelhochdeutsche Novelle vom Studentenabenteuer,* 198–216. Palaestra, 67. Berlin: Mayer & Müller, 1909.

Thomas von Kandelberg. In GA, 3: 577–86.

Thomasin von Zerclaere. [*Welscher Gast*] *Der Wälsche Gast des Thomasin von Zirclaria.* Ed. Heinr[ich] Rückert. Bibl.d.ges.dt.Nat.-Lit., 30. Quedlinburg: Basse, 1852. Reprint. Berlin: de Gruyter, 1965.

Trierer *Floyris.* In G. De Smet and M. Gysseling, "Die Trierer Floyris-Bruchstücke," 159–69. *Studia Germanica Gandensia* 9 (1967): 157–96.

[*Ulmer Schwesternbuch*]. In Roth, "Aufzeichnungen," 123–48.

Ulrich von [Etzenbach] Eschenbach. *Alexander.* Ed. Wendelin Toischer. StLV 183. Tübingen: Litterarischer Verein, 1888. Reprint. Hildesheim: Olms, 1974.

———. *Wilhelm von Wenden.* Ed. Hans-Friedrich Rosenfeld. DTM 49. Berlin: Akademie-Verlag, 1957.

Ulrich von Liechtenstein. *Frauendienst.* Ed. Franz Viktor Spechtler. GAG 485. Göppingen: Kümmerle, 1987.

Ulrich von Türheim. *Rennewart.* Ed. Alfred Hübner. DTM 39. Berlin: Weidmann, 1938. Reprint. Berlin: Weidmann, 1964.

Ulrich von dem Türlin. *Willehalm.* Ed. S[amuel] Singer. Bibliothek der mittelhochdeutschen Litteratur in Bœhmen, 4. Prague: Verein für Geschichte der Deutschen in Böhmen, 1893. Reprint. Hildesheim: Olms, 1970.

———. [*Willehalm*]. In Werner Schröder, *'Arabel'-Studien I: Prolegomena zu einer neuen Ausgabe Ulrichs von dem Türlin,* 103–31. Akademie der Wissenschaften und der Literatur, Mainz. Abhandlungen der geistes- und sozialwissenschaftlichen Klasse, 1982, 6. Wiesbaden: Steiner, 1982.

Ulrich von Zatzikhoven. *Lanzelet.* Ed. K. A. Hahn. Frankfurt am Main: Brönner, 1845. Reprint. Berlin: de Gruyter, 1965.

Das Väterbuch. Ed. Karl Reissenberger. DTM 22. Berlin: Weidmann, 1914. Reprint. Dublin: Weidmann, 1967.

Virginal. In Julius Zupitza, *Dietrichs Abenteuer von Albrecht von Kemenaten nebst den Bruchstücken von Dietrich und Wenezlan,* 1–200. *Deutsches Heldenbuch,* pt. 5. Berlin: Weidmann, 1870.

Von Christi Geburt. In Kraus, *Deutsche Gedichte,* 3–6.

Von sent Dorothea. In Busse, *Dorothea,* 30–41.

Die Vorauer Bücher Mosis. In Joseph Diemer, *Deutsche Gedichte des XI. und XII.*

Jahrhunderts aufgefunden im regulierten Chorherrenstifte zu Vorau, 1–86. Vienna: Braumüller, 1849. Reprint. Wissenschaftliche Buchgesellschaft, 1968.

Die Vorauer Novelle. In Anton E. Schönbach, *Studien zur Erzählungsliteratur des Mittelalters*, 42–68. WSB 140.4. Vienna: Gerold, 1899.

[*Wallersteiner Margareta-Legende*] *Wetzels* [sic] *heilige Margarete*. Ed. Karl Bartsch. *Germanistische Studien* 1 (1872): 10–25.

Walther von Rheinau. *Das Marienleben Walthers von Rheinau*. Ed. Edit Perjus. 2nd ed. Acta Academiae Aboensis: Humaniora, 17.1. Åbo: Åbo Akademi, 1949.

Walther von der Vogelweide. *Die Gedichte Walthers von der Vogelweide.* Ed. Karl Lachmann, 13th ed. Hugo Kuhn. Berlin: de Gruyter, 1965.

Die Warnung. Ed. Moriz Haupt. ZfdA 1 (1841): 438–537.

Wernher, Priester. *Maria: Bruchstücke und Umarbeitungen.* Ed. Carl Wesle, 2nd ed. Hans Fromm. ATB 26. Tübingen: Niemeyer, 1969.

Wernher der Gartenære. *Helmbrecht.* Ed. Friedrich Panzer, 8th ed. Kurt Ruh. ATB 11. Tübingen: Niemeyer, 1968.

Wetzel von Bernau. *Margareta.* In Gerrit Gijsbertus van den Andel, *Die Margaretalegende in ihren mittelalterlichen Versionen: Eine vergleichende Studie*, 125–56. Groningen: Noordhoff, 1933.

Wigamur. Ed. Danielle Buschinger. GAG 320. Göppingen: Kümmerle, 1987.

Winsbecke. In *Winsbeckische Gedichte*, 1–45.

Winsbeckin. In *Winsbeckische Gedichte*, 46–66.

Winsbeckische Gedichte nebst Tirol und Fridebrant. Ed. Albert Leitzmann, 3rd ed. Ingo Reiffenstein. ATB 9. Tübingen: Niemeyer, 1962.

Wirnt von Gravenberc. *Wigalois: Der Ritter mit dem Rade.* Ed. J.M.N. Kapteyn. Rheinische Beiträge und Hülfsbücher zur germanischen Philologie und Volkskunde, 9. Bonn: Klopp, 1926.

Wisse, Claus and Philipp Colin. [*Rappoltsteiner*] *Parzifal.* Ed. Karl Schorbach. Elsässische Litteraturdenkmäler aus dem XIV–XVII. Jahrhundert, 5. Strassburg: Trübner, 1888. Reprint. Berlin: de Gruyter, 1974.

Wolfdietrich A. In Amelung and Jänicke, *Ortnit und die Wolfdietriche*, 1:79–163.

Wolfdietrich B. In Amelung and Jänicke, *Ortnit und die Wolfdietriche*, 1:165–301.

Wolfdietrich D. In Amelung und Jänicke, *Ortnit und die Wolfdietriche*, 2:13–236.

Wolfram von Eschenbach. *Parzival.* In *Wolfram von Eschenbach*, 1–3, ed. Albert Leitzmann, 6th ed. (vol. 1) 7th ed. (vol. 2–3) Wilhelm Deinert, ATB 12–14. Tübingen: Niemeyer, 1961, 1963, 1965.

———. *Titurel.* In *Wolfram von Eschenbach*, 5, ed. Albert Leitzmann, 5th ed., ATB 16, 161–84. Tübingen: Niemeyer, 1963.

———. *Willehalm.* In *Wolfram von Eschenbach*, 4–5, ed. Albert Leitzmann, 5th ed., ATB 15–16. Tübingen: Niemeyer, 1963.

Der Würzburger Totentanz. In Hellmut Rosenfeld, *Der mittelalterliche Totentanz: Entstehung—Entwicklung—Bedeutung*, 308–18. Beihefte zum Archiv für Kulturgeschichte, 3. Münster: Böhlau, 1954.

Zwingäuer, Der. [*Des Mönches Not*] *Der swanger münch.* In GA, 2:53–69.

OTHER TEXTS

Alberic de Pisançon. *Alexandre*. In Karl Kinzel, *Lamprechts Alexander nach den drei Texten mit dem Fragment des Alberic von Besançon*, 26–41. Germanistische Handbibliothek, 6. Halle: Buchhandlung des Waisenhauses, 1884.

Alexandre-Bidon, Danièle and Monique Closson. *L'enfant à l'ombre des cathédrales*. Lyon: Presses Universitaires de Lyon, 1985.

Aliscans. Ed. Erich Weinbeck, Wilhelm Hartnacke, and Paul Rasch. Halle: Niemeyer, 1903.

Alter, Robert and Frank Kermode, eds. *The Literary Guide to the Bible*. Cambridge, MA: Harvard University Press, 1987.

Amundsen, Darrel W. and Carol Jean Diers. "The Age of Menarche in Medieval Europe." *Human Biology* 45 (1973): 363–69.

Andersen, Elizabeth A. "Väter und Söhne im 'Prosa-Lancelot.'" In *Wolfram-Studien IX: Schweinfurter 'Lancelot'-Kolloquium 1984*, ed. Werner Schröder, 213–27. Berlin: Schmidt, 1986.

Andersson, Theodore M. "Rüdiger von Munre's 'Irregang und Girregar': A Courtly Parody?" PBB (Tüb) 93 (1971): 311–50.

———. *A Preface to the Nibelungenlied*. Stanford, CA: Stanford University Press, 1987.

Appiah, Kwame Anthony. "Race." In *Critical Terms for Literary Study*, ed. Frank Lentricchia and Thomas McLaughlin, 274–87. Chicago: University of Chicago Press, 1990.

Ariès, Philippe. *Centuries of Childhood: A Social History of Family Life*. Trans. Robert Baldick. New York: Vintage, 1962. French: *L'enfant et la vie familiale sous l'ancien régime*. Paris: Plon, 1960. German: *Geschichte der Kindheit*. Trans. Caroline Neubaur and Karin Kersten. Munich: Hanser, 1975.

Ariès, Philippe, with Michel Winock. *Un historien du dimanche*. Paris: Seuil, 1980.

Aristotle. *Politics*. In *The Complete Works of Aristotle: The Revised Oxford Translation*, ed. Jonathan Barnes, 2:1986–2129. Bollingen Series, 71,2. Princeton, NJ: Princeton University Press, 1984.

Arnold, Klaus. *Kind und Gesellschaft in Mittelalter und Renaissance: Beiträge und Texte zur Geschichte der Kindheit*. Sammlung Zebra, B,2. Paderborn: Schöningh; Munich: Lurz, 1980.

———. "Kindheit im europäischen Mittelalter." In Martin and Nitschke, *Sozialgeschichte*, 443–67.

———. "Mentalität und Erziehung—Geschlechtsspezifische Arbeitsteilung und Geschlechtersphären als Gegenstand der Sozialisation im Mittelalter." In *Mentalitäten im Mittelalter: Methodische und inhaltliche Probleme*, ed. František Graus, 257–88. Vorträge und Forschungen, 35. Sigmaringen: Thorbecke, 1987.

Augustine. *St. Augustine's Confessions*. Trans. William Watts. 2 vols. Loeb Classical Library, 26. Cambridge, MA: Harvard University Press, 1977.

———. *The Literal Meaning of Genesis*. Trans. John Hammond Taylor. Ancient Christian Writers: The Works of the Fathers in Translation, 42. New York: Newman Press, 1982.

Bach, Adolf. *Geschichte der deutschen Sprache*. 9th ed. Heidelberg: Quelle und Meyer, 1970.

Baecker, Linde. "Die Sage von Wolfdietrich und das Gedicht Wolfdietrich A." ZfdA 92 (1963): 31–82.

Beckers, Hartmut. "Karls erster Zweikampf—Literaturgeschichtliche Bemerkungen zu einer zentralen Episode des 'Karl und Galie'-Romans samt Textabdruck und textkritischem Kommentar." In *Aspekte der Germanistik: Festschrift für Hans-Friedrich Rosenfeld zum 90. Geburtstag*, ed. Walter Tauber, 185–206. GAG 521. Göppingen: Kümmerle, 1989.

Behr, Hans-Joachim. "Literatur und Politik am Böhmerhof: Ulrich von Etzenbach, 'Herzog Ernst D' und der sogenannte 'Anhang' zum 'Alexander.'" ZfdPh 96 (1977): 410–29.

Bellingham, Bruce. "The History of Childhood Since the 'Invention of Childhood': Some Issues in the Eighties." *Journal of Family History* 13 (1988): 347–58.

Benecke, Georg, Wilhelm Müller, and Friedrich Zarncke. *Mittelhochdeutsches Wörterbuch*. Leipzig: Hirzel, 1854–66. Reprint. Hildesheim: Olms, 1963.

Berkvam, Doris Desclais. *Enfance et maternité dans la littérature française des XIIe et XIIIe siècles*. Paris: Champion, 1981.

———. "*Nature* and *Norreture*: A Notion of Medieval Childhood and Education." *Mediaevalia* 9 (1983): 165–80.

Bindschedler, Maria. "Der Bildungsgedanke im Mittelalter." DVjs 29 (1955): 20–36.

Bischoff, Bernhard. "The Study of Foreign Languages in the Middle Ages." *Speculum* 36 (1961): 209–24.

Boehm, Laetitia. "Das mittelalterliche Erziehungs- und Bildungswesen." In *Die mittelalterliche Welt: 600–1400*, Propyläen Geschichte der Literatur: Literatur und Gesellschaft der westlichen Welt, 2:143–81. Berlin: Propyläen, 1982.

Borck, Karl Heinz. "Adel, Tugend und Geblüt: Thesen und Beobachtungen zur Vorstellung des Tugendadels in der deutschen Literatur des 12. und 13. Jahrhunderts." PBB (Tüb) 100 (1978): 423–57.

Borst, Arno. *Barbaren, Ketzer und Artisten: Welten des Mittelalters*. Munich: Piper, 1988.

Borst, Otto. *Alltagsleben im Mittelalter*. Frankfurt am Main: Insel, 1983.

Bosl, Karl. "Die 'Familia' als Grundstruktur der mittelalterlichen Gesellschaft." *Zeitschrift für bayerische Landesgeschichte* 38 (1975): 403–24.

Boswell, John E. "*Expositio* and *Oblatio*: The Abandonment of Children and the Ancient and Medieval Family." *American Historical Review* 89 (1984): 10–33.

———. *The Kindness of Strangers: The Abandonment of Children in Western Europe from Late Antiquity to the Renaissance*. New York: Pantheon, 1988.

Bourdieu, Pierre. *Distinction: A Social Critique of the Judgement of Taste*. Trans. Richard Nice. Cambridge, MA: Harvard University Press, 1984.

———. "Fieldwork in Philosophy." In *In Other Words: Essays Towards a Reflexive Sociology*, trans. Matthew Adamson, 3–33. Stanford, CA: Stanford University Press, 1990.

———. *Outline of a Theory of Practice*. Trans. Richard Nice. Cambridge, MA: Cambridge University Press, 1977.

————. "Rites of Institution." In Bourdieu, *Language and Symbolic Power*, ed. John B. Thompson, trans. Gino Raymond and Matthew Adamson, 117–26. Cambridge, MA: Harvard University Press, 1991.

Brackert, Helmut. *"Da stuont daz minne wol gezam*: Minnebriefe im späthöfischen Roman." ZfdPh 93 (1974, Sonderheft): 1–18.

————. *Rudolf von Ems: Dichtung und Geschichte*. Heidelberg: Winter, 1968.

Brandt, Rüdiger. *Konrad von Würzburg*. Erträge der Forschung, 249. Darmstadt: Wissenschaftliche Buchgesellschaft, 1987.

Brandt, Wolfgang. "Landgraf Hermann I. von Thüringen in Paris? Abbau einer germanistischen Legende." In *Zur Sprache und Literatur Mitteldeutschlands, Festschrift für Friedrich von Zahn*, ed. Reinhold Olesch and Ludwig Erich Schmitt with Joachim Göschel, 2:200–22. Mitteldeutsche Forschungen 50,2. Cologne: Böhlau, 1971.

Brundage, James A. *Law, Sex, and Christian Society in Medieval Europe*. Chicago: University of Chicago Press, 1987.

Bruner, Jerome. *Acts of Meaning*. Cambridge, MA: Harvard University Press, 1990.

————. *Actual Minds, Possible Worlds*. Cambridge, MA: Harvard University Press, 1986.

Brunner, Horst. "Genealogische Phantasien: Zu Konrads von Würzburg 'Schwanritter' und 'Engelhard.'" ZfdA 110 (1981): 274–99.

Buchda, Gerhard. "Kinder und Jugendliche im deutschen Recht (Mittelalter und neuere Zeit): Ihre Fähigkeit zu Rechtsgeschäften und der Einfluss unehelicher Geburt auf ihre Rechtsstellung." In *L'enfant*, 2, 381–415.

Bumke, Joachim. *Geschichte der deutschen Literatur im hohen Mittelalter*. Munich: Deutscher Taschenbuch Verlag, 1990.

————. *Höfische Kultur: Literatur und Gesellschaft im hohen Mittelalter*. Munich: Deutscher Taschenbuch Verlag, 1986.

————. "Höfische Kultur: Versuch einer kritischen Bestandsaufnahme." PBB 114 (1992): 414–92.

————. *Mäzene im Mittelalter: Die Gönner und Auftraggeber der höfischen Literatur in Deutschland 1150–1300*. Munich: Beck, 1979.

————. "Parzivals 'Schwertleite.'" In *Taylor Stark Festschrift*, ed. Werner Betz, Evelyn S. Coleman, and Kenneth Northcott, 235–45. The Hague: Mouton, 1964.

————. *Studien zum Ritterbegriff im 12. und 13. Jahrhundert*. Beihefte zum Euphorion, 1. Heidelberg: Winter, 1964.

————. *Wolfram von Eschenbach*. 3rd ed. SM 36. Stuttgart: Metzler, 1970.

Buntz, Herwig. *Die deutsche Alexanderdichtung des Mittelalters*. SM 123. Stuttgart: Metzler, 1973.

Burrow, J[ohn] A. *The Ages of Man: A Study in Medieval Writing and Thought*. Oxford: Clarendon, 1986.

Bynum, Caroline Walker. *Fragmentation and Redemption: Essays on Gender and the Human Body in Medieval Religion*. New York: Zone, 1991.

Campbell, Ian. "*Kudrun*'s wilder Hagen, Vâlant aller Künige." *Seminar* 6 (1970): 1–14.

Chisholm, James S. and Martin Richards. "Swaddling, Cradleboards and the Development of Children." *Early Human Development* 2 (1978): 255–75.

Chrétien de Troyes. *Le Conte du Graal (Perceval).* Ed. Félix Lecoy. 2 vols. Les
Romans de Chrétien de Troyes, 5–6. Paris: Champion, 1975.

———. *Erec et Enide.* Ed. Mario Roques. Les Romans de Chrétien de Troyes, 1.
Paris: Champion, 1973.

Classen, Albrecht. "Der komische Held Wigamur—Ironie oder Parodie? Struk-
turelle und thematische Untersuchungen zu einem spätmittelalterlichen
Artus-Roman." *Euphorion* 87 (1993): 200–24.

Coale, Ansley J. "The History of the Human Population." *Scientific American* 231
(Sept. 1974): 40–51.

Combridge, Rosemary Norah. *Das Recht im 'Tristan' Gottfrieds von Strassburg.* 2nd
ed. Phil.Stud.u.Qu., 15. Berlin: Schmidt, 1964.

Constable, Giles. Introduction to Burchard of Bellevaux, *Apologia de barbis.* In
Apologiae duae, ed. R. B. C. Huygens, 47–130. Corpus Christianorum Con-
tinuatio Mediaevalis, 62. Turnholt: Brepols, 1985.

Cormeau, Christoph. *Hartmanns von Aue 'Armer Heinrich' und 'Gregorius': Studien
zur Interpretation mit dem Blick auf die Theologie zur Zeit Hartmanns.* MTU 15.
Munich: Beck, 1966.

———. "Quellenkompendium oder Erzählkonzept? Eine Skizze zu Konrads von
Würzburg 'Trojanerkrieg.'" In Grubmüller, *Befund und Deutung,* 303–19.

———. "'Tandareis und Flordibel' von dem Pleier: Eine poetologische Refle-
xion über Liebe im Artusroman." In Schulze-Belli and Dallapiazza, *Liebe und
Aventiure,* 23–38.

———. *'Wigalois' und 'Diu Crône': Zwei Kapitel zur Gattungsgeschichte des nach-
klassischen Aventiureromans.* MTU 57. Munich: Artemis, 1977.

———. "Zur Rekonstruktion der Leserdisposition am Beispiel des deutschen
Artusromans." *Poetica* 8 (1976): 120–33.

Cormeau, Christoph and Wilhelm Störmer. *Hartmann von Aue: Epoche—Werk—
Wirkung.* Munich: Beck, 1985.

Curschmann, Michael. "Dichtung über Heldendichtung: Bermerkungen zur Diet-
richepik des 13. Jahrhunderts." In *Akten des V. Internationalen Germanisten-
Kongresses: Cambridge 1975, Jahrbuch für Internationale Germanistik, A, 2,* ed.
Leonard Forster and Hans-Gert Roloff, 4:17–21. Bern: Lang, 1976.

———. *Der Münchener Oswald und die deutsche spielmännische Epik.* MTU 6. Munich: Beck, 1964.

———. *"Spielmannsepik": Wege und Ergebnisse der Forschung von 1907–1965.* DVjs 40
(1966): 434–78, 595–647. Reprint. Stuttgart: Metzler, 1968.

Curtius, Ernst Robert. *European Literature and the Latin Middle Ages.* Trans.
Willard R. Trask. Bollingen Series, 36. Princeton, NJ: Princeton University
Press, 1953.

de Boor, Helmut. "Die Chronologie der Werke Konrads von Würzburg, insbeson-
dere die Stellung des Turniers von Nantes." PBB (Tüb) 89 (1967): 210–69.

———. *Die deutsche Literatur im späten Mittelalter: Zerfall und Neubeginn: Erster Teil 1250–1350. Geschichte der deutschen Literatur von den Anfängen bis zur
Gegenwart,* ed. Helmut de Boor and Richard Newald, 3.1. Munich: Beck, 1973.

Deißmann-Merten, Marieluise. "Zur Sozialgeschichte des Kindes im antiken Griechenland." In Martin and Nitschke, *Sozialgeschichte*, 267–316.

Demaitre, Luke. "The Idea of Childhood and Child Care in Medical Writings of the Middle Ages." *Journal of Psychohistory* 4 (1976–77): 461–90.

de Mause, Lloyd, ed. *The History of Childhood*. New York: Psychohistory Press, 1974. Reprint. New York: Harper & Row, 1975.

Demos, John. "Developmental Perspectives on the History of Childhood." In Rabb and Rotberg, *Family in History*, 127–39.

―――. *A Little Commonwealth: Family Life in Plymouth Colony*. Oxford: Oxford University Press, 1970.

―――. *Past, Present, and Personal: The Family and the Life Course in American History*. New York: Oxford University Press, 1986.

De Smet, Gilbert. "Der Trierer Floyris und seine französische Quelle." *Festschrift für Ludwig Wolff zum 70. Geburtstag*, ed. Werner Schröder, 203–16. Neumünster: Wachholtz, 1962.

Dittmann, Wolfgang. *Hartmanns Gregorius: Untersuchungen zur Überlieferung, zum Aufbau und Gehalt*. Phil.Stud.u.Qu., 32. Berlin: Schmidt, 1966.

Duby, Georges. *The Chivalrous Society*. Trans. Cynthia Postan. London: Arnold, 1977.

―――. *The Knight, the Lady and the Priest: The Making of Modern Marriage in Medieval France*. Trans. Barbara Bray. New York: Pantheon, 1983.

―――. "The Structure of Kinship and Nobility: Northern France in the Eleventh and Twelfth Centuries." In Duby, *Chivalrous Society*, 134–48.

―――. "Youth in Aristocratic Society: Northwestern France in the Twelfth Century." In Duby, *Chivalrous Society*, 112–22.

Ebenbauer, Alfred. "Tschionatulander und Artus: Zur Gattungsstruktur und zur Interpretation des Tschionatulanderlebens im 'Jüngeren Titurel.'" ZfdA 108 (1979): 374–407.

―――. "Wigamur und die Familie." In Wolfzettel, *Artusrittertum*, 28–46.

Eggers, Hans. *Deutsche Sprachgeschichte*. Rowohlts Enzyklopädie, 425. Reinbek bei Hamburg: Rowohlt, 1986.

Ehrismann, Gustav. *Geschichte der deutschen Literatur bis zum Ausgang des Mittelalters*; Second Part: *Die mittelhochdeutsche Literatur*; First Section: *Frühmittelhochdeutsche Zeit*. Munich: Beck, 1922. Reprint. Munich: Beck, 1954.

Eis, Gerhard. "Fragment eines frühmittelhochdeutschen Predigtwerks." *Journal of English and Germanic Philology* 49 (1950): 549–56.

Elias, Norbert. *The Civilizing Process*. Vol. 1: *The History of Manners*. Vol. 2: *Power and Civility*. Trans. Edmund Jephcott. New York: Pantheon, 1982.

Eneas. Ed. J.-J. Salverda de Grave. 2 vols. Classiques Français du Moyen Age, 44, 62. Paris: Champion, 1964, 1968.

L'enfant, 2. Recueils de la Société Jean Bodin pour l'histoire comparative des institutions, 36. Brussels: Librairie Encyclopedique, 1976.

Enfant et sociétés. Annales de démographie historique (1973).

Erben, Wilhelm. *Schwertleite und Ritterschlag: Beiträge zu einer Rechtsgeschichte der Waffen*. Dresden: von Baensch Stiftung, 1919. Originally: *Zeitschrift für historische Waffenkunde* 8 (1918–20): 105–68.

Erikson, Erik H. *The Life Cycle Completed: A Review*. New York: Norton, 1985.
von Ertzdorff, Xenja. "Fräulein Obilot: Zum siebten Buch von Wolframs Parzival." *Wirkendes Wort* 12 (1962): 129–40.
———. *Rudolf von Ems: Untersuchungen zum höfischen Roman im 13. Jahrhundert*. Munich: Fink, 1967.
Excidium Troiae. Ed. E. Bagby Atwood and Virgil K. Whitaker. Mediaeval Academy of America, Publication 44. Cambridge, MA: Mediaeval Academy, 1944.
Eyben, Emiel. "Sozialgeschichte des Kindes im römischen Altertum." In Martin and Nitschke, *Sozialgeschichte*, 317–63.
Fechter, Werner. *Lateinische Dichtkunst und deutsches Mittelalter: Forschungen über Ausdrucksmittel, poetische Technik und Stil mittelhochdeutscher Dichtungen*. Phil.Stud.u.Qu., 23. Berlin: Schmidt, 1964.
Feilzer, Heinrich. *Jugend in der mittelalterlichen Ständegesellschaft: Ein Beitrag zum Problem der Generationen*. Wiener Beiträge zur Theologie, 36. Vienna: Herder, 1971.
Feistner, Edith. *Ottes "Eraclius" vor dem Hintergrund der französischen Quelle*. GAG 470. Göppingen: Kümmerle, 1987.
Fenske, Lutz. "Der Knappe: Erziehung und Funktion." In Fleckenstein, *Curialitas*, 55–127.
Ferrante, Joan M. "The Education of Women in the Middle Ages in Theory, Fact, and Fantasy." In *Beyond Their Sex: Learned Women of the European Past*, ed. Patricia H. Labalme, 9–42. New York: New York University Press, 1980.
Fischer, Hanns. *Studien zur deutschen Märendichtung*. Tübingen: Niemeyer, 1968.
Fishman, Sterling. "Changing the History of Childhood: A Modest Proposal." *Journal of Psychohistory* 13 (1985–86): 65–78.
Flandrin, Jean-Louis. "L'attitude à l'égard du petit enfant et les conduites sexuelles dans la civilisation occidentale: structures anciennes et évolution." In *Enfant et sociétés*, 143–210.
———. *Families in Former Times: Kinship, Household and Sexuality*. Trans. Richard Southern. Cambridge: Cambridge University Press, 1979.
Fleckenstein, Josef, ed. *Curialitas: Studien zu Grundfragen der höfisch-ritterlichen Kultur*. Veröffentlichungen des Max-Planck-Instituts für Geschichte, 100. Göttingen: Vandenhoeck und Ruprecht, 1990.
———. "Friedrich Barbarossa und das Rittertum: Zur Bedeutung der großen Mainzer Hoftage von 1184 und 1188." In *Das Rittertum im Mittelalter*, ed. Arno Borst, 392–418. Wege der Forschung, 349. Darmstadt: Wissenschaftliche Buchgesellschaft, 1976.
———. "Miles und clericus am Königs- und Fürstenhof: Bemerkungen zu den Voraussetzungen, zur Entstehung und zur Trägerschaft der höfisch-ritterlichen Kultur." In Fleckenstein, *Curialitas*, 302–25.
———. *Ordnungen und formende Kräfte des Mittelalters: Ausgewählte Beiträge*. Göttingen: Vandenhoeck & Ruprecht, 1989.
———. "Rittertum und höfische Kultur: Entstehung—Bedeutung—Nachwirkung." In Fleckenstein, *Ordnungen*, 421–36.
———. "Zum Problem der Abschließung des Ritterstandes." In Fleckenstein, *Ordnungen*, 357–76.

Flitner, Andreas and Walter Hornstein. "Kindheit und Jugendalter in geschicht-licher Betrachtung." *Zeitschrift für Pädagogik* 10 (1964): 311–39.

Forsyth, Ilene H. "Children in Early Medieval Art: Ninth Through Twelfth [sic] Centuries." *Journal of Psychohistory* 4 (1976–77): 31–70.

Foucault, Michel. *The Use of Pleasure. The History of Sexuality*, 2. Trans. Robert Hurley. New York: Pantheon, 1985.

Freed, John B. *The Counts of Falkenstein: Noble Self-Consciousness in Twelfth-Century Germany*. Transactions of the American Philosophical Society, 74,6. Philadel-phia: American Philosophical Society, 1984.

———. "German Source Collections: The Archdiocese of Salzburg as a Case Study." In *Medieval Women and the Sources of Medieval History*, ed. Joel T. Rosenthal, 80–121. Athens: University of Georgia Press, 1990.

Freud, Sigmund. *Abriss der Psychoanalyse*. In Freud, *Gesammelte Werke*, 17:63–138.

———. *Drei Abhandlungen zur Sexualtheorie*. In Freud, *Gesammelte Werke*, 5:27–145.

———. *Der Mann Moses und die monotheistische Religion*. In *Gesammelte Werke*, 16:101–246.

———. *Vorlesungen zur Einführung in die Psychoanalyse*. In Freud, *Gesammelte Werke*, vol. 11.

———. *Gesammelte Werke chronologisch geordnet*. London: Imago, 1940–52. Re-print. Frankfurt am Main: Fischer, 1960-.

———. "Zur sexuellen Aufklärung der Kinder." In Freud, *Gesammelte Werke*, 7:17–27.

Fried, Johannes, ed. *Schulen und Studium im sozialen Wandel des hohen und späten Mittelalters*. Vorträge und Forschungen, 30. Sigmaringen: Thorbecke, 1986.

Fromm, Hans. "Die Erzählkunst des *Rother*-Epikers." *Euphorion* 54 (1960): 347–79.

Frosch-Freiburg, Frauke. *Schwankmären und Fabliaux: Ein Stoff- und Motivvergleich*. GAG 49. Göppingen: Kümmerle, 1971.

Gallatin, Judith E. *Adolescence and Individuality: A Conceptual Approach to Adolescent Psychology*. New York: Harper & Row, 1975.

Gärtner, Kurt. "Philipps 'Marienleben' und die 'Weltchronik' Heinrichs von Mün-chen." In *Wolfram-Studien VIII*, ed. Werner Schröder, 199–218. Berlin: Schmidt, 1984.

Gärtner, Kurt and Joachim Heinzle, eds. *Studien zu Wolfram von Eschenbach: Fest-schrift für Werner Schröder zum 75. Geburtstag*. Tübingen: Niemeyer, 1989.

Geering, Agnes. *Die Figur des Kindes in der mittelhochdeutschen Dichtung*. Gesell-schaft für deutsche Sprache in Zürich, Abhandlungen, 4. Zürich: Speidel, 1899.

Geith, Karl-Ernst, *Carolus Magnus: Studien zur Darstellung Karls des Großen in der deutschen Literatur des 12. und 13. Jahrhunderts*. Bibliotheca Germanica, 19. Bern: Francke, 1977.

Gillis, John R. *Youth and History: Tradition and Change in European Age Relations: 1770-Present*. New York: Academic Press, 1974.

Glier, Ingeborg, ed. *Die deutsche Literatur im späten Mittelalter: 1250–1370: Reim-paargedichte, Drama, Prosa. Geschichte der deutschen Literatur von den Anfängen bis zur Gegenwart*, ed. Helmut de Boor and Richard Newald, 3.2. Munich: Beck, 1987.

Goethe, Johann Wolfgang. *Die Leiden des jungen Werther*. Ed. Erich Trunz. In *Goethes Werke*, Hamburger Ausgabe, 6:7–124. Hamburg: Wegner, 1951.

Golden, Mark. *Children and Childhood in Classical Athens*. Baltimore: Johns Hopkins University Press, 1990.

Goodich, Michael. "Bartholomaeus Anglicus on Child-Rearing." *History of Childhood Quarterly: The Journal of Psychohistory* 3 (1975–76): 75–84.

———. *Vita Perfecta: The Ideal of Sainthood in the Thirteenth Century*. Monographien zur Geschichte des Mittelalters, 25. Stuttgart: Hiersemann, 1982.

Goody, Jack. *The Development of the Family and Marriage in Europe*. Cambridge: Cambridge University Press, 1983.

Graff, Harvey J. "The History of Childhood and Youth: Beyond Infancy?" *History of Education Quarterly* 26 (1986): 95–109.

Gravdal, Kathryn. *Ravishing Maidens: Writing Rape in Medieval French Literature and Law*. Philadelphia: University of Pennsylvania Press, 1991.

Gray, Ursula. *Das Bild des Kindes im Spiegel der altdeutschen Dichtung und Literatur: Mit textkritischer Ausgabe von Metlingers "Regiment der jungen Kinder."* Europäische Hochschulschriften, 1.91. Bern: Lang, 1974.

Green, Dennis. "Parzival's Departure—Folktale and Romance." *Frühmittelalterliche Studien* 14 (1980): 352–409.

———. "The Young Parzival—Naming and Anonymity." In *Interpretation und Edition deutscher Texte des Mittelalters: Festschrift für John Asher zum 60. Geburtstag*, ed. Kathryn Smits, Werner Besch, and Victor Lange, 103–18. Berlin: Schmidt, 1981.

Grimm, Gunter. "Die Eheschließungen in der Kudrun: Zur Frage der Verlobten- und Gattentreue Kudruns." ZfdPh 90 (1971): 48–70.

Grimm, Jacob and Wilhelm Grimm. *Deutsches Wörterbuch*. Leipzig: Hirzel, 1854-.

———. *Kinder- und Hausmärchen*. Munich: Winkler, n.d.

Groos, Arthur. "Parzival's 'swertleite.'" *Germanic Review* 50 (1975): 245–59.

Grubmüller, Klaus. "Die Viten der Schwestern zu Töß und Elsbeth Stagel (Überlieferung und literarische Einheit)." ZfdA 98 (1969): 171–204.

Grubmüller, Klaus, Ernst Hellgardt, Heinrich Jellissen, and Marga Reis, eds. *Befund und Deutung: Zum Verhältnis von Empirie und Interpretation in Sprach- und Literaturwissenschaft* [Festschrift für Hans Fromm]. Tübingen: Niemeyer, 1979.

Grundmann, Herbert. "Die Frauen und die Literatur im Mittelalter: Ein Beitrag zur Frage nach der Entstehung des Schrifttums in der Volkssprache." *Archiv für Kulturgeschichte* 26 (1936): 129–61.

Grylls, David. *Guardians and Angels: Parents and Children in Nineteenth-Century Literature*. London: Faber and Faber, 1978.

Haacke, Diether. "Konrads Rolandslied und Strickers Karl der Große." PBB (Tüb) 81 (1959): 274–94.

Hamilton, G.L. "La source d'un épisode de Baudouin de Sebourc." *Zeitschrift für romanische Philologie* 36 (1912): 129–59.

Hanawalt, Barbara A. "Childrearing Among the Lower Classes of Late Medieval England." *Journal of Interdisciplinary History* 8 (1977): 1–22.

———. *Growing Up in Medieval London: The Experience of Childhood in History.* Oxford: Oxford University Press, 1993.

———. *The Ties That Bound: Peasant Families in Medieval England.* New York: Oxford University Press, 1986.

Harkness, Sara and Charles M. Super. "The Cultural Construction of Child Development: A Framework for the Socialization of Affect." *Ethos* 11 (1983): 221–31.

Harms, Wolfgang. " 'Epigonisches' im 'Reinfried von Braunschweig.' " ZfdA 94 (1965): 307–16.

———. *Der Kampf mit dem Freund oder Verwandten in der deutschen Literatur bis um 1300.* MA 1. Munich: Eidos, 1963.

Harms, Wolfgang and L. Peter Johnson, eds. *Deutsche Literatur des späten Mittelalters: Hamburger Colloquium 1973.* Berlin: Schmidt, 1975.

Hart, Georg. *Ursprung und Verbreitung der Pyramus- und Thisbe-Saga.* Passau: Bucher, 1889.

Haug, Walter. "Erzählen vom Tod her: Sprachkrise, gebrochene Handlung und zerfallende Welt in Wolframs 'Titurel.' " In *Wolfram-Studien VI*, ed. Werner Schröder, 8–24. Berlin: Schmidt, 1980.

———. "Höfische Idealität und heroische Tradition im Nibelungenlied." In *Colloquio ital-germanico sul tema: I Nibelunghi*, 35–50. Atti dei convegni lincei, 1. Rome: Accademia Nazionale dei Lincei, 1974.

———. "Rudolfs 'Willehalm' und Gottfrieds 'Tristan': Kontrafaktur als Kritik." In Harms and Johnson, *Deutsche Literatur des späten Mittelalters*, 83–98.

———. "Von der Idealität des arthurischen Festes zur apokalyptischen Orgie in Wittenwilers *Ring*." In *Das Fest*, ed. Walter Haug and Rainer Warning, 157–79. Munich: Fink, 1989.

Haug, Walter and Burghart Wachinger. *Positionen des Romans im späten Mittelalter.* Tübingen: Niemeyer, 1991.

Haupt, Joseph. *Ueber das mitteldeutsche Buch der Väter.* WSB 69 (1871): 71–146.

Hausen, Karin. "Familie als Gegenstand Historischer Sozialwissenschaft: Bemerkungen zu einer Forschungsstrategie." *Geschichte und Gesellschaft: Zeitschrift für Historische Sozialwissenschaft* 1 (1975): 171–209.

Heinzle, Joachim. *Stellenkommentar zu Wolframs Titurel: Beiträge zum Verständnis des überlieferten Textes.* Hermaea, n.s. 30. Tübingen: Niemeyer, 1972.

———. *Wandlungen und Neuansätze im 13. Jahrhundert. Geschichte der deutschen Literatur von den Anfängen bis zum Beginn der Neuzeit*, ed. Joachim Heinzle, 2,2. Königstein/Ts.: Athenäum, 1984.

Helm, Karl and Walther Ziesemer. *Die Literatur des Deutschen Ritterordens.* Gießener Beiträge zur deutschen Philologie, 94. Gießen: Schmitz, 1951.

Hennig, Ursula. "Die Gurnemanzlehren und die unterlassene Frage Parzivals." PBB (Tüb) 97 (1975): 312–32.

Herlem-Prey, Brigitte. "Der Dialog Abt-Gregorius in der Legende vom guten Sünder." In *La littérature d'inspiration religieuse: Théâtre et vies de siants*, Actes du Colloque d'Amiens des 16, 17 et 18 janvier 1987, ed. Danielle Buschinger, 61–80. GAG 493. Göppingen: Kümmerle, 1988.

——. "Neues zur Quelle von Hartmanns 'Gregorius.'" ZfdPh 97 (1978): 414–26.

Herlihy, David. "Family." *American Historical Review* 96 (1991): 1–16.

——. "Medieval Children." In *The Walter Prescott Webb Memorial Lectures [12]: Essays on Medieval Civilization*, ed. Bede Karl Lackner and Kenneth Roy Philip, 109–41. Austin: University of Texas Press, 1978.

——. *Medieval Households*. Cambridge, MA: Harvard University Press, 1985.

Herter, Hans. "Das unschuldige Kind." *Jahrbuch für Antike und Christentum* 4 (1961): 146–62.

Hirschberg, Dagmar. "Zur Struktur von Hartmanns 'Gregorius.'" In Grubmüller, *Befund und Deutung*, 240–67.

Historia de preliis. In Oswald Zingerle, *Die Quellen zum Alexander des Rudolf von Ems*, 129–256. Germ.Abh. 4. Breslau: Koebner, 1885.

Hoffmann, Werner. "Die Hauptprobleme der neueren 'Kudrun'-Forschung." *Wirkendes Wort* 14 (1964): 183–96, 233–43.

——. *Kudrun: Ein Beitrag zur Deutung der nachnibelungischen Heldendichtung*. Germ.Abh., 17. Stuttgart: Metzler, 1967.

——. *Mittelhochdeutsche Heldendichtung*. Grundlagen der Germanistik, 14. Berlin: Schmidt, 1974.

Hofmeister, Adolf. "Puer, iuvenis, senex: Zum Verständnis der mittelalterlichen Altersbezeichnungen." In *Papsttum und Kaisertum: Forschungen zur politischen Geschichte und Geisteskultur des Mittelalters: Paul Kehr zum 65. Geburtstag*, ed. Albert Brackmann, 287–316. Munich: Münchner Drucke, 1926.

Hofmeister, Wernfried. "'Der Jüngling' Konrads von Haslau: Versuch einer Neubewertung." *Sprachkunst* 15 (1984): 1–13.

Hohmann, Karl. *Beiträge zum Väterbuch*. Hermaea, 7. Halle: Niemeyer, 1909.

Holmes, Urban T. "Medieval Children" [review of Ariès, *Centuries*]. *Journal of Social History*, 2 (1968/69): 164–72.

Horrent, Jacques. *Les versions françaises et étrangères des Enfances de Charlemagne*. Académie Royale de Belgique, Mémoires de la classe des lettres, series 2, 64.1. Brussels: n.p., 1979.

Huber, Christoph. "Bemerkungen Hugos von Trimberg zum Reisen." In *Reisen und Welterfahrung in der deutschen Literatur des Mittelalters: Vorträge des XI. Anglo-deutschen Colloquiums, 11.-15. September 1989, Universität Liverpool*, ed. Dietrich Huschenbett and John Margetts, 110–24. Würzburger Beiträge zur deutschen Philologie, 7. Würzburg: Königshausen & Neumann, 1991.

——. *Gottfried von Straßburg: 'Tristan und Isolde': Eine Einführung*. Artemis Einführungen, 24. Munich: Artemis, 1986.

Hübner, Arthur. "Alexander der Große in der deutschen Dichtung des Mittelalters." *Die Antike* 9 (1933): 32–48.

Huby, Michel. "Nochmals zu Parzivals 'Entwicklung.'" In Gärtner and Heinzle, *Studien zu Wolfram*, 257–69.

——. "Wolframs Bearbeitungstechnik im 'Parzival' (Buch III)." In *Wolfram-Studien III: Schweinfurter Kolloquium 1972*, ed. Werner Schröder, 40–51. Berlin: Schmidt, 1975.

Hunt, David. *Parents and Children in History: The Psychology of Family Life in Early Modern France*. New York: Harper, 1972.

Jackson, Timothy R. *The Legends of Konrad von Würzburg: Form, Content, Function*. Erlanger Studien, 45. Erlangen: Palm & Enke, 1983.

Jaeger, C. Stephen. "Der Magister in der Moralphilosophie des Mittelalters und der Renaissance." In *Entzauberung der Welt: Deutsche Literatur 1200–1500*, ed. James F. Poag and Thomas C. Fox, 119–31. Tübingen: Francke, 1989.

———. *The Origins of Courtliness: Civilizing Trends and the Formation of Courtly Ideals 939–1210*. Philadelphia: University of Pennsylvania Press, 1985.

Jefferis, Sibylle. "'Aristoteles (and Phyllis)': *Fabliau, Maere, Spiel*." In *The Medieval Text: Methods and Hermeneutics: A Volume of Essays in Honor of Edelgard E. DuBruck*, ed. William C. McDonald and Guy R. Mermier. *Fifteenth-Century Studies* 17 (1990): 169–83.

Johanek, Peter. "Klosterstudien im 12. Jahrhundert." In Fried, *Schulen*, 35–68.

Johansen, Erna M. *Betrogene Kinder: Eine Sozialgeschichte der Kindheit*. Frankfurt am Main: Fischer, 1978.

Jordan, Karl. *Heinrich der Löwe: Eine Biographie*. Munich: Beck, 1979.

Kagan, Jerome. *The Nature of the Child*. New York: Basic, 1984.

Kantorowicz, Ernst. *Frederick the Second 1194–1250*. Trans. E. O. Lorimer. New York: Ungar, 1957.

Karnein, Alfred. "Minne, Aventiure und Artus-Idealität in den Romanen des späten 13. Jahrhunderts." In Wolfzettel, *Artusrittertum*, 114–25.

Kartschoke, Dieter. *Geschichte der deutschen Literatur im frühen Mittelalter*. Munich: Deutscher Taschenbuch Verlag, 1990.

Kästner, Hannes. *Mittelalterliche Lehrgespräche: Textlinguistische Analysen, Studien zur poetischen Funktion und pädagogischen Intention*. Phil.Stud.u.Qu., 94. Berlin: Schmidt, 1978.

Kern, Peter. *Die Artusromane des Pleier: Untersuchungen über den Zusammenhang von Dichtung und literarischer Situation*. Phil.Stud.u.Qu., 100. Berlin: Schmidt, 1981.

Kessel, Frank S. and Alexander W. Siegel, eds. *The Child and Other Cultural Inventions*. Houston Symposium, 4 [1981]. New York: Praeger, 1983.

Kessen, William. "The American Child and Other Cultural Inventions." In Kessel and Siegel, *Cultural Inventions*, 261–70.

———. *The Child*. Perspectives in Psychology. New York: Wiley, 1965.

———. "The Child and Other Cultural Inventions." In Kessel and Siegel, *Cultural Inventions*, 26–39.

Kett, Joseph F. "Adolescence and Youth in Nineteenth-Century America." In Rabb and Rotberg, *Family in History*, 93–110.

Klapisch, Christiane. "Attitudes devant l'enfant." In *Enfant et sociétés*, 63–67.

Klingenberg, Eva. "*helt* Flore." ZfdA 92 (1963): 275–76.

Kluge, Friedrich. *Etymologisches Wörterbuch der deutschen Sprache*. 20th ed. Walther Mitzka. Berlin: de Gruyter, 1967.

Knape, Joachim. "Zur Typik historischer Personen-Erinnerung in der mittelhoch-deutschen Weltchronistik des 12. und 13. Jahrhunderts." In *Geschichtsbewußtsein in der deutschen Literatur des Mittelalters: Tübinger Colloquium 1983*, ed. Christoph Gerhardt, Nigel F. Palmer, and Burghart Wachinger, 17–36. Tübingen: Niemeyer, 1985.

Knapp, Fritz Peter. "Drei Bruchstücke einer Handschrift des 'Märterbuches' aus dem 13. Jahrhundert." ZfdA 100 (1971): 432–44.

Knapp, Gerhard P. *Hector und Achill: Die Rezeption des Trojastoffes im deutschen Mittelalter: Personenbild und struktureller Wandel.* Utah Studies in Literature and Linguistics, 1. Bern: Lang, 1974.

Koebner, Richard. "Die Eheauffassung des ausgehenden deutschen Mittelalters." *Archiv für Kulturgeschichte* 9 (1911): 136–98, 279–318.

Köhn, Rolf. "Schulbildung und Trivium im lateinischen Hochmittelalter und ihr möglicher praktischer Nutzen." In Fried, *Schulen*, 203–84.

Könneker, Barbara. "Erzähltypus und epische Struktur des *Engelhard*: Ein Beitrag zur literarhistorischen Stellung Konrads von Würzburg." *Euphorion* 62 (1968): 239–77.

Konner, Melvin. *Childhood.* Boston: Little, Brown, 1991.

Konrad von Megenberg. *Yconomica.* Ed. Sabine Krüger. MGH, Staatsschriften des späteren Mittelalters, 3.5.1. Stuttgart: Hiersemann, 1973.

Kotzenberg, Walther. *man, frouwe, juncfrouwe: Drei Kapitel aus der mittelhochdeutschen Wortgeschichte.* Berliner Beiträge zur germanischen und romanischen Philologie, 33. Berlin: Ebering, 1907.

Kreutzer, Gert. *Kindheit und Jugend in der altnordischen Literatur.* Münster: Kleinheinrich, 1987.

Kroll, Jerome. "The Concept of Childhood in the Middle Ages." *Journal of the History of the Behavioral Sciences* 13 (1977): 384–93.

Krüger, Sabine. "'Verhöflichter Krieger' und miles illitteratus." In Fleckenstein, *Curialitas*, 326–49.

Kuhn, Hugo. "Aspekt des 13. Jahrhunderts." In Hugo Kuhn, *Minnesangs Wende*, 2nd ed., 159–96. Tübingen: Niemeyer, 1967. Reprint. Kuhn, *Entwürfe*, 19–56.

———. *Aspekte des dreizehnten Jahrhunderts in der deutschen Literatur* [Akademievortrag]. MSB 1967, 5. Reprint. Kuhn, *Entwürfe*, 1–18.

———. "Determinanten der Minne." *Zeitschrift für Literaturwissenschaft und Linguistik* 26, 7 (1977): 83–94.

———. *Entwürfe zu einer Literatursystematik des Spätmittelalters.* Tübingen: Niemeyer, 1980.

———. "Frühmittelhochdeutsche Literatur." In Kuhn, *Text und Theorie*, 141–57.

———. "Kudrun." In Kuhn, *Text und Theorie*, 206–15.

———. *Text und Theorie.* Stuttgart: Metzler, 1969.

———. *Tristan, Nibelungenlied, Artusstruktur.* MSB 1973, 5.

Kunze, Konrad. "Die Hauptquelle des Märterbuches." ZfdPh 88 (1969): 45–57.

———. "Das Märterbuch: Grundlinien einer Interpretation." ZfdPh 90 (1971): 429–49.

———. *Studien zur Legende der heiligen Maria Aegyptiaca im deutschen Sprachgebiet.* Phil.Stud.u.Qu., 49. Berlin: Schmidt, 1969.

Langer, Otto. "Meister Eckharts Lehre von der Gottesgeburt und vom Durchbruch in die Gottheit und seine Kritik mystischer Erfahrung." In *"Eine Höhe, über die nichts geht": Spezielle Glaubenserfahrung in der Frauenmystik?* ed. Margot Schmidt and Dieter R. Bauer, 135–61. Mystik in Geschichte und Gegenwart, 1.4. Stuttgart-Bad Cannstatt: Frommann-Holzboog, 1986.

Le Goff, Jacques. *Medieval Civilization: 400–1500.* Trans. Julia Barrow. Oxford: Blackwell, 1988.

Le Roy Ladurie, Emmanuel. *Montaillou: The Promised Land of Error.* Trans. Barbara Bray. New York: Braziller, 1978.

LeVine, Robert A., with James Caron and Rebecca New. "Anthropology and Child Development." In *Anthropological Perspectives on Child Development,* ed. Charles M. Super and Sara Harkness, 71–86. New Directions for Child Development, 8. San Francisco: Jossey-Bass, 1980.

Lewis, C. S. *The Allegory of Love: A Study in Medieval Tradition.* Oxford: Clarendon Press, 1936.

Limmer, Rudolf. *Bildungszustände und Bildungsideen des 13. Jahrhunderts.* Munich: Oldenbourg, 1928.

Loerzer, Eckart. *Eheschließung und Werbung in der 'Kudrun'.* MTU 37. Munich: Beck, 1971.

Loffl-Haag, Elisabeth. *Hört ihr die Kinder lachen? Zur Kindheit im Spätmittelalter.* Forum Sozialgeschichte, 3. Pfaffenweiler: Centaurus, 1991.

Lofmark, Carl. *Rennewart in Wolfram's 'Willehalm': A Study of Wolfram von Eschenbach and His Sources.* Cambridge: Cambridge University Press, 1972.

Lotman, Jurij. *The Structure of the Artistic Text.* Trans. Ronald Vroon. Michigan Slavic Contributions, 7. Ann Arbor: Department of Slavic Languages and Literatures, 1977.

Lüdicke, Victor. *Vorgeschichte und Nachleben des Willehalm von Orlens von Rudolf von Ems.* Hermaea, 8. Halle: Niemeyer, 1910.

Maine: Revised Statutes Annotated 1964. Vol. 8. St. Paul, MN: West, 1980.

Mann, Thomas. *Buddenbrooks: Verfall einer Familie.* Frankfurt am Main: Fischer, 1960.

Martin, Jochen and August Nitschke. *Zur Sozialgeschichte der Kindheit.* Veröffentlichungen des "Instituts für Historische Anthropologie E.V.," 4. Freiburg: Alber, 1986.

Masser, Achim. *Bibel, Apokryphen und Legenden: Geburt und Kindheit Jesu in der religiösen Epik des deutschen Mittelalters.* Berlin: Schmidt, 1969.

——. *Bibel- und Legendenepik des deutschen Mittelalters.* Grundlagen der Germanistik, 19. Berlin: Schmidt, 1976.

——. "Gahmuret und Belakane: Bemerkungen zur Problematik von Eheschließung und Minnebeziehungen in der höfischen Literatur." In Schulze-Belli and Dallapiazza, *Liebe und Aventiure,* 109–32.

——. "Marien- und Leben-Jesu-Dichtung." In Glier, *Geschichte,* 142–52.

——. "Zum sogenannten Grazer Marienleben." In *Studien zur deutschen Literatur des Mittelalters,* ed. Rudolf Schützeichel, 542–52. Bonn: Grundmann, 1979.

Mayser, Eugen. *Studien zur Dichtung Johanns von Würzburg.* Germanische Studien, 101. Berlin: Ebering, 1931.

McLaughlin, Mary Martin. "Survivors and Surrogates: Children and Parents from the Ninth to the Thirteenth Centuries." In de Mause, *History of Childhood*, 101–81.

Mead, Margaret. *Coming of Age in Samoa: A Psychological Study of Primitive Youth for Western Civilisation.* n.p.: Morrow, 1961.

Mergell, Bodo. *Wolfram von Eschenbach und seine französischen Quellen: Teil 1: Wolframs Willehalm.* Forschungen zur deutschen Sprache und Dichtung, 6. Münster: Aschendorff, 1936.

Metz, René. "L'enfant dans le droit canonique médiéval: Orientations de recherche." In *L'enfant*, 2, 9–96.

Mitterauer, Michael. *Sozialgeschichte der Jugend.* Frankfurt am Main: Suhrkamp, 1986.

Mitterauer, Michael and Reinhard Sieder. *The European Family: Patriarchy to Partnership from the Middle Ages to the Present.* Trans. Karla Oosterveen, Manfred Hörzinger. Chicago: University of Chicago Press, 1982.

Mohr, Wolfgang. "Obie und Meljanz: Zum 7. Buch von Wolframs Parzival." In *Gestaltprobleme der Dichtung*, ed. Richard Alewyn, Hans-Egon Hass, Clemens Heselhaus, 9–20. Bonn: Bouvier, 1957.

———. "Tristan und Isolde." *Germanisch-romanische Monatsschrift* n.s. 26 (1976): 54–83.

Morvay, Karin. *Die Albanuslegende: Deutsche Fassungen und ihre Beziehungen zur lateinischen Überlieferung.* MA 32. Munich: Fink, 1977.

Morvay, Karin and Dagmar Grube. *Bibliographie der deutschen Predigt des Mittelalters: Veröffentlichte Predigten.* MTU 47. Munich: Beck, 1974.

Néraudau, Jean-Pierre. *Etre enfant à Rome.* Paris: Société d'Edition "Les Belles Lettres," 1984.

Neumann, Friedrich. "Wann verfaßte Wirnt den 'Wigalois'?" ZfdA 93 (1964): 31–62.

Nicholas, David. *The Domestic Life of a Medieval City: Women, Children, and the Family in Fourteenth-Century Ghent.* Lincoln: University of Nebraska Press, 1985.

Niewöhner, Heinrich. *Der Sperber und verwandte mhd. Novellen.* Palaestra, 119. Berlin: Mayer & Müller, 1913.

Novalis. "Blüthenstaub." In Novalis, *Schriften*, ed. Richard Samuel with Hans-Joachim Mähl and Gerhard Schulz, 2:413–63. Stuttgart: Kohlhammer, 1960.

Oessenich, Maria. "Die Elisabethlegende im gereimten Passional." ZfdPh 49 (1921–26): 181–95.

Oettli, Peter. "Zur Quellengeschichte von Konrads von Würzburg *Engelhard*." *Etudes Germaniques* 31 (1976): 1–7.

Ohlenroth, Derk. "'Reinfried von Braunschweig': Vorüberlegungen zu einer Interpretation." In Haug and Wachinger, *Positionen*, 67–96.

Ohly, Ernst Friedrich. *Sage und Legende in der Kaiserchronik: Untersuchungen über Quellen und Aufbau der Dichtung.* Forschungen zur deutschen Sprache und Dichtung, 10. Münster: Aschendorff, 1940. Reprint. Darmstadt: Wissenschaftliche Buchgesellschaft, 1968.

Opie, Iona and Peter Opie. *The Oxford Dictionary of Nursery Rhymes*. London: Oxford University Press, 1975.

Opitz, Claudia. *Frauenalltag im Mittelalter: Biographien des 13. und 14. Jahrhunderts*. Ergebnisse der Frauenforschung, 5. 2nd ed. Weinheim: Beltz, 1987.

Orme, Nicholas. *From Childhood to Chivalry: The Education of the English Kings and Aristocracy 1066–1530*. London: Methuen, 1984.

Orth, Elsbet. "Formen und Funktionen der höfischen Rittererhebung." In Fleckenstein, *Curialitas*, 128–70.

Päpke, Max. *Das Marienleben des Schweizers Wernher: Mit Nachträgen zu Vögtlins Ausgabe der Vita Marie Rhythmica*. Palaestra, 81. Berlin: Mayer & Müller, 1913.

Pérennec, René. "Artusroman und Familie: *daz welsche buoch von Lanzelete*." *Acta Germanica* 11 (1979): 1–51.

Peters, Ursula. "Historische Anthropologie und mittelalterliche Literatur: Schwerpunkte einer interdisziplinären Forschungsdiskussion." In *Festschrift für Walter Haug und Burghart Wachinger*, ed. Johannes Janota, Paul Sappler, Frieder Schanze, Konrad Vollmann, Gisela Vollmann-Profe, Hans-Joachim Ziegeler, 1:63–86. Tübingen: Niemeyer, 1992.

——. "Von der Sozialgeschichte zur Familienhistorie: Georges Dubys Aufsatz über die Jeunes und seine Bedeutung für ein funktionsgeschichtliches Verständnis der höfischen Literatur." PBB 112 (1990): 404–36.

Plomin, Robert. "Environment and Genes: Determinants of Behavior." *American Psychologist* 44 (1989): 105–11.

Poag, James F. and Thomas C. Fox, eds. *Entzauberung der Welt: Deutsche Literatur 1200–1500*. Tübingen: Francke, 1989.

Pollock, Linda A. *Forgotten Children: Parent-Child Relations from 1500 to 1900*. Cambridge: Cambridge University Press, 1983.

Post, J. B. "Ages at Menarche and Menopause: Some Medieval Authorities." *Population Studies* 25 (1971): 83–87.

Rabb, Theodore K. and Robert I. Rotberg, eds. *The Family in History: Interdisciplinary Essays*. New York: Harper & Row, 1973. Originally: *Journal of Interdisciplinary History* 2 (1971).

Ragotzky, Hedda. *Studien zur Wolfram-Rezeption: Die Entstehnug und Verwandlung der Wolfram-Rolle in der deutschen Literatur des 13. Jahrhunderts*. Studien zur Poetik und Geschichte der Literatur, 20. Stuttgart: Kohlhammer, 1971.

Rank, Otto. *Der Mythus von der Geburt des Helden: Versuch einer psychologischen Mythendeutung*. 2nd ed. Schriften zur angewandten Seelenkunde, 5. Leipzig: Deuticke, 1922.

Reyerson, Kathryn L. "The Adolescent Apprentice/Worker in Medieval Montpellier." *Journal of Family History* 17 (1992): 353–70.

Riché, Pierre. "L'enfant dans le haut moyen âge." In *Enfant et sociétés*, 95–98.

Richey, Margaret Fitzgerald. "The Independence of Wolfram von Eschenbach in Relation to Chrestien de Troyes as Shown in 'Parzival,' Books III–VI." MLR 47 (1952): 350–61.

Richter, Dieter. *Das fremde Kind: Zur Entstehung der Kindheitsbilder des bürgerlichen Zeitalters*. Frankfurt am Main: Fischer, 1987.

Ringler, Siegfried. *Viten- und Offenbarungsliteratur in Frauenklöstern des Mittelalters*. MTU 72. Munich: Artemis, 1980.

Röcke, Werner. "Minne, Weltflucht und Herrschaftslegitimation: Wandlungen des späthöfischen Romans am Beispiel der 'Guten Frau' und Veit Warbecks 'Magelone.'" In *Germanistik—Forschungsstand und Perspektiven: Vorträge des Deutschen Germanistentages 1984*, ed. Georg Stötzel, 2:144–59. Berlin: de Gruyter, 1985.

Rogoff, Barbara and Gilda Morelli. "Perspectives on Children's Development from Cultural Psychology." *American Psychologist* 44 (1989): 343–48.

Rösener, Werner. "Die höfische Frau im Hochmittelalter." In Fleckenstein, *Curialitas*, 171–230.

Rosenfeld, Hans-Friedrich. *'Herzog Ernst' und die deutsche Kaiserkrone*. Societas Scientiarum Fennica, Arsbok-Vuosikirja, 39 B,9. Helsinki: n.p., 1961.

——. *Mittelhochdeutsche Novellenstudien: I. Der Hellerwertwitz; II. Der Schüler von Paris*. Palaestra, 153. Leipzig: Mayer & Müller, 1927.

Rosenfeld, Hellmut. "Aristoteles und Phillis: Eine neu aufgefundene Benediktbeurer Fassung um 1200." ZfdPh 89 (1970): 321–36.

——. *Legende*. 3rd ed. SM 9. Stuttgart: Metzler, 1972.

Ruh, Kurt. "Bemerkungen zur Liebessprache in Wolframs 'Titurel.'" In Gärtner and Heinzle, *Studien zu Wolfram*, 501–12.

——. "Der Gralsheld in der 'Quest del Saint Graal.'" In *Wolfram-Studien* [I], ed. Werner Schröder, 240–63. Berlin: Schmidt, 1970.

——. *Von den Anfängen bis zu Hartmann von Aue. Höfische Epik des deutschen Mittelalters*, 1. Grundlagen der Germanistik, 7. Berlin: Schmidt, 1967.

Ruh, Kurt, with Gundolf Keil, Werner Schröder, Burghart Wachinger, and Franz Josef Worstbrock, eds. *Die deutsche Literatur des Mittelalters: Verfasserlexikon*. 2nd ed. Berlin: de Gruyter, 1978-.

Russell, J. C. "Population in Europe 500–1500." In *The Middle Ages*, ed. Carlo M. Cipolla, 45–47. Fontana Economic History of Europe, 1. New York: Barnes and Noble, 1976.

Sablonier, Roger. "Zur wirtschaftlichen Situation des Adels im Spätmittelalter." In *Adelige Sachkultur des Spätmittelalters*, Internationaler Kongress Krems an der Donau 22. bis 25. September 1980, WSB 400 (1982): 9–34.

Sappler, Paul. "'Friedrich von Schwaben.'" In Haug and Wachinger, *Positionen*, 136–45.

Scheludko, D. "Versuch neuer Interpretation des Wolfdietrichstoffes." ZfdPh 55 (1930): 1–49.

Schindele, Gerhard. "'Helmbrecht': Bäuerlicher Aufstieg und landesherrliche Gewalt." In *Literatur im Feudalismus*, ed. Dieter Richter, 131–211. Literaturwissenschaft und Sozialwissenschaften, 5. Stuttgart: Metzler, 1975.

——. *Tristan: Metamorphose und Tradition*. Studien zur Poetik und Geschichte der Literatur, 12. Stuttgart: Kohlhammer, 1971.

Schirmer, Karl-Heinz. *Stil- und Motivuntersuchungen zur mittelhochdeutschen Versnovelle*. Hermaea, n.s. 26. Tübingen: Niemeyer, 1969.

Schmid, Elisabeth. "Mutterrecht und Vaterliebe: Spekulationen über Eltern und

Kinder im *Lanzelet* des Ulrich von Zatzikhoven." *Archiv für das Studium der neueren Sprachen und Literaturen* 144 (1992): 241–54.

————. "Obilot als Frauengeber." *Germanisch-romanische Monatsschrift* n.s. 41 (1991): 46–60

Schmid, Karl. "Zur Problematik von Familie, Sippe und Geschlecht, Haus und Dynastie beim mittelalterlichen Adel: Vorfragen zum Thema 'Adel und Herrschaft im Mittelalter.'" *Zeitschrift für die Geschichte des Oberrheins* 105 (1957): 1–62.

Schmidt-Wiegand, Ruth. "Knecht." In *Handwörterbuch zur deutschen Rechtsgeschichte*, ed. Adalbert Erler, Ekkehard Kaufmann, 2:895–98. Berlin: Schmidt, 1978.

Schneider, Hermann. *Die Gedichte und die Sage von Wolfdietrich: Untersuchungen über ihre Entstehungsgeschichte*. Munich: Beck, 1913.

————. *Germanische Heldensage*, 1. *Grundriß der germanischen Philologie*, ed. Hermann Paul, 10,1. Berlin: de Gruyter, 1928.

————. *Heldendichtung Geistlichendichtung Ritterdichtung. Geschichte der deutschen Literatur*, ed. Albert Köster and Julius Petersen, 1. Heidelberg: Winter, 1925.

Schnell, Rüdiger. "Die 'höfische' Liebe als 'höfscher' Diskurs über die Liebe." In Fleckenstein, *Curialitas*, 231–301.

————. "Strickers 'Karl der Grosse': Literarische Tradition und politische Wirklichkeit." ZfdPh 93 (1974, Sonderheft): 50–80.

Schnyder, André. "'Des Mönches Not': Mit Michel Foucault neu gelesen." *Wirkendes Wort* 37 (1987): 269–84.

Schönbach, Anton. Review essay on Tischendorf's *Evangelia apocrypha*. AfdA 2 (1876): 149–212.

Schottmann, Hans. "Gregorius und Grégoire." ZfdA 94 (1965): 81–108.

Schouwink, Wilfried. *Fortuna im Alexanderroman Rudolfs von Ems: Studien zum Verhältnis von Fortuna und Virtus bei einem Autor der späten Stauferzeit.* GAG 212. Göppingen: Kümmerle, 1977.

Schreiner, Klaus. "'Hof' (*curia*) und 'höfische Lebensführung' (*vita curialis*) als Herausforderung an die christliche Theologie und Frömmigkeit." In *Höfische Literatur, Hofgesellschaft, höfische Lebensformen um 1200*, ed. Gert Kaiser and Jan-Dirk Müller, 67–138. Studia humaniora, 6. Düsseldorf: Droste, 1986.

Schröder, Franz Rolf. "Die Sage von Hetel und Hilde." DVjs 32 (1958): 38–70.

Schröder, Werner. *'Arabel'-Studien I: Prolegomena zu einer neuen Ausgabe Ulrichs von dem Türlin*. Akademie der Wissenschaften und der Literatur, Mainz. Abhandlungen der geistes- und sozialwissenschaftlichen Klasse, 1982, 6. Wiesbaden: Steiner, 1982.

————. *Wolfram-Nachfolge im 'Jüngeren Titurel': Devotion oder Arroganz.* Frankfurter wissenschaftliche Beiträge, Kulturwissenschaftliche Reihe, 15. Frankfurt am Main: Klostermann, 1982.

Schultz, James A. "Medieval Adolescence: The Claims of History and the Silence of German Narrative." *Speculum* 66 (1991): 519–39.

————. *The Shape of the Round Table: Structures of Middle High German Arthurian Romance.* Toronto: University of Toronto Press, 1983.

Schulze-Belli, Paola and Michael Dallapiazza, eds. *Liebe und Aventiure im Artus-roman des Mittelalters: Beiträge der Triester Tagung 1988*. GAG 532. Göppingen: Kümmerle, 1990.

Schwab, Dieter. "Familie." In *Geschichtliche Grundbegriffe: Historisches Lexikon zur politisch-sozialen Sprache in Deutschland*, ed. Otto Brunner, Werner Conze, and Reinhart Koselleck, 2:253–301. Stuttgart: Klett, 1975.

Schwietering, Julius. "Natur und *art*." ZfdA 91 (1961–62): 108–37.

Scott, Joan Wallach. *Gender and the Politics of History*. New York: Columbia University Press, 1988.

Sears, Elizabeth. *The Ages of Man: Medieval Interpretations of the Life Cycle*. Princeton, NJ: Princeton University Press, 1986.

Shahar, Shulamith. *Childhood in the Middle Ages*. London: Routledge, 1990.

———. *Die Frau im Mittelalter*. Trans. Ruth Achlama. Frankfurt am Main: Fischer, 1983.

Shorter, Edward. *The Making of the Modern Family*. New York: Basic Books, 1975.

Siefken, Hinrich. *Überindividuelle Formen und der Aufbau des Kudrunepos*. MA 11. Munich: Fink, 1967.

Southern, R[ichard] W[illiam]. *Western Society and the Church in the Middle Ages*. Harmondsworth: Penguin, 1970.

Spechtler, Franz Viktor. "Biterolf und Dietleib: Dietrichdichtung und Roman im 13. Jahrhundert." In *Deutsche Heldenepik in Tirol: König Laurin und Dietrich von Bern in der Dichtung des Mittelalters; Beiträge der Neustifter Tagung 1977 des Südtiroler Kulturinstitutes*, ed. Egon Kühebacher and Karl H. Vigl, 253–74. Schriften des Südtiroler Kulturinstitutes, 7. Bozen: Athesia, 1979.

Spiecker, Ben and Leendert F. Groenendijk. "Betrogene Kinder? Projektionen in der heutigen Historiographie der Kindheit." *Neue Sammlung* 25 (1985): 450–64.

Spieß, Karl-Heinz. "Königshof und Fürstenhof: Der Adel und die Mainzer Erzbischöfe im 12. Jahrhundert." In *Deus qui mutat tempora: Menschen und Institutionen im Wandel des Mittelalters: Festschrift für Alfons Becker zu seinem fünfundsechzigsten Geburtstag*, ed. Ernst-Dieter Hehl, Hubertus Seibert, Franz Staab, 203–34. Sigmaringen: Thorbecke, 1987.

Spock, Benjamin. *Dr. Spock's Baby and Child Care*. Fortieth anniversary edition with Michael B. Rothenberg. New York: Pocket Books, 1985.

Sprandel, Rolf. "Die Diskriminierung der unehelichen Kinder im Mittelalter." In Martin and Nitschke, *Sozialgeschichte*, 487–502.

Stackmann, Karl. "Dietrich von Bern in der Kaiserchronik: Struktur als Anweisung zur Deutung." In *Idee Gestalt Geschichte: Festschrift Klaus von See: Studien zur europäischen Kulturtradition, Studies in European Cultural Tradition*, ed. Gerd Wolfgang Weber, 137–42. Odense: Odense University Press, 1988.

Stammler, Wolfgang and Karl Langosch, eds. *Die deutsche Literatur des Mittelalters: Verfasserlexikon*. Berlin: de Gruyter, 1953.

Statius. *Achilleid*. In *Statius*, ed. J. H. Mozley, 2:507–95. Loeb Classical Library. Cambridge, MA: Harvard University Press, 1928.

Steer, Georg. "Geistliche Prosa." In Glier, *Geschichte*, 306–70.

Stehmann, Wilhelm. *Die mittelhochdeutsche Novelle vom Studentenabenteuer*. Palaestra, 67. Berlin: Mayer & Müller, 1909.

Steinberg, Laurence, Jay Belsky, and Roberta B. Meyer. *Infancy, Childhood, and Adolescence: Development in Context*. New York: McGraw-Hill, 1991.

Steinhoff, Hans-Hugo. "Artusritter und Gralsheld: Zur Bewertung des höfischen Rittertums im *Prosa-Lancelot*." In *The Epic in Medieval Society: Aesthetic and Moral Values*, ed. Harald Scholler, 271–89. Tübingen: Niemeyer, 1977.

Stone, Lawrence. "Family History in the 1980s: Past Achievements and Future Trends." *Journal of Interdisciplinary History* 12 (1981): 51–87.

———. *The Family, Sex and Marriage in England 1500–1800*. Abridged edition. New York: Harper, 1979.

———. "The Massacre of the Innocents." *New York Review of Books* 21 (14 November 1974): 25–31.

Suchier, Hermann. *Ueber die Quelle Ulrichs von dem Türlin und die älteste Gestalt der prise d'Orenge*. Paderborn: Schöningh, 1873.

Swanson, Jenny. "Childhood and Childrearing in *ad status* Sermons by Later Thirteenth-Century Friars." *Journal of Medieval History* 16 (1990): 309–31.

Ta-Shma, Israel. "Children in Medieval German Jewry: A Perspective on Ariès from Jewish Sources." *Studies in Medieval and Renaissance History* n.s. 12 (1991): 261–80.

Thomas Aquinas. *Summa Theologiae*. Vol. 31, ed. and trans. T. C. O'Brien. New York: Blackfriars, 1974.

Tiedemann, Ernst. *Passional und Legenda aurea*. Palaestra, 87. Berlin: Mayer & Müller, 1909.

Tobler, Eva. "*daz er si sîn gemahel hiez*: Zum *Armen Heinrich* Hartmanns von Aue." *Euphorion* 81 (1987): 315–29.

Toischer, W[endelin]. *Ueber die Alexandreis Ulrichs von Eschenbach*. WSB 97 (1880): 311–408.

Turner, Ralph V. "The Children of Anglo-Norman Royalty and Their Upbringing." *Medieval Prosopography* 11.2 (1990): 17–52.

van den Andel, Gerrit Gijsbertus. *Die Margaretalegende in ihren mittelalterlichen Versionen: Eine vergleichende Studie*. Groningen: Noordhoff, 1933.

van der Lee, A. *Zum literarischen Motiv der Vatersuche*. Verhandelingen der Koninklijke Nederlandse Akademie van Wetenschappen, Afd. Letterkunde, n.s. 63, 3. Amsterdam: Noord-hollandsche Uitgevers Maatschappij, 1957.

Vauchez, André. "'Beata stirps': Sainteté et lignage en occident aux XIIIe et XIVe siècles." In *Famille et parenté dans l'occident médiéval*, ed. Georges Duby and Jacques Le Goff, 2:397–407. Collection de L'École Française de Rome, 30. Rome: École Française de Rome, 1977.

———. "The Saint." In *Medieval Callings*, ed. Jacques Le Goff, trans. Lydia G. Cochrane, 313–45. Chicago: University of Chicago Press, 1990.

———. *La sainteté en occident aux derniers siècles du moyen âge: D'après les procès de canonisation et les documents hagiographiques*. Rome: École Française de Rome, 1981.

Verlinden, Charles. "L'enfant esclave dans l'Europe médiévale." In *L'enfant*, 2, 107–25.

Vogt, Friedrich. "Über die Margaretalegenden." PBB 1 (1874): 263–87.

Vollmann-Profe, Gisela. *Wiederbeginn volkssprachiger Schriftlichkeit im hohen Mittelalter (1050/60–1160/70)*. *Geschichte der deutschen Literatur von den Anfängen bis zum Beginn der Neuzeit*, ed. Joachim Heinzle, 1, 2. Königstein/Ts.: Athenäum, 1986.

von der Burg, Udo. *Strickers Karl der Große als Bearbeitung des Rolandsliedes*. GAG 131. Göppingen: Kümmerle, 1974.

Wachinger, Burghart. *Sängerkrieg: Untersuchungen zur Spruchdichtung des 13. Jahrhunderts*. MTU 42. Munich: Beck, 1973.

——. *Studien zum Nibelungenlied: Vorausdeutungen, Aufbau, Motivierung*. Tübingen: Niemeyer, 1960.

——. "Zur Rezeption Gottfrieds von Straßburg im 13. Jahrhundert." In Harms and Johnson, *Deutsche Literatur des späten Mittelalters*, 56–82.

Wailes, Stephen L. "The Childishness of Till: Hermen Bote's *Ulenspiegel*." *German Quarterly* 64 (1991): 127–37.

Wartofsky, Marx. "The Child's Construction of the World and the World's Construction of the Child: From Historical Epistemology to Historical Psychology." In Kessel and Siegel, *Cultural Inventions*, 188–215.

Wehrli, Max. *Geschichte der deutschen Literatur vom frühen Mittelalter bis zum Ende des 16. Jahrhunderts*. *Geschichte der deutschen Literatur von den Anfängen bis zur Gegenwart*, 1. Stuttgart: Reclam, 1980.

——. "Herzog Ernst." In Wehrli, *Formen mittelalterlicher Erzählung: Aufsätze*, 141–53. Zürich: Atlantis, 1969.

——. *Literatur im deutschen Mittelalter: Eine poetologische Einführung*. Stuttgart: Reclam, 1984.

——. *Wolframs 'Titurel.'* Rheinisch-Westfälische Akademie der Wissenschaften, Vorträge, G194. Opladen: Westdeutscher Verlag, 1974.

Weinstein, Donald and Rudolph M. Bell. *Saints and Society: The Two Worlds of Western Christendom, 1000–1700*. Chicago: University of Chicago Press, 1982.

Wells, D. A. *The Vorau Moses and Balaam: A Study of their Relationship to Exegetical Tradition*. Cambridge: Modern Humanities Research Association, 1970.

Wendehorst, Alfred. "Wer konnte im Mittelalter lesen und schreiben?" In Fried, *Schulen*, 9–33.

Wenzel, Horst. "Höfische Repräsentation: Zu den Anfängen der Höflichkeit im Mittelalter." In *Kultur und Alltag*, ed. Hans-Georg Soeffner, 105–19. *Soziale Welt*, Sonderband 6. Göttingen: Schwartz, 1988.

——. "'kindes zuht und wibes reht': Zu einigen Aspekten von Kindheit im Mittelalter." In *Ordnung und Lust: Bilder von Liebe, Ehe und Sexualität in Spätmittelalter und Früher Neuzeit*, ed. Hans-Jürgen Bachorski, 141–63. Trier: Wissenschaftlicher Verlag, 1991.

Werner, Otmar. "Tristan sprach auch Altnordisch: Fremdsprachen in Gottfrieds Roman." ZfdA 114 (1985): 166–87.

Wesener, Gunter. "Die Rechtsstellung des unehelichen Kindes in Österreich (Vom Mittelalter bis zur Gegenwart)." In *L'enfant*, 2, 493–515.

White, Hayden. *Tropics of Discourse: Essays in Cultural Criticism*. Baltimore: Johns Hopkins University Press, 1978.

Whiting, Beatrice B. and John W. M. Whiting. *Children of Six Cultures: A Psycho-Cultural Analysis.* Cambridge, MA: Harvard University Press, 1975.

Wiedemann, Thomas. *Adults and Children in the Roman Empire.* London: Routledge, 1989.

Williams-Krapp, Werner. *Die deutschen und niederländischen Legendare des Mittelalters: Studien zu ihrer Überlieferungs-, Text- und Wirkungsgeschichte.* Texte und Textgeschichte, 20. Tübingen: Niemeyer, 1986.

Wilson, Adrian. "The Infancy of the History of Childhood: An Appraisal of Philippe Ariès." *History and Theory* 19 (1980): 132–53.

Wilson, Stephen. "The Myth of Motherhood a Myth: The Historical View of European Child-Rearing." *Social History* 9 (1984): 181–98.

Winkelman, J. H. *Die Brückenpächter- und die Turmwächterepisode im 'Trierer Floyris' und in der 'Version Aristocratique' des altfranzösischen Florisromans.* Amsterdamer Publikationen zur Sprache und Literatur, 27. Amsterdam: Rodopi, 1977.

Winter, Matthias. *Kindheit und Jugend im Mittelalter.* Hochschulsammlung Philosophie: Geschichte, 6. Freiburg (Breisgau): Hochschulverlag, 1984.

Wisbey, Roy. "Die Aristotelesrede bei Walter von Châtillon und Rudolf von Ems." ZfdA 85 (1955): 304–22. Reprint. Wisby, *Das Alexanderbild Rudolfs von Ems*, Phil.Stud.u.Qu., 31, 100–108. Berlin: Schmidt, 1966.

Wisniewski, Roswitha. *Mittelalterliche Dietrichdichtung.* SM 205. Stuttgart: Metzler, 1986.

Wolfzettel, Friedrich, ed. *Artusrittertum im späten Mittelalter: Ethos und Ideologie.* Beiträge zur deutschen Philologie, 57. Gießen: Schmitz, 1984.

———. "Zur Stellung und Bedeutung der *Enfances* in der altfranzösischen Epik." *Zeitschrift für französische Sprache und Literatur* [Part 1] 83 (1973): 317–48, [Part 2] 84 (1974): 1–32.

Wyss, Ulrich. *Theorie der mittelhochdeutschen Legendenepik.* Erlanger Studien, 1. Erlangen: Palm & Enke, 1973.

Yeandle, David N. *Commentary on the Soltane and Jeschute Episodes in Book III of Wolfram von Eschenbach's Parzival (116,5–138,8).* Heidelberg: Winter, 1984.

Ziegeler, Hans-Joachim. *Erzählen im Spätmittelalter: Mären im Kontext von Minnereden, Bispeln und Romanen.* MTU 87. Munich: Artemis, 1985.

Zingerle, I[gnaz] V. *Das deutsche Kinderspiel im Mittelalter.* 2nd ed. Innsbruck: Wagner, 1873.

Index of Middle High German Children

Anonymous children are listed under Maiden or Youth, as appropriate, or Child, where the sex is unknown, and are distinguished by the name of work in which they appear.

General Index

Names in parentheses refer to entries in the Index of Middle High German Children.

Mann, Thomas, *Buddenbrooks*, 244, 249–50,
  267–68
Manners, education in, 80, 81 n.55
Margaretenlegende des XII. Jahrhunderts, 102,
  206 (Margaret)
Das Marienleben der Königsberger Hs. 905, 230
  (Jesus, Mary)
Marriage, 113–14, 120, 155–61, 171, 253, 258,
  261; to Christ, 163–64, 164 n.100; refu-
  sal of, 143–44, 167, 179, 188–89. *See also*
  Bride, childhood of; Arranged marriage;
  Courtship-pattern marriage; Knightly-
  combat marriage
Die Marter der heiligen Margareta, 229
  (Margaret)
Martin, Jochen, 9 n.37
Martyr, childhood of (genre), 178–80,
  189–90, 197–98, 247, 256, 260
Martyrs, 46, 166, 253
Mary of Egypt, Saint, 60, 197
Masser, Achim, 207 n.42
Mathilda (wife of Henry the Lion), 156
Mead, Margaret, 12
Mechthild von Magdeburg, 258
Menarche, 11, 156
Merchants, children of, 58, 154
Midwives, 109–10
Milk, maternal, 76
Miracles: performed on children, 46, 49–
  50, 68; performed by children, 66–67, 67
  n.154
Mitteldeutsche Predigten, 205, 205 n.31 (Jesus)
Mittelfränkische Reimbibel, 199–201, 209
  (Jesus)
Modesty of children, 53–54,
Monastic education, 79, 91, 204
Monastic life, 138, 265
moraliteit, 102
Morelli, Gilda, 265
Mortality, 266; child, 3, 46; parental, 109,
  121, 124, 264
Moses, 174–75, 196
Der Münchner Oswald, 203 (Oswald, Paug)
Music, 77, 81
Mystical writers, 239–40, 242

Die Nachtigall A, 236 (maiden, youth)
Naming, 112–13, 113 n.40
Natural exfiliation, 117–21
Nature, 247; of children, 45–54, 103; im-

mutability of, 252, 254–55, 264; inherited
from the noble lineage, 54–61, 86, 252; and
nurture, 43–44, 44 n.2, 98–105; pecul-
iar to the individual hero/ine, 61–69,
252; revelation of, 70, 245, 252, 255, 264.
See also Deficiency; Discretion, lack of;
Foolishness; Gullibility; Restraint, lack
of; Seriousness, lack of; Special nature;
Weakness
Das Nibelungenlied, 85, 211–12 (Kriemhild,
  maiden, Siegfried)
Niewöhner, Heinrich, 225 n.143
Nikolaus von Jeroschin, *Sent Adalbrechtes
  leben*, 238 (Adalbert)
Nitschke, August, 9 n.37
Nobility, 104
Novalis, 249
Nurses, 75, 122, 136–37, 248, 266
Nursing, 11, 73, 75–76, 253; as heroic sign, 65,
  66, 67 n.154
Nurture, and nature, 98–102, 103–5
Nurturers, 137, 142

Oberaltaicher Predigtsammlung, 111–12
  (Jesus)
Oblation, 91, 122, 164–65, 253, 264
Only children, 114 n.42
Ordination, 169, 169 n.122
Orendel, 202 (Orendel)
Orth, Elsbet, 151
Otte, *Eraclius*, 218–19 (Eraclius)
Otto II. von Freising, *Der Laubacher Bar-
  laam*, 124, 218 (Josaphat)
Ottokar von Steiermark, *Steirische Reim-
  chronik*, 13, 120, 159, 162, 182 n.45, 183 n.46,
  237 (Elizabeth of Glogau, Guta, maiden,
  Wenzel)
Ovid, *Metamorphoses*, 235

Paradisus anime intelligentis, 240
Parents, 137, 248, 213–14; conflict with chil-
  dren, 129–32; love for children, 3–4, 7
  n.32, 9 n.37, 110–11, 129, 216, 260, 265
Paris, University of, 35
Partonopeu de Blois, 222
Passienbüchlein von den vier Hauptjungfrauen,
  238 (Dorothy, Margaret)
Passional, 66, 89, 112, 188, 218, 231–33, 235,
  239, 241–42 (Agatha, Agnes, Ambrose,
  Benedict, Dominic, Gregory, Jerome,

University of Pennsylvania Press
MIDDLE AGES SERIES
Ruth Mazo Karras and Edward Peters, General Editors

F. R. P. Akehurst, trans. *The* Coutumes de Beauvaisis *of Philippe de Beaumanoir*. 1992

Peter L. Allen. *The Art of Love: Amatory Fiction from Ovid to the* Romance of the Rose. 1992

David Anderson. *Before the Knight's Tale: Imitatin of Classical Epic in Boccaccio's* Teseida. 1988

Benjamin Arnold. *Count and Bishop in Medieval Germany: A Study of Regional Power, 1100–1350*. 1991

Mark C. Bartusis. *The Late Byzantine Army: Arms and Society, 1204–1453*. 1992

Thomas N. Bisson, ed. *Cultures of Power: Lordship, Status, and Process in Twelfth-Century Europe*. 1995

Uta-Renate Blumenthal. *The Investiture Controversy: Church and Monarchy from the Ninth to the Twelfth Century*. 1988

Daniel Bornstein, trans. *Dino Compagni's* Chronicle *of Florence*. 1986

Maureen Boulton. *The Song in the Story: Lyric Insertions in French Narrative Fiction, 1200–1400*. 1993

Betsy Bowden. *Chaucer Aloud: The Varieties of Textual Interpretation*. 1987

Charles R. Bowlus. *Franks, Moravians, and Magyars: The Struggle for the Middle Danube, 788–907*. 1995

James William Brodman. *Ransoming Captives in Crusader Spain: The Order of Merced on the Christian-Islamic Frontier*. 1986

Kevin Brownlee and Sylvia Huot, eds. *Rethinking the* Romance of the Rose*: Text, Image, Reception*. 1992

Matilda Tomaryn Bruckner. *Shaping Romance: Interpretation, Truth, and Closure in Twelfth-Century French Fictions*. 1993

Otto Brunner (Howard Kaminsky and James Van Horn Melton, eds. and trans.). *Land and Lordship: Structures of Governance in Medieval Austria*. 1992

Rober I. Burns, S.J., ed. *Emperor of Culture: Alfonso X the Learned of Castile and His Thirteenth-Century Renaissance*. 1990

David Burr. *Olivi and Franciscan Poverty: The Origins of the* Usus Pauper *Controversy*. 1989

David Burr. *Olivi's Peaceable Kingdom: A Reading of the Apocalypse Commentary*. 1993

Thomas Cable. *The English Alliterative Tradition*. 1991

Anthony K. Cassell and Victoria Kirkham, eds. and trans. *Diana's Hunt/Caccia di Diana: Boccaccio's First Fiction*. 1991

John C. Cavadini. *The Last Christology of the West: Adoptionism in Spain and Gaul, 785–820*. 1993

Brigitte Cazelles. *The Lady as Saint: A Collection of French Hagiographic Romances of the Thirteenth Century.* 1991

Karen Cherewatuk and Ulrike Wiethaus, eds. *Dear Sister: Medieval Women and the Epistolary Genre.* 1993

Anne L. Clark. *Elisabeth of Schönau: A Twelfth-Century Visionary.* 1992

Willene B. Clark and Meradith T. McMunn, eds. *Beasts and Birds of the Middle Ages: The Bestiary and Its Legacy.* 1989

Richard C. Dales. *The Scientific Achievement of the Middle Ages.* 1973

Charles T. David. *Dante's Italy and Other Essays.* 1984

William J. Dohar. *The Black Death and Pastoral Leadership: The Diocese of Hereford in the Fourteenth Century.* 1994

Katherine Fischer Drew, trans. *The Burgundian Code.* 1972

Katherine Fischer Drew, trans. *The Laws of the Salian Franks.* 1991

Katherine Fischer Drew, trans. *The Lombard Laws.* 1973

Nancy Edwards. *The Archaeology of Early Medieval Ireland.* 1990

Richard K. Emmerson and Ronald B. Herzman. *The Apocalyptic Imagination in Medieval Literature.* 1992

Theodore Evergates. *Feudal Society in Medieval France: Documents from the County of Champagne.* 1993

Felipe Fernández-Armesto. *Before Columbus: Exploration and Colonization from the Mediterranean to the Atlantic, 1229–1492.* 1987

Jerold C. Frakes. *Brides and Doom: Gender, Property, and Power in Medieval Women's Epic.* 1994

R. D. Fulk. *A History of Old English Meter.* 1992

Patrick J. Geary. *Aristocracy in Provence: The Rhône Basin at the Dawn of the Carolingian Age.* 1985

Peter Heath. *Allegory and Philosophy in Avicenna (Ibn Sînâ), with a Translation of the Book of the Prophet Muḥammad's Ascent to Heaven.* 1992

J. N. Hillgarth, ed. *Christianity and Paganism, 350–750: The Conversion of Western Europe.* 1986

Richard C. Hoffmann. *Land, Liberties, and Lordship in a Late Medieval Countryside: Agrarian Structures and Change in the Duchy of Wrocław.* 1990

Robert Hollander. *Boccaccio's Last Fiction:* Il Corbaccio. 1988

John Y. B. Hood. *Aquinas and the Jews.* 1995

Edward B. Irving, Jr. *Rereading* Beowulf. 1989

Richard A. Jackson, ed. Ordines Coronationis Franciae: *Texts and Ordines for the Coronation of Frankish and French Kings and Queens in the Middle Ages,* Vol. I. 1995

C. Stephen Jaeger. *The Envy of Angels: Cathedral Schools and Social Ideals in Medieval Europe, 950–1200.* 1994

C. Stephen Jaeger. *The Origins of Courtliness: Civilizing Trends and the Formation of Courtly Ideals, 939–1210.* 1985

Donald J. Kagay, trans. *The Usatges of Barcelona: The Fundamental Law of Catalonia.* 1994

Richard Kay. *Dante's Christian Astrology.* 1994

Ellen E. Kittell. *From* Ad Hoc *to* Routine: *A Case Study in Medieval Bureaucracy.* 1991

Alan C. Kors and Edward Peters, eds. *Witchcraft in Europe, 1100–1700: A Documentary History.* 1972

Barbara M. Kreutz. *Before the Normans: Southern Italy in the Ninth and Tenth Centuries.* 1992

Michael P. Kuczynski. *Prophetic Song: The Psalms as Moral Discourse in Late Medieval England.* 1995

E. Ann Matter. *The Voice of My Beloved: The Song of Songs in Western Medieval Christianity.* 1990

A. J. Minnis. *Medieval Theory of Authorship.* 1988

Lawrence Nees. *A Tainted Mantle: Hercules and the Classical Tradition at the Carolingian Court.* 1991

Lynn H. Nelson, trans. *The Chronicle of San Juan de la Peña: A Fourteenth-Century Official History of the Crown of Aragon.* 1991

Barbara Newman. *From Virile Woman to WomanChrist: Studies in Medieval Religion and Literature.* 1995

Joseph F. O'Callaghan. *The Cortes of Castile-León, 1188–1350.* 1989

Joseph F. O'Callaghan. *The Learned King: The Reign of Alfonso X of Castile.* 1993

Odo of Tournai (Irven M. Resnick, trans.). *Two Theological Treatises:* On Original Sin *and* A Disputation with the Jew, Leo, Concerning the Advent of Christ, the Son of God. 1994

David M. Olster. *Roman Defeat, Christian Response, and the Literary Construction of the Jew.* 1994

William D. Paden, ed. *The Voice of the Trobairitz: Perspectives on the Women Troubadours.* 1989

Edward Peters. *The Magician, the Witch, and the Law.* 1982

Edward Peters, ed. *Christian Society and the Crusades, 1198–1229: Sources in Translation, including* The Capture of Damietta *by Oliver of Paderborn.* 1971

Edward Peters, ed. *Heresy and Authority in Medieval Europe.* 1980

James M. Powell. *Albertanus of Brescia: The Pursuit of Happiness in the Early Thirteenth Century.* 1992

James M. Powell. *Anatomy of a Crusade, 1213–1221.* 1986

Susan A. Rabe. *Faith, Art, and Politics at Saint-Riquier: The Symbolic Vision of Angilbert.* 1995

Jean Renart (Patricia Terry and Nancy Vine Durling, trans.). *The Romance of the Rose or Guillaume de Dole.* 1993

Michael Resler, trans. Erec *by Hartmann von Aue.* 1987

Pierre Riché (Michael Idomir Allen, trans.). *The Carolingians: A Family Who Forged Europe.* 1993

Jonathan Riley-Smith. *The First Crusade and the Idea of Crusading.* 1986

Joel T. Rosenthal. *Patriarchy and Families of Privilege in Fifteenth-Century England.* 1991

Teofilo F. Ruiz. *Crisis and Continuity: Land and Town in Late Medieval Castile.* 1994

James A. Rushing, Jr. *Images of Adventure: Ywain in the Visual Arts.* 1995

Steven D. Sargent, ed. and trans. *On the Threshold of Exact Science: Selected Writings of Anneliese Maier on Late Medieval Natural Philosophy.* 1982

James A. Schultz. *The Knowledge of Childhood in the German Middle Ages, 1100–1350*. 1995

Pamela Sheingorn, ed. and trans. *The Book of Sainte Foy*. 1995

Robin Chapman Stacey. *The Road to Judgment: From Custom to Court in Medieval Ireland and Wales*. 1994

Sarah Stanbury. *Seeing the* Gawain-*Poet: Description and the Act of Perception*. 1992

Robert D. Stevick. *The Earliest Irish and English Bookarts: Visual and Poetic Forms Before A.D. 1000*. 1994

Thomas C. Stillinger. *The Song of Troilus: Lyric Authority in the Medieval Book*. 1992

Susan Mosher Stuard. *A State of Deference: Ragusa/Dubrovnik in the Medieval Centuries*. 1992

Susan Mosher Stuard, ed. *Women in Medieval History and Historiography*. 1987

Susan Mosher Stuard, ed. *Women in Medieval Society*. 1976

Jonathan Sumption. *The Hundred Years War: Trial by Battle*. 1992

Ronald E. Surtz. *The Guitar of God: Gender, Power, and Authority in the Visionary World of Mother Juana de la Cruz (1481–1534)*. 1990

Ronald E. Surtz. *Writing Women in Late Medieval and Early Modern Spain: The Mothers of Saint Teresa of Avila*. 1995

Del Sweeney, ed. *Agriculture in the Middle Ages: Technology, Practice, and Representation*. 1995

William H. TeBrake. *A Plague of Insurrection: Popular Politics and Peasant Revolt in Flanders, 1323–1328*. 1993

Patricia Terry, trans. *Poems of the Elder Edda*. 1990

Hugh M. Thomas. *Vassals, Heiresses, Crusaders, and Thugs: The Gentry of Angevin Yorkshire, 1154–1216*. 1993

Ralph V. Turner. *Men Raised from the Dust: Administrative Service and Upward Mobility in Angevin England*. 1988

Mary F. Wack. *Lovesickness in the Middle Ages: The* Viaticum *and Its Commentaries*. 1990

Benedicta Ward. *Miracles and the Medieval Mind: Theory, Record, and Event, 1000–1215*. 1982

Suzanne Fonay Wemple. *Women in Frankish Society: Marriage and the Cloister, 500–900*. 1981

Kenneth Baxter Wolf. *Making History: The Normans and Their Historians in Eleventh-Century Italy*. 1995

Jan M. Ziolkowski. *Talking Animals: Medieval Latin Beast Poetry 750–1150*. 1993

This book has been set in Linotron Galliard. Galliard was designed for Mergenthaler in 1978 by Matthew Carter. Galliard retains many of the features of a sixteenth-century typeface cut by Robert Granjon but has some modifications that give it a more contemporary look.

Printed on acid-free paper.